Forget Me Not

4

ORIGINAL STORY:
Mag Hsu

ART:
Nao Emoto

4

CONTENTS

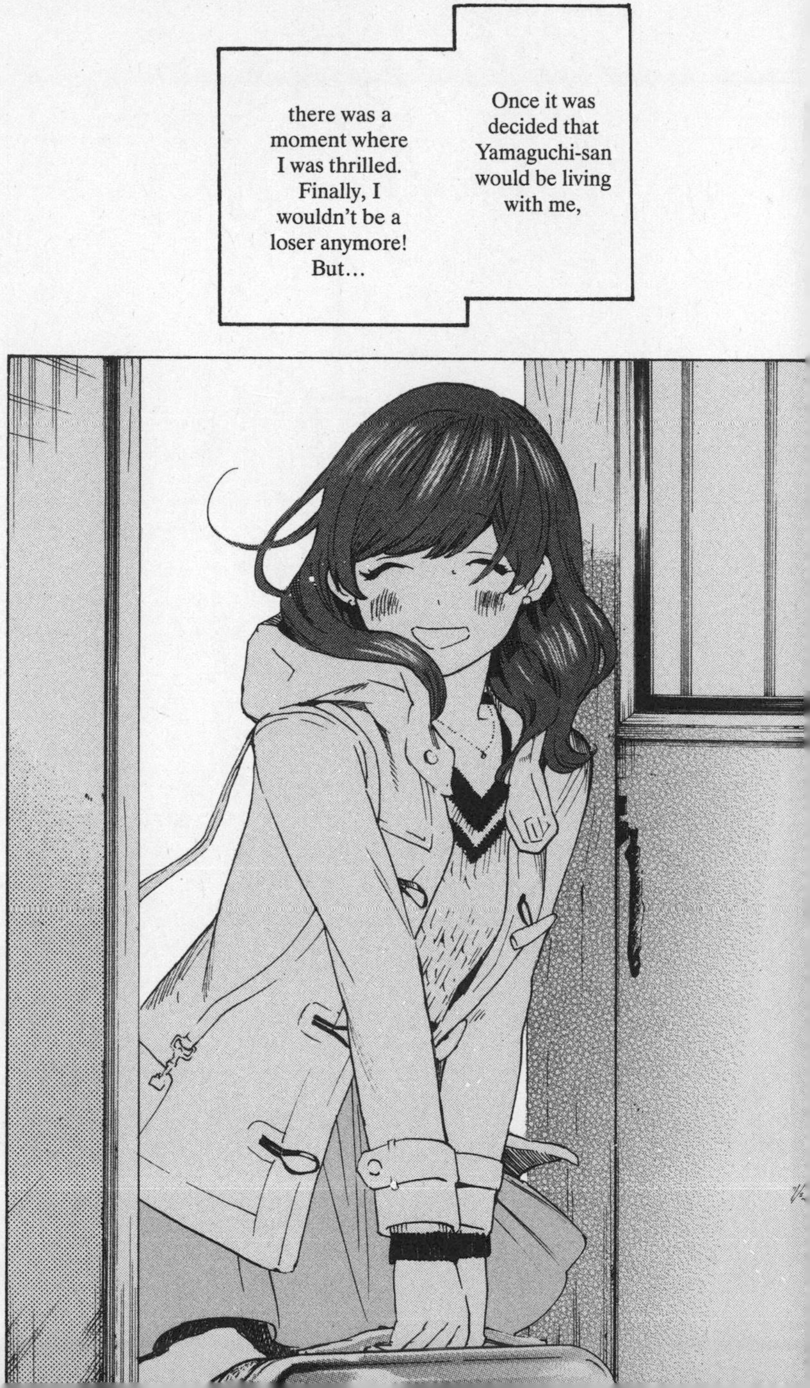
Once it was decided that Yamaguchi-san would be living with me,
there was a moment where I was thrilled. Finally, I wouldn't be a loser anymore! But…

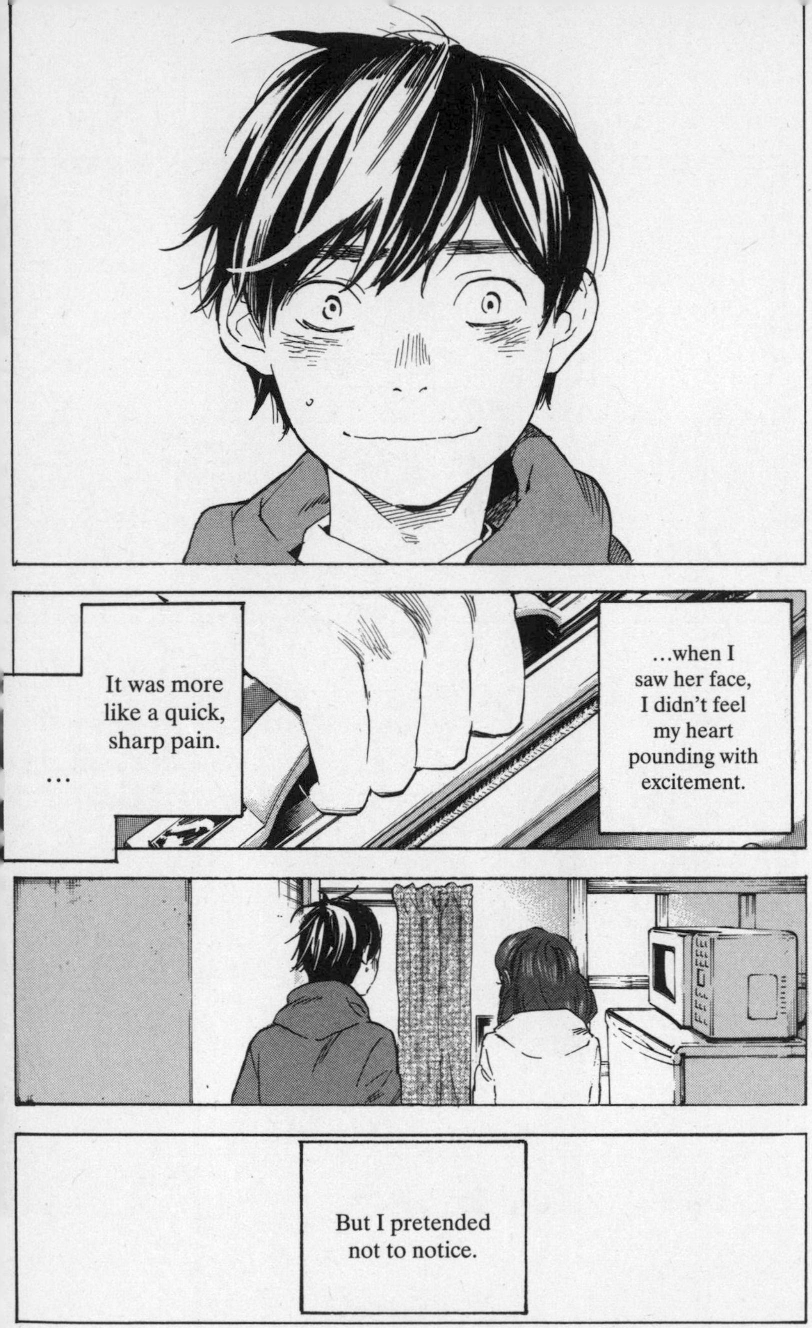
…when I saw her face, I didn't feel my heart pounding with excitement.
It was more like a quick, sharp pain.
…
But I pretended not to notice.

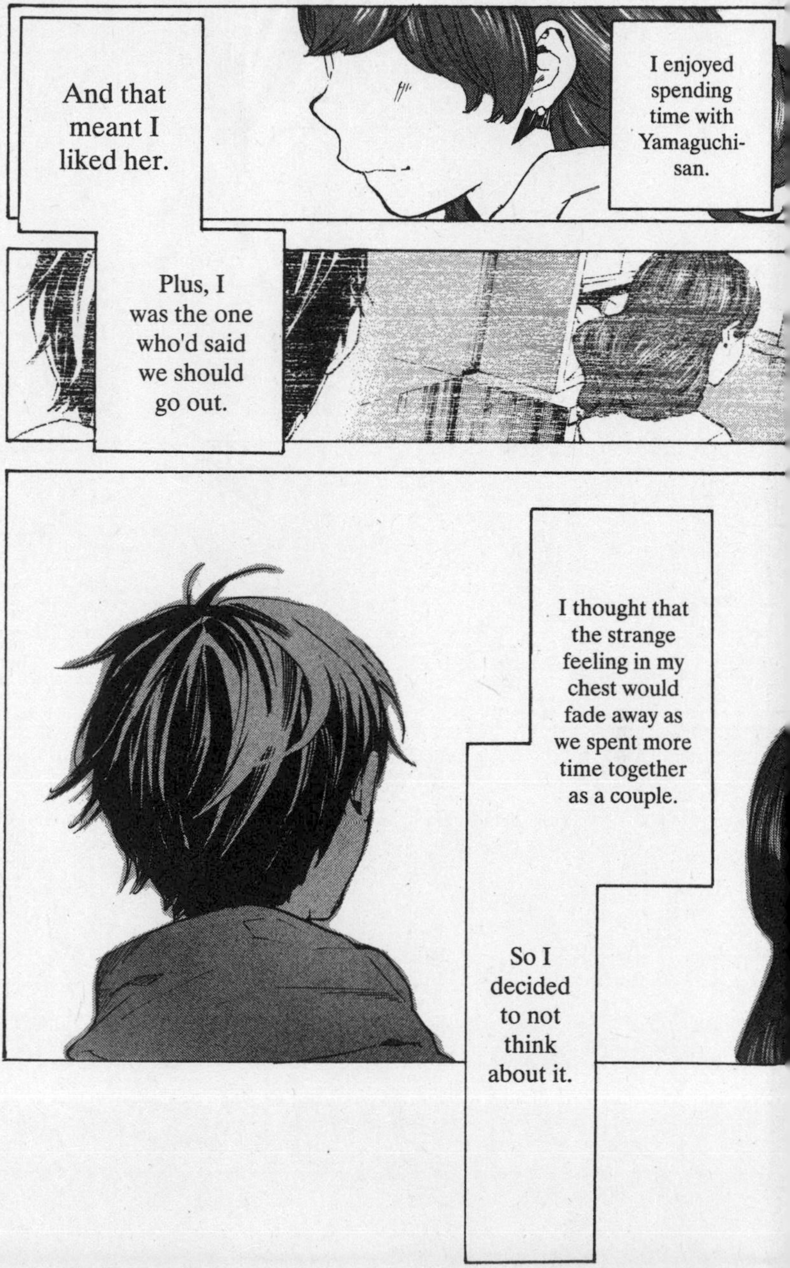
I enjoyed spending time with Yamaguchi-san.
And that meant I liked her.
Plus, I was the one who'd said we should go out.
I thought that the strange feeling in my chest would fade away as we spent more time together as a couple.
So I decided to not think about it.

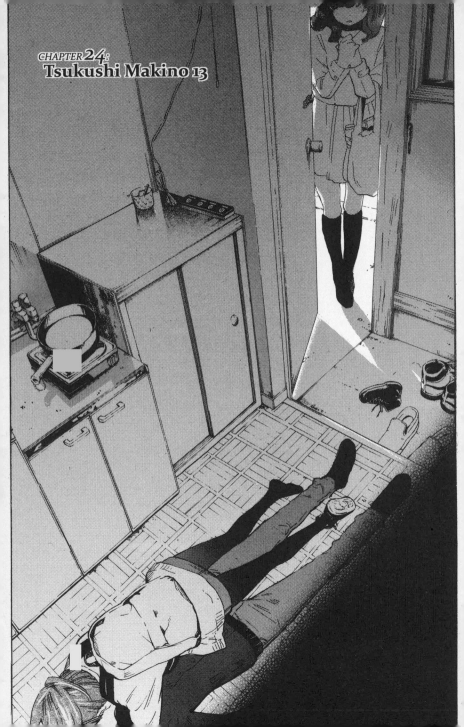

CHAPTER *24*:
Tsukushi Makino 13

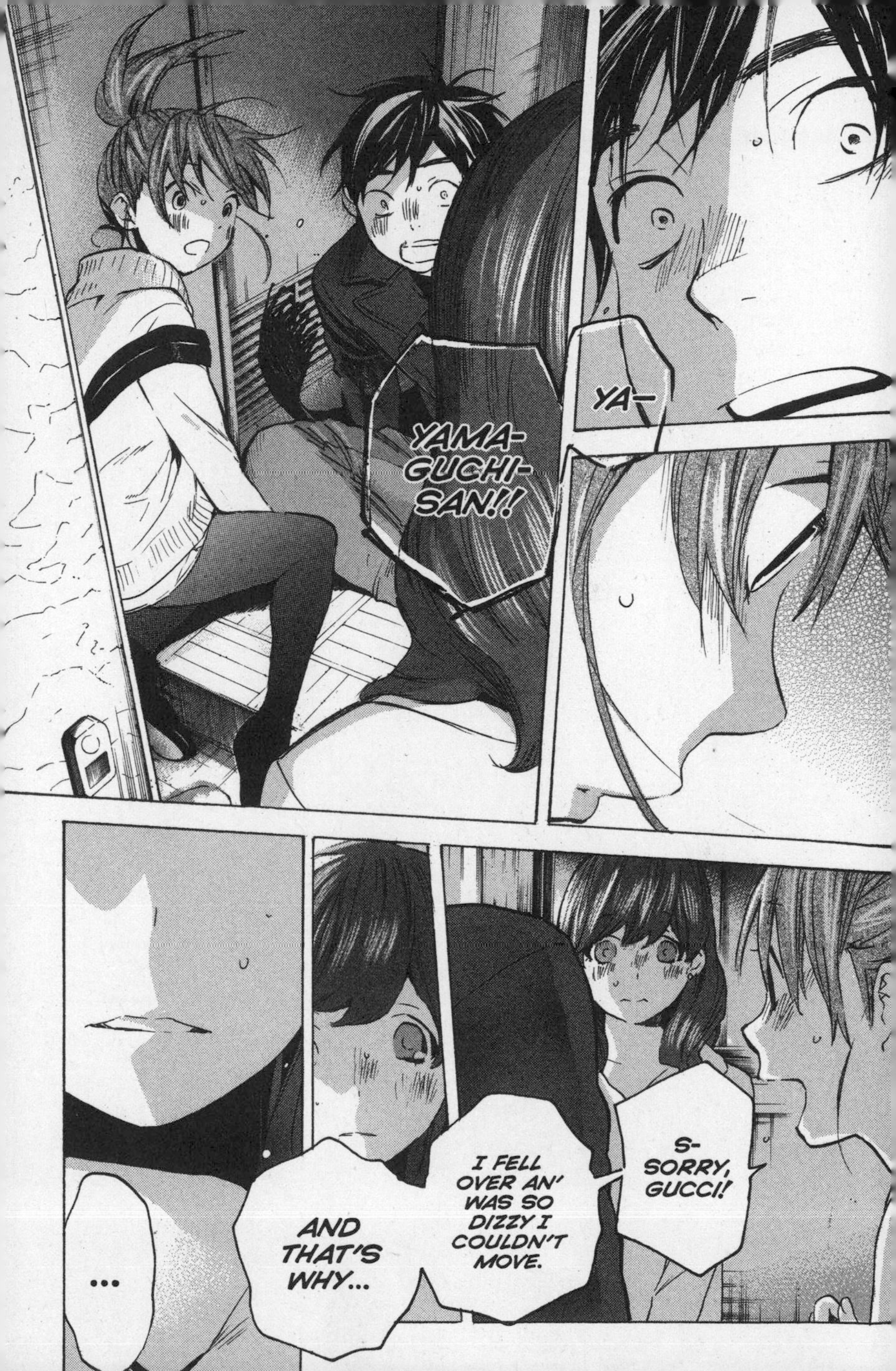
YA—
YAMA-GUCHI-SAN!!
S-SORRY, GUCCI!
I FELL OVER AN' WAS SO DIZZY I COULDN'T MOVE.
AND THAT'S WHY...
...

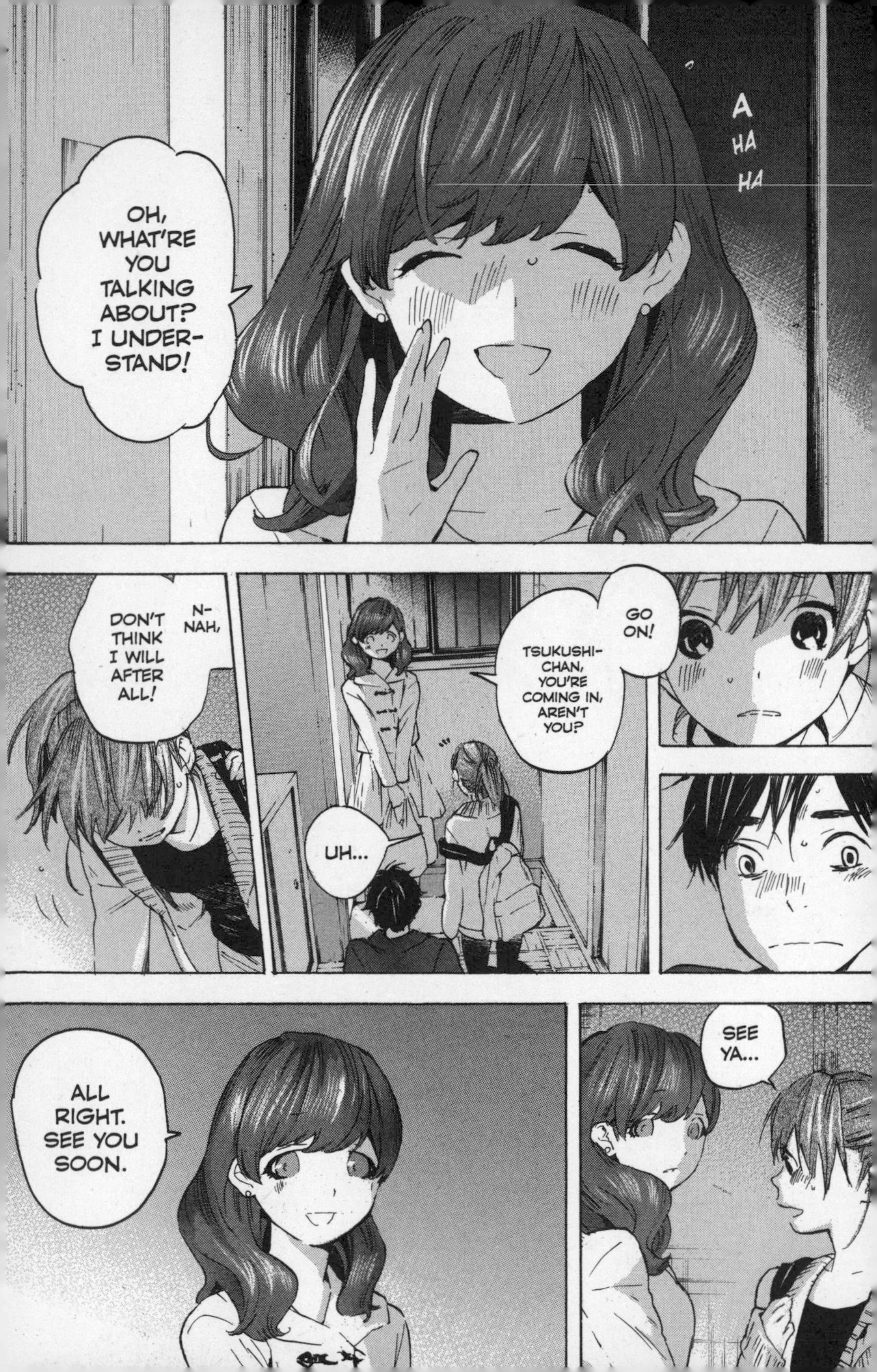
A HA HA
OH, WHAT'RE YOU TALKING ABOUT? I UNDER-STAND!
GO ON!
TSUKUSHI-CHAN, YOU'RE COMING IN, AREN'T YOU?
UH...
N-NAH,
DON'T THINK I WILL AFTER ALL!
SEE YA...
ALL RIGHT. SEE YOU SOON.

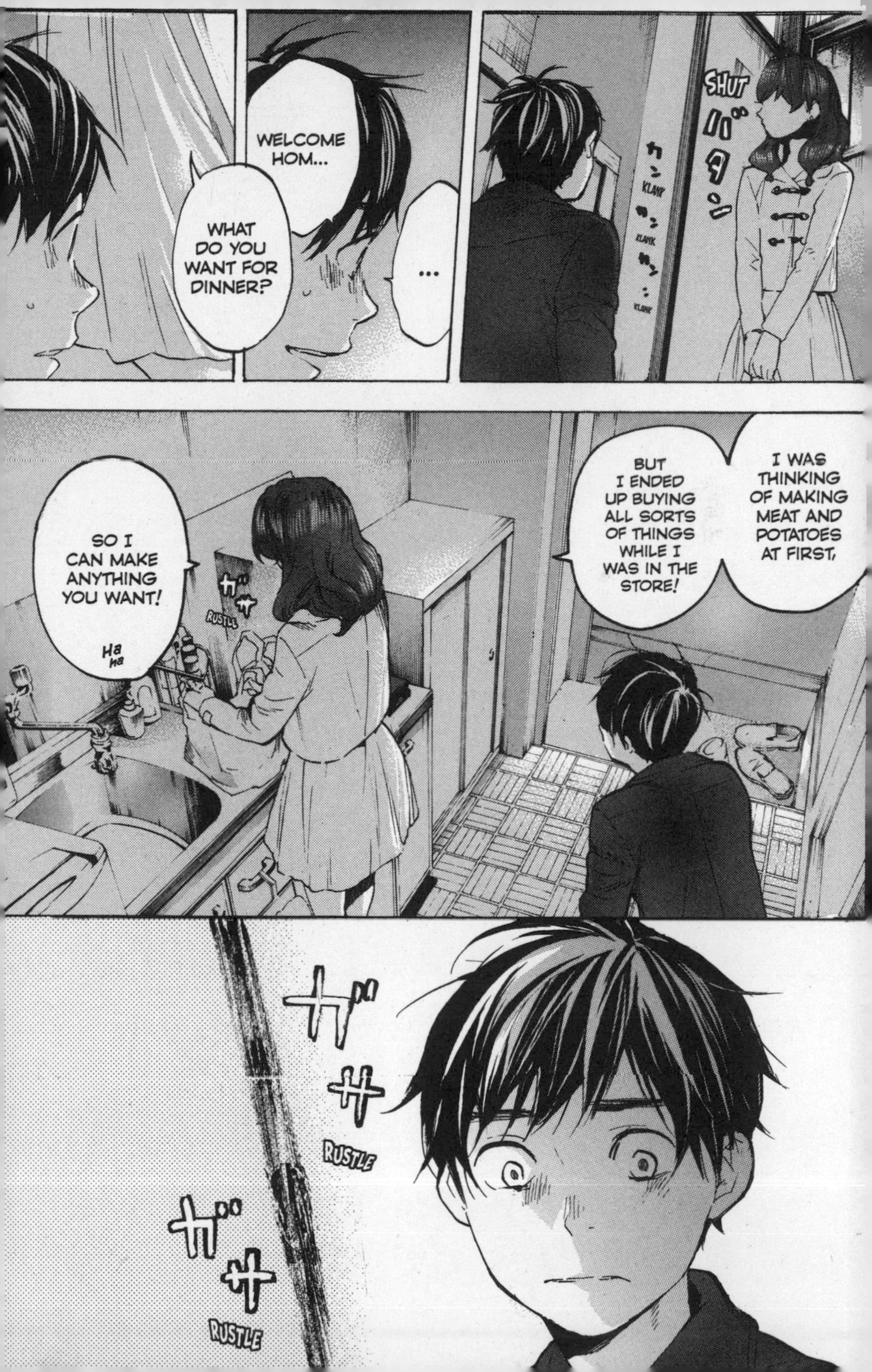
SHUT
KLANK
KLANK
KLANK
WELCOME HOM...
...
WHAT DO YOU WANT FOR DINNER?
I WAS THINKING OF MAKING MEAT AND POTATOES AT FIRST,
BUT I ENDED UP BUYING ALL SORTS OF THINGS WHILE I WAS IN THE STORE!
SO I CAN MAKE ANYTHING YOU WANT!
Ha ha
RUSTLE
RUSTLE
RUSTLE

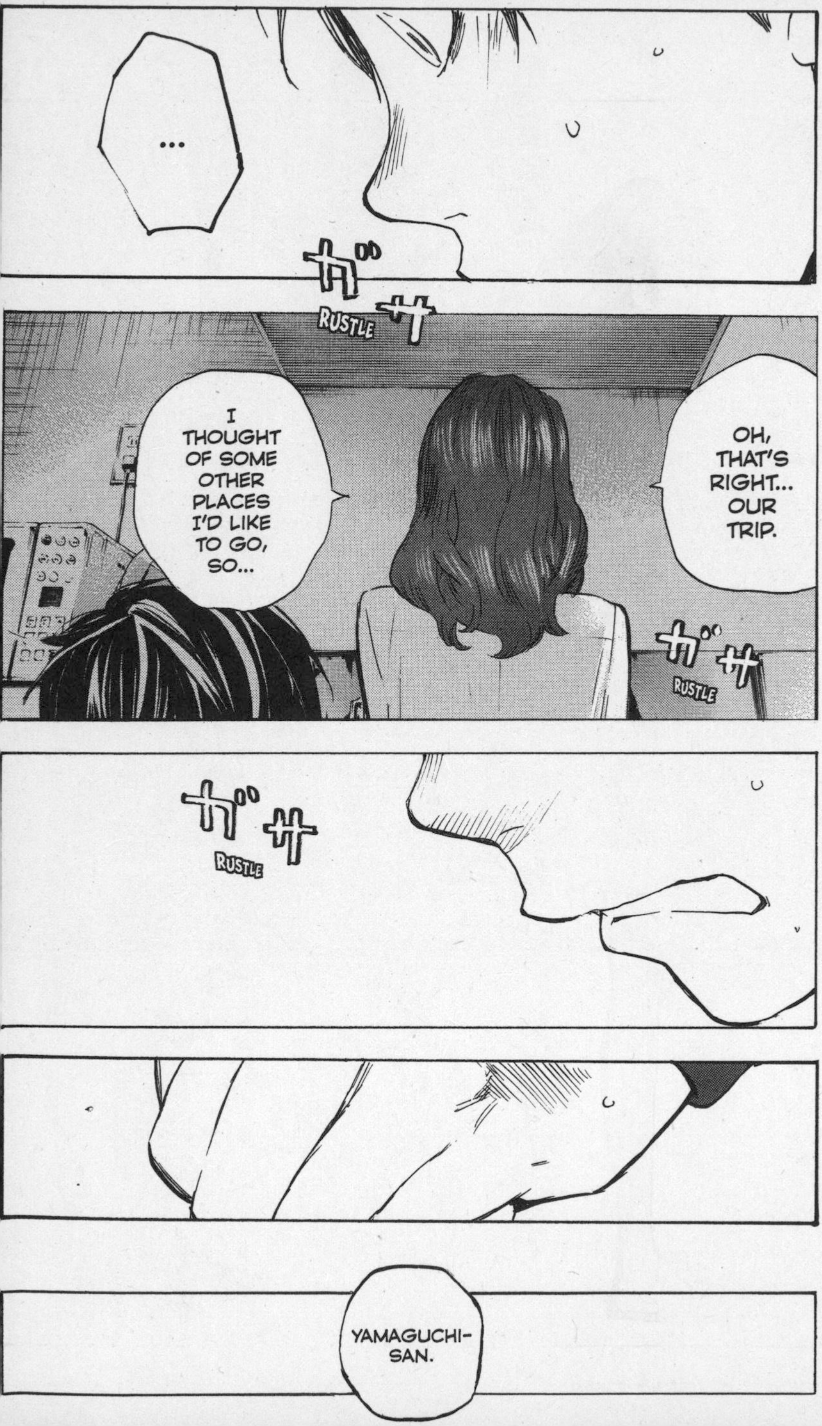
...
RUSTLE
OH, THAT'S RIGHT... OUR TRIP.
I THOUGHT OF SOME OTHER PLACES I'D LIKE TO GO, SO...
RUSTLE
RUSTLE
YAMAGUCHI-SAN.

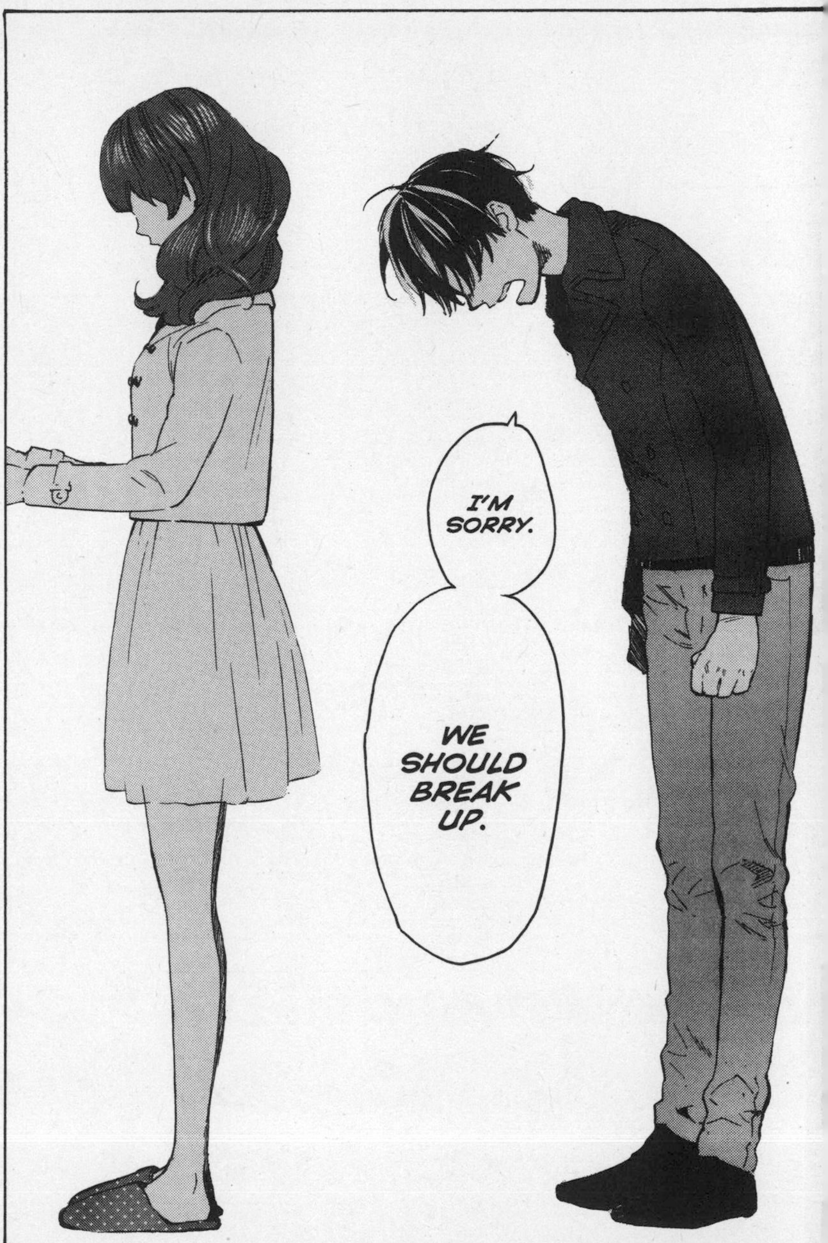
I'M SORRY.
WE SHOULD BREAK UP.

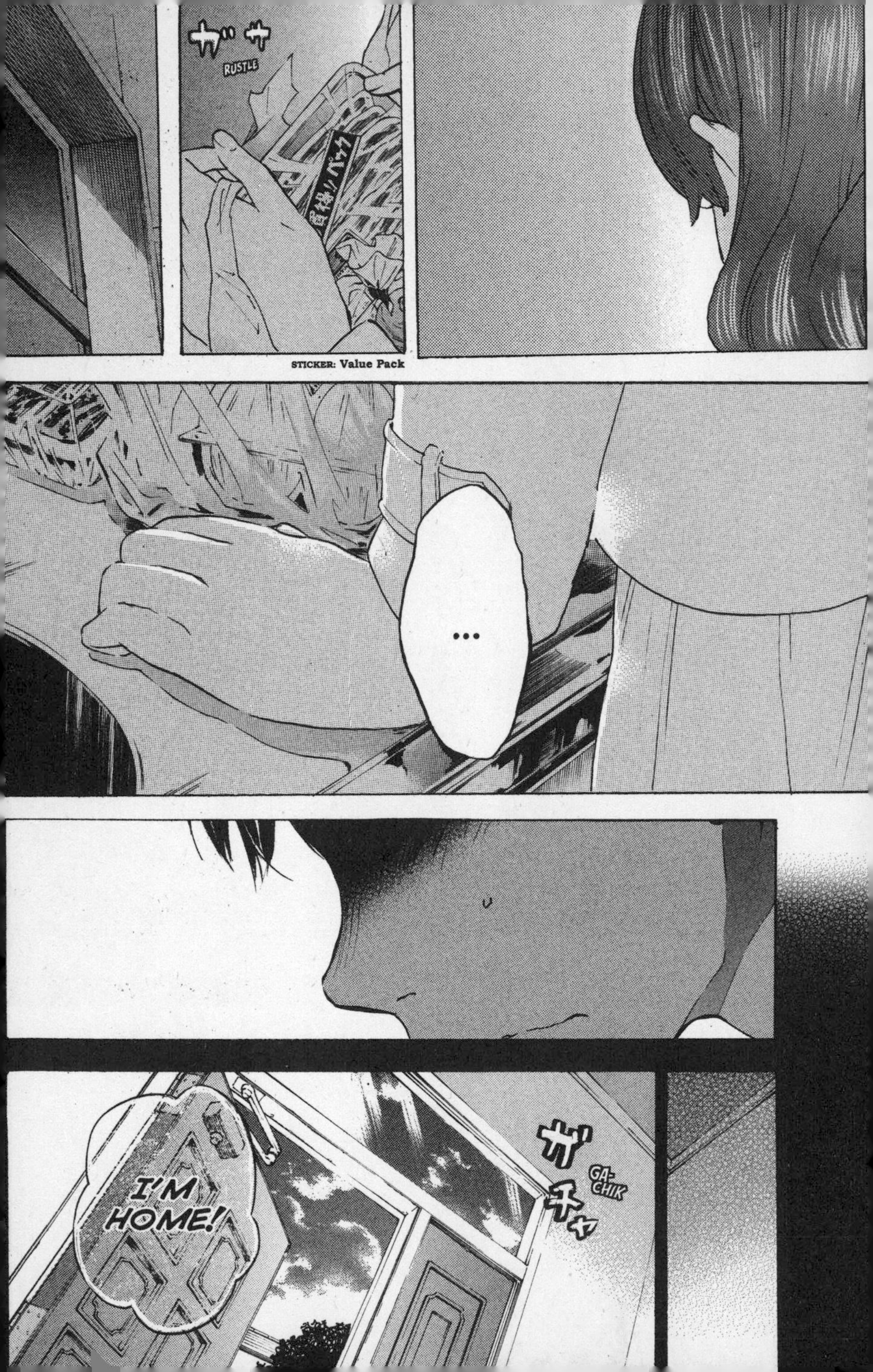
ガサ
RUSTLE
STICKER: Value Pack
...
I'M HOME!
ガチャ
GA-CHIK

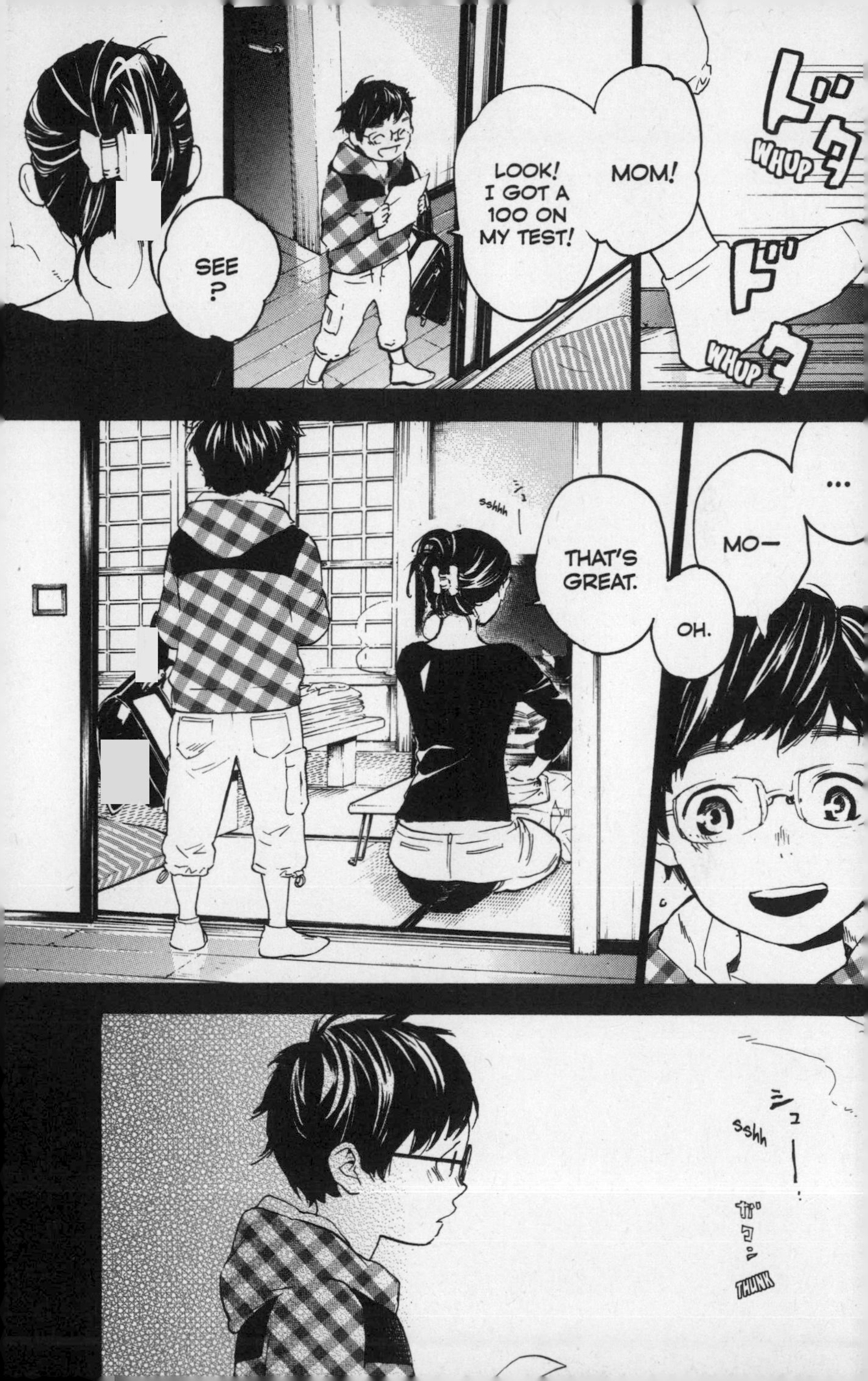
ドタ
WHUP
WHUP
MOM!
LOOK! I GOT A 100 ON MY TEST!
SEE?
...
MO—
OH.
THAT'S GREAT.
sshh
sshh
THUNK

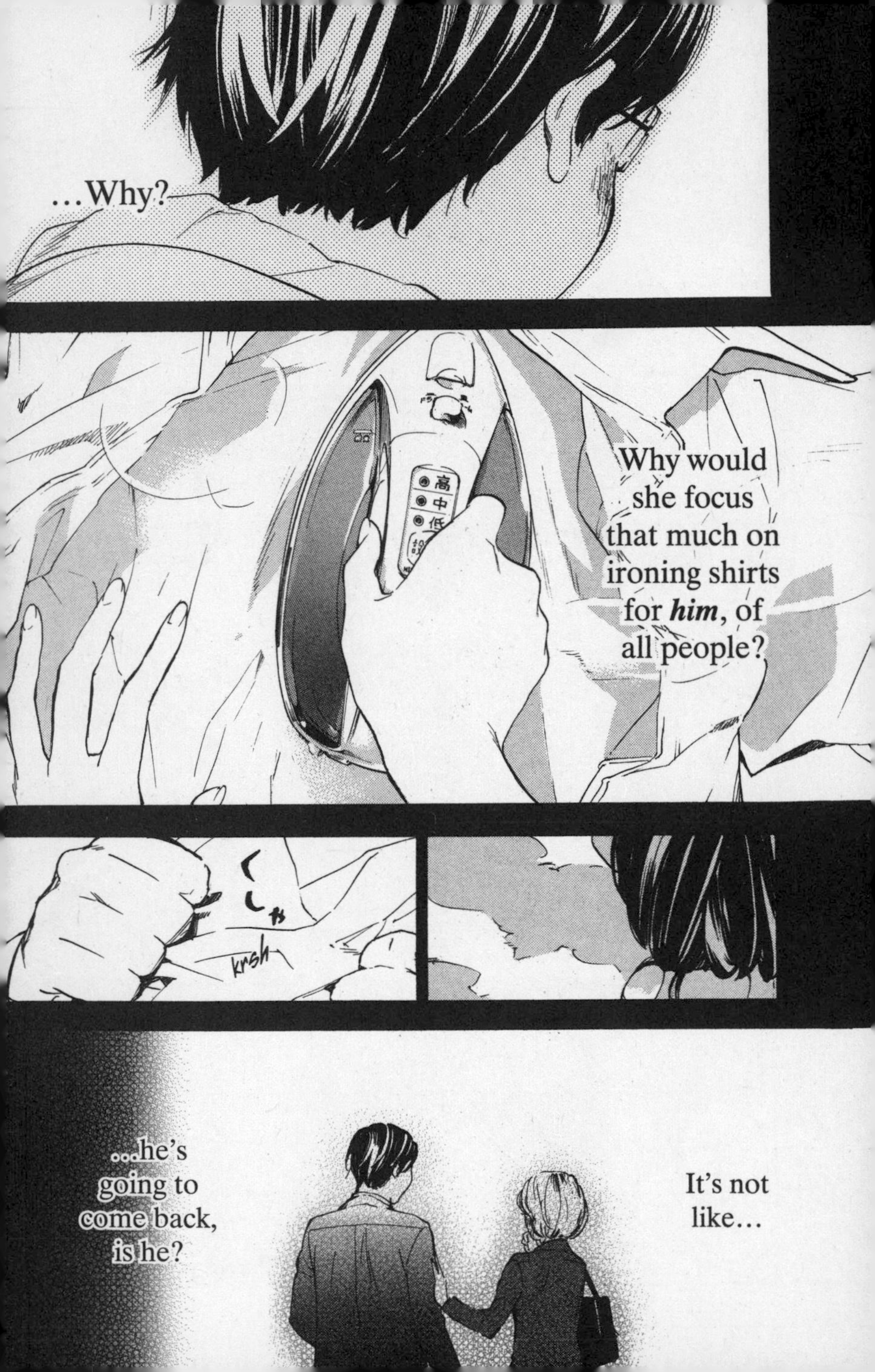
…Why?
Why would she focus that much on ironing shirts for *him*, of all people?
くしゃ
krsh
It's not like…
…he's going to come back, is he?

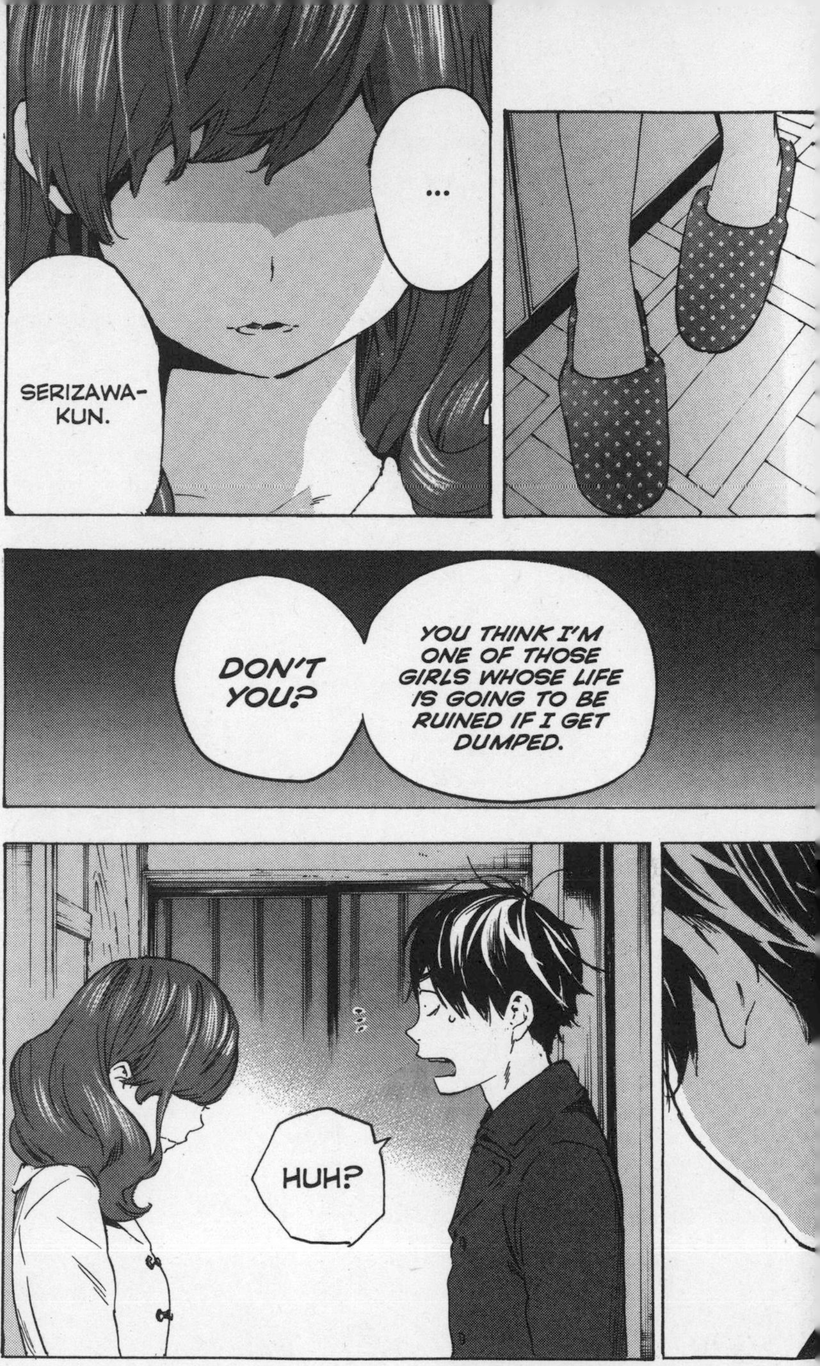
...
SERIZAWA-KUN.
YOU THINK I'M ONE OF THOSE GIRLS WHOSE LIFE IS GOING TO BE RUINED IF I GET DUMPED.
DON'T YOU?
HUH?

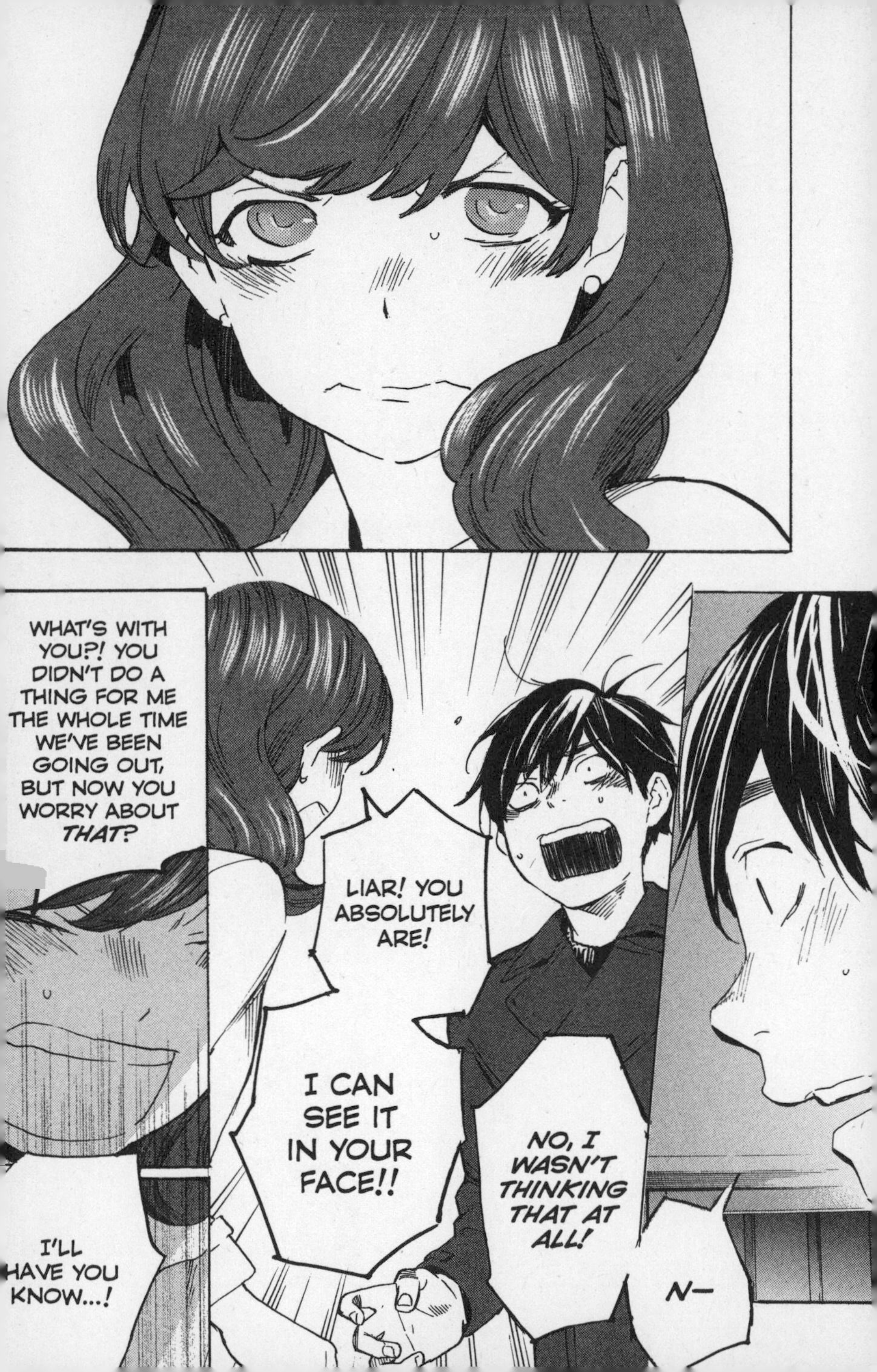
N—
NO, I WASN'T THINKING THAT AT ALL!
LIAR! YOU ABSOLUTELY ARE!
I CAN SEE IT IN YOUR FACE!!
WHAT'S WITH YOU?! YOU DIDN'T DO A THING FOR ME THE WHOLE TIME WE'VE BEEN GOING OUT, BUT NOW YOU WORRY ABOUT *THAT*?
I'LL HAVE YOU KNOW...!

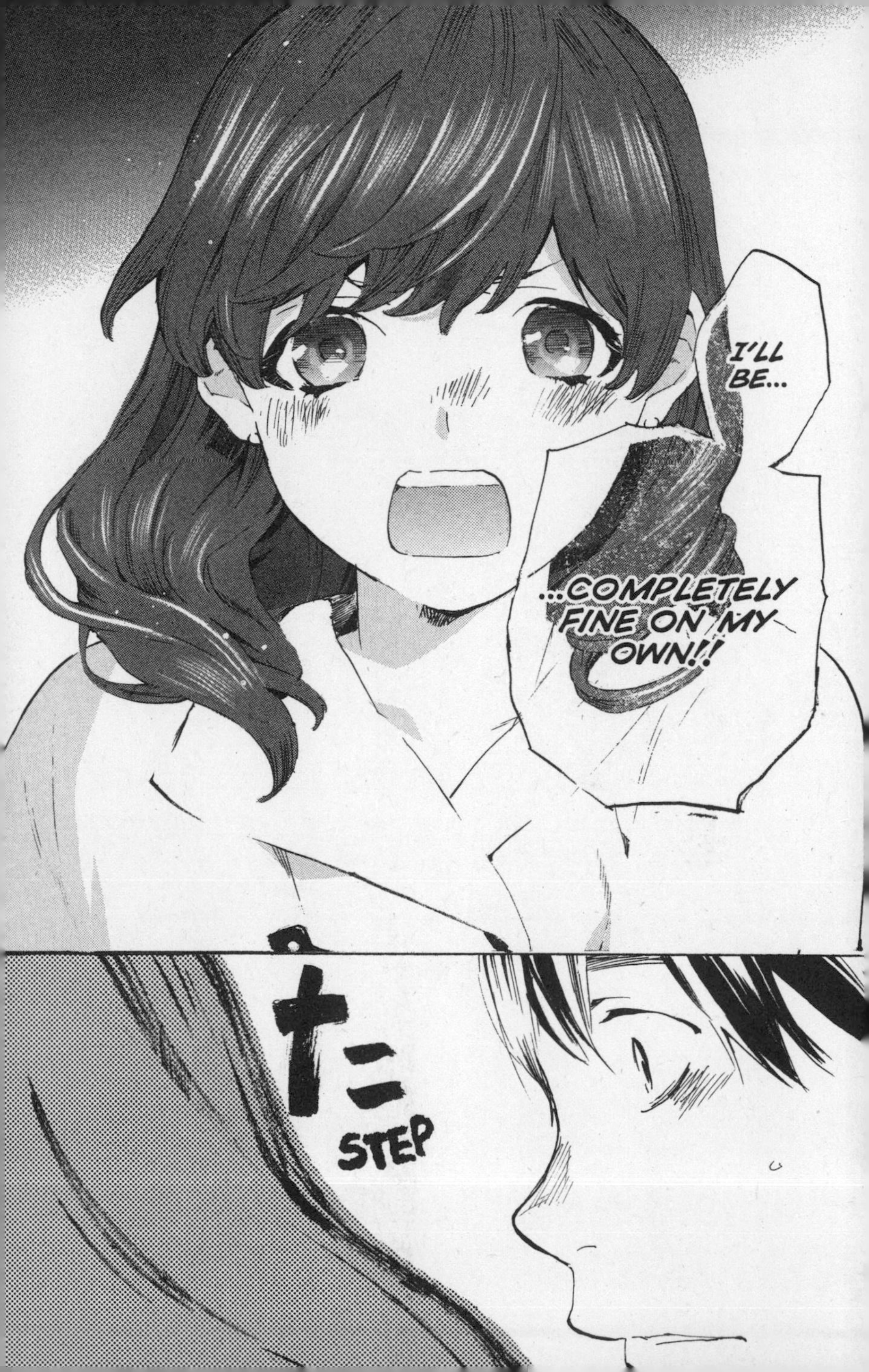
I'LL BE...
...COMPLETELY FINE ON MY OWN!!
た
STEP

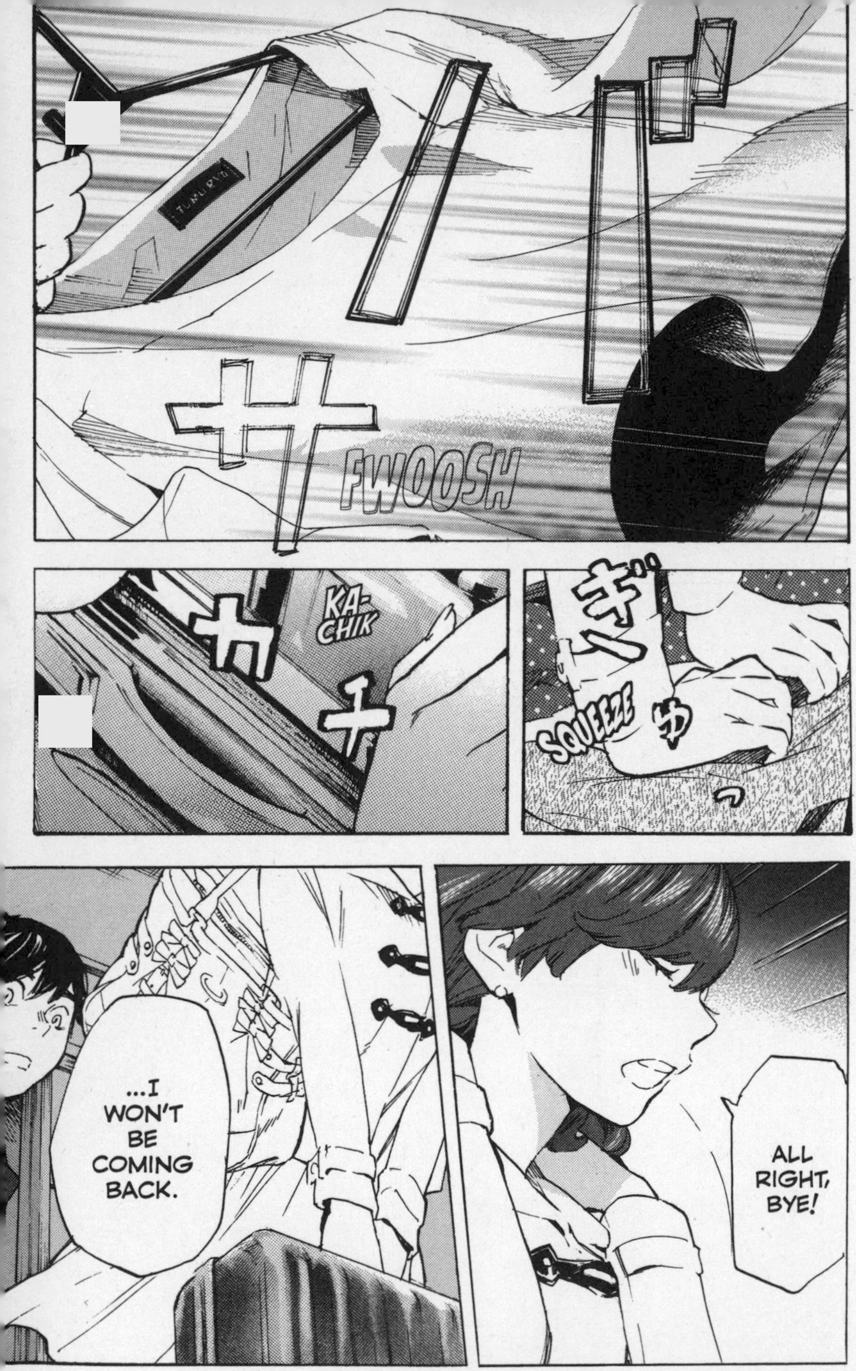
FWOOSH
SQUEEZE
KA-CHIK
ALL RIGHT, BYE!
...I WON'T BE COMING BACK.

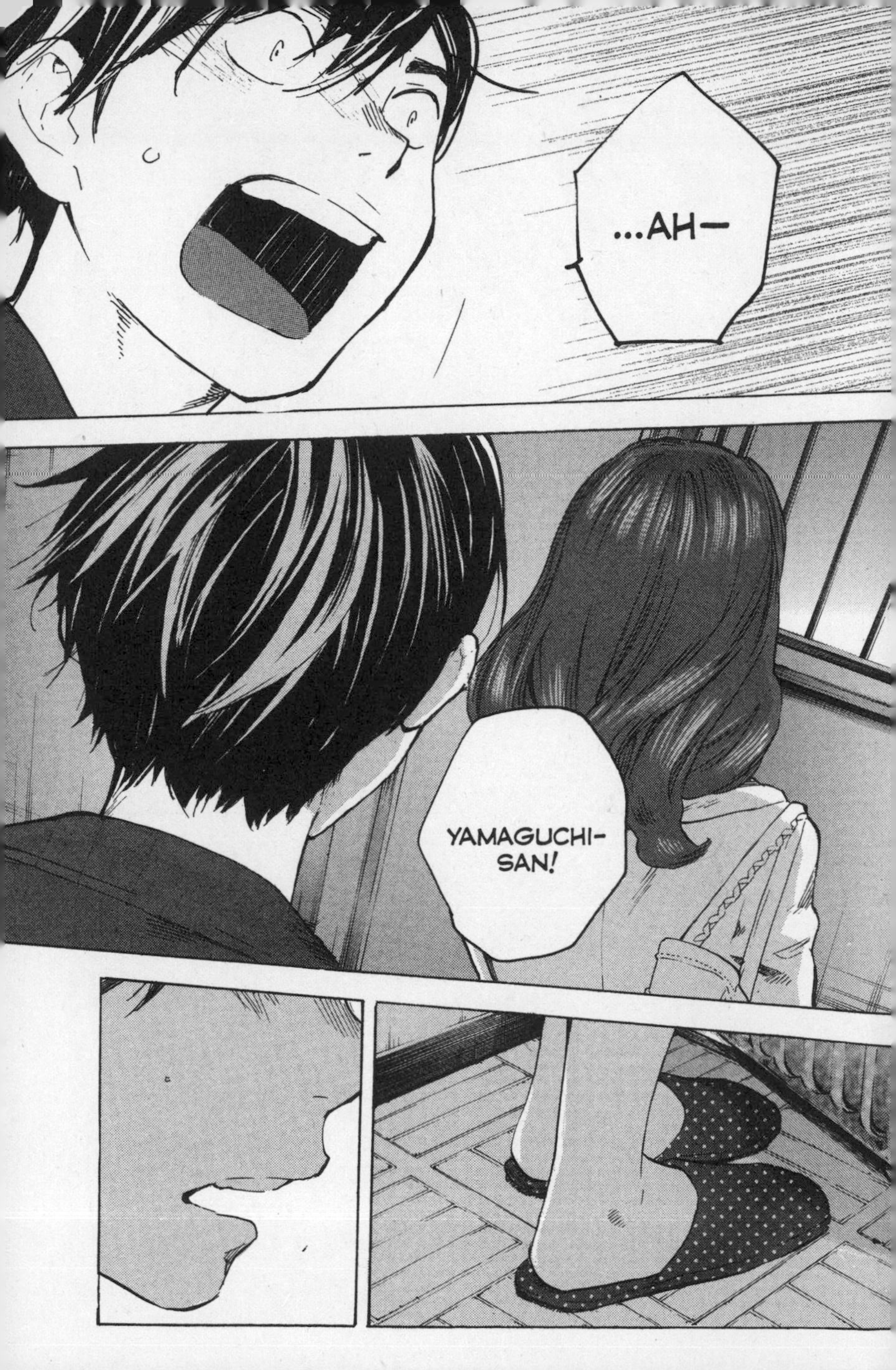
...AH—
YAMAGUCHI-SAN!

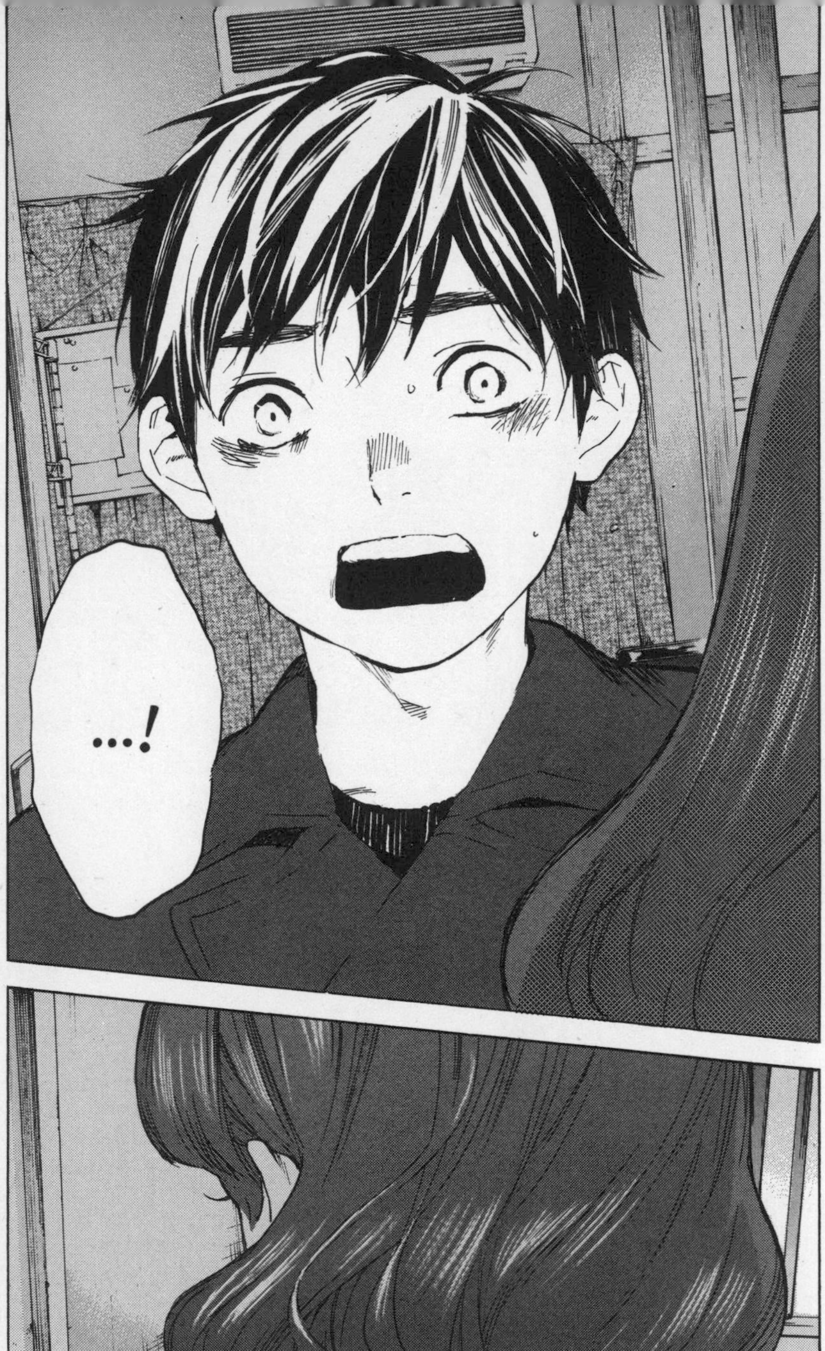
...!

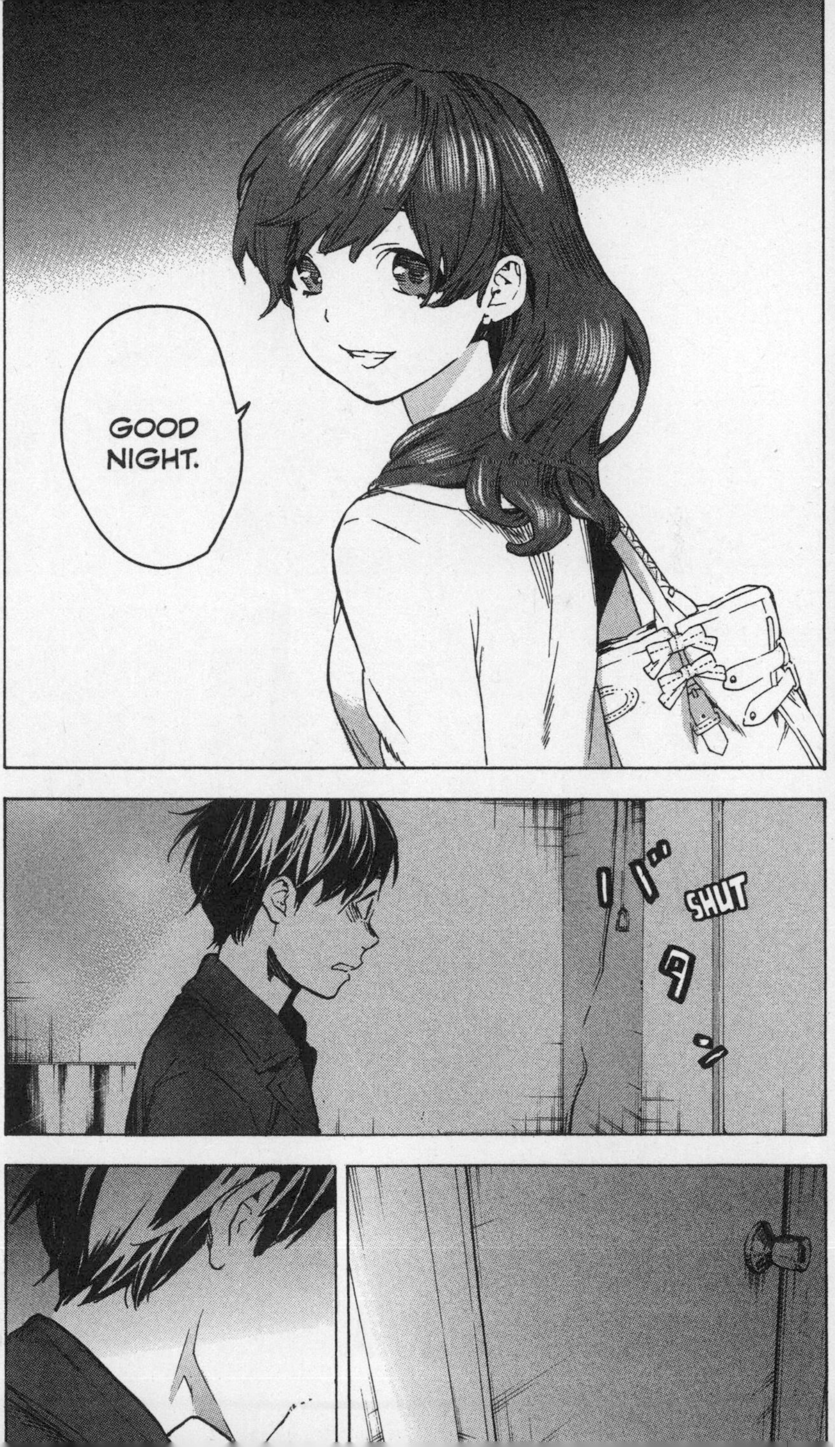
GOOD NIGHT.
SHUT

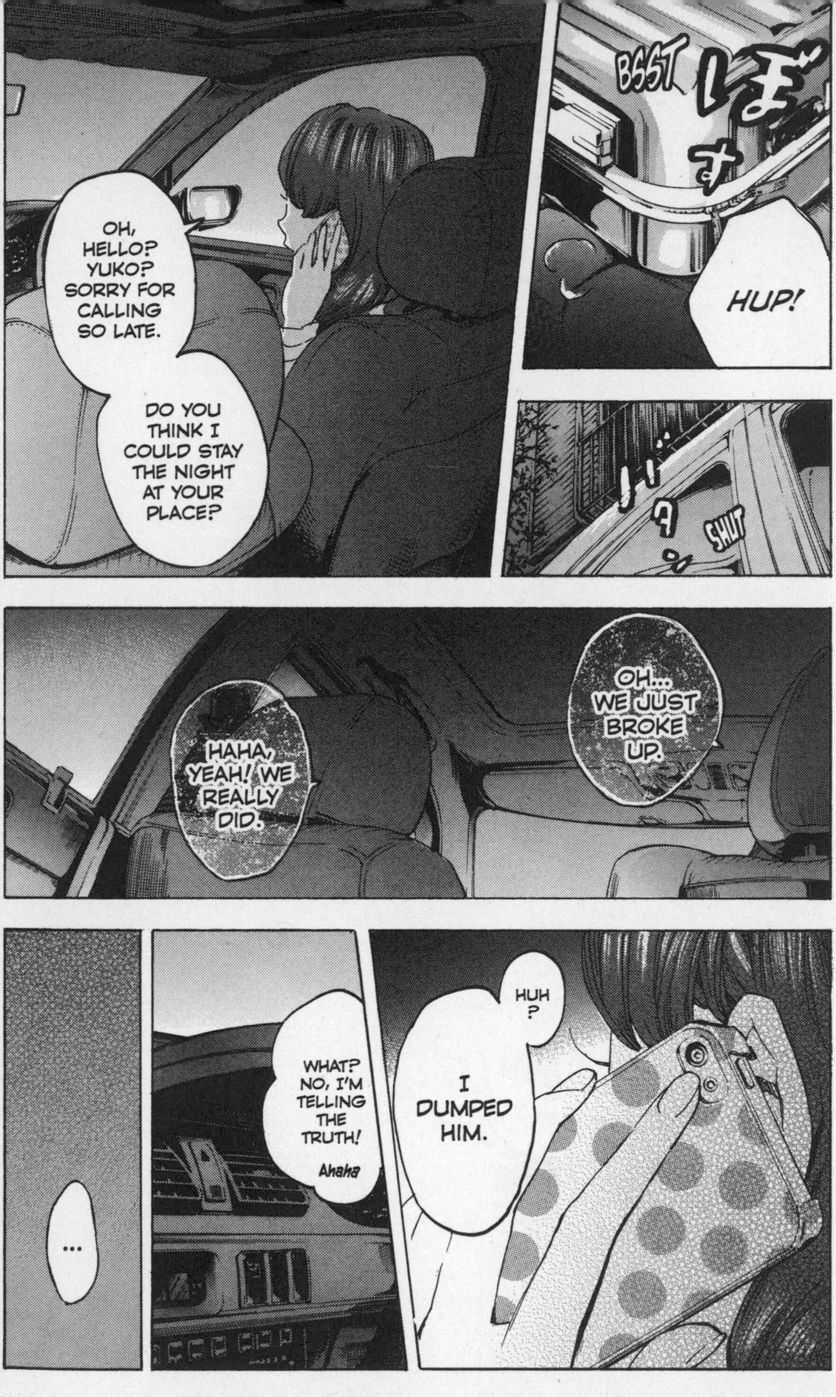
BSST
HUP!
SHUT
OH, HELLO? YUKO? SORRY FOR CALLING SO LATE.
DO YOU THINK I COULD STAY THE NIGHT AT YOUR PLACE?
OH... WE JUST BROKE UP.
HAHA, YEAH! WE REALLY DID.
HUH?
I DUMPED HIM.
WHAT? NO, I'M TELLING THE TRUTH!
Ahaha
...

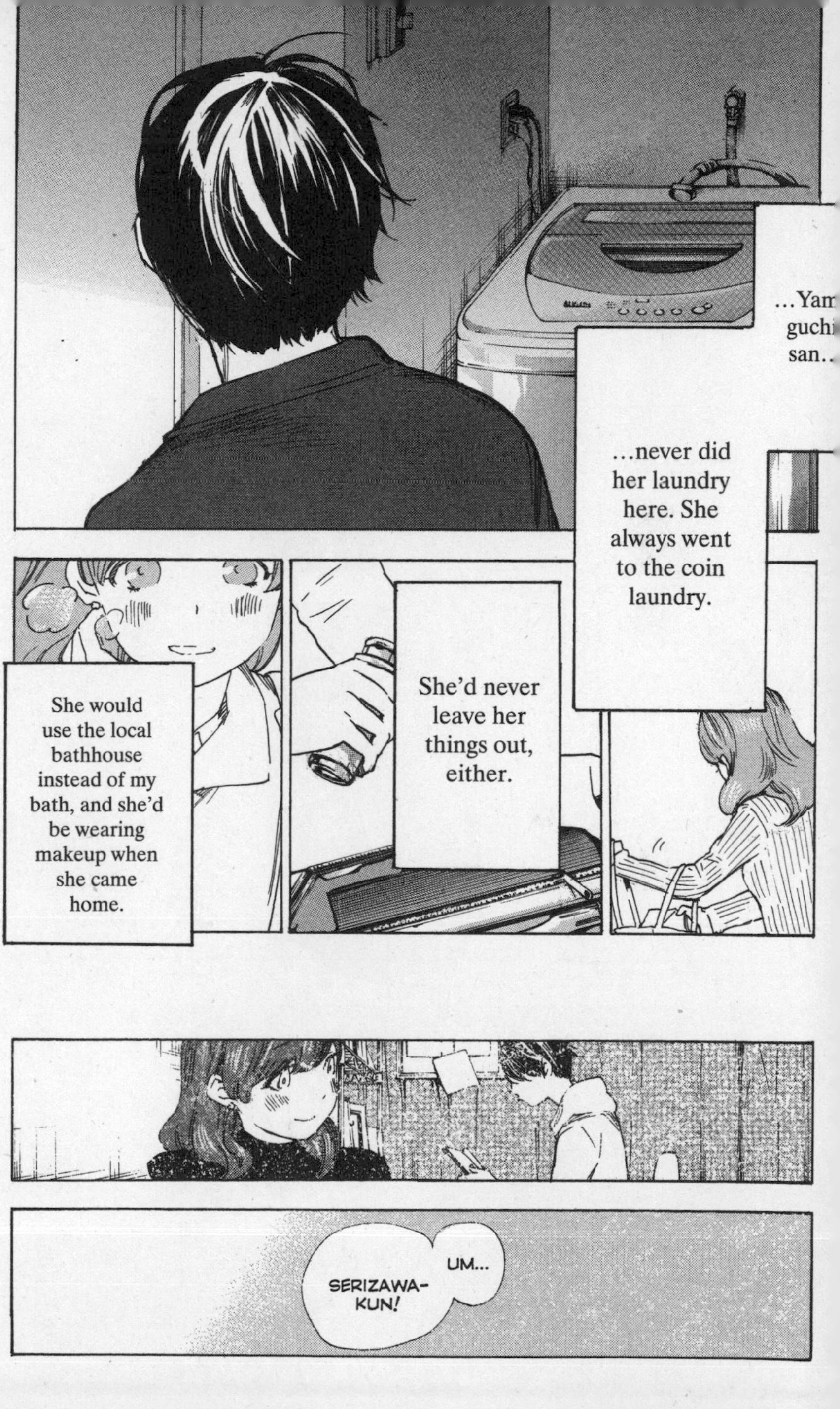
…Yam
guchi
san…
…never did her laundry here. She always went to the coin laundry.
She'd never leave her things out, either.
She would use the local bathhouse instead of my bath, and she'd be wearing makeup when she came home.
UM… SERIZAWA-KUN!

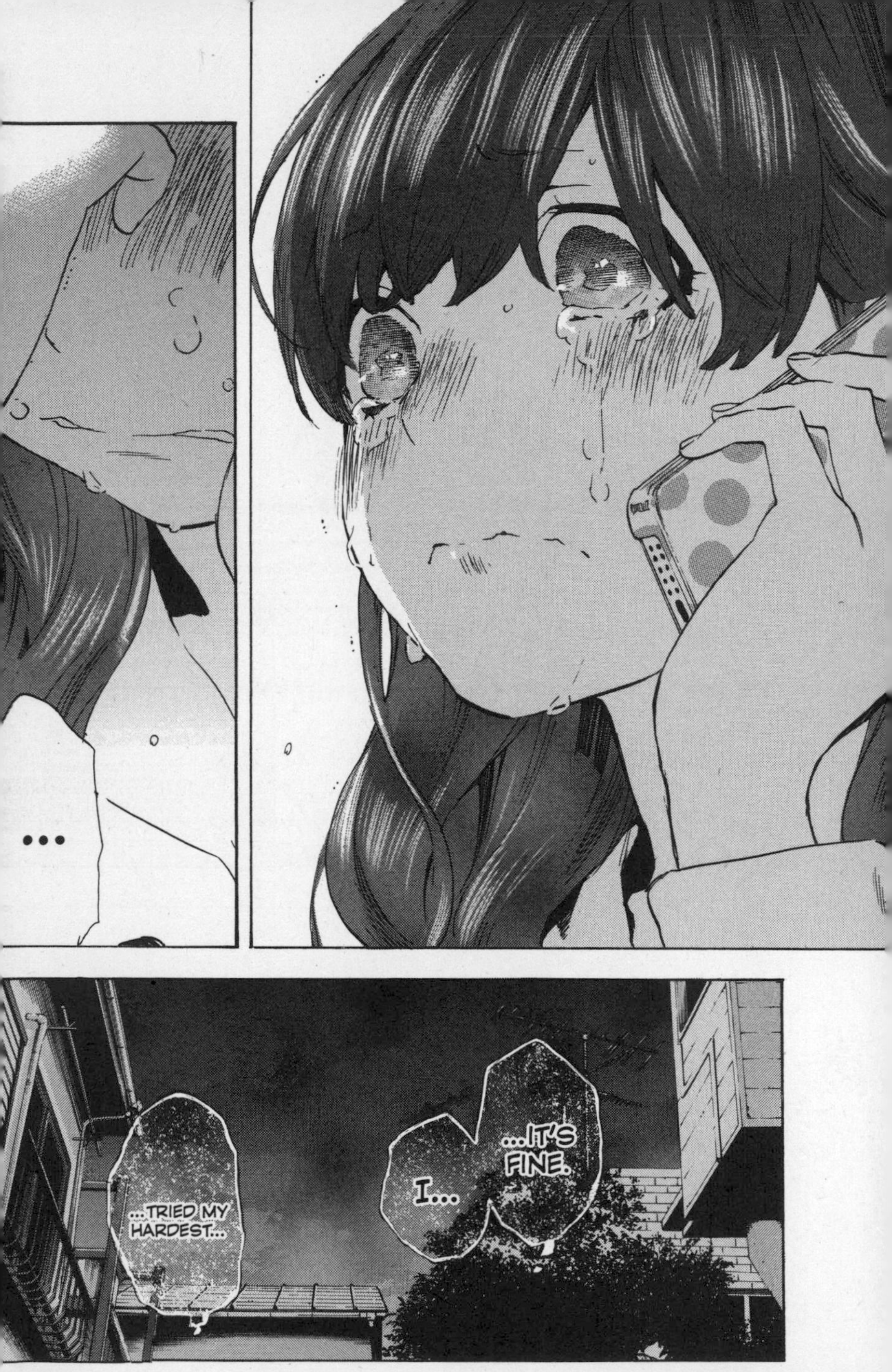
...
...IT'S FINE.
I...
...TRIED MY HARDEST...

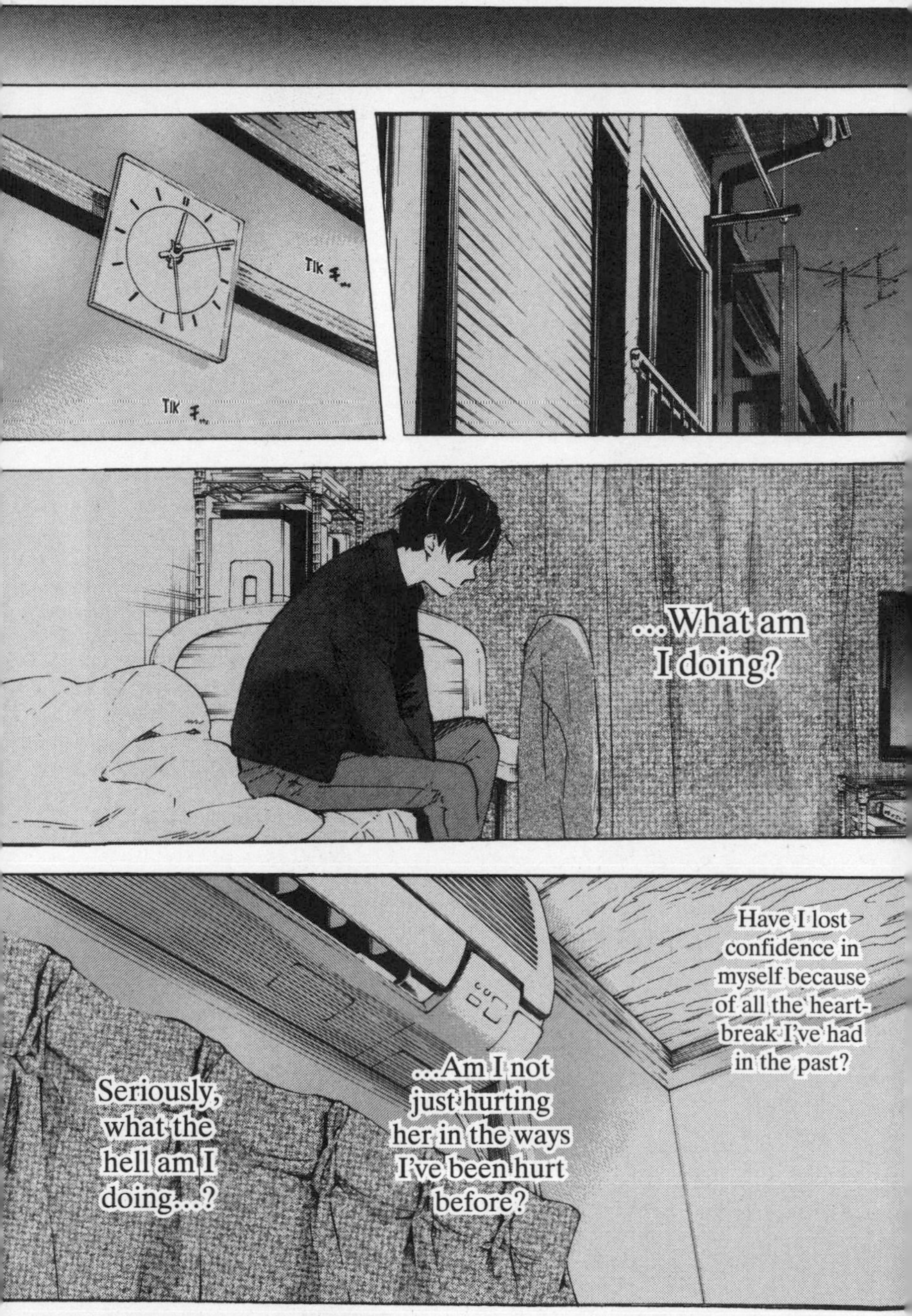
TIK
TIK
...What am I doing?
Have I lost confidence in myself because of all the heart-break I've had in the past?
...Am I not just hurting her in the ways I've been hurt before?
Seriously, what the hell am I doing...?

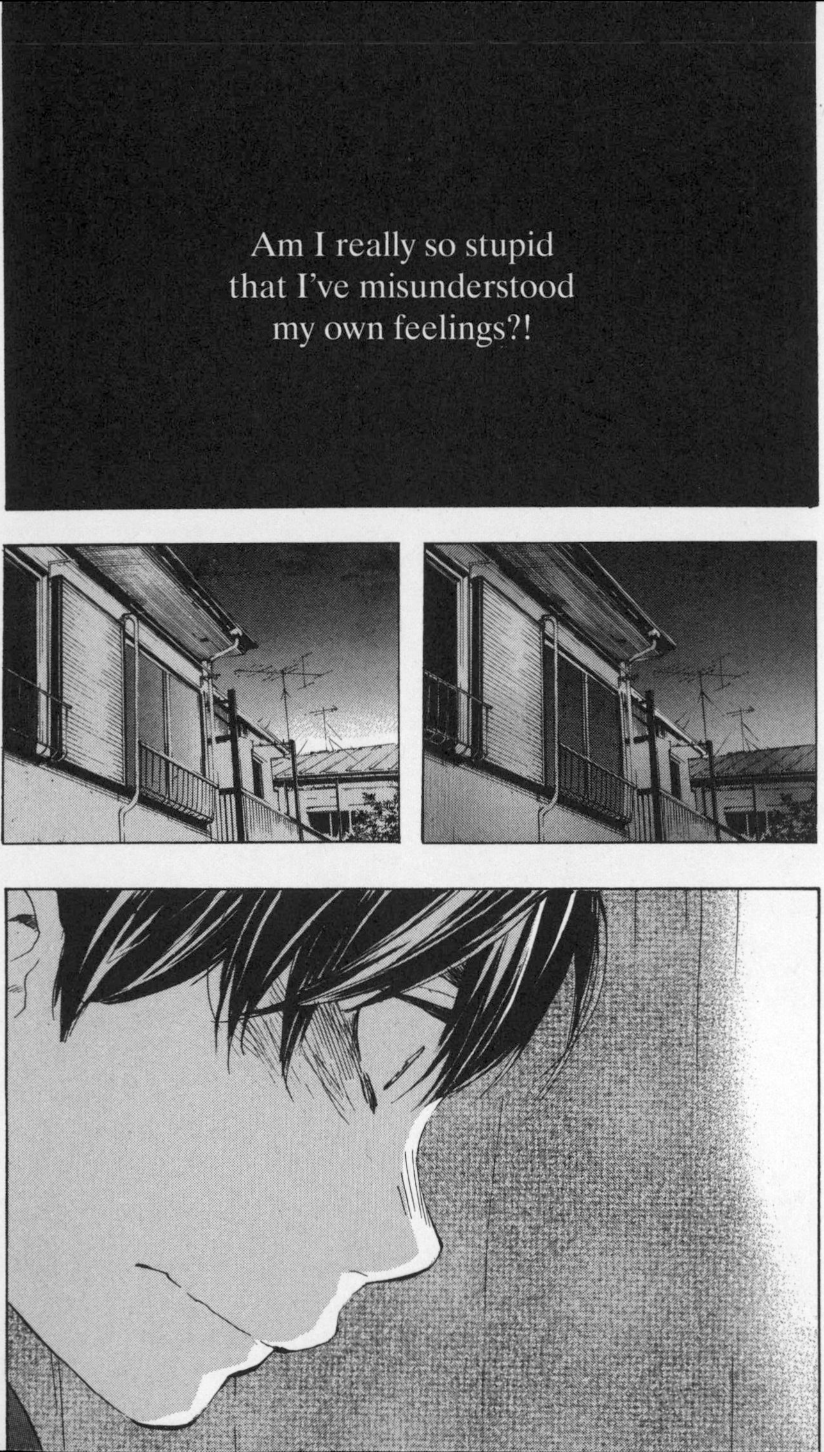
Am I really so stupid that I've misunderstood my own feelings?!

Forget Me Not

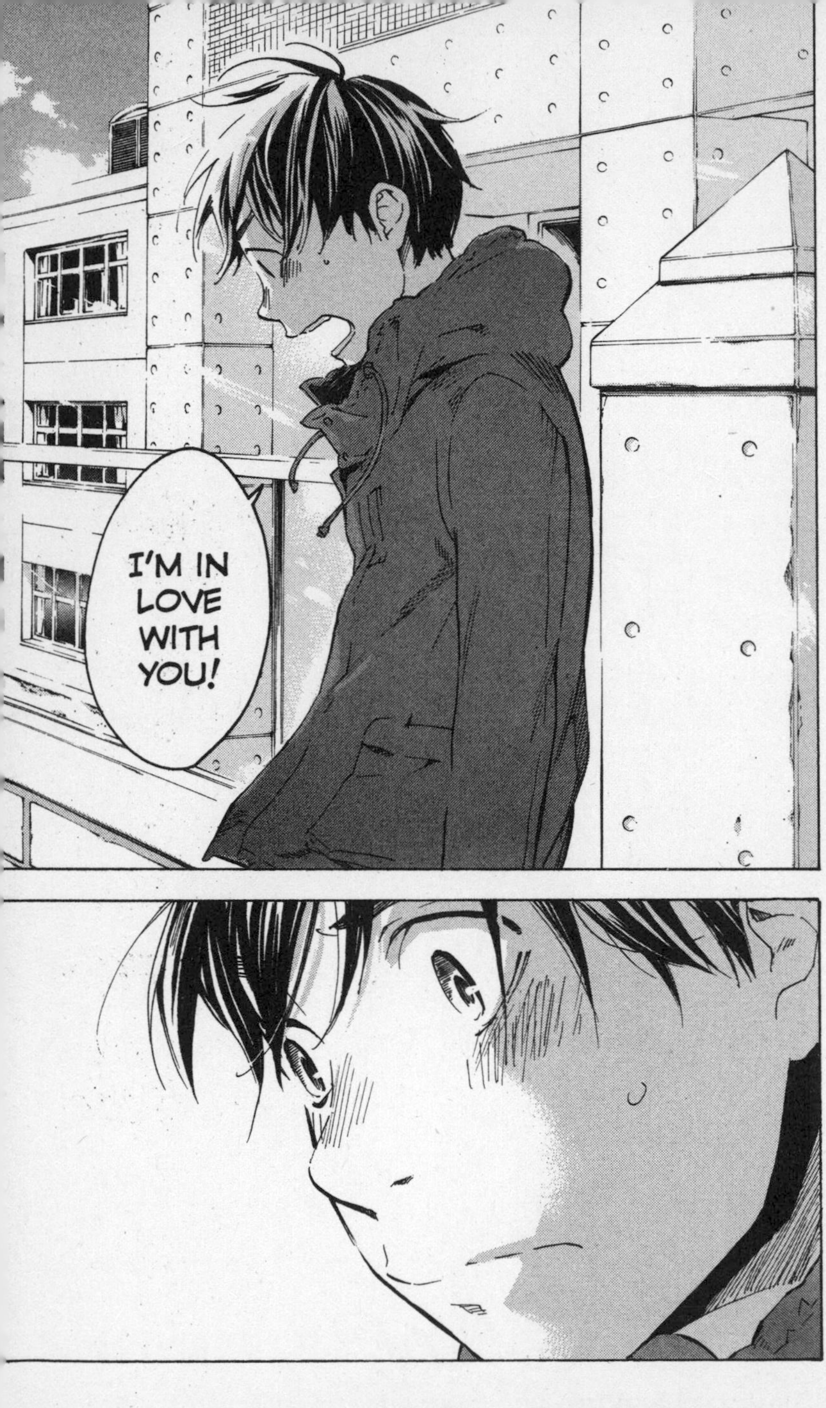
I'M IN LOVE WITH YOU!

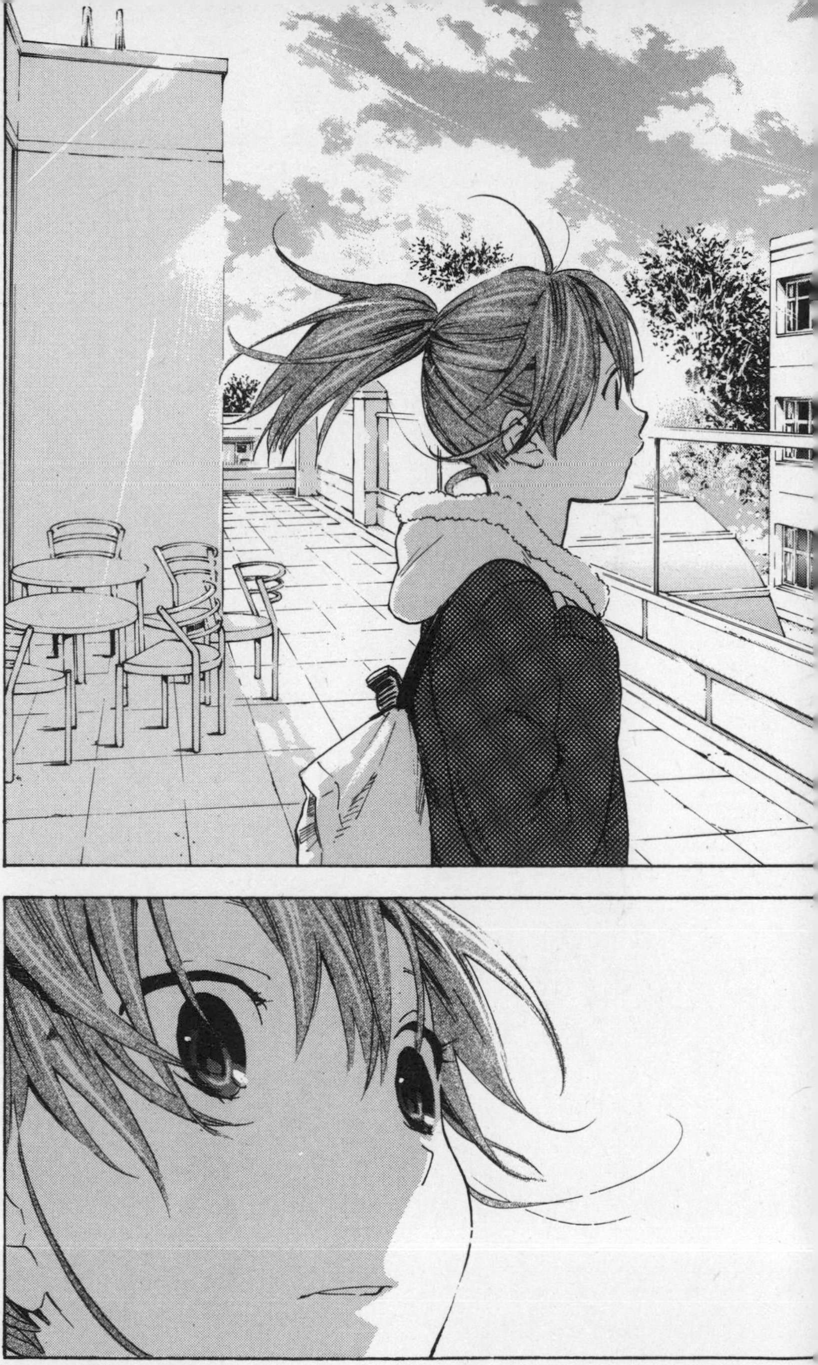

CHAPTER 25:

Tsukushi Makino 14

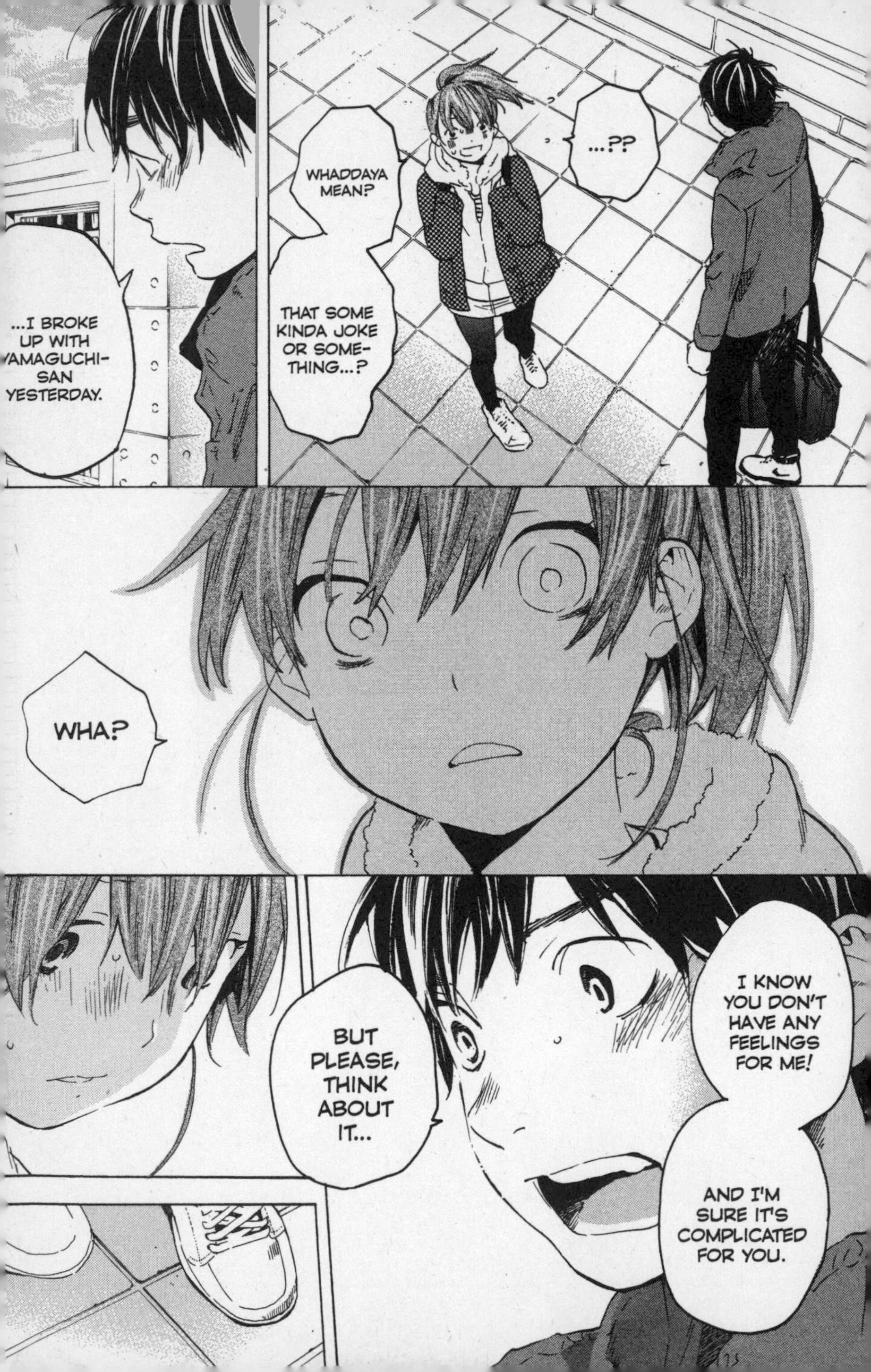
...??
WHADDAYA MEAN?
THAT SOME KINDA JOKE OR SOMETHING...?
...I BROKE UP WITH YAMAGUCHI-SAN YESTERDAY.
WHA?
I KNOW YOU DON'T HAVE ANY FEELINGS FOR ME!
AND I'M SURE IT'S COMPLICATED FOR YOU.
BUT PLEASE, THINK ABOUT IT...

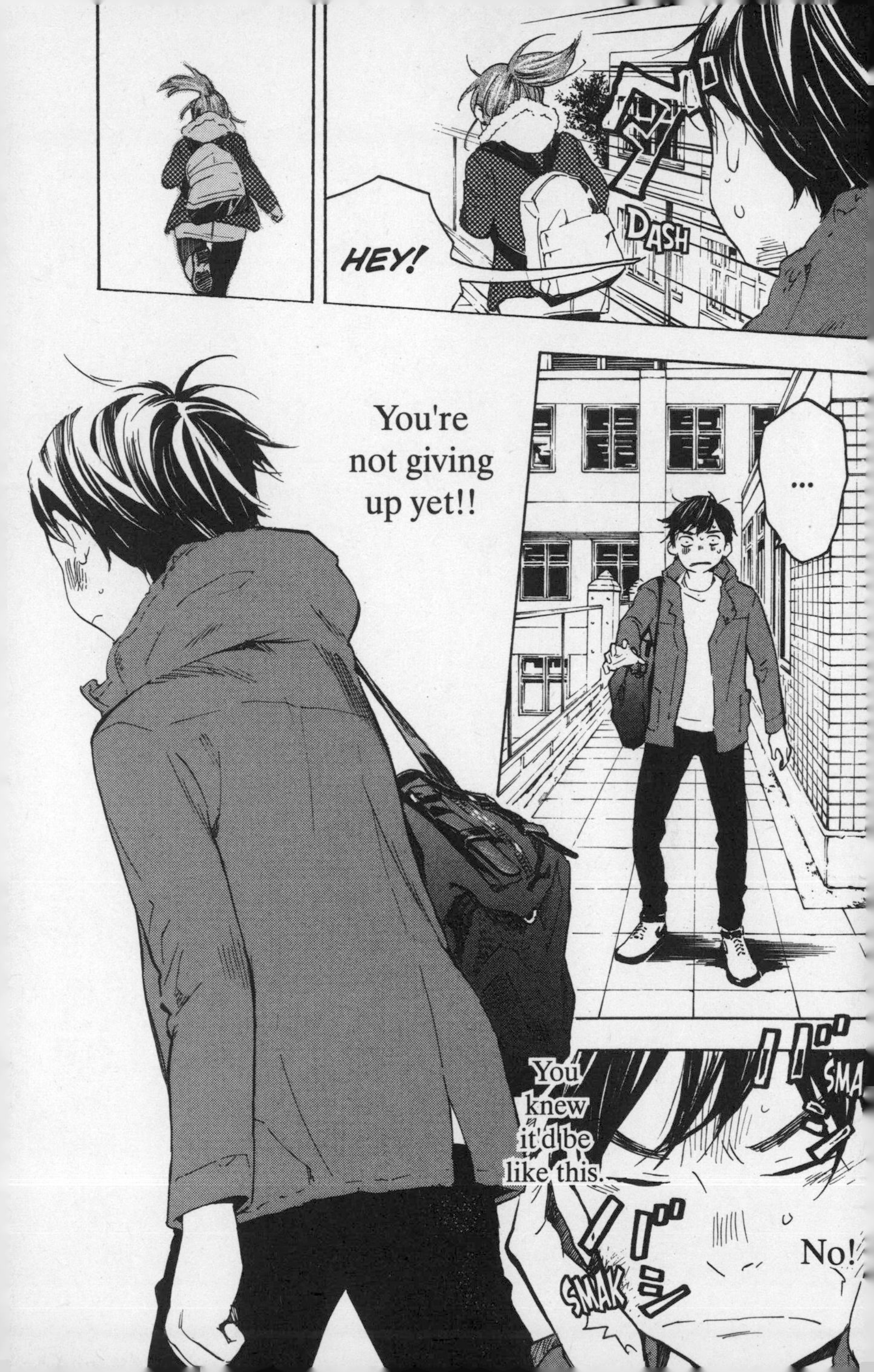
DASH
HEY!
...
SMA
You knew it'd be like this.
No!
SMAK
You're not giving up yet!!

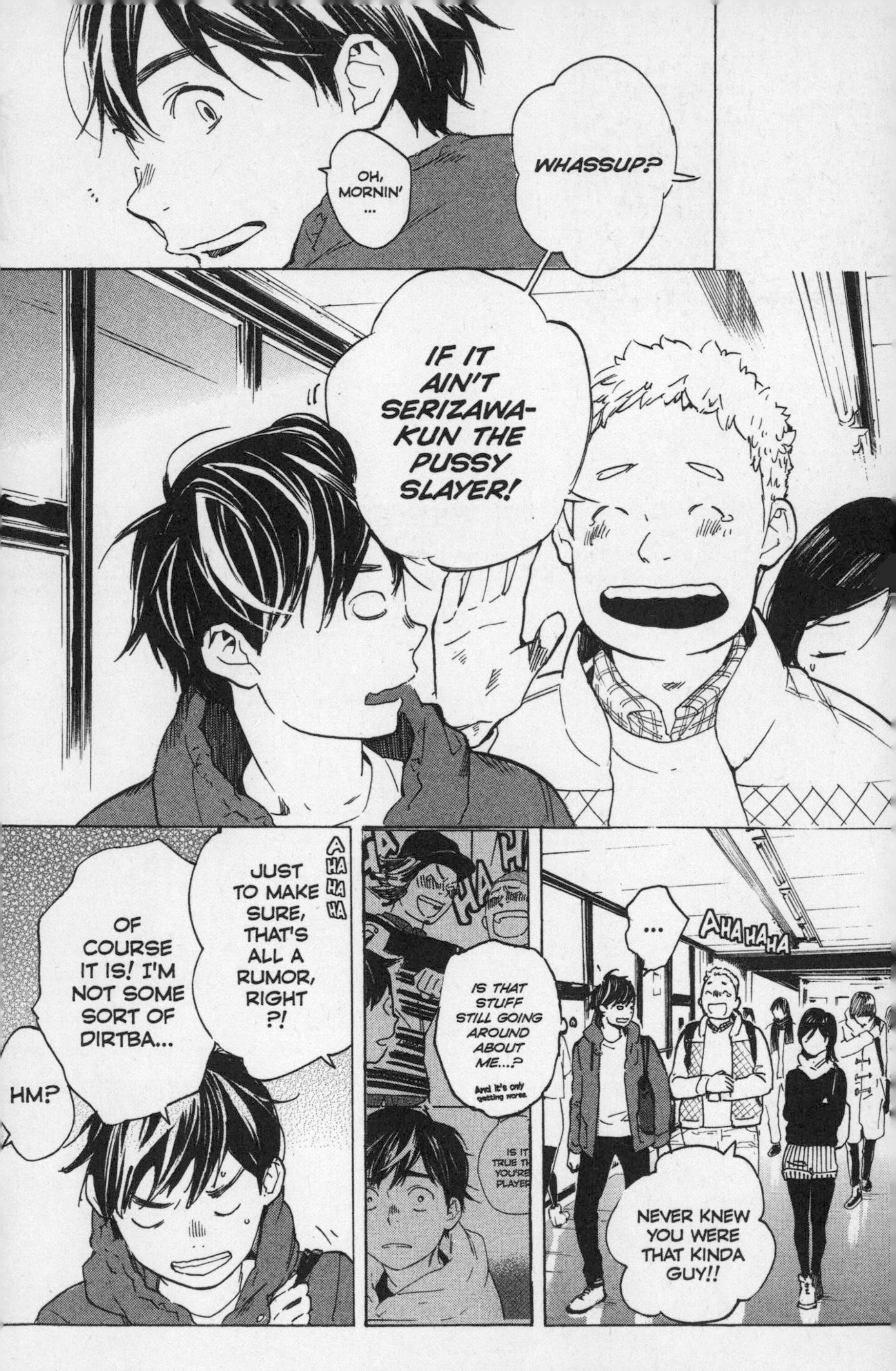
WHASSUP?
OH, MORNIN' ...
IF IT AIN'T SERIZAWA-KUN THE PUSSY SLAYER!
...
AHAHAHA
NEVER KNEW YOU WERE THAT KINDA GUY!!
IS THAT STUFF STILL GOING AROUND ABOUT ME...?
And it's only getting worse.
AHAHAHA
JUST TO MAKE SURE, THAT'S ALL A RUMOR, RIGHT?!
OF COURSE IT IS! I'M NOT SOME SORT OF DIRTBA...
HM?

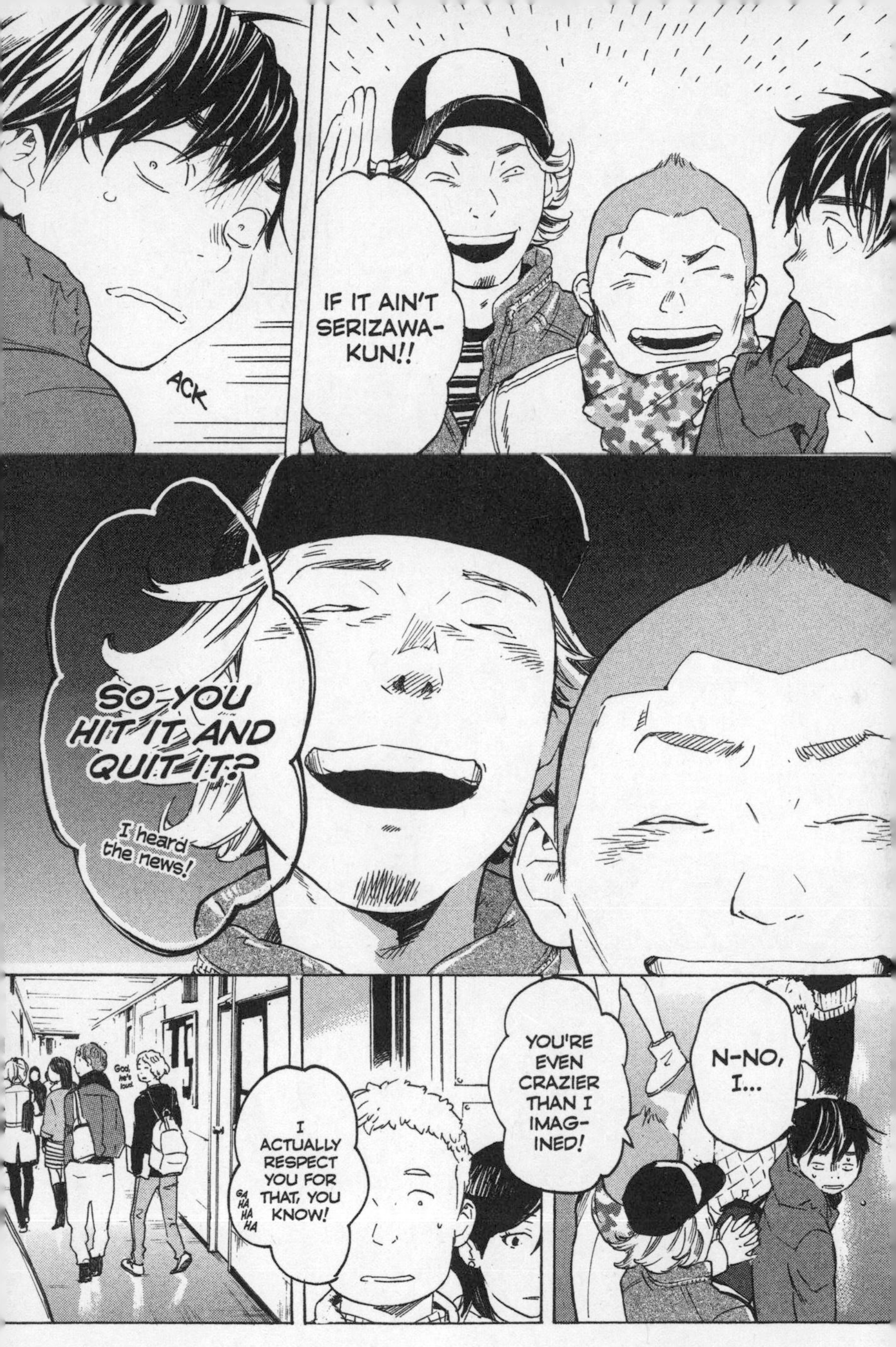
IF IT AIN'T SERIZAWA-KUN!!
ACK
SO YOU HIT IT AND QUIT IT?
I heard the news!
N-NO, I...
YOU'RE EVEN CRAZIER THAN I IMAG-INED!
I ACTUALLY RESPECT YOU FOR THAT, YOU KNOW!
GA HA HA HA
God, he's loud.

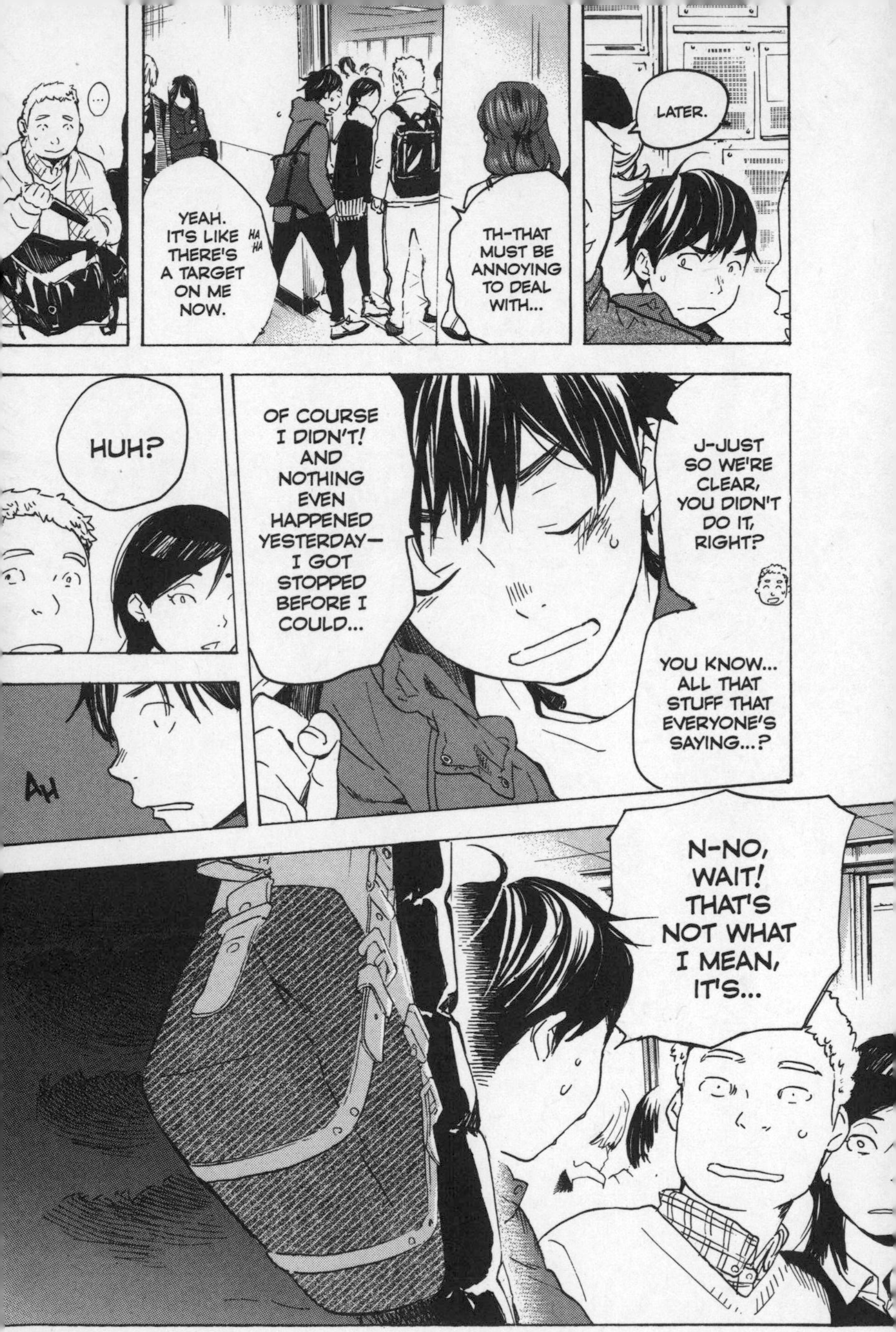
LATER.
TH-THAT MUST BE ANNOYING TO DEAL WITH...
YEAH. IT'S LIKE THERE'S A TARGET ON ME NOW.
HA HA
...
J-JUST SO WE'RE CLEAR, YOU DIDN'T DO IT, RIGHT?
YOU KNOW... ALL THAT STUFF THAT EVERYONE'S SAYING...?
OF COURSE I DIDN'T! AND NOTHING EVEN HAPPENED YESTERDAY— I GOT STOPPED BEFORE I COULD...
HUH?
AH
N-NO, WAIT! THAT'S NOT WHAT I MEAN, IT'S...

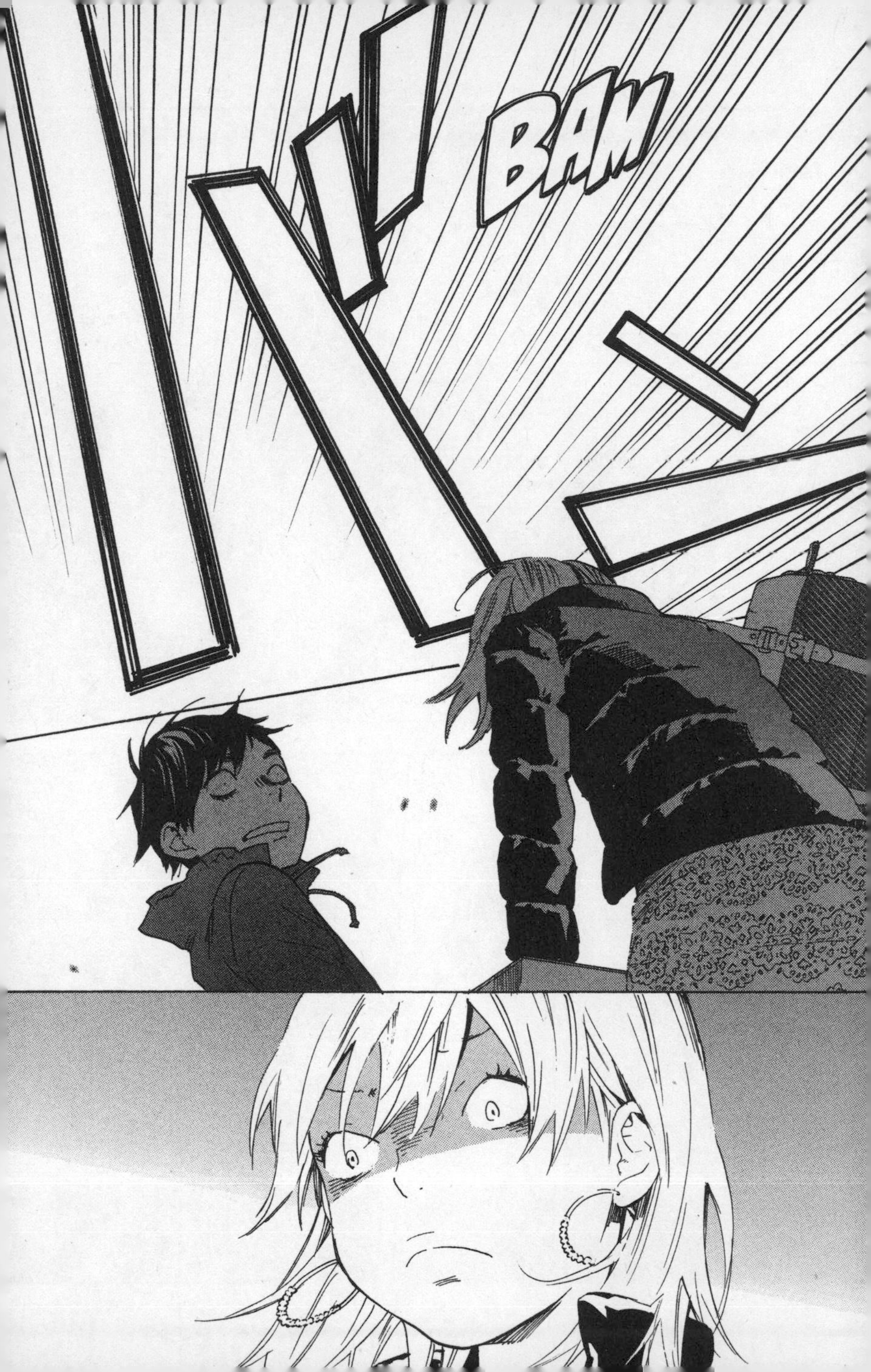
BAM

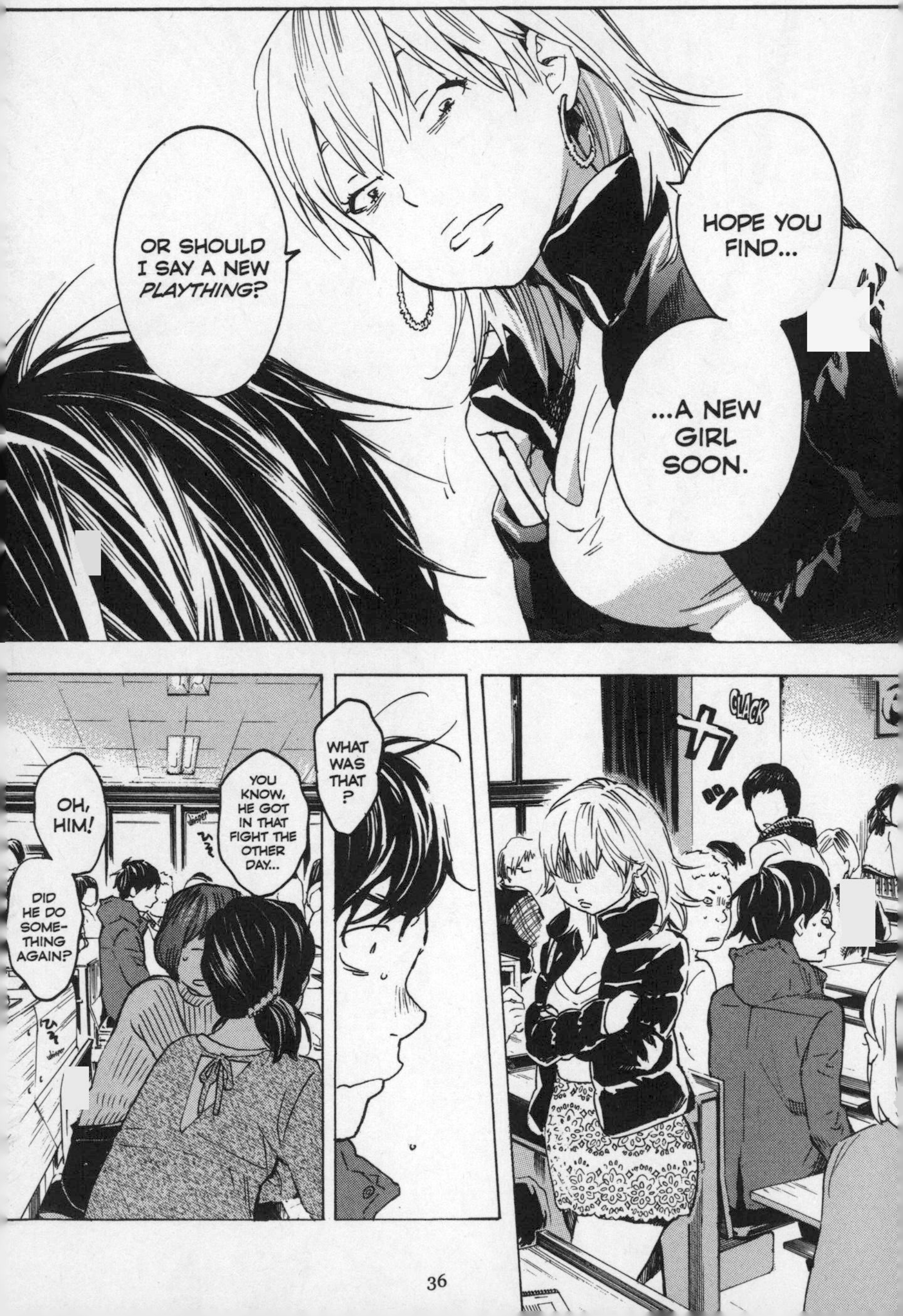
HOPE YOU FIND...
...A NEW GIRL SOON.
OR SHOULD I SAY A NEW *PLAYTHING*?
CLACK
WHAT WAS THAT?
YOU KNOW, HE GOT IN THAT FIGHT THE OTHER DAY...
OH, HIM!
DID HE DO SOME-THING AGAIN?

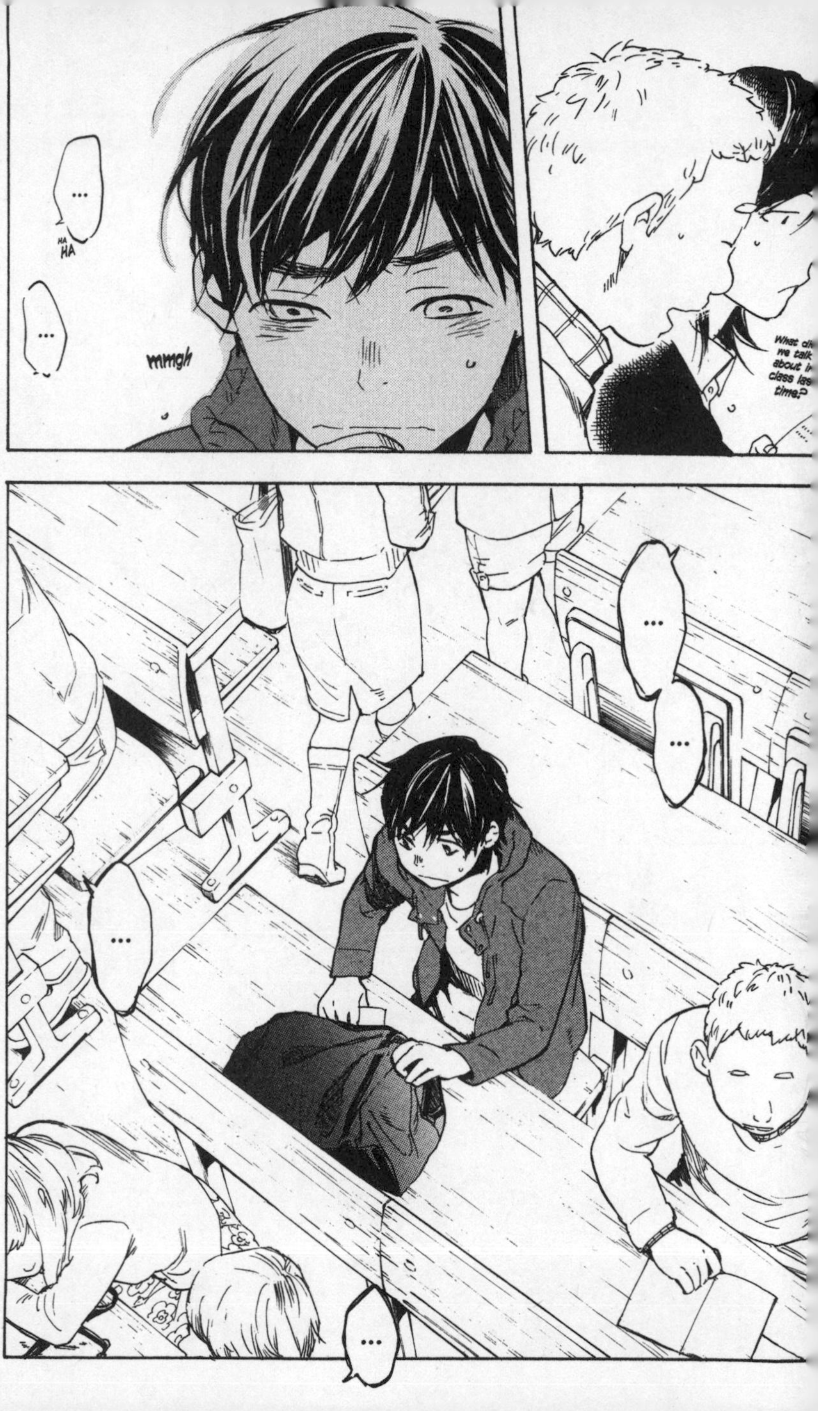
What di
we talk
about i
class las
time?
...
HA HA
...
mmgh
...
...
...
...

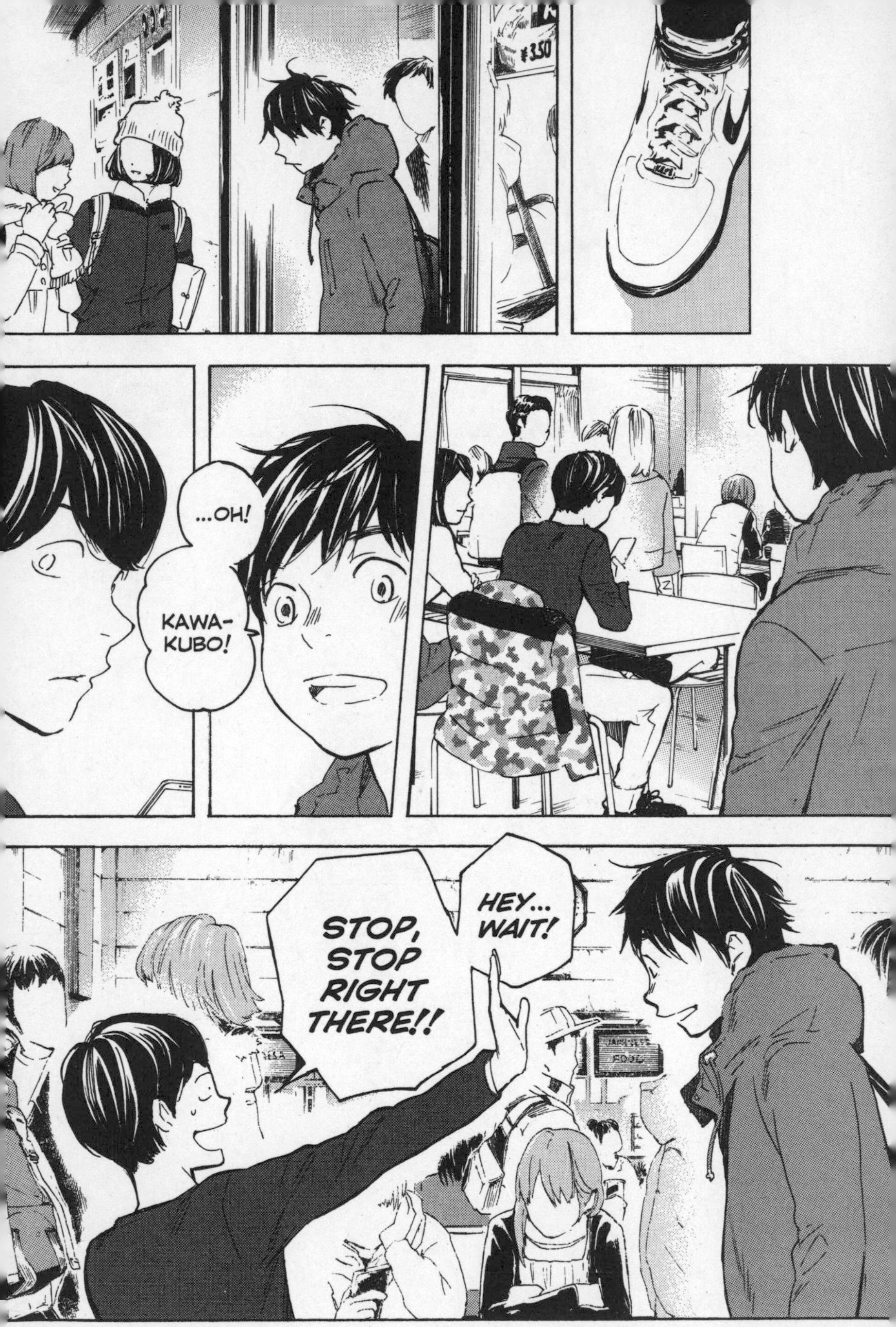
¥350
...OH!
KAWA-KUBO!
HEY... WAIT!
STOP, STOP RIGHT THERE!!

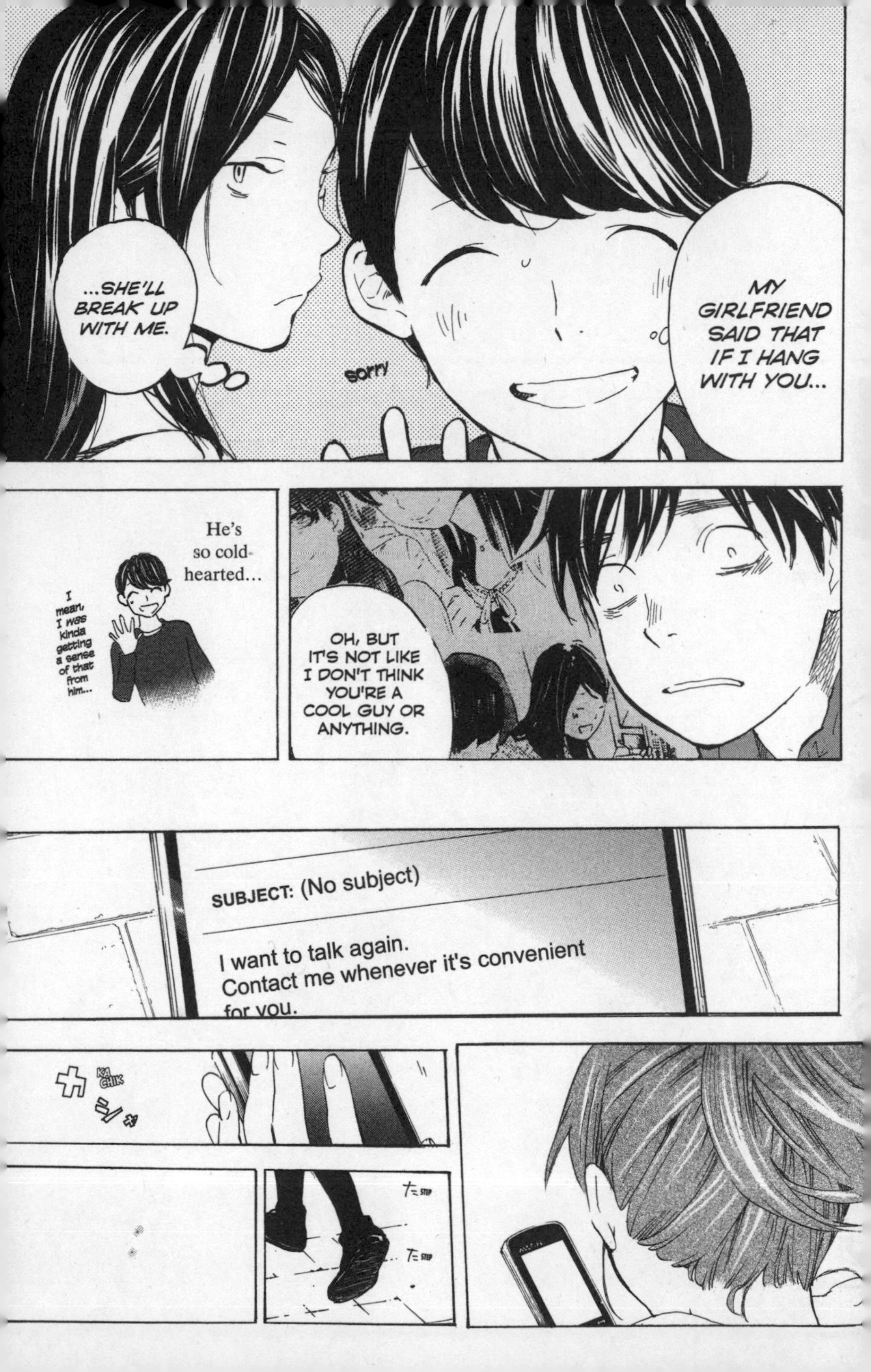
MY GIRLFRIEND SAID THAT IF I HANG WITH YOU...
sorry
...SHE'LL BREAK UP WITH ME.
OH, BUT IT'S NOT LIKE I DON'T THINK YOU'RE A COOL GUY OR ANYTHING.
He's so cold-hearted...
I mean, I was kinda getting a sense of that from him...
SUBJECT: (No subject)
I want to talk again.
Contact me whenever it's convenient for you.
KA CHIK
STEP
STEP

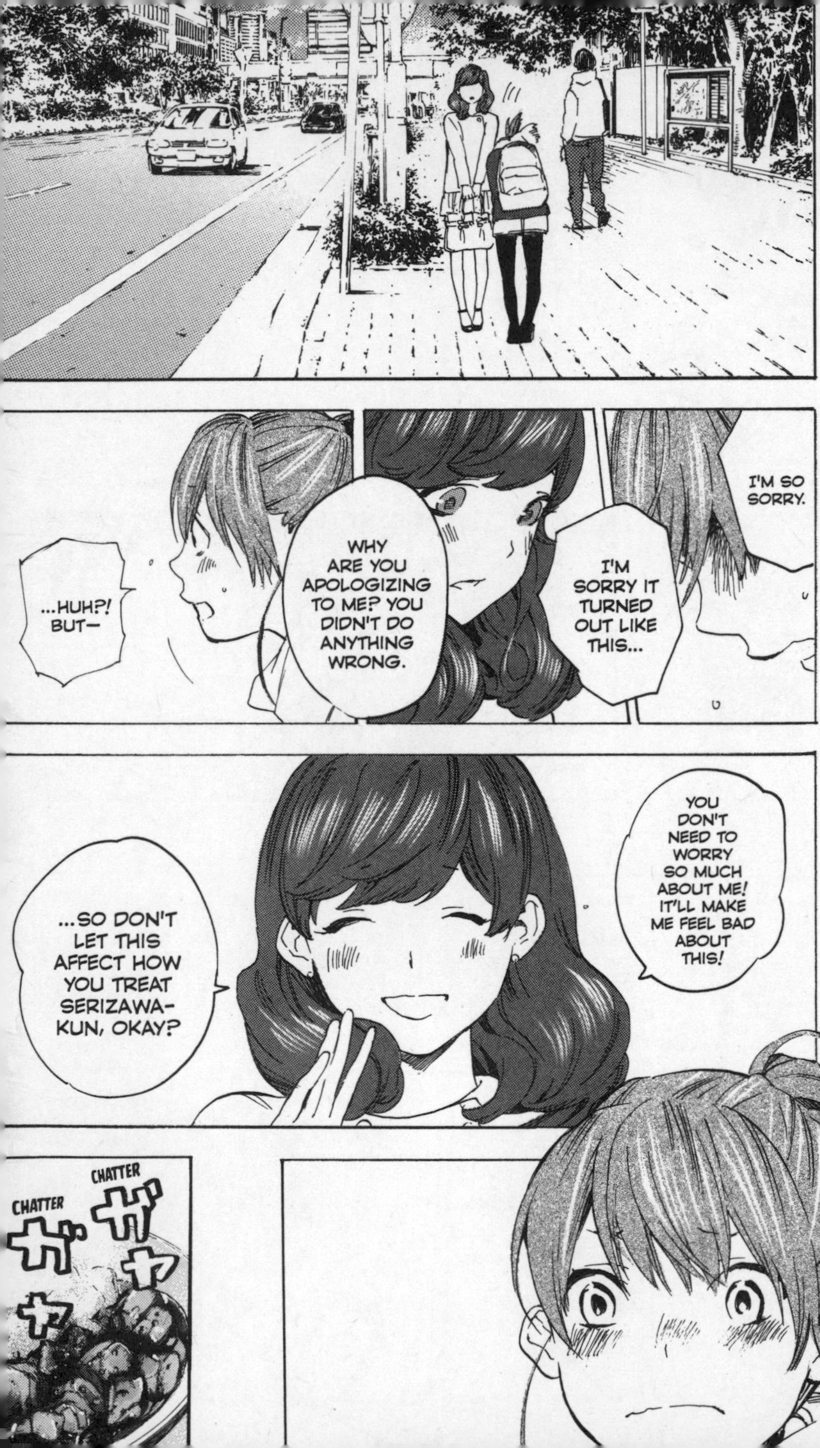
I'M SO SORRY.
I'M SORRY IT TURNED OUT LIKE THIS...
WHY ARE YOU APOLOGIZING TO ME? YOU DIDN'T DO ANYTHING WRONG.
...HUH?! BUT—
YOU DON'T NEED TO WORRY SO MUCH ABOUT ME! IT'LL MAKE ME FEEL BAD ABOUT THIS!
...SO DON'T LET THIS AFFECT HOW YOU TREAT SERIZAWA-KUN, OKAY?
CHATTER
CHATTER

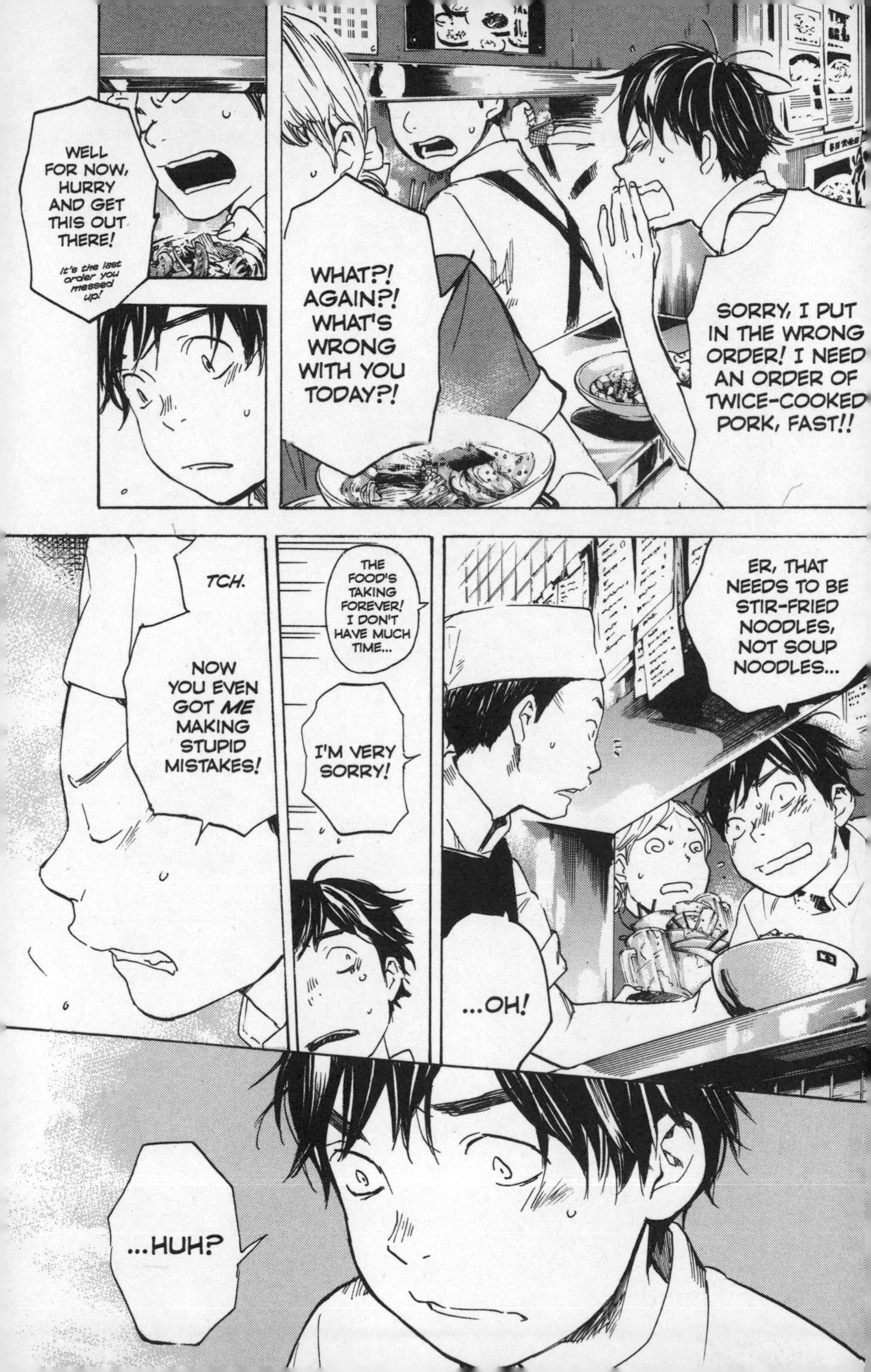
SORRY, I PUT IN THE WRONG ORDER! I NEED AN ORDER OF TWICE-COOKED PORK, FAST!!
WHAT?! AGAIN?! WHAT'S WRONG WITH YOU TODAY?!
WELL FOR NOW, HURRY AND GET THIS OUT THERE!
It's the last order you messed up!
ER, THAT NEEDS TO BE STIR-FRIED NOODLES, NOT SOUP NOODLES...
...OH!
THE FOOD'S TAKING FOREVER! I DON'T HAVE MUCH TIME...
I'M VERY SORRY!
TCH.
NOW YOU EVEN GOT *ME* MAKING STUPID MISTAKES!
...HUH?

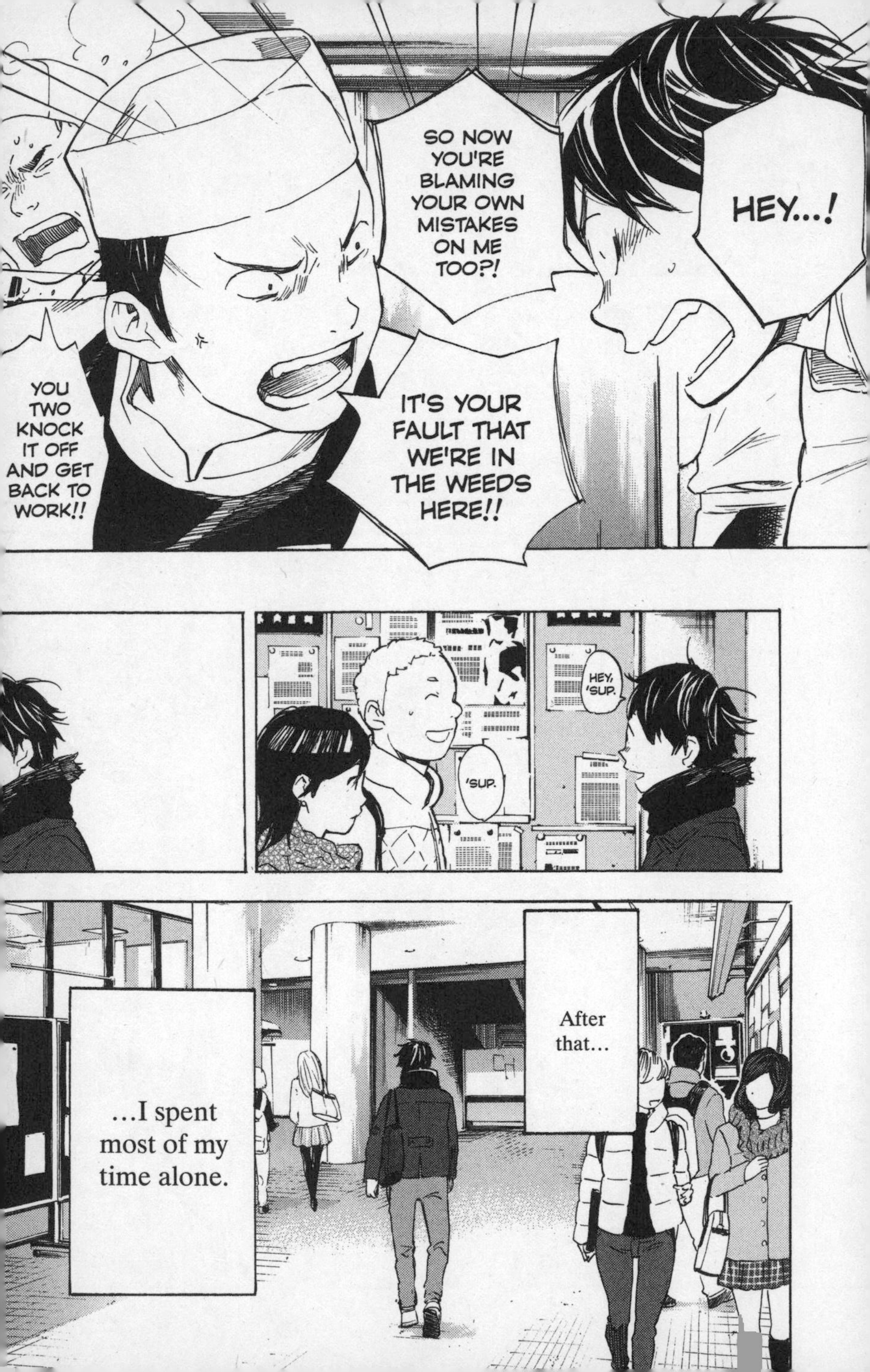
HEY...!
SO NOW YOU'RE BLAMING YOUR OWN MISTAKES ON ME TOO?!
IT'S YOUR FAULT THAT WE'RE IN THE WEEDS HERE!!
YOU TWO KNOCK IT OFF AND GET BACK TO WORK!!
HEY, 'SUP.
'SUP.
After that...
...I spent most of my time alone.

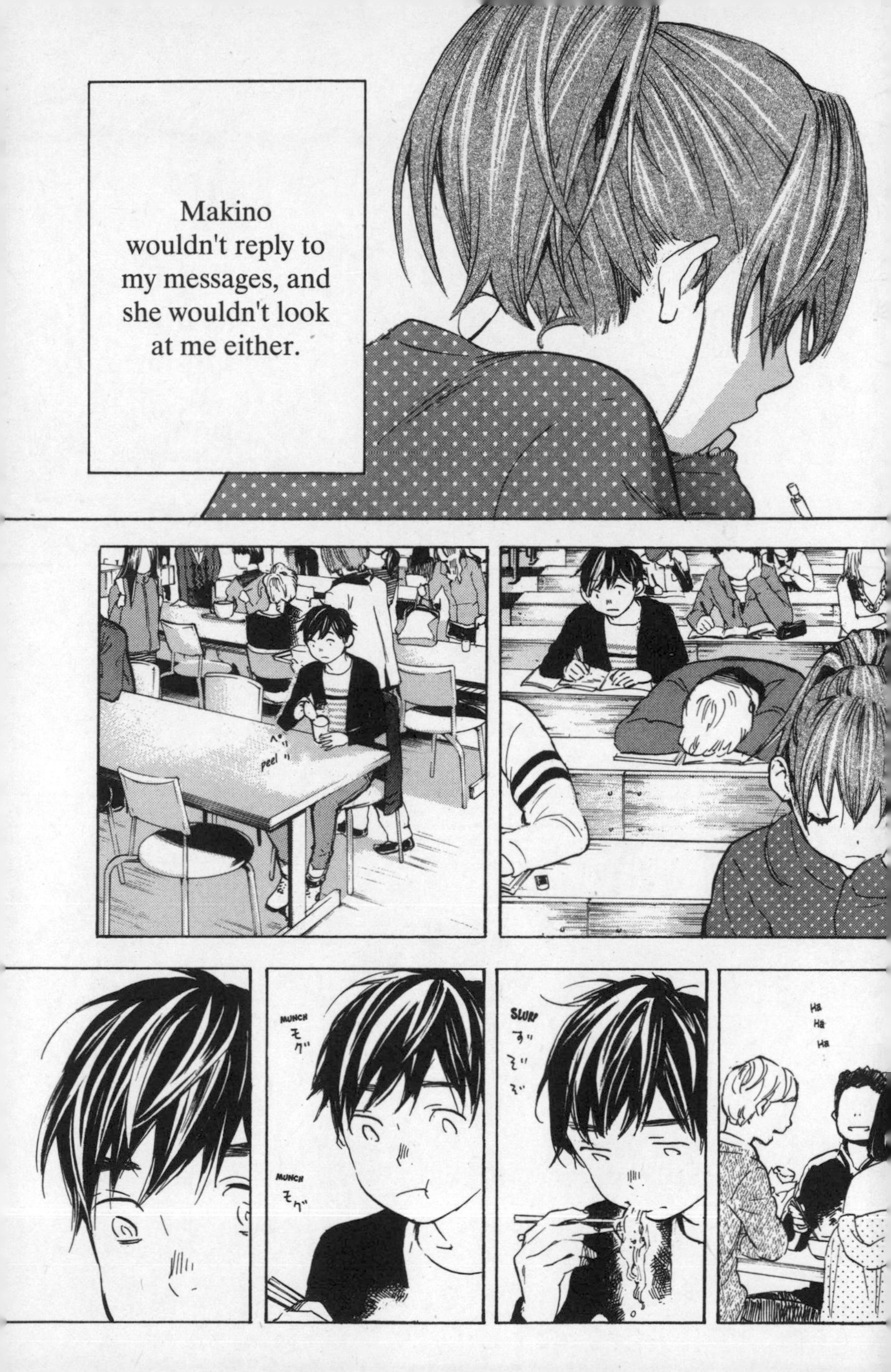
Makino wouldn't reply to my messages, and she wouldn't look at me either.
peel
Ha
Ha
Ha
SLURP
MUNCH
MUNCH

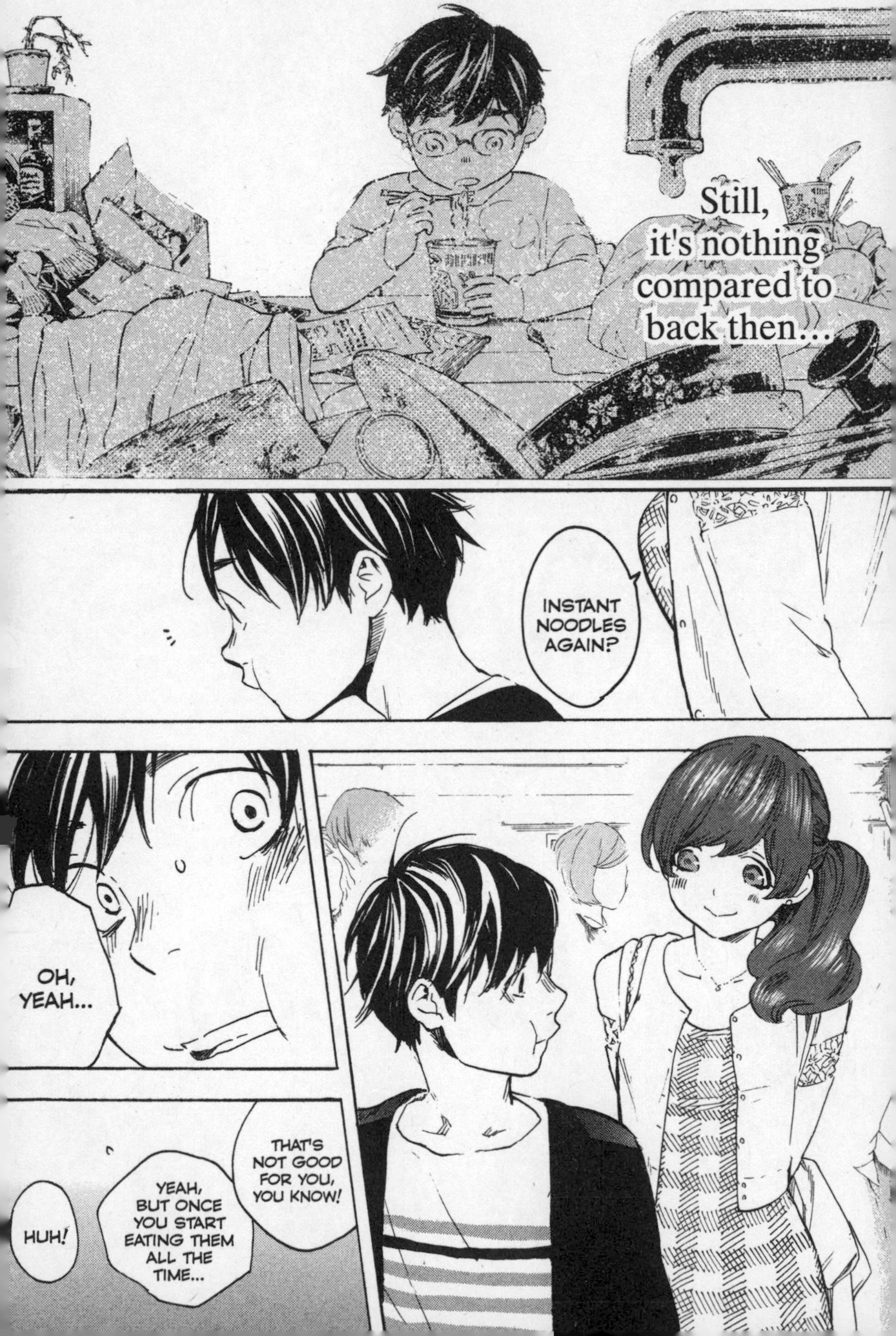
Still, it's nothing compared to back then...
INSTANT NOODLES AGAIN?
OH, YEAH...
THAT'S NOT GOOD FOR YOU, YOU KNOW!
YEAH, BUT ONCE YOU START EATING THEM ALL THE TIME...
HUH!

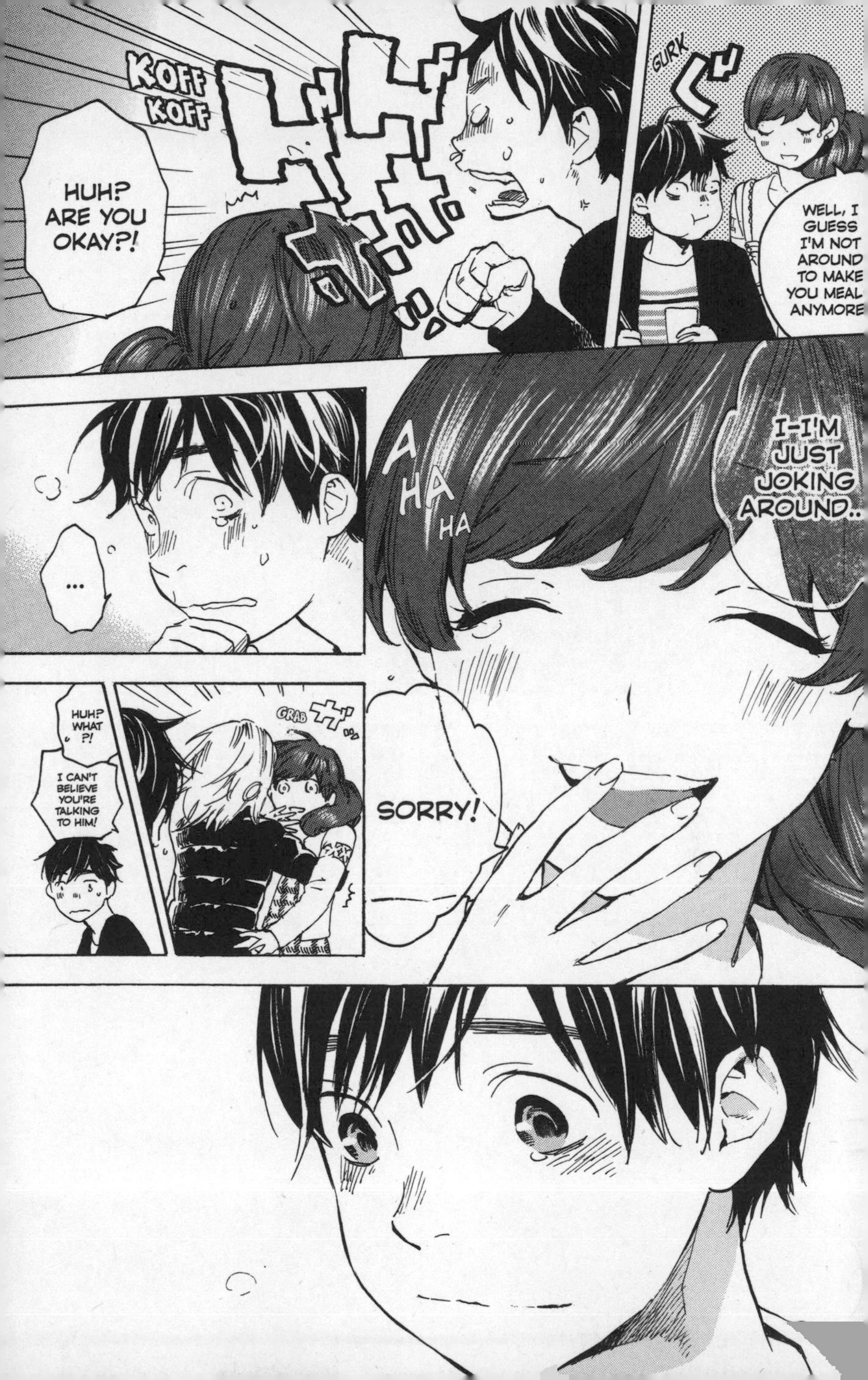
GURK
WELL, I GUESS I'M NOT AROUND TO MAKE YOU MEAL ANYMORE
KOFF KOFF
HUH? ARE YOU OKAY?!
I-I'M JUST JOKING AROUND..
AHAHA
SORRY!
...
GRAB
HUH? WHAT?!
I CAN'T BELIEVE YOU'RE TALKING TO HIM!

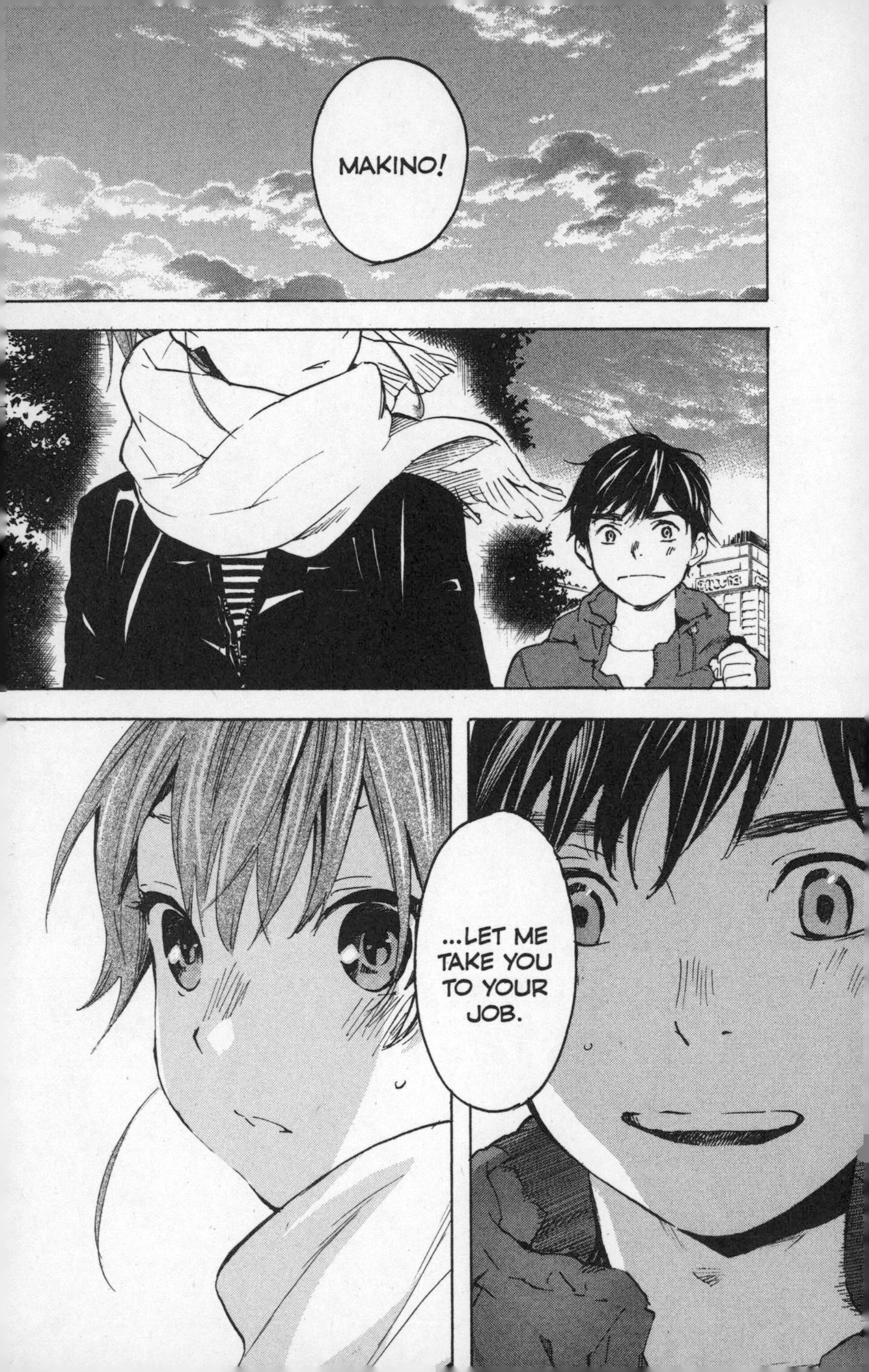
MAKINO!
...LET ME TAKE YOU TO YOUR JOB.

Forget Me Not

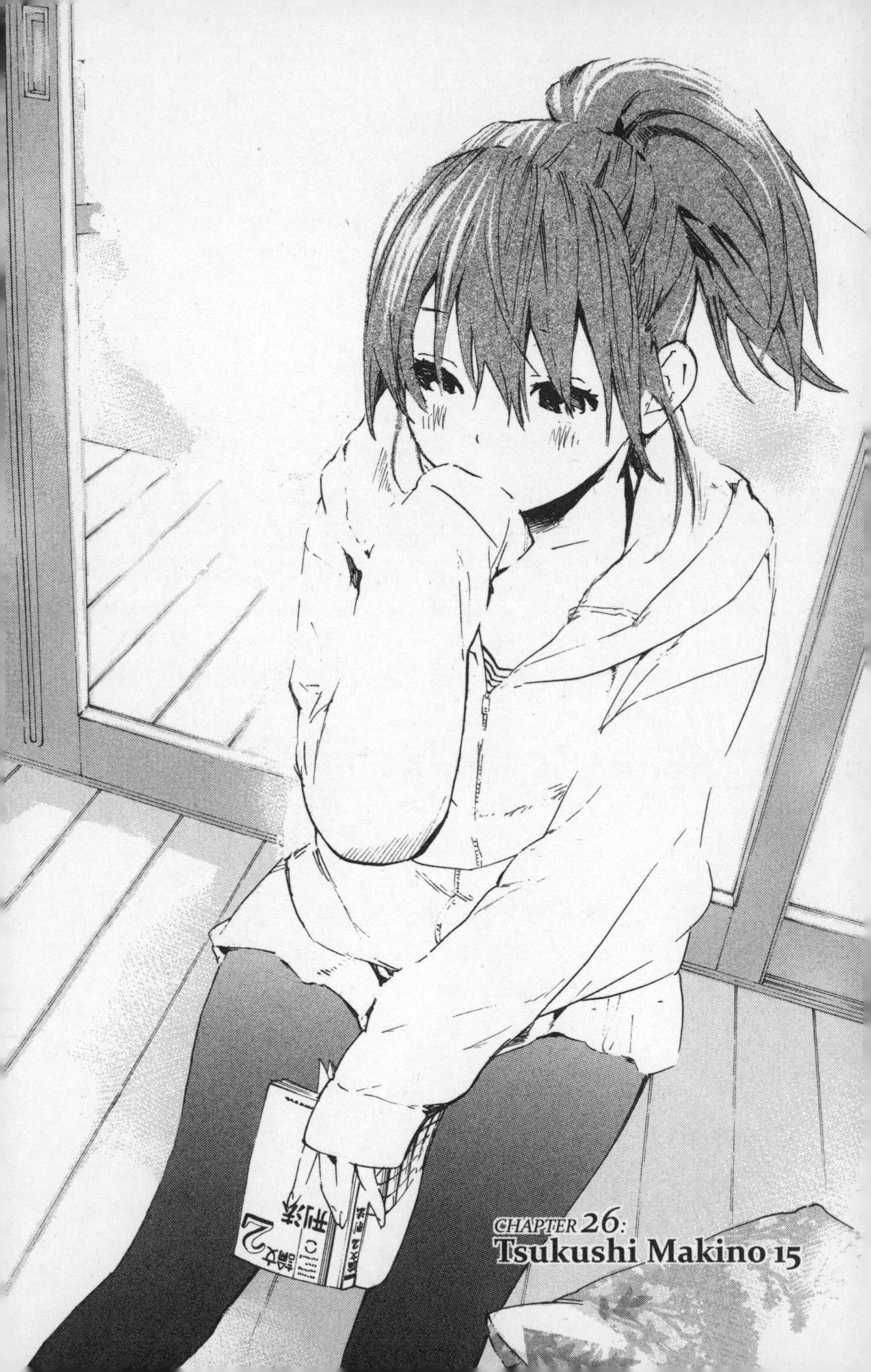

CHAPTER 26: Tsukushi Makino 15

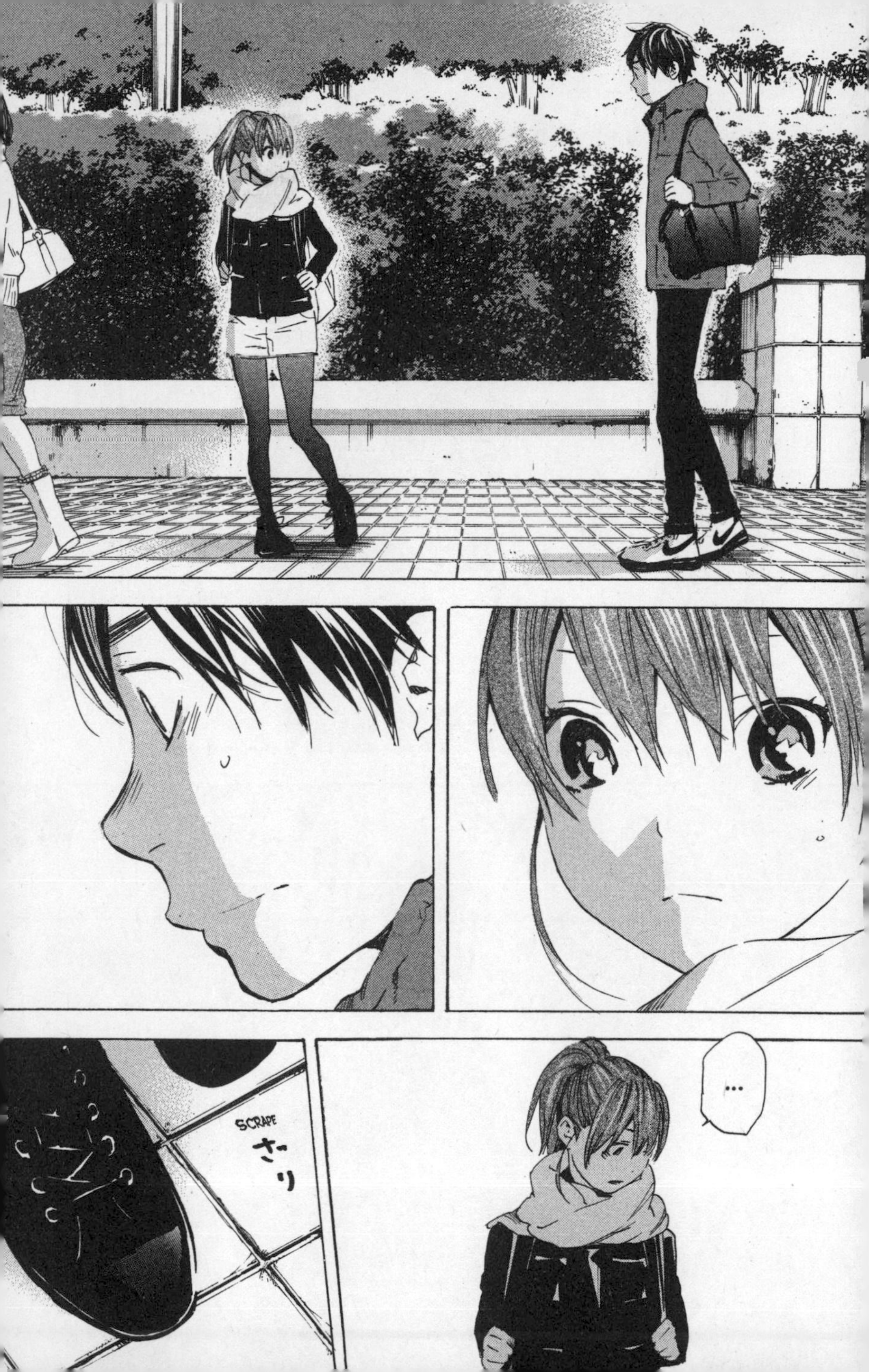
...
SCRAPE
さり

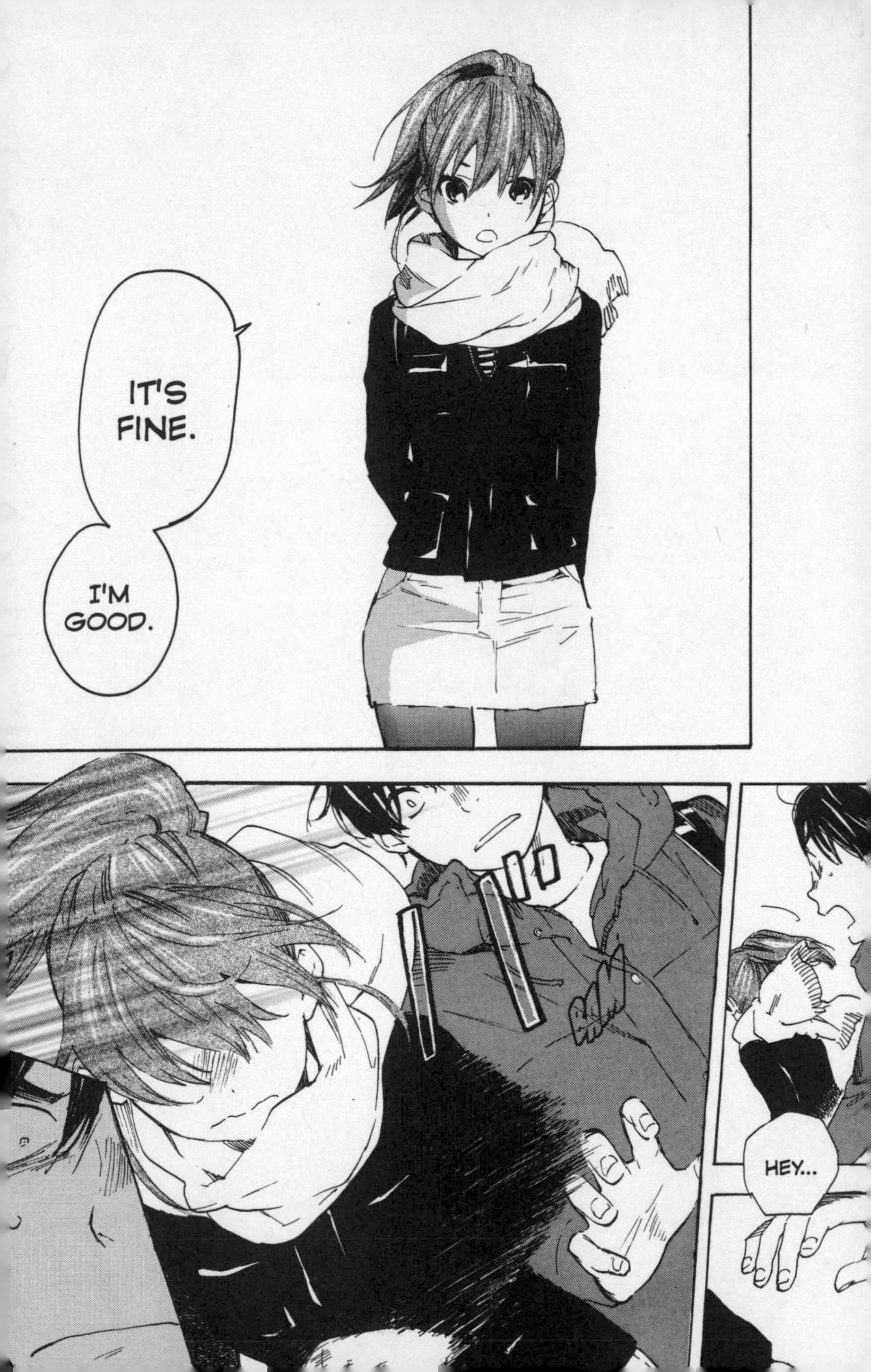
IT'S FINE.
I'M GOOD.
HEY...

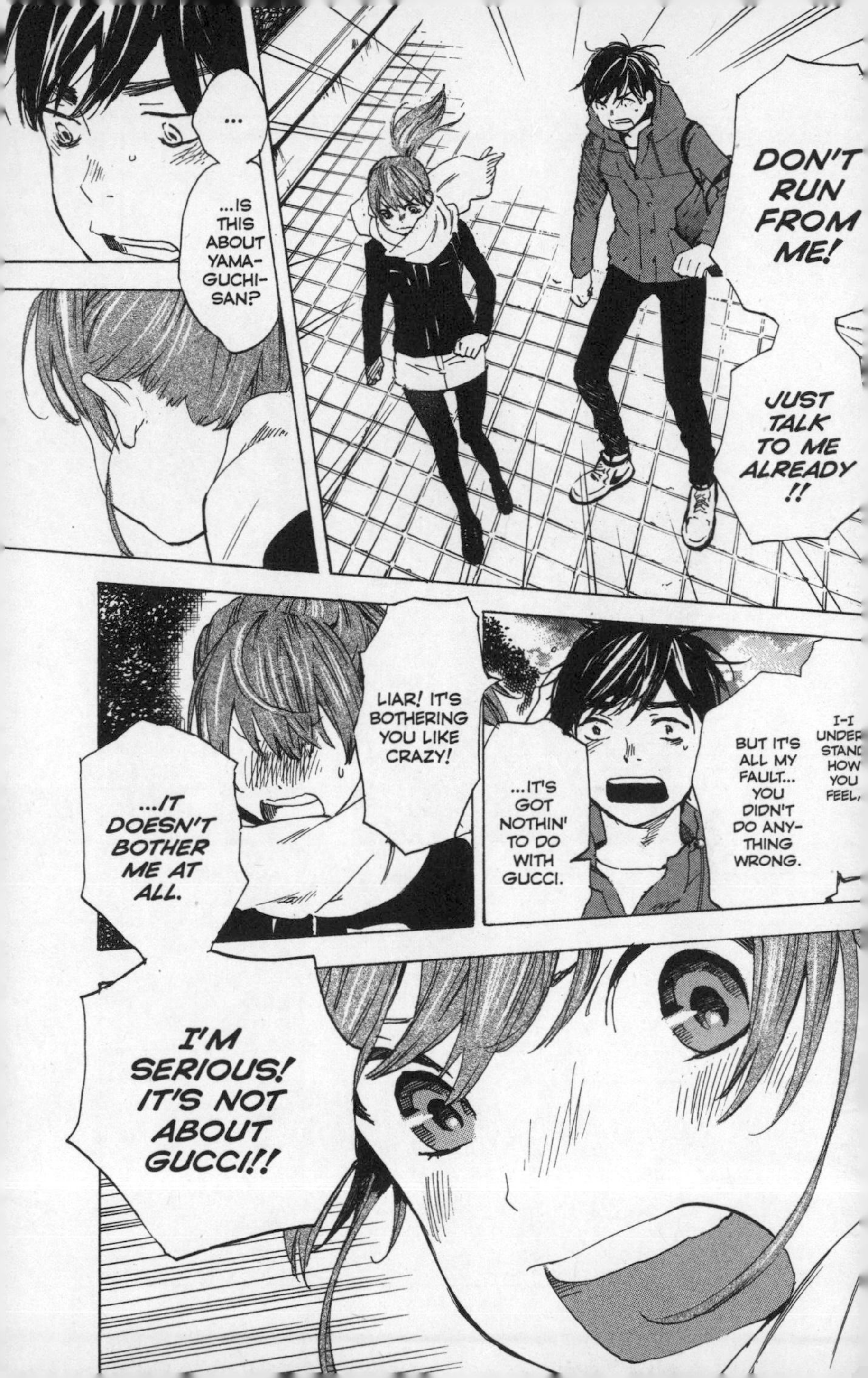
DON'T RUN FROM ME!
JUST TALK TO ME ALREADY!!
...
...IS THIS ABOUT YAMA-GUCHI-SAN?
I-I UNDERSTAND HOW YOU FEEL,
BUT IT'S ALL MY FAULT... YOU DIDN'T DO ANYTHING WRONG.
...IT'S GOT NOTHIN' TO DO WITH GUCCI.
LIAR! IT'S BOTHERING YOU LIKE CRAZY!
...IT DOESN'T BOTHER ME AT ALL.
I'M SERIOUS! IT'S NOT ABOUT GUCCI!!

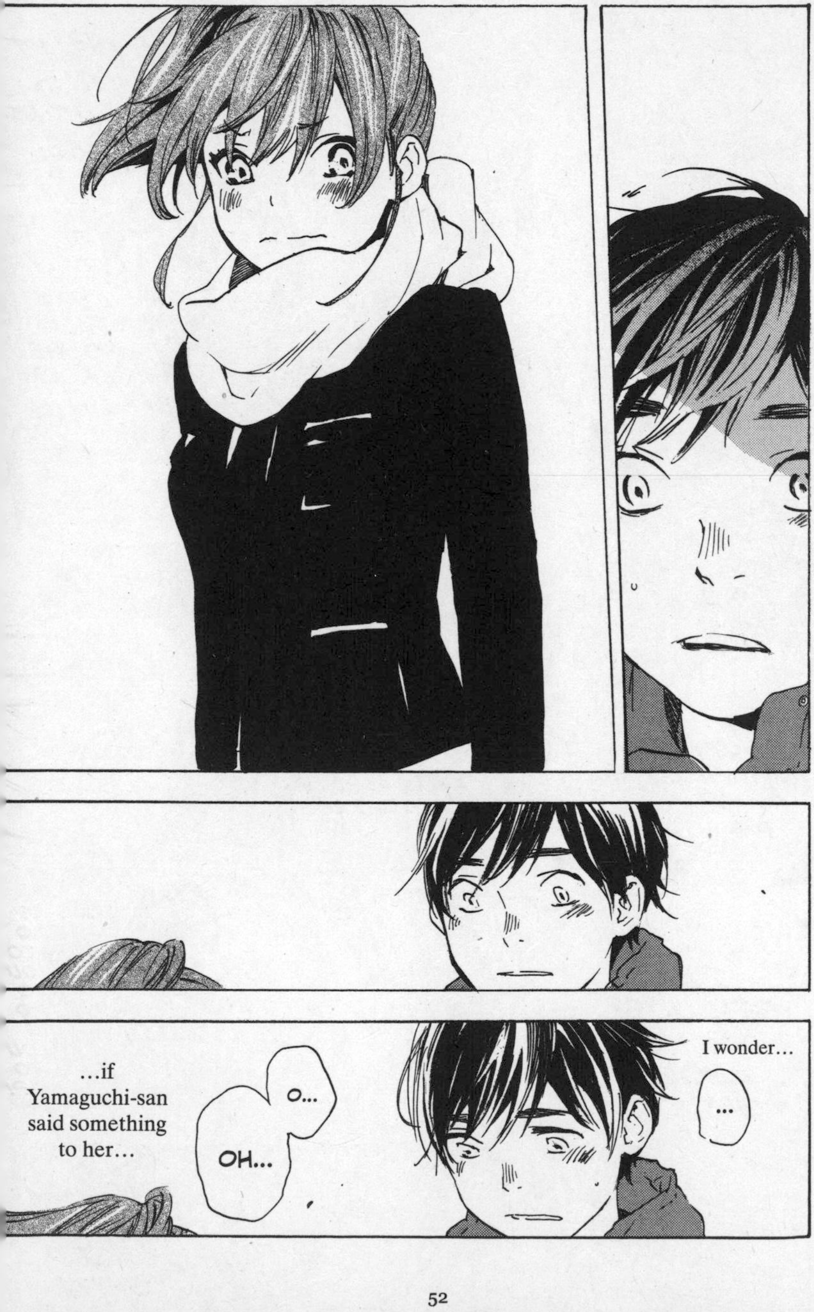
I wonder…
…
O…
OH…
…if Yamaguchi-san said something to her…

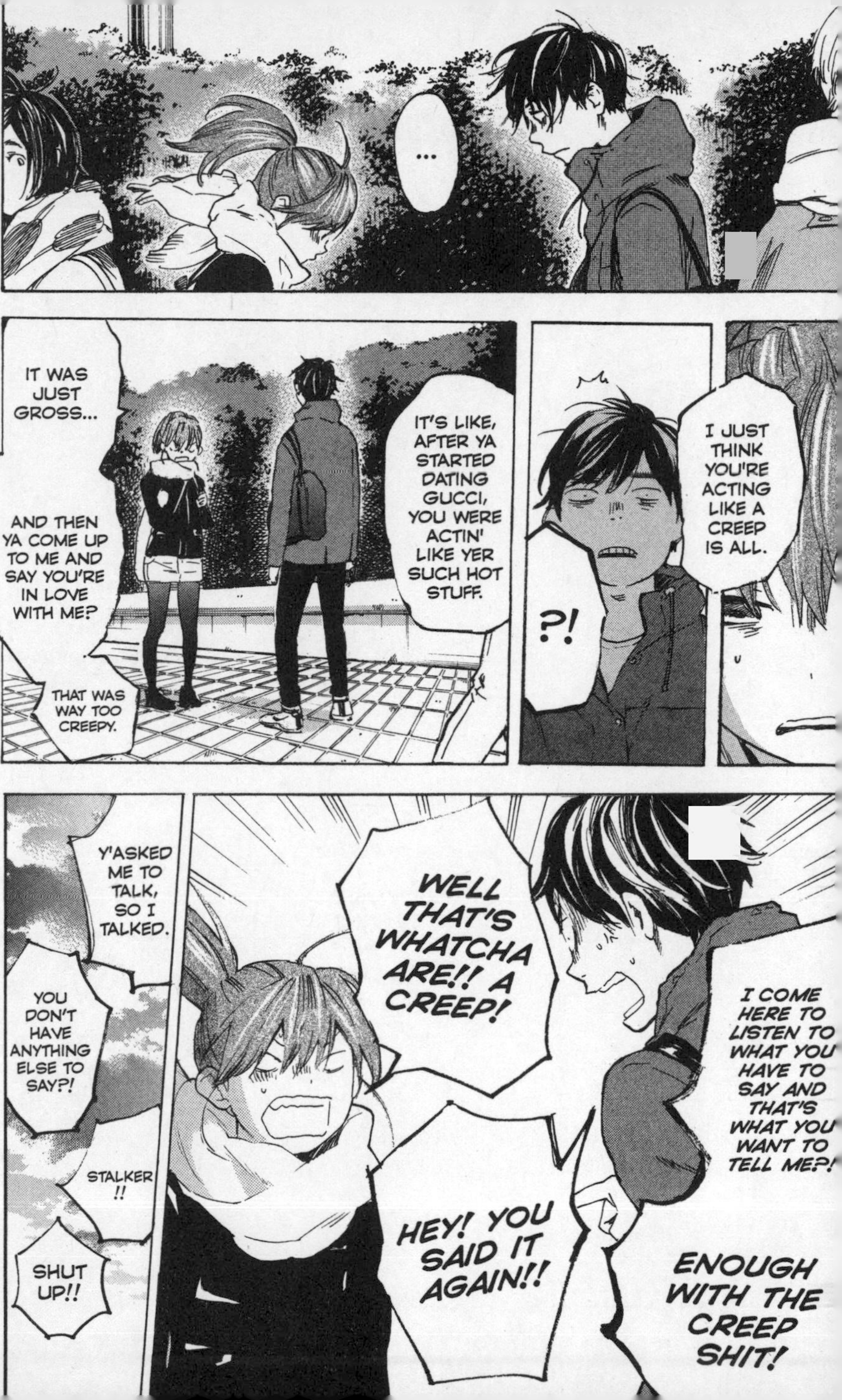
...
I JUST THINK YOU'RE ACTING LIKE A CREEP IS ALL.
?!
IT'S LIKE, AFTER YA STARTED DATING GUCCI, YOU WERE ACTIN' LIKE YER SUCH HOT STUFF.
IT WAS JUST GROSS...
AND THEN YA COME UP TO ME AND SAY YOU'RE IN LOVE WITH ME?
THAT WAS WAY TOO CREEPY.
I COME HERE TO LISTEN TO WHAT YOU HAVE TO SAY AND THAT'S WHAT YOU WANT TO TELL ME?!
WELL THAT'S WHATCHA ARE!! A CREEP!
ENOUGH WITH THE CREEP SHIT!
HEY! YOU SAID IT AGAIN!!
Y'ASKED ME TO TALK, SO I TALKED.
YOU DON'T HAVE ANYTHING ELSE TO SAY?!
STALKER !!
SHUT UP!!

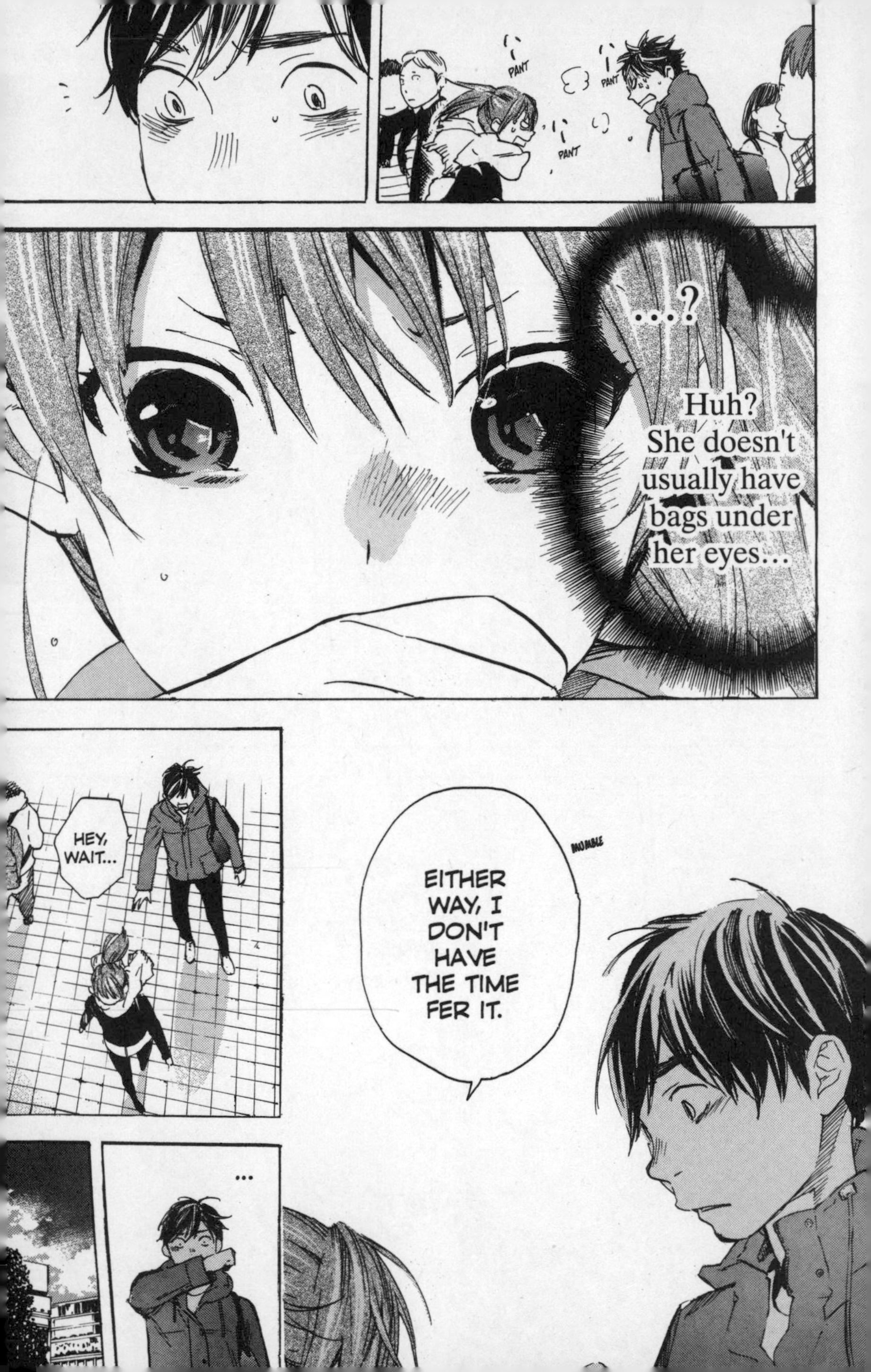
PANT
PANT
PANT
...?
Huh? She doesn't usually have bags under her eyes...
MUMBLE
EITHER WAY, I DON'T HAVE THE TIME FER IT.
HEY, WAIT...
...

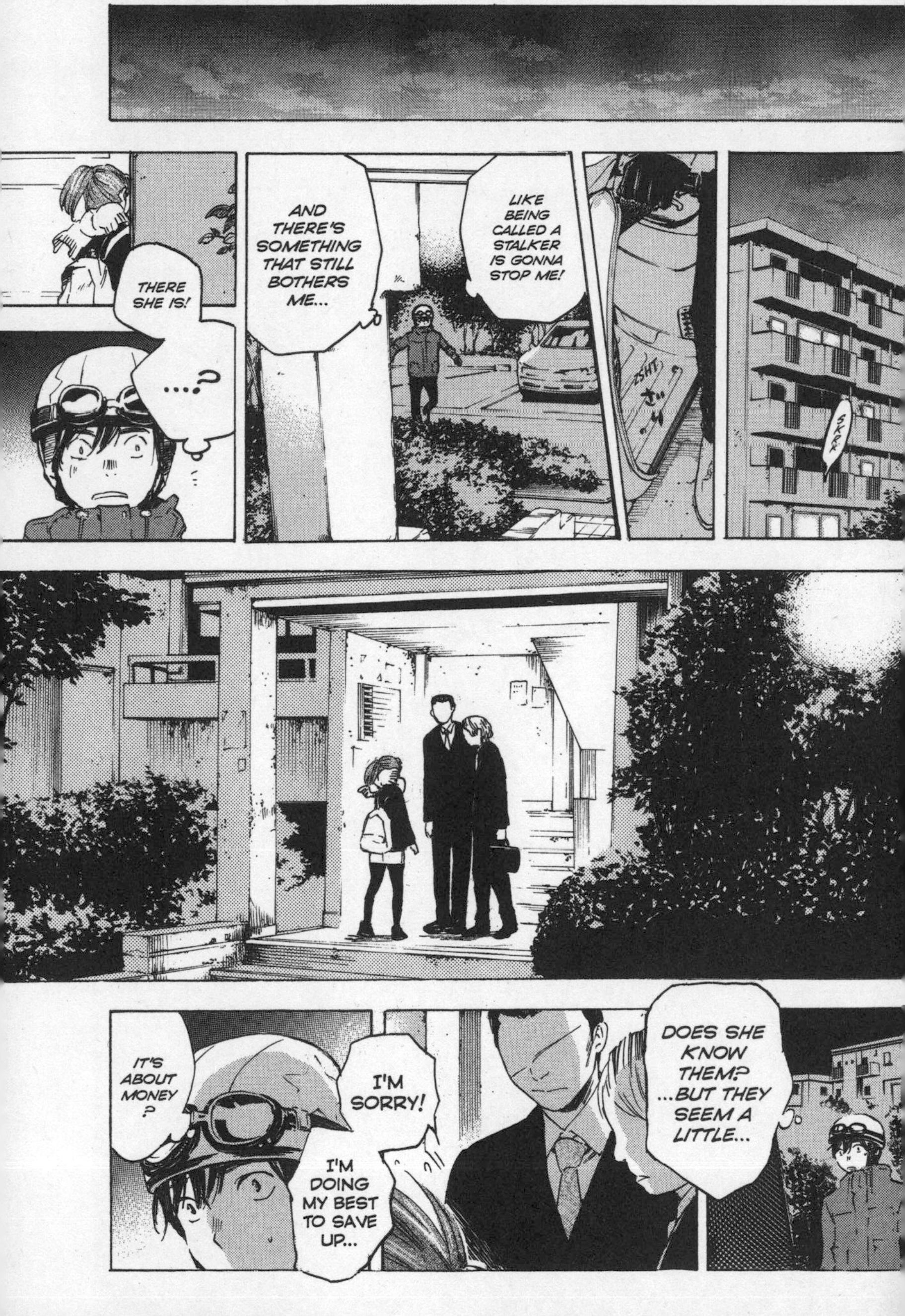
SKRK
ZSHT
LIKE BEING CALLED A STALKER IS GONNA STOP ME!
AND THERE'S SOMETHING THAT STILL BOTHERS ME...
THERE SHE IS!
...?
DOES SHE KNOW THEM? ...BUT THEY SEEM A LITTLE...
I'M SORRY!
I'M DOING MY BEST TO SAVE UP...
IT'S ABOUT MONEY?

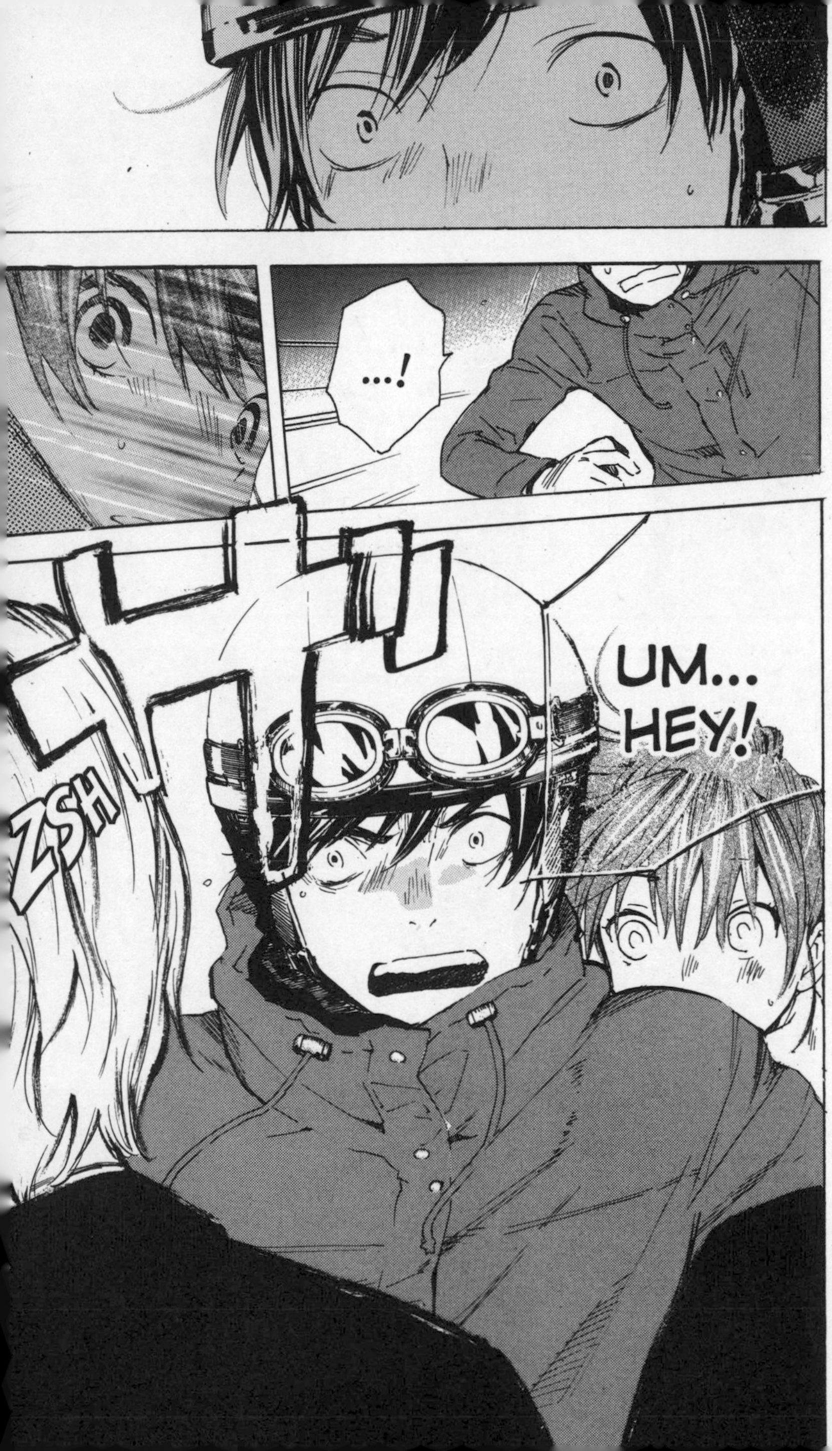
...!
UM... HEY!
ZSH

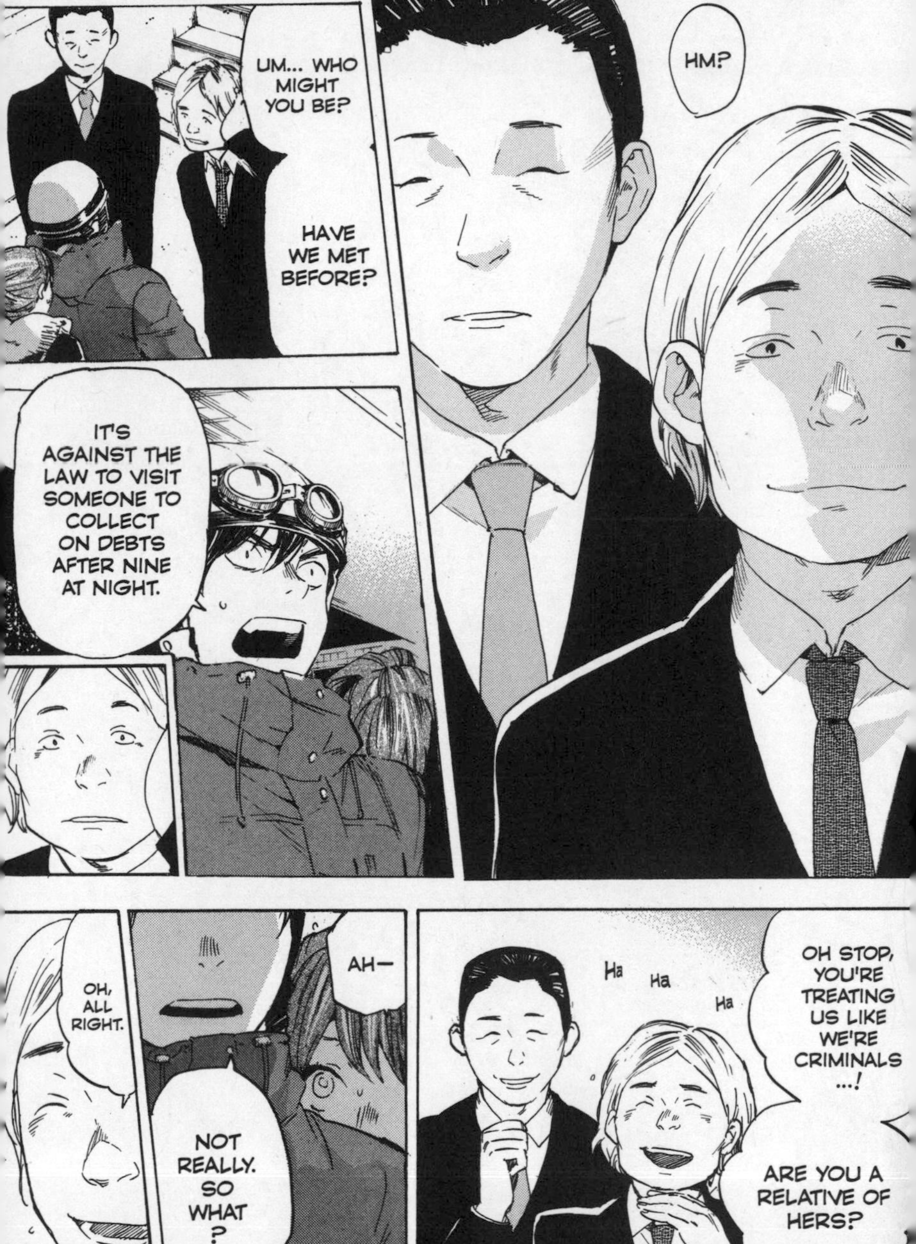
HM?
UM... WHO MIGHT YOU BE?
HAVE WE MET BEFORE?
IT'S AGAINST THE LAW TO VISIT SOMEONE TO COLLECT ON DEBTS AFTER NINE AT NIGHT.
OH STOP, YOU'RE TREATING US LIKE WE'RE CRIMINALS ...!
Ha Ha Ha
ARE YOU A RELATIVE OF HERS?
AH—
NOT REALLY. SO WHAT?
OH, ALL RIGHT.

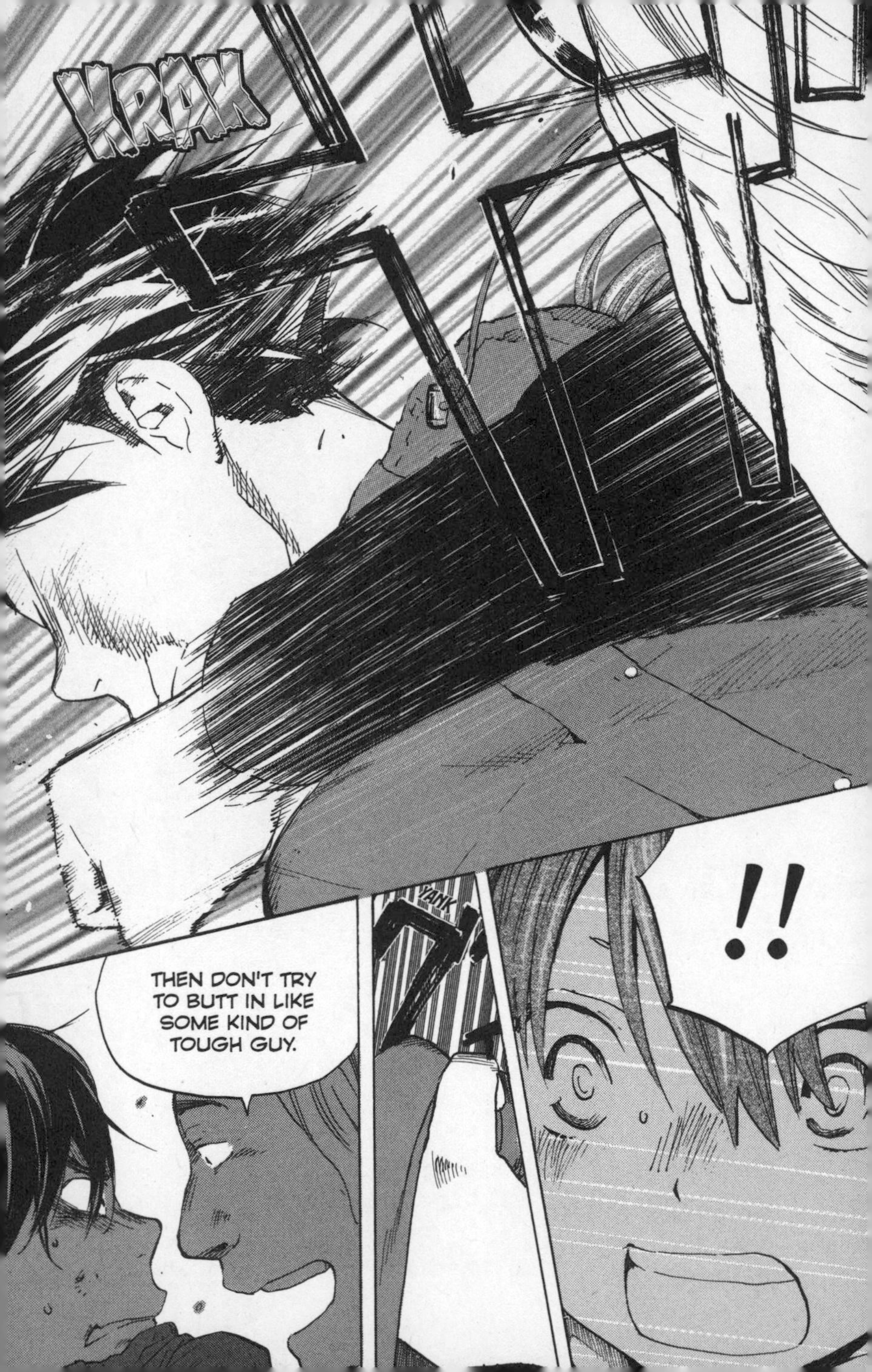
KRAK
!!
YANK
THEN DON'T TRY TO BUTT IN LIKE SOME KIND OF TOUGH GUY.

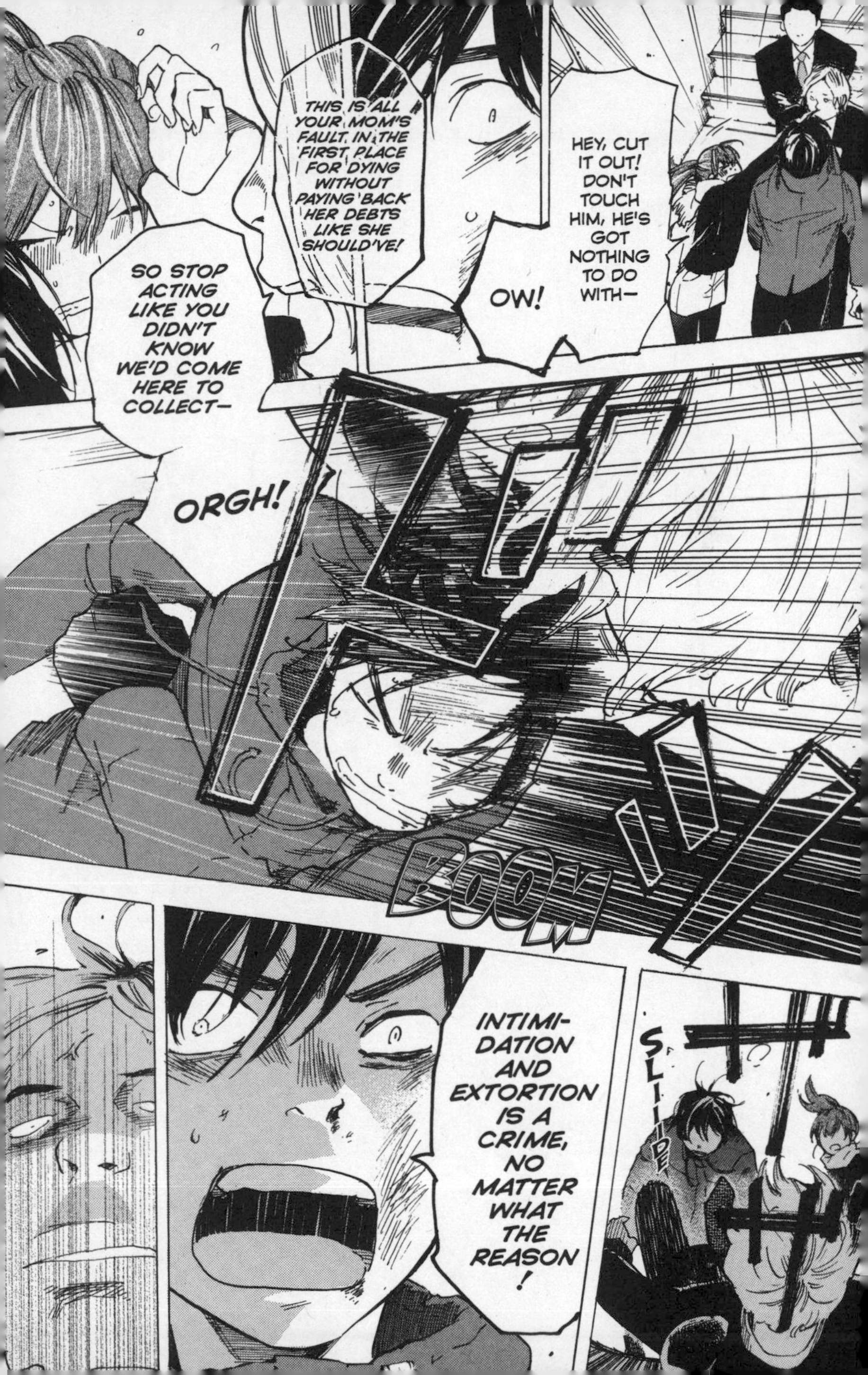
HEY, CUT IT OUT! DON'T TOUCH HIM, HE'S GOT NOTHING TO DO WITH—
OW!
THIS IS ALL YOUR MOM'S FAULT IN THE FIRST PLACE FOR DYING WITHOUT PAYING BACK HER DEBTS LIKE SHE SHOULD'VE!
SO STOP ACTING LIKE YOU DIDN'T KNOW WE'D COME HERE TO COLLECT—
ORGH!
BOOM
SLIIDE
INTIMIDATION AND EXTORTION IS A CRIME, NO MATTER WHAT THE REASON!

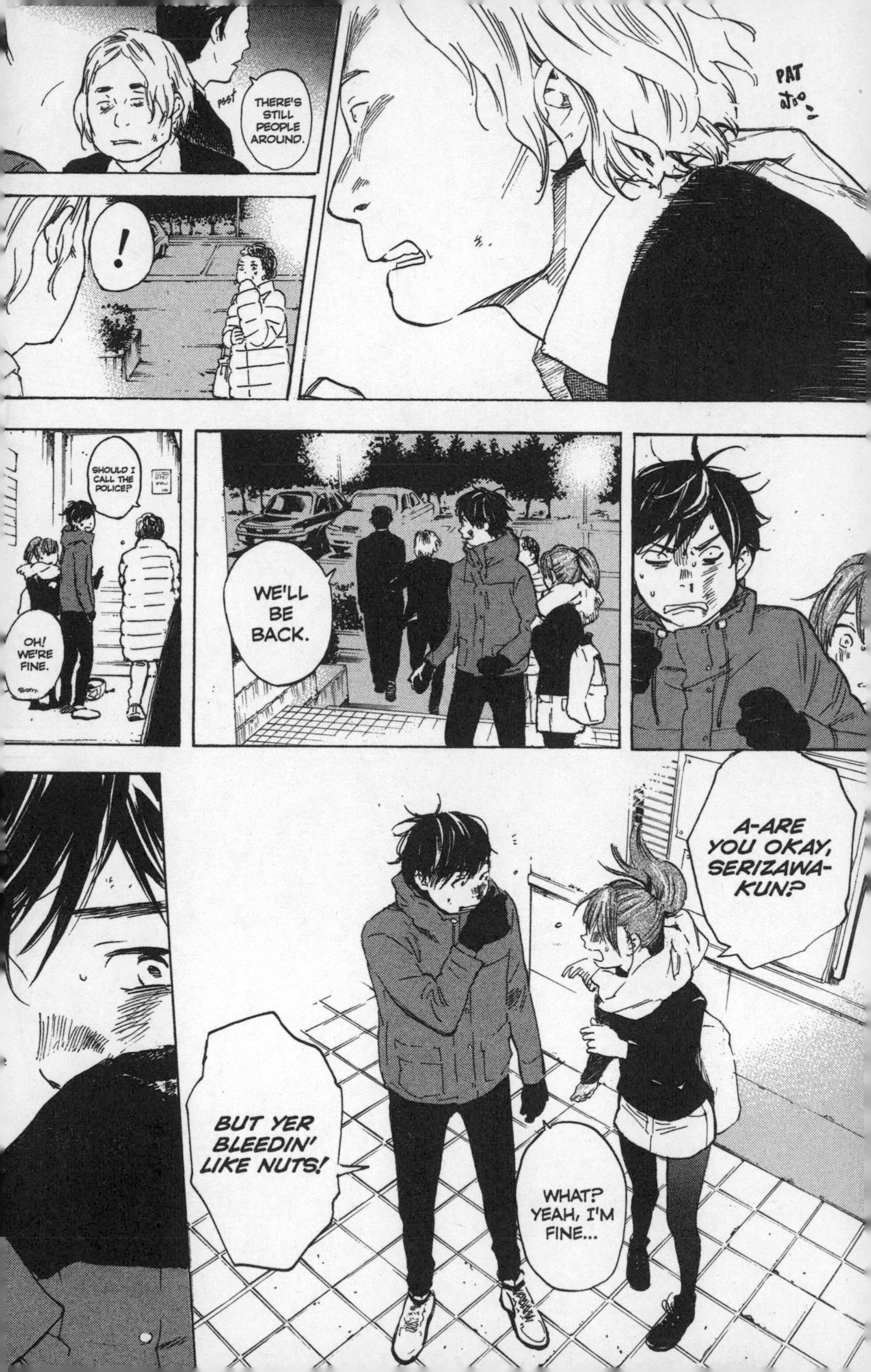
PAT
psst
THERE'S STILL PEOPLE AROUND.
!
WE'LL BE BACK.
SHOULD I CALL THE POLICE?
OH! WE'RE FINE.
Sorry.
A-ARE YOU OKAY, SERIZAWA-KUN?
WHAT? YEAH, I'M FINE...
BUT YER BLEEDIN' LIKE NUTS!

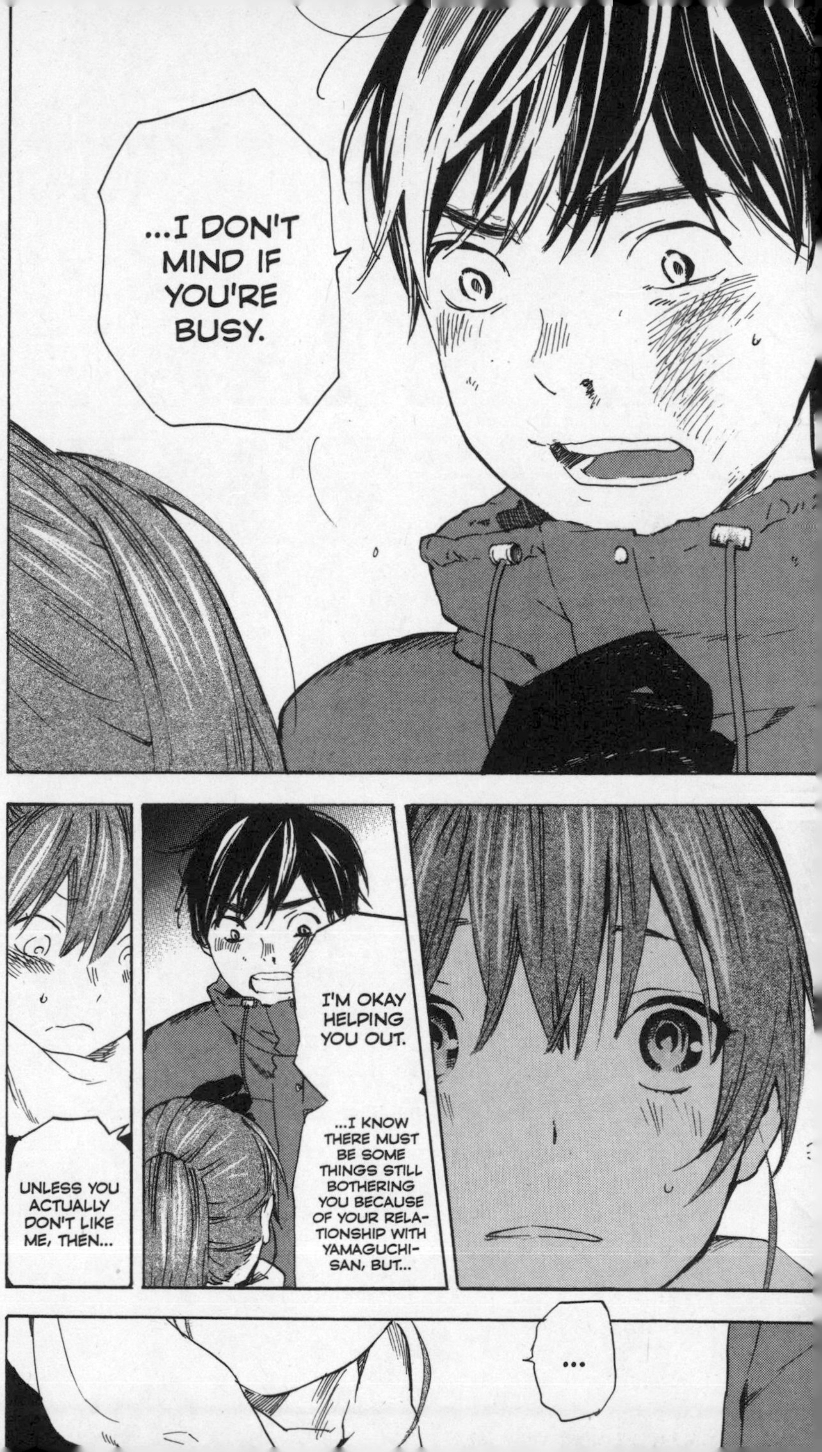
...I DON'T MIND IF YOU'RE BUSY.
I'M OKAY HELPING YOU OUT.
...I KNOW THERE MUST BE SOME THINGS STILL BOTHERING YOU BECAUSE OF YOUR RELATIONSHIP WITH YAMAGUCHI-SAN, BUT...
UNLESS YOU ACTUALLY DON'T LIKE ME, THEN...
...

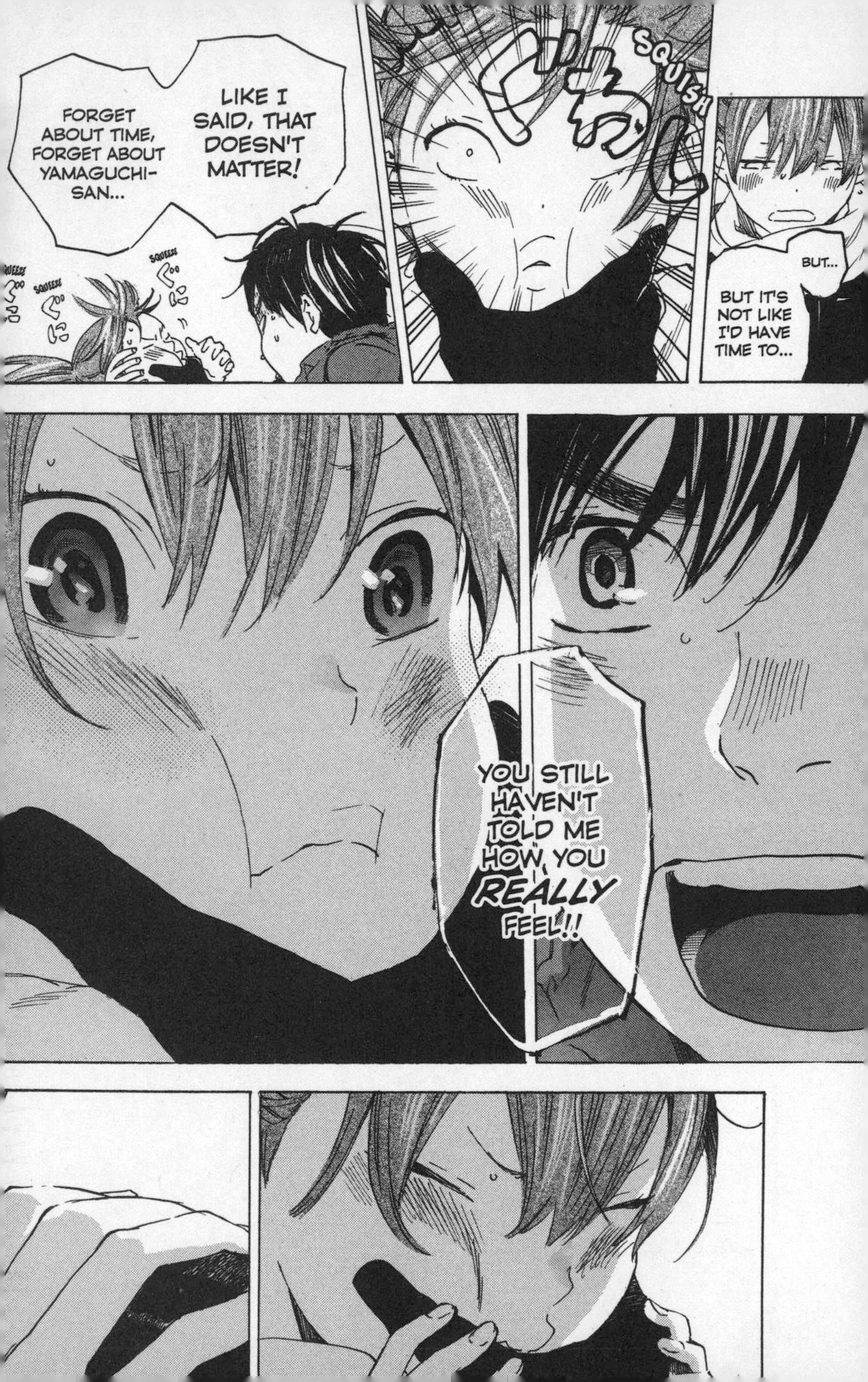
BUT...
BUT IT'S NOT LIKE I'D HAVE TIME TO...
SQUISH
LIKE I SAID, THAT DOESN'T MATTER!
FORGET ABOUT TIME, FORGET ABOUT YAMAGUCHI-SAN...
SQUEEZE
SQUEEZE
YOU STILL HAVEN'T TOLD ME HOW YOU REALLY FEEL!!

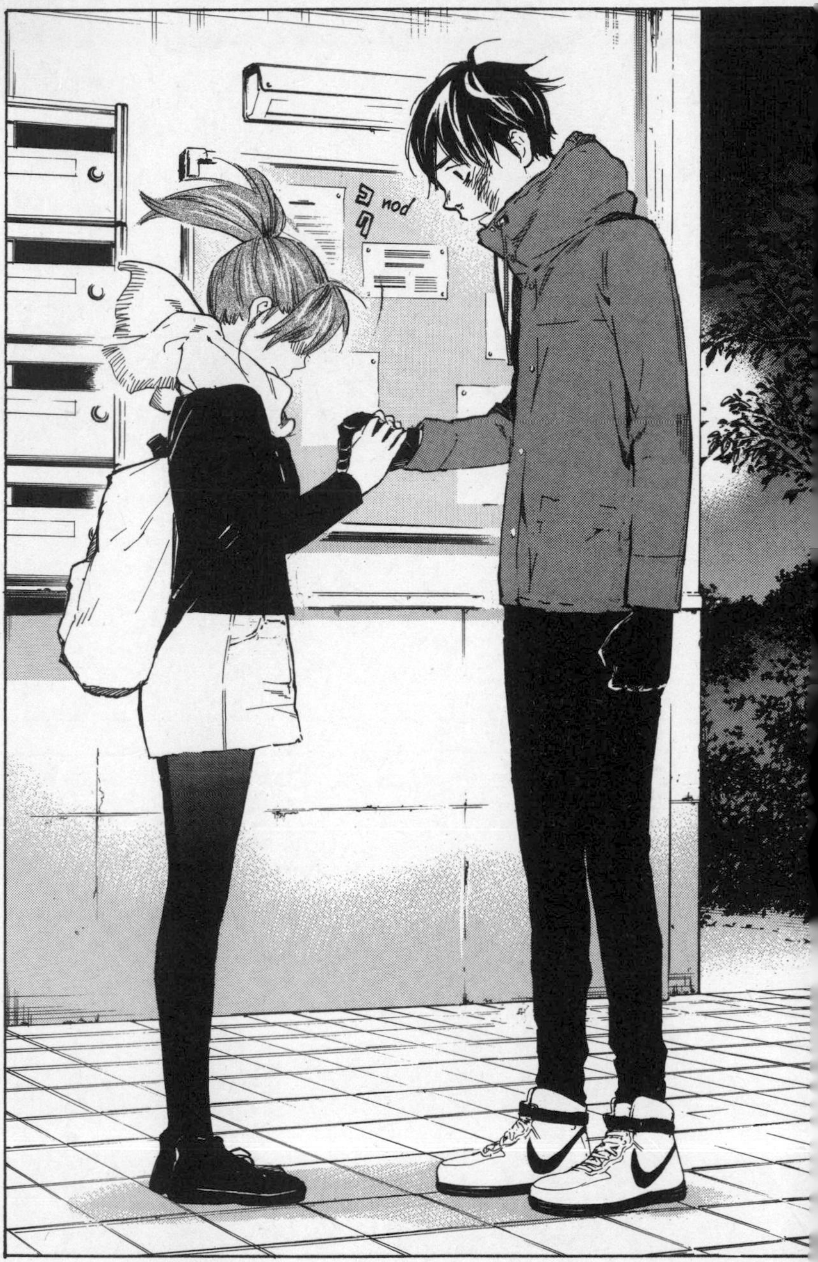
nod
nod

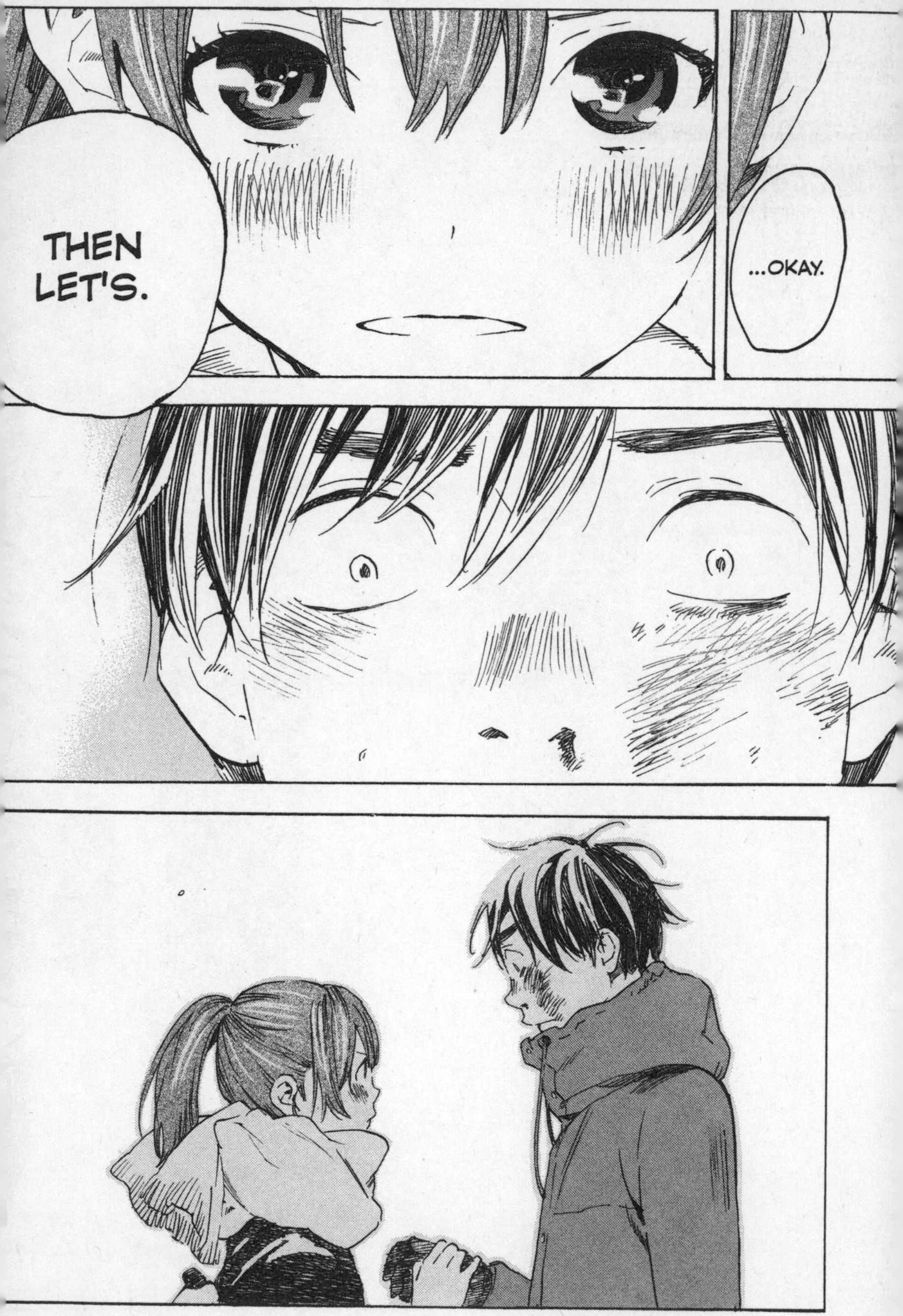
...OKAY.
THEN LET'S.

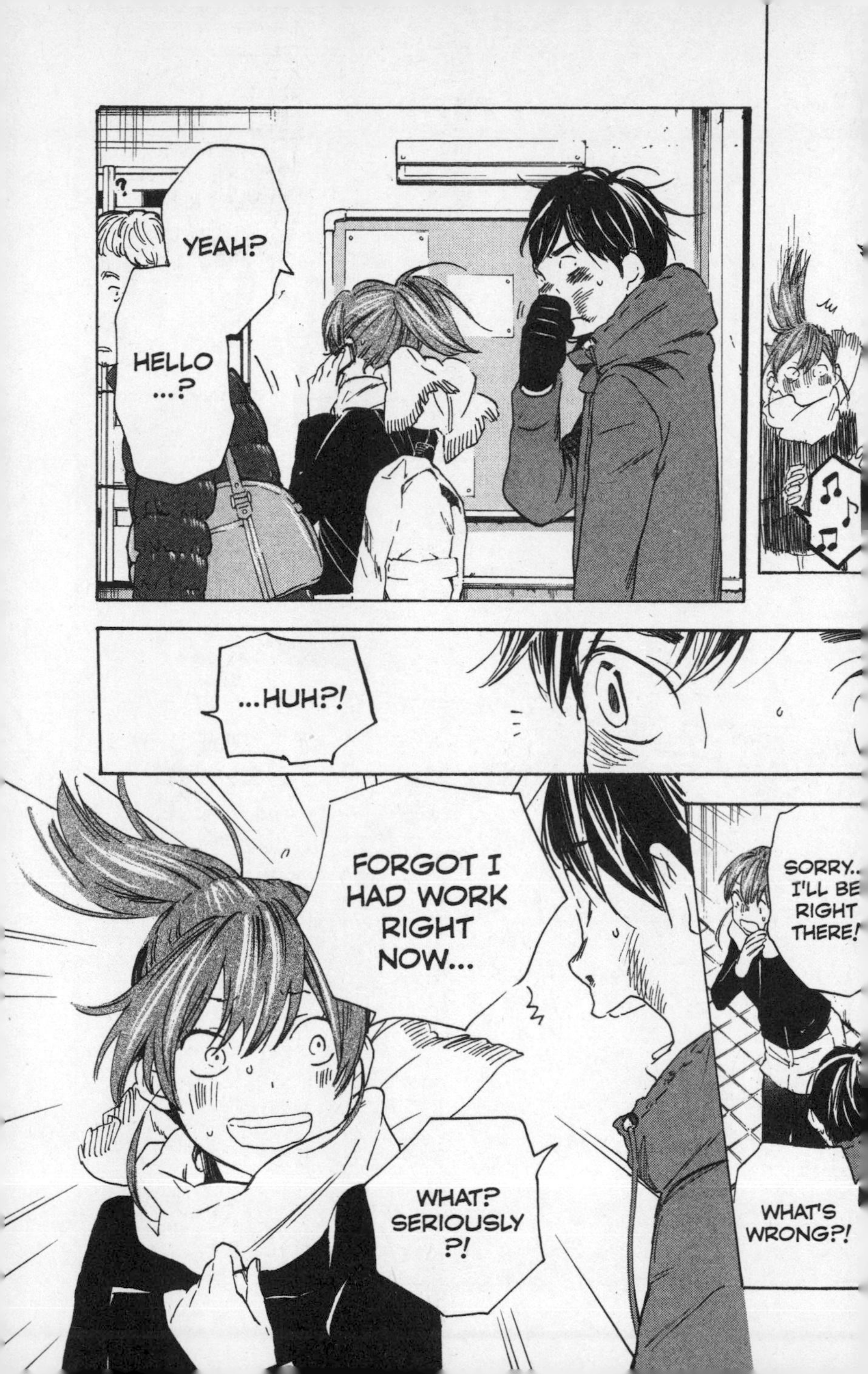
YEAH?
HELLO ...?
...HUH?!
SORRY... I'LL BE RIGHT THERE!
WHAT'S WRONG?!
FORGOT I HAD WORK RIGHT NOW...
WHAT? SERIOUSLY ?!

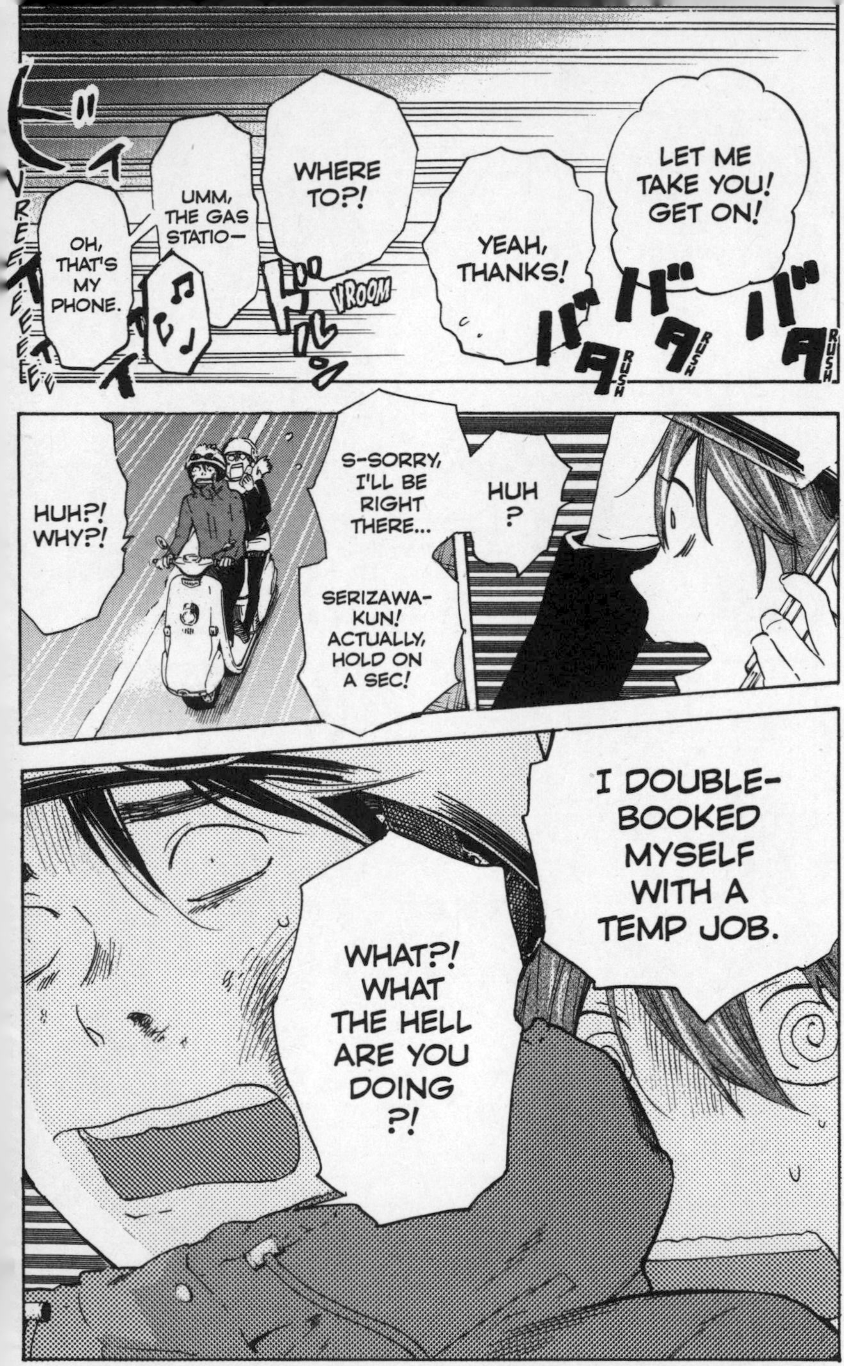
LET ME TAKE YOU! GET ON!
RUSH
RUSH
RUSH
YEAH, THANKS!
WHERE TO?!
VROOM
UMM, THE GAS STATIO—
OH, THAT'S MY PHONE.
VREEEEEEEE
HUH ?
S-SORRY, I'LL BE RIGHT THERE...
SERIZAWA-KUN! ACTUALLY, HOLD ON A SEC!
HUH?! WHY?!
I DOUBLE-BOOKED MYSELF WITH A TEMP JOB.
WHAT?! WHAT THE HELL ARE YOU DOING ?!

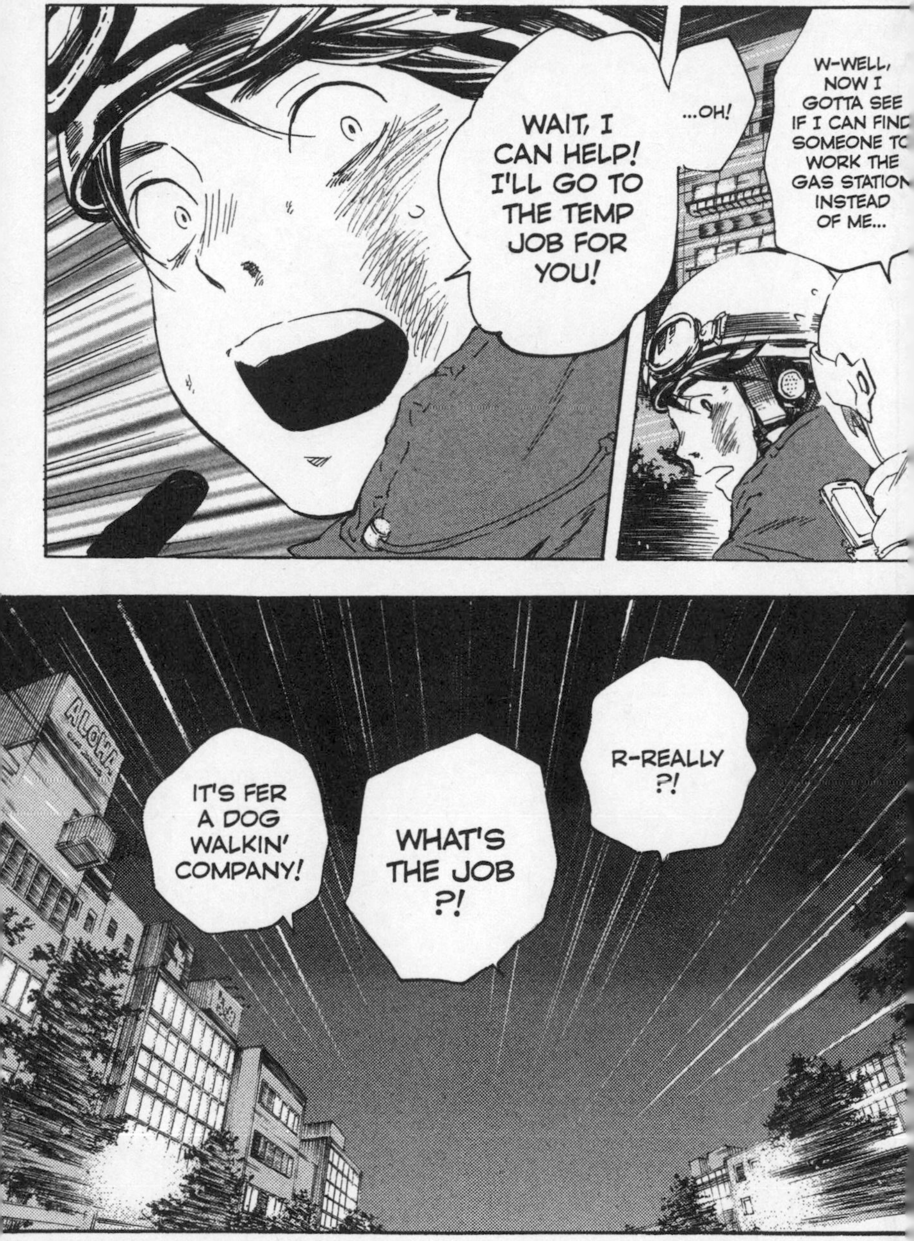
W-WELL, NOW I GOTTA SEE IF I CAN FIND SOMEONE TO WORK THE GAS STATION INSTEAD OF ME...
...OH!
WAIT, I CAN HELP! I'LL GO TO THE TEMP JOB FOR YOU!
R-REALLY ?!
WHAT'S THE JOB ?!
IT'S FER A DOG WALKIN' COMPANY!

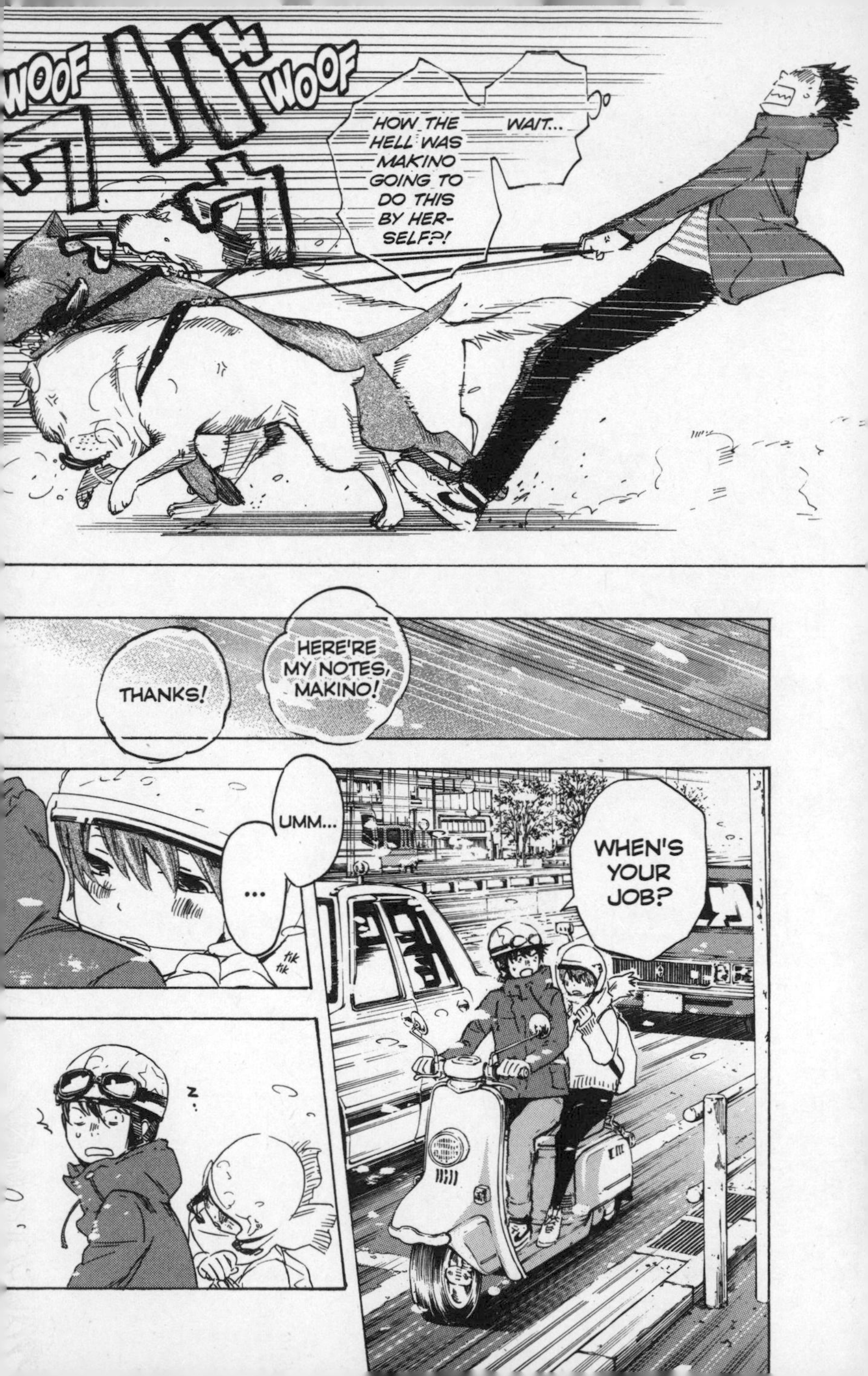
WOOF
WOOF
WAIT...
HOW THE HELL WAS MAKINO GOING TO DO THIS BY HER-SELF?!
HERE'RE MY NOTES, MAKINO!
THANKS!
WHEN'S YOUR JOB?
UMM...
...
tik tik

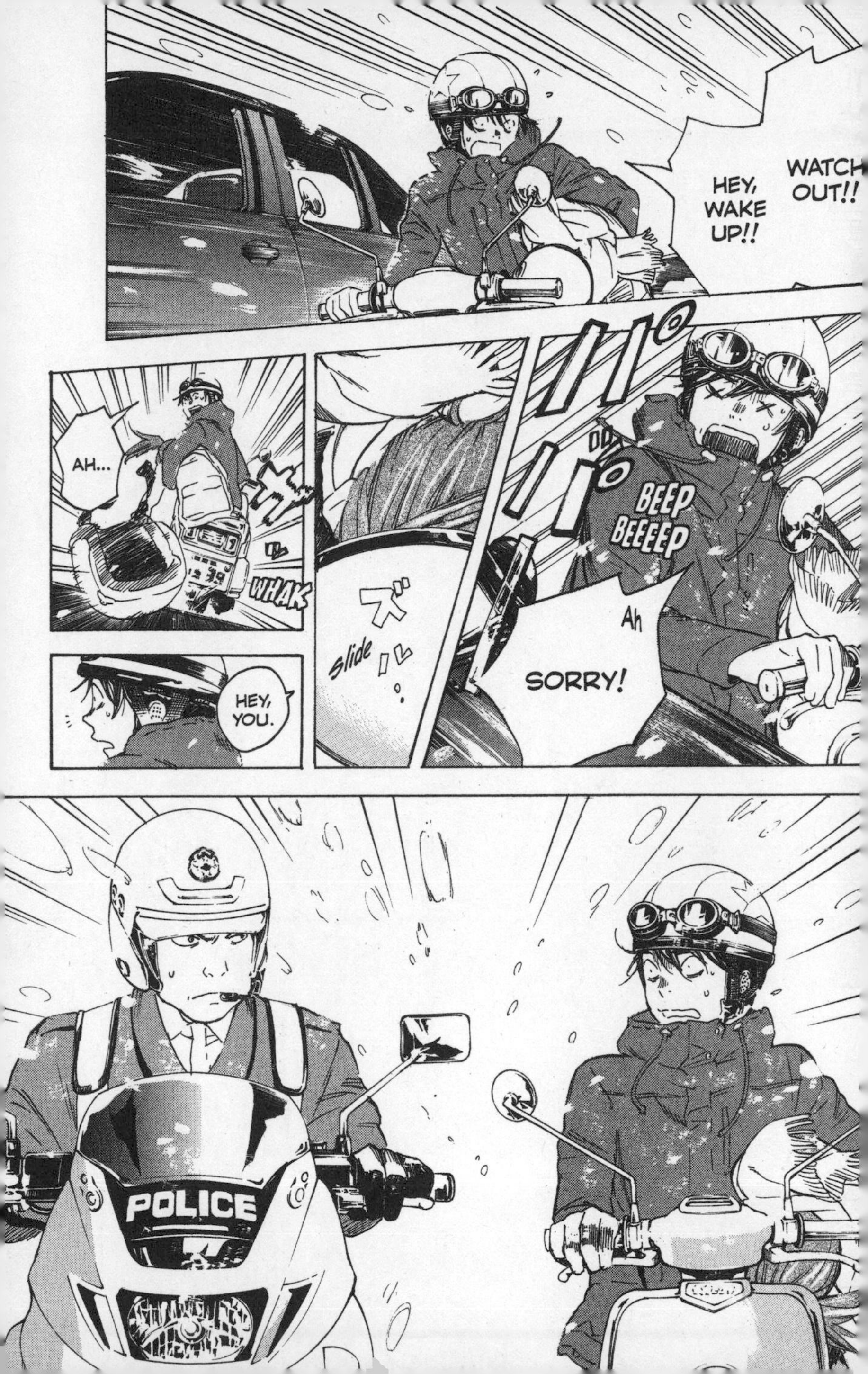
WATCH OUT!!
HEY, WAKE UP!!
BEEP BEEEEP
Ah
SORRY!
ズ
Slide
ル
AH...
WHAK
HEY, YOU.
POLICE

TE:
e Road Traffic Act (in Japan) forbids passengers from
ing along on a bicycle unless they are children under
age of six or otherwise exempt.

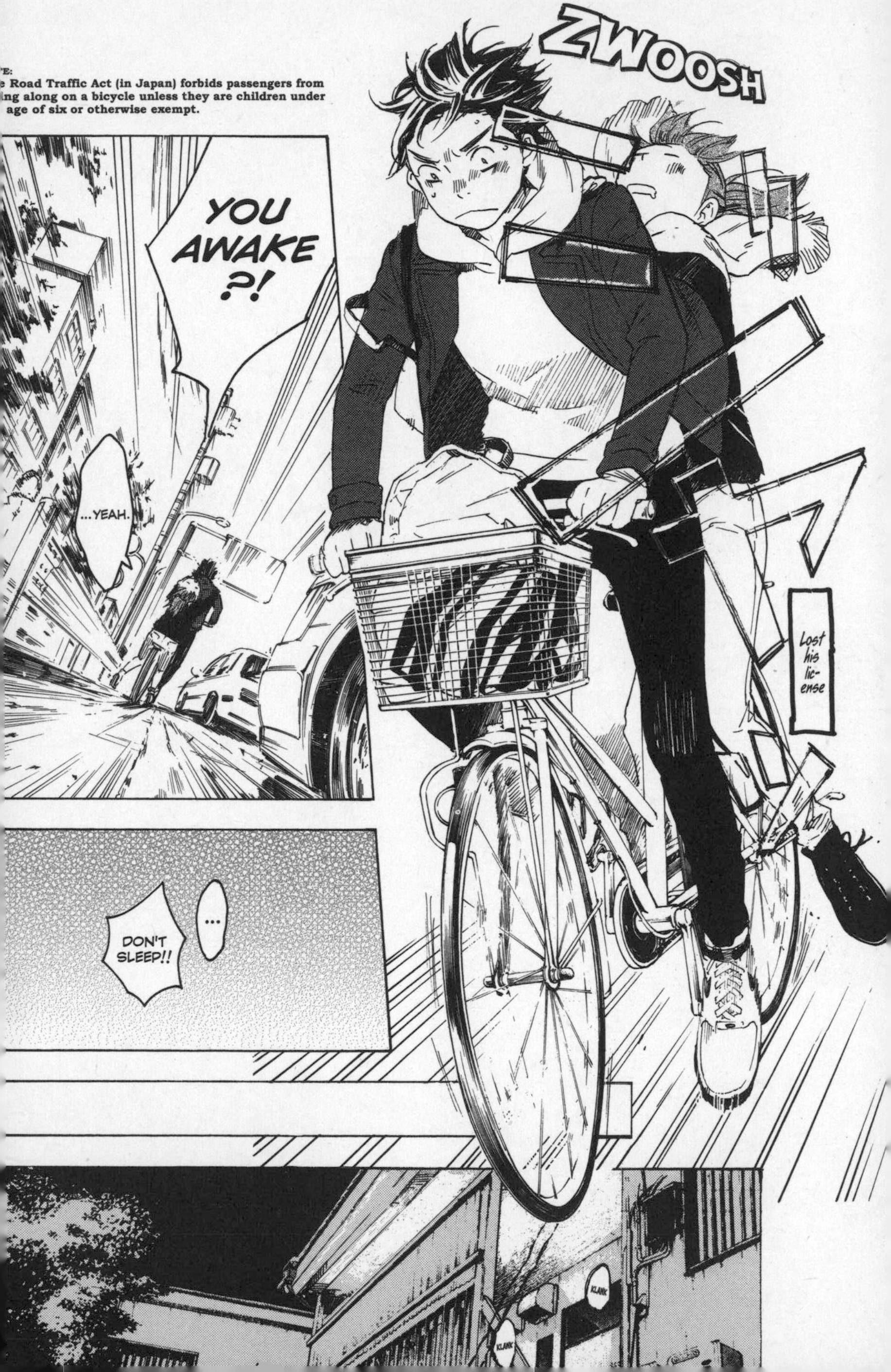
ZWOOSH
YOU AWAKE ?!
...YEAH.
Lost his lic-ense
...
DON'T SLEEP!!
KLANK
KLANK

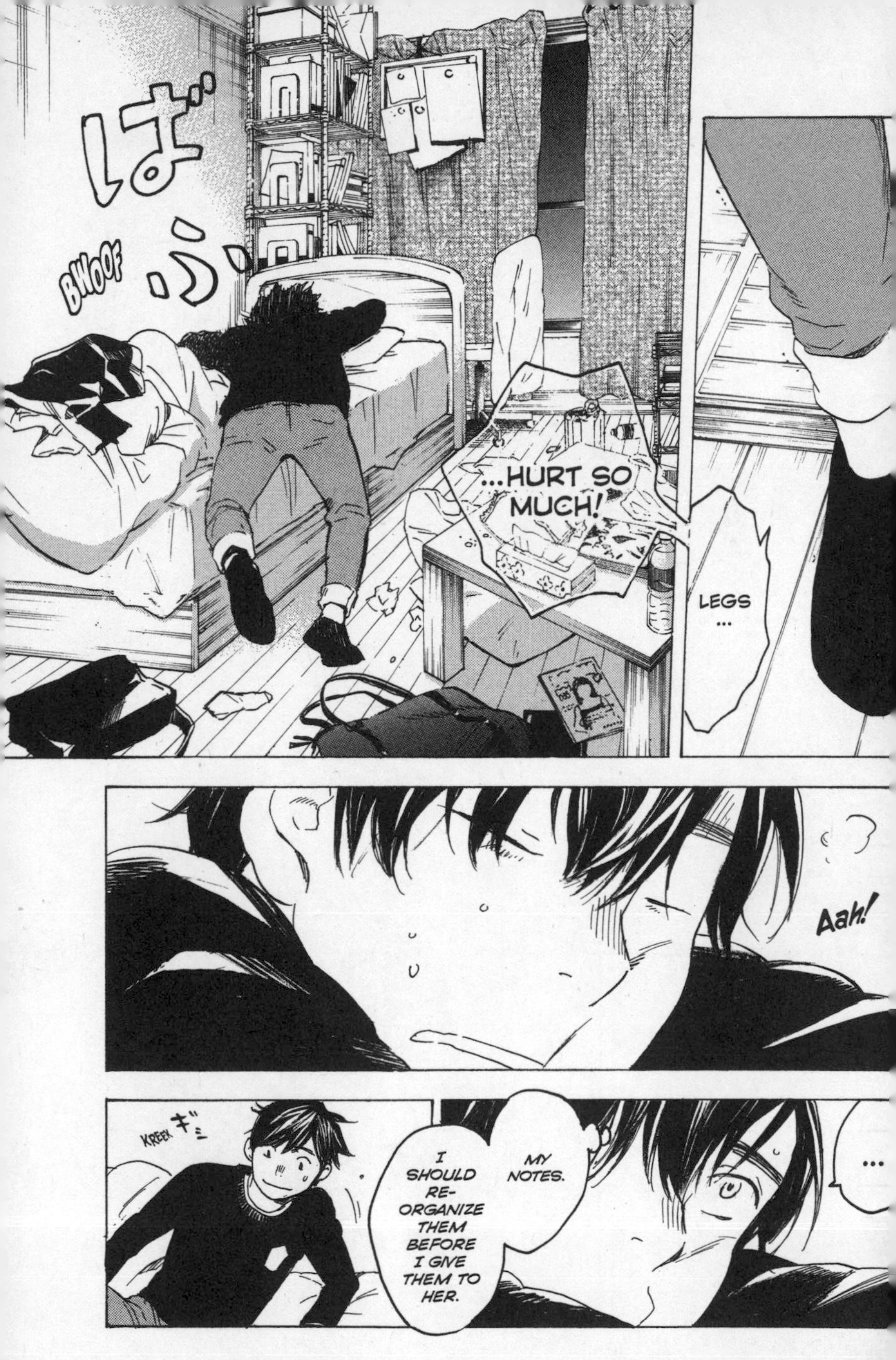
LEGS ...
...HURT SO MUCH!
ばふ
BWOOF
Aah!
...
MY NOTES.
I SHOULD RE-ORGANIZE THEM BEFORE I GIVE THEM TO HER.
KREEK

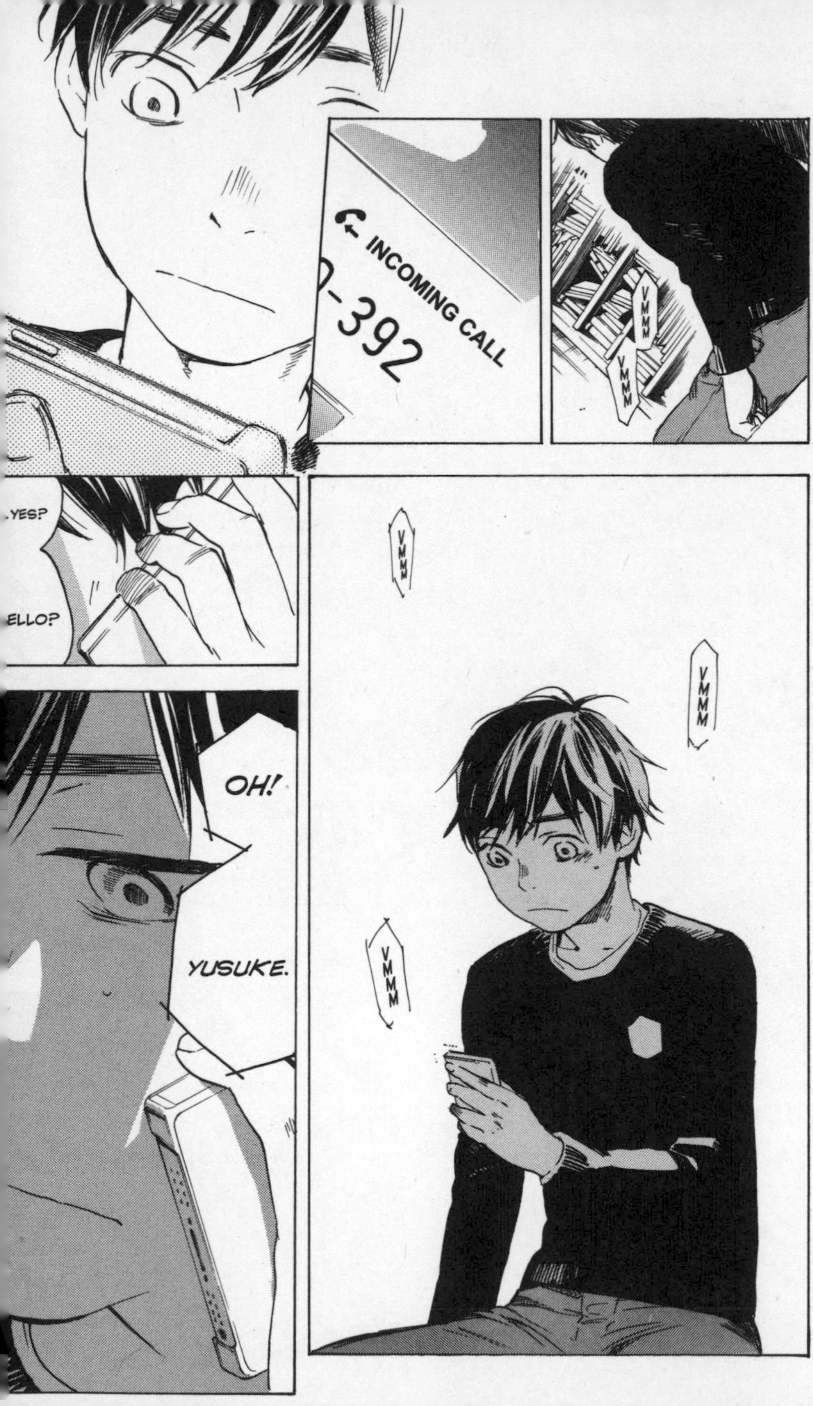
VMMM
VMMM
INCOMING CALL
-392
VMMM
VMMM
VMMM
.YES?
ELLO?
OH!
YUSUKE.

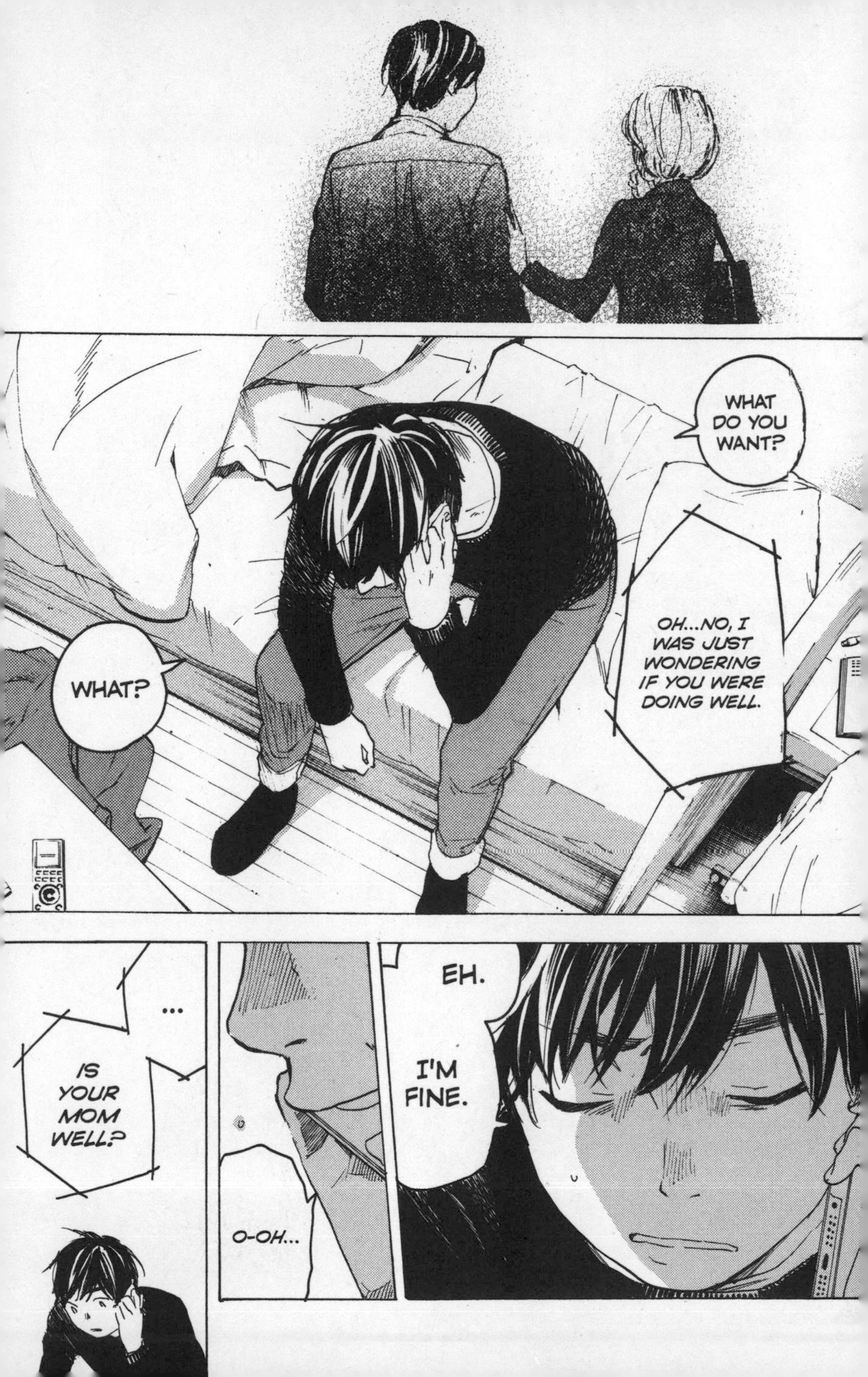
WHAT DO YOU WANT?
OH...NO, I WAS JUST WONDERING IF YOU WERE DOING WELL.
WHAT?
EH.
I'M FINE.
O-OH...
...
IS YOUR MOM WELL?

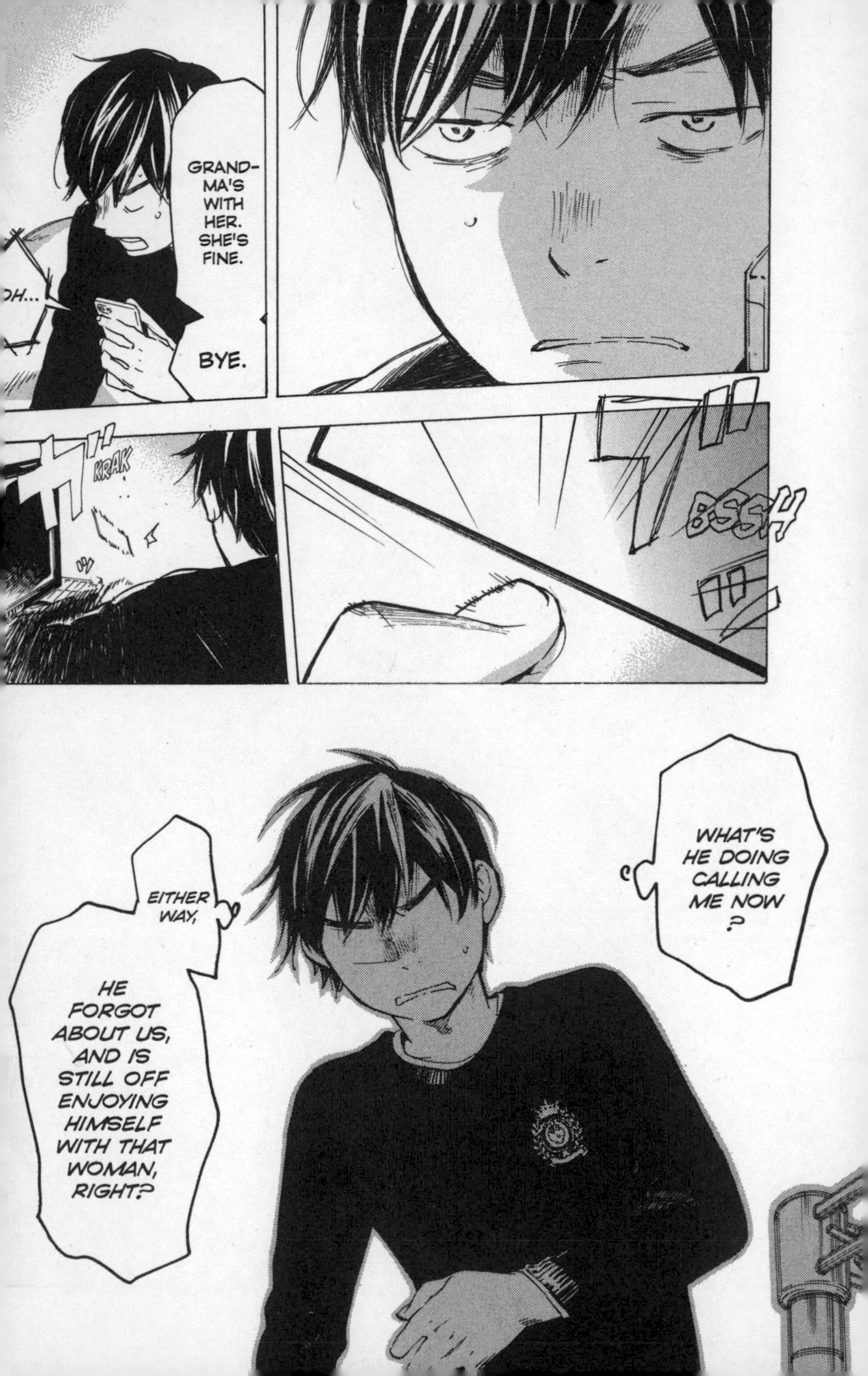
GRAND-MA'S WITH HER. SHE'S FINE.
OH...
BYE.
BSSH
KRAK
WHAT'S HE DOING CALLING ME NOW?
EITHER WAY,
HE FORGOT ABOUT US, AND IS STILL OFF ENJOYING HIMSELF WITH THAT WOMAN, RIGHT?

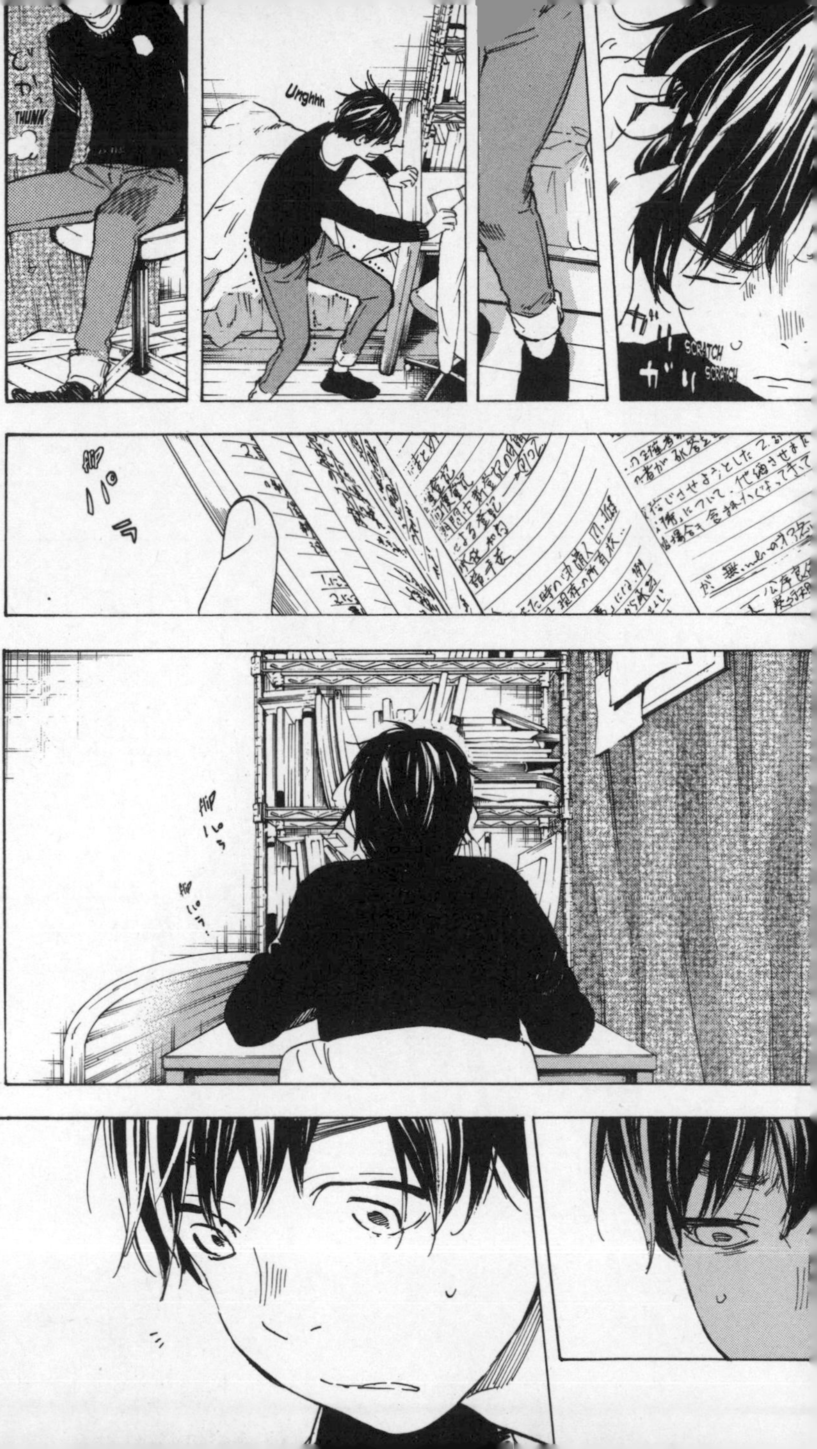
ガリ
ガリ
SCRATCH
SCRATCH
Unghhh
どかっ
THUNK
FLIP
パラ
FLIP
FLIP

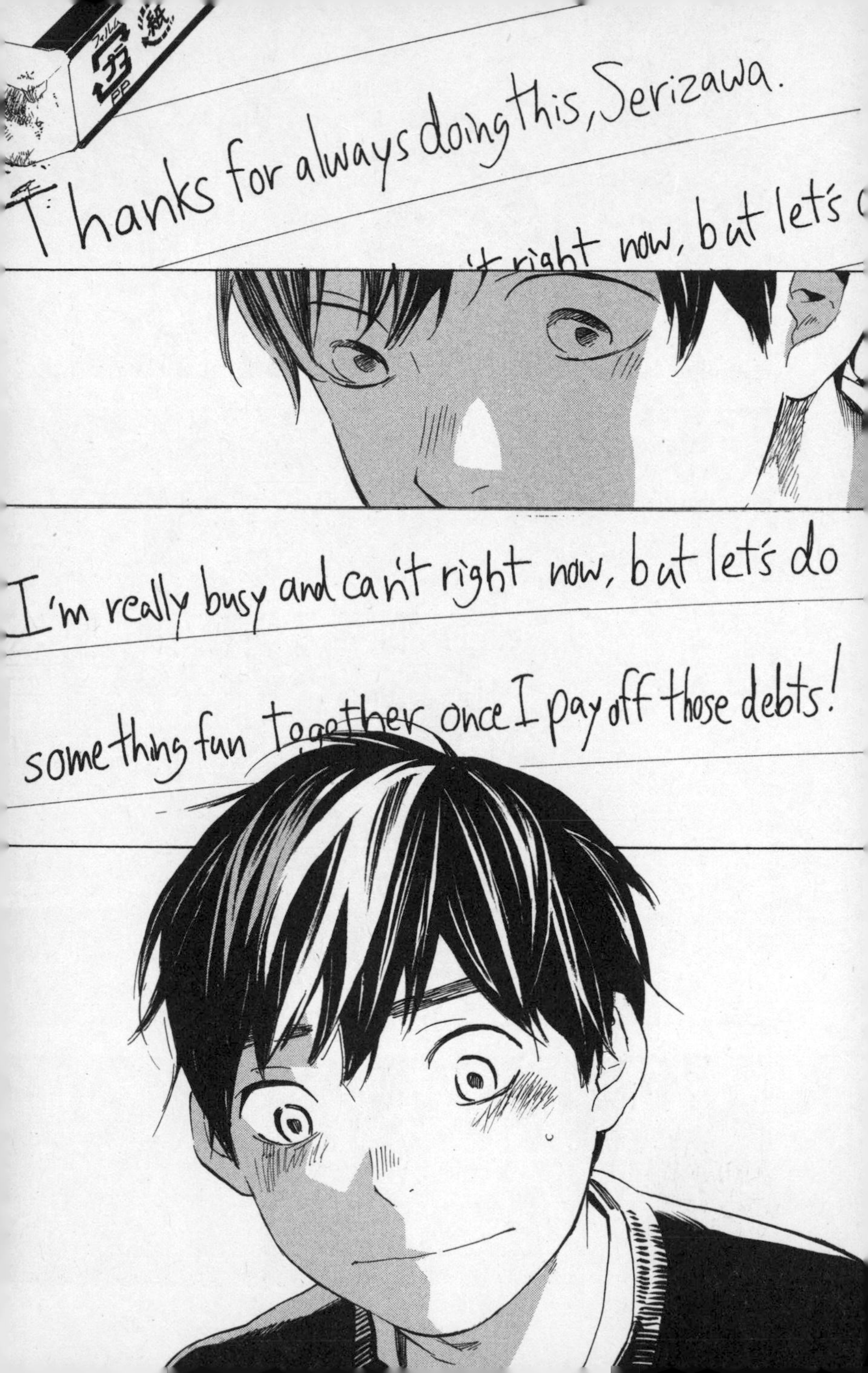

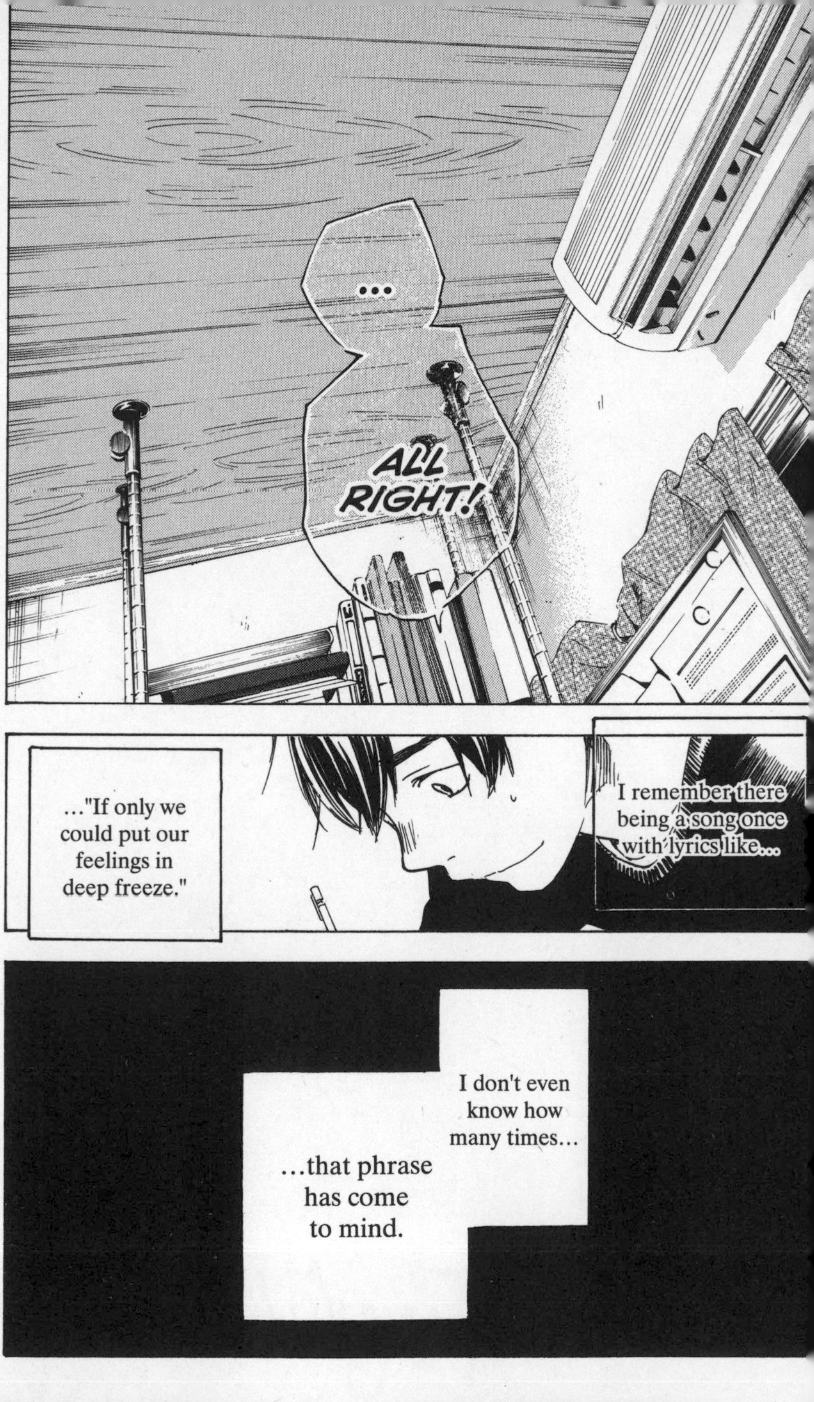
...
ALL RIGHT!
I remember there being a song once with lyrics like...
..."If only we could put our feelings in deep freeze."
I don't even know how many times...
...that phrase has come to mind.

Forget Me Not

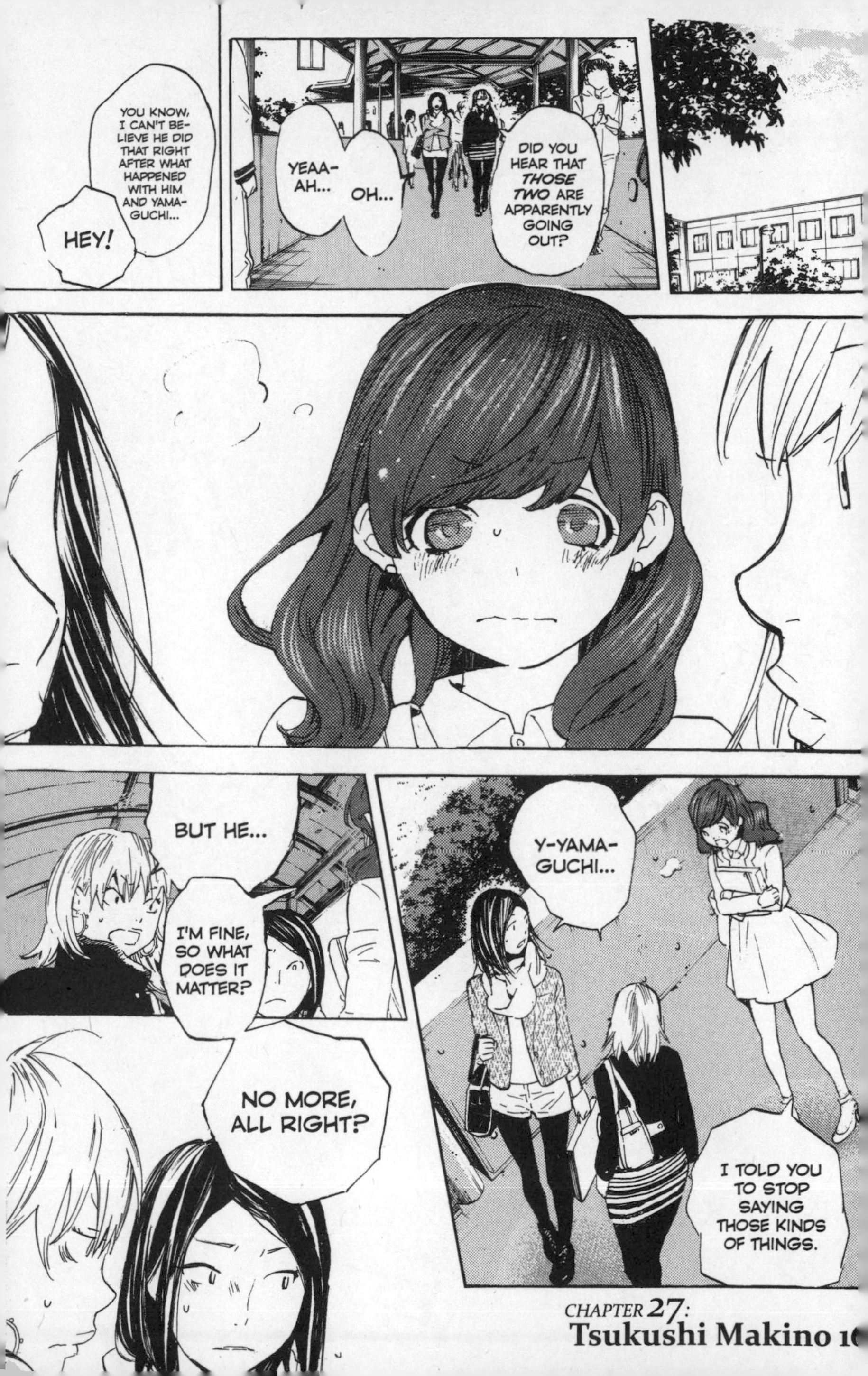
DID YOU HEAR THAT *THOSE TWO* ARE APPARENTLY GOING OUT?
OH...
YEAA-AH...
YOU KNOW, I CAN'T BELIEVE HE DID THAT RIGHT AFTER WHAT HAPPENED WITH HIM AND YAMAGUCHI...
HEY!
Y-YAMAGUCHI...
I TOLD YOU TO STOP SAYING THOSE KINDS OF THINGS.
BUT HE...
I'M FINE, SO WHAT DOES IT MATTER?
NO MORE, ALL RIGHT?

CHAPTER 27: Tsukushi Makino 1

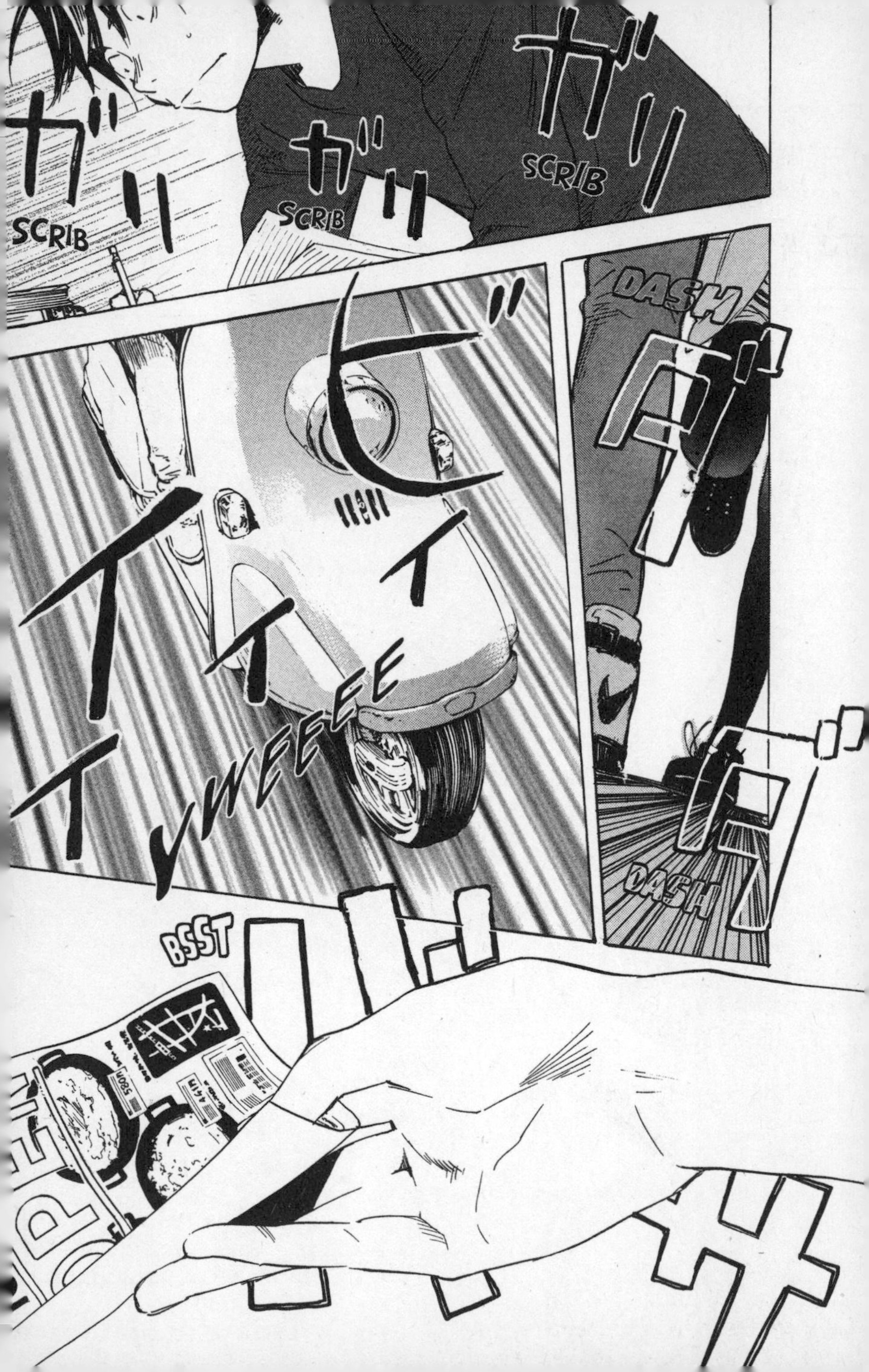
ガリ
SCRIB
ガリ
SCRIB
ガリ
SCRIB
DASH
DASH
ビイイイ
VWEEEE
BSST

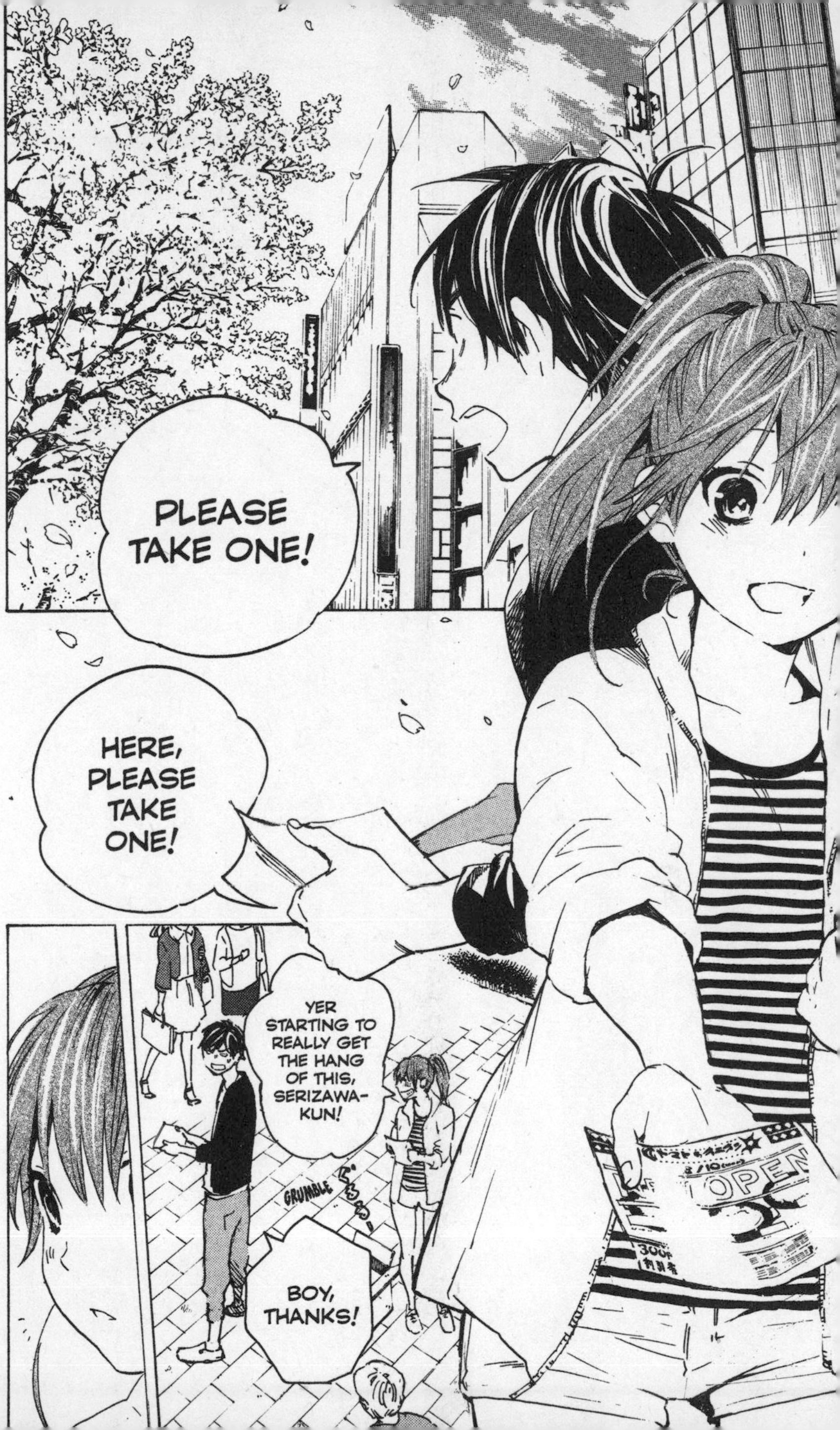
PLEASE TAKE ONE!
HERE, PLEASE TAKE ONE!
OPEN
YER STARTING TO REALLY GET THE HANG OF THIS, SERIZAWA-KUN!
GRUMBLE
BOY, THANKS!

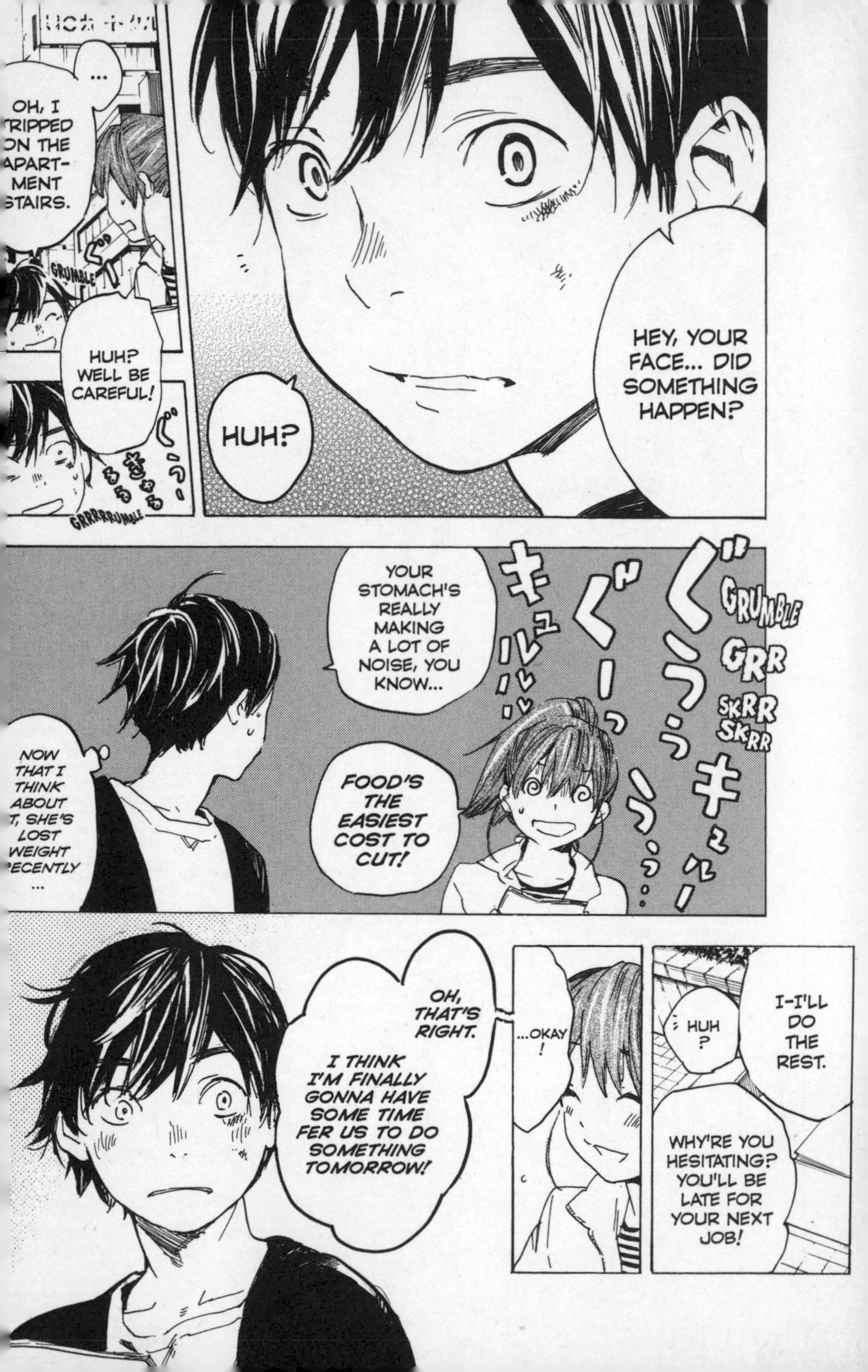
HEY, YOUR FACE... DID SOMETHING HAPPEN?
HUH?
...
OH, I TRIPPED ON THE APARTMENT STAIRS.
GRUMBLE
HUH? WELL BE CAREFUL!
GRRRRRUMBLE
GRUMBLE
GRR
SKRR
SKRR
YOUR STOMACH'S REALLY MAKING A LOT OF NOISE, YOU KNOW...
FOOD'S THE EASIEST COST TO CUT!
NOW THAT I THINK ABOUT IT, SHE'S LOST WEIGHT RECENTLY...
I-I'LL DO THE REST.
HUH?
WHY'RE YOU HESITATING? YOU'LL BE LATE FOR YOUR NEXT JOB!
...OKAY!
OH, THAT'S RIGHT.
I THINK I'M FINALLY GONNA HAVE SOME TIME FER US TO DO SOMETHING TOMORROW!

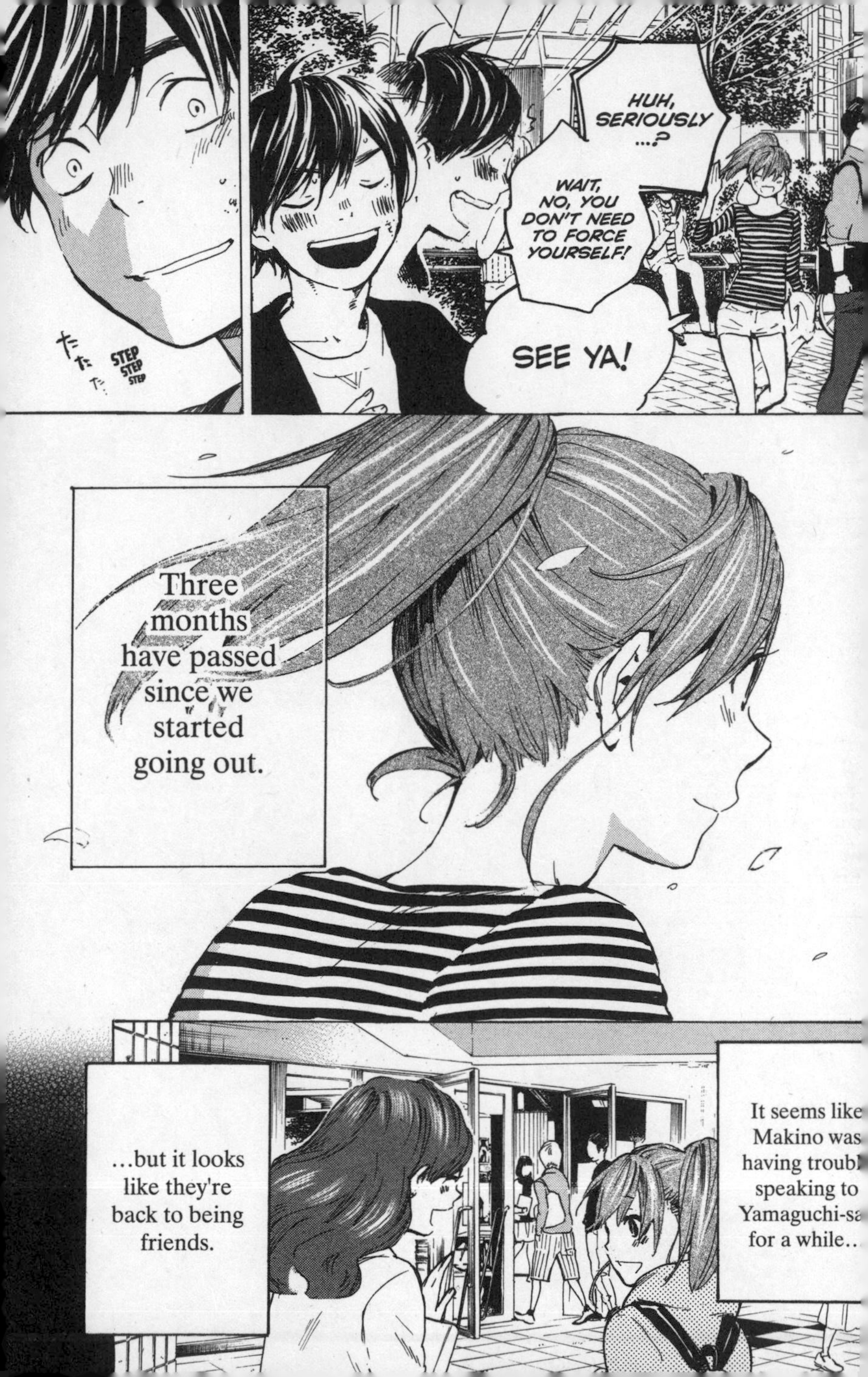
HUH, SERIOUSLY ...?
WAIT, NO, YOU DON'T NEED TO FORCE YOURSELF!
SEE YA!
STEP STEP STEP
Three months have passed since we started going out.
It seems like Makino was having troubl speaking to Yamaguchi-sa for a while..
...but it looks like they're back to being friends.

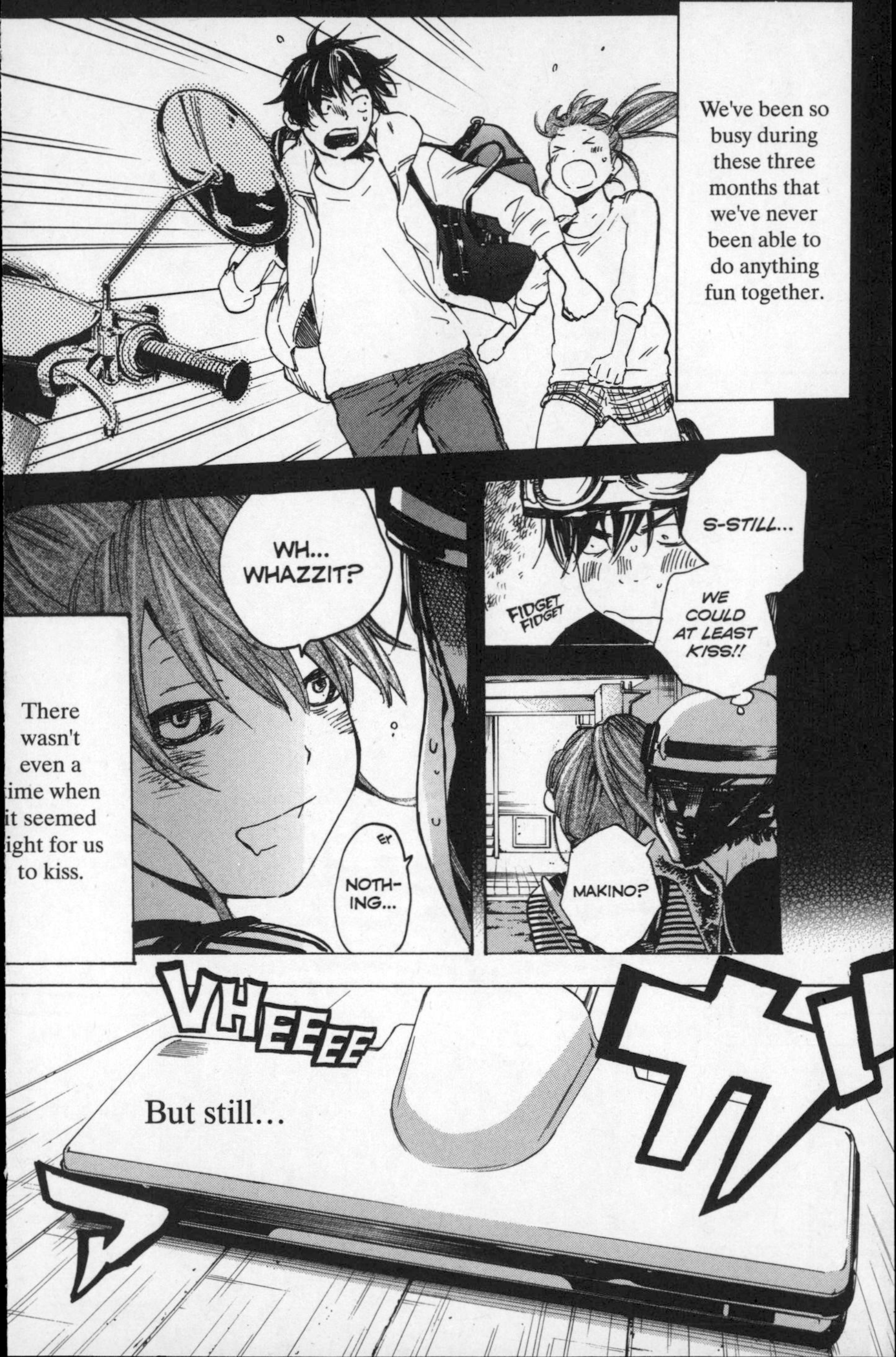
We've been so busy during these three months that we've never been able to do anything fun together.
S-STILL...
FIDGET FIDGET
WE COULD AT LEAST KISS!!
MAKINO?
WH... WHAZZIT?
Er
NOTH-ING...
There wasn't even a ime when it seemed ight for us to kiss.
VHEEEE
But still…

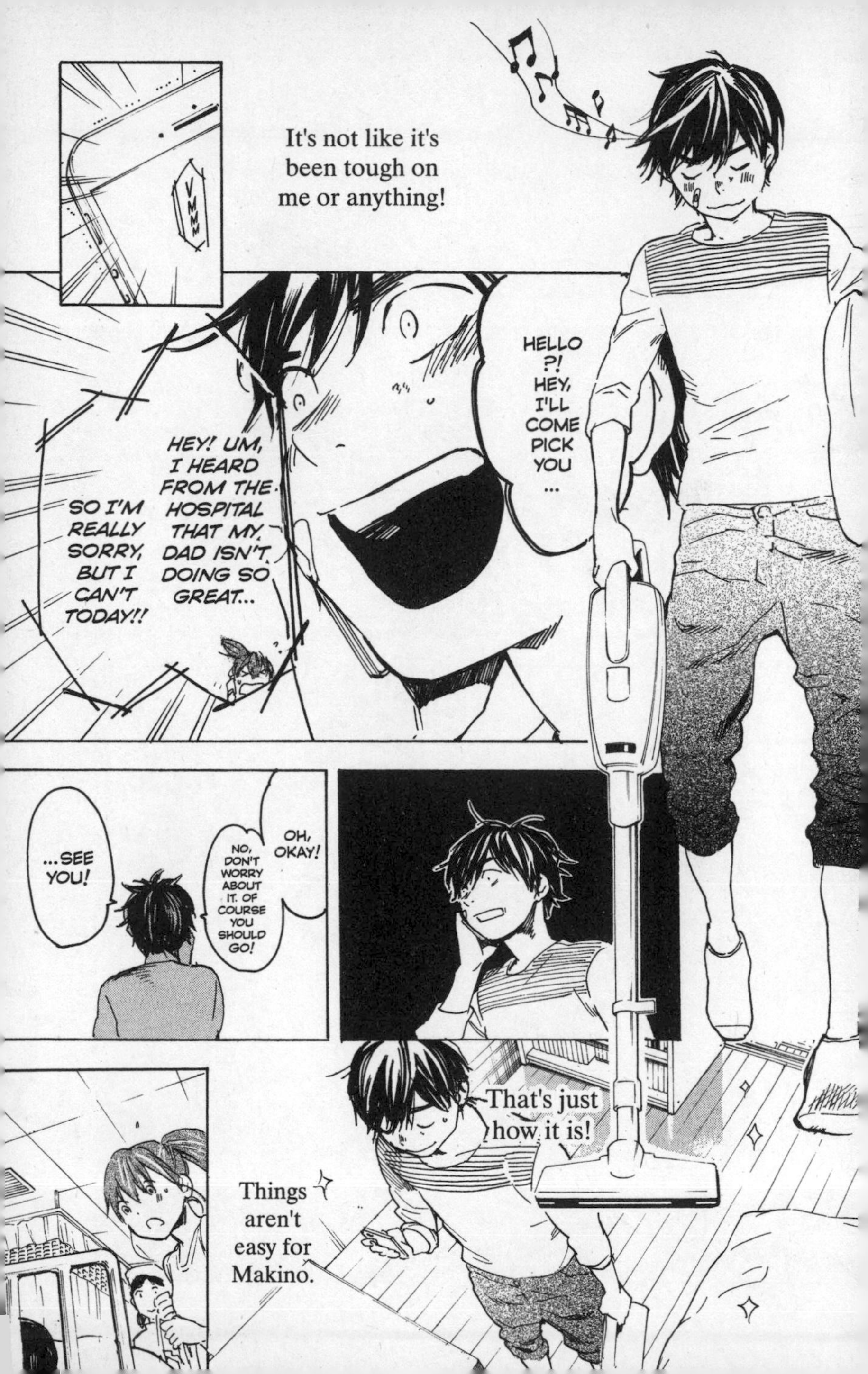
It's not like it's been tough on me or anything!
VMMM
HELLO?! HEY, I'LL COME PICK YOU...
HEY! UM, I HEARD FROM THE HOSPITAL THAT MY DAD ISN'T DOING SO GREAT...
SO I'M REALLY SORRY, BUT I CAN'T TODAY!!
OH, OKAY!
NO, DON'T WORRY ABOUT IT. OF COURSE YOU SHOULD GO!
...SEE YOU!
That's just how it is!
Things aren't easy for Makino.

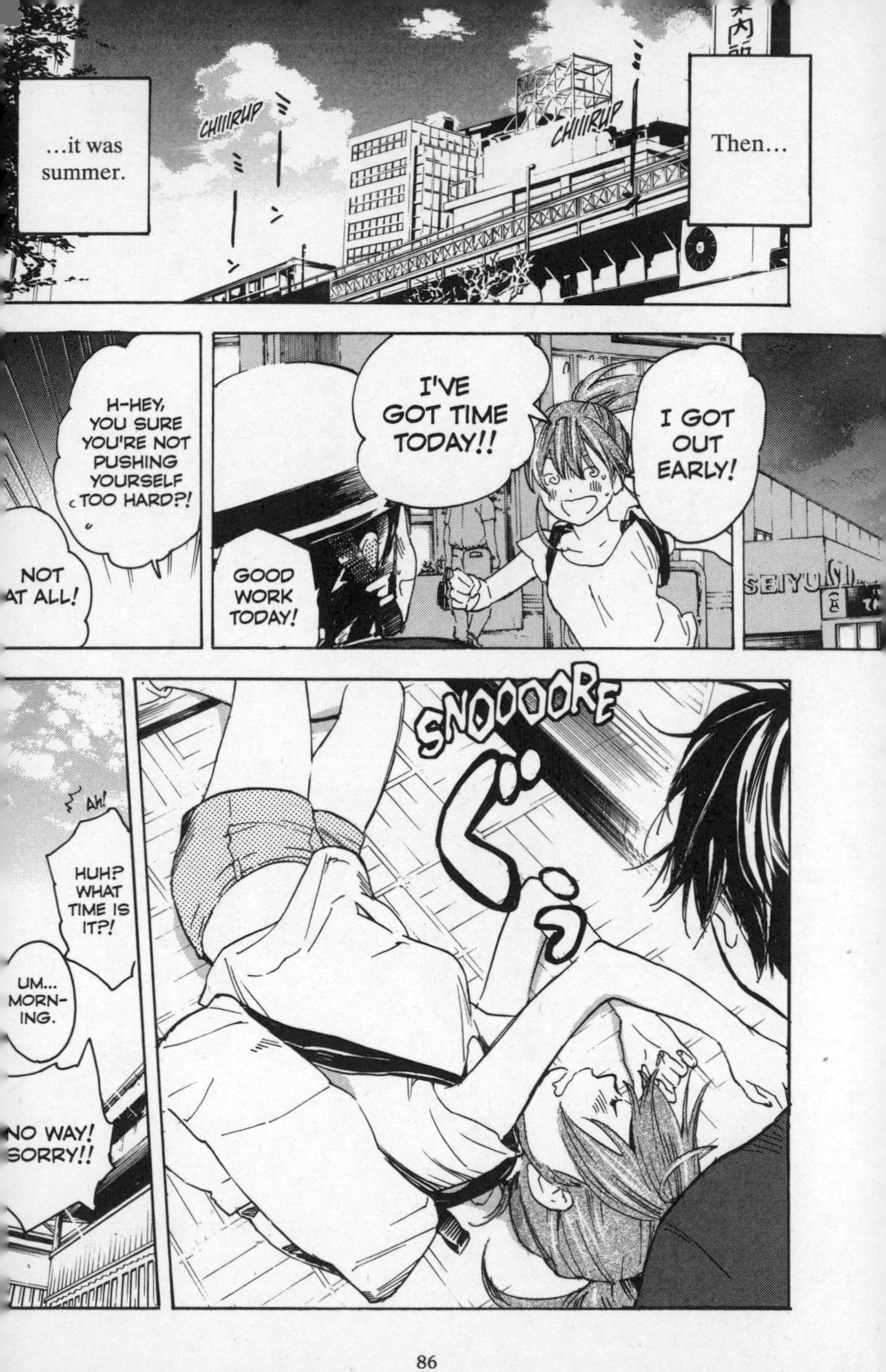
Then…
…it was summer.
CHIIIRUP
CHIIIRUP
I GOT OUT EARLY!
I'VE GOT TIME TODAY!!
GOOD WORK TODAY!
H-HEY, YOU SURE YOU'RE NOT PUSHING YOURSELF TOO HARD?!
NOT AT ALL!
SNOOOORE
AH!
HUH? WHAT TIME IS IT?!
UM... MORNING.
NO WAY! SORRY!!

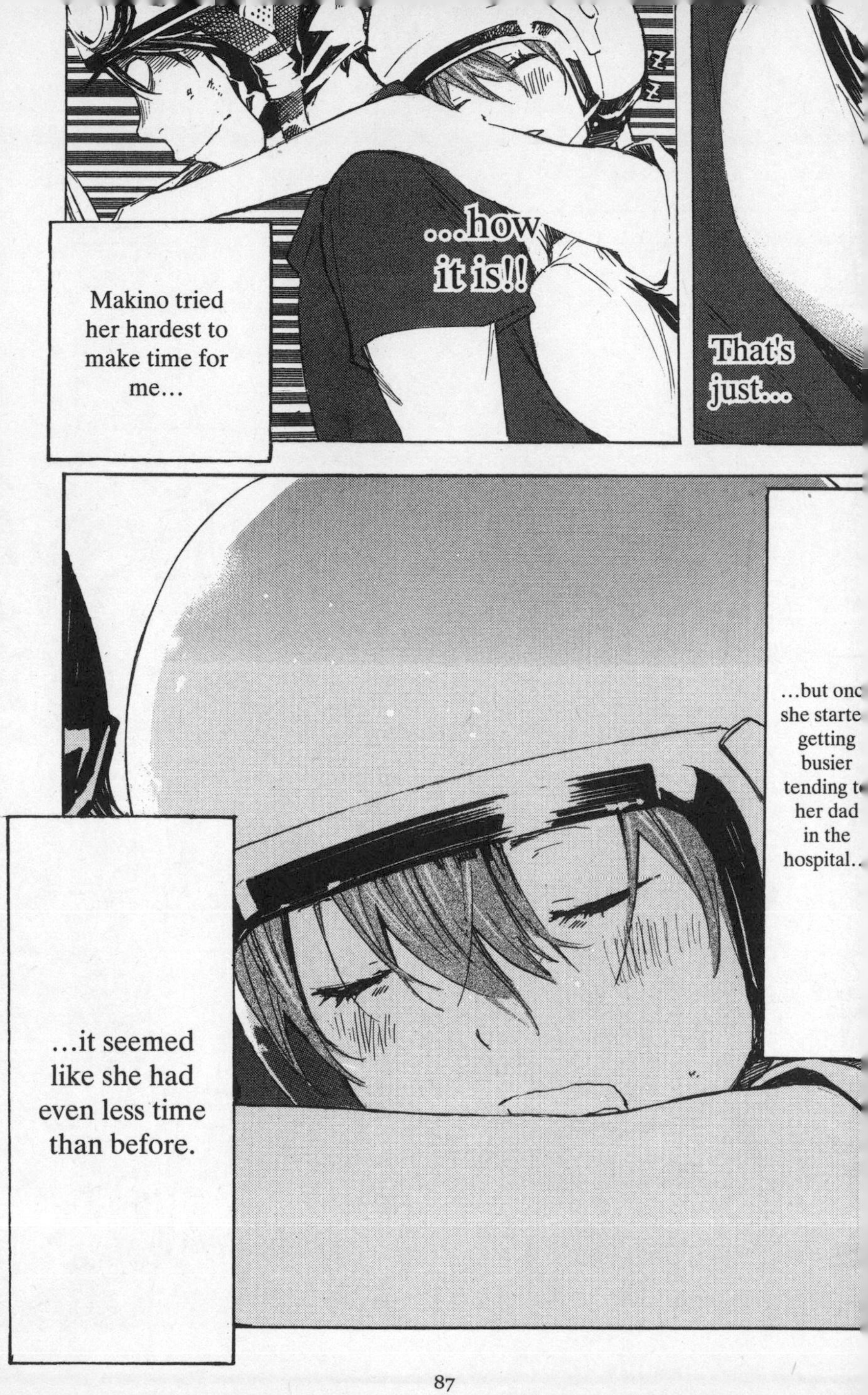
That's just...
...how it is!!
Makino tried her hardest to make time for me...
...but onc she starte getting busier tending t her dad in the hospital..
...it seemed like she had even less time than before.

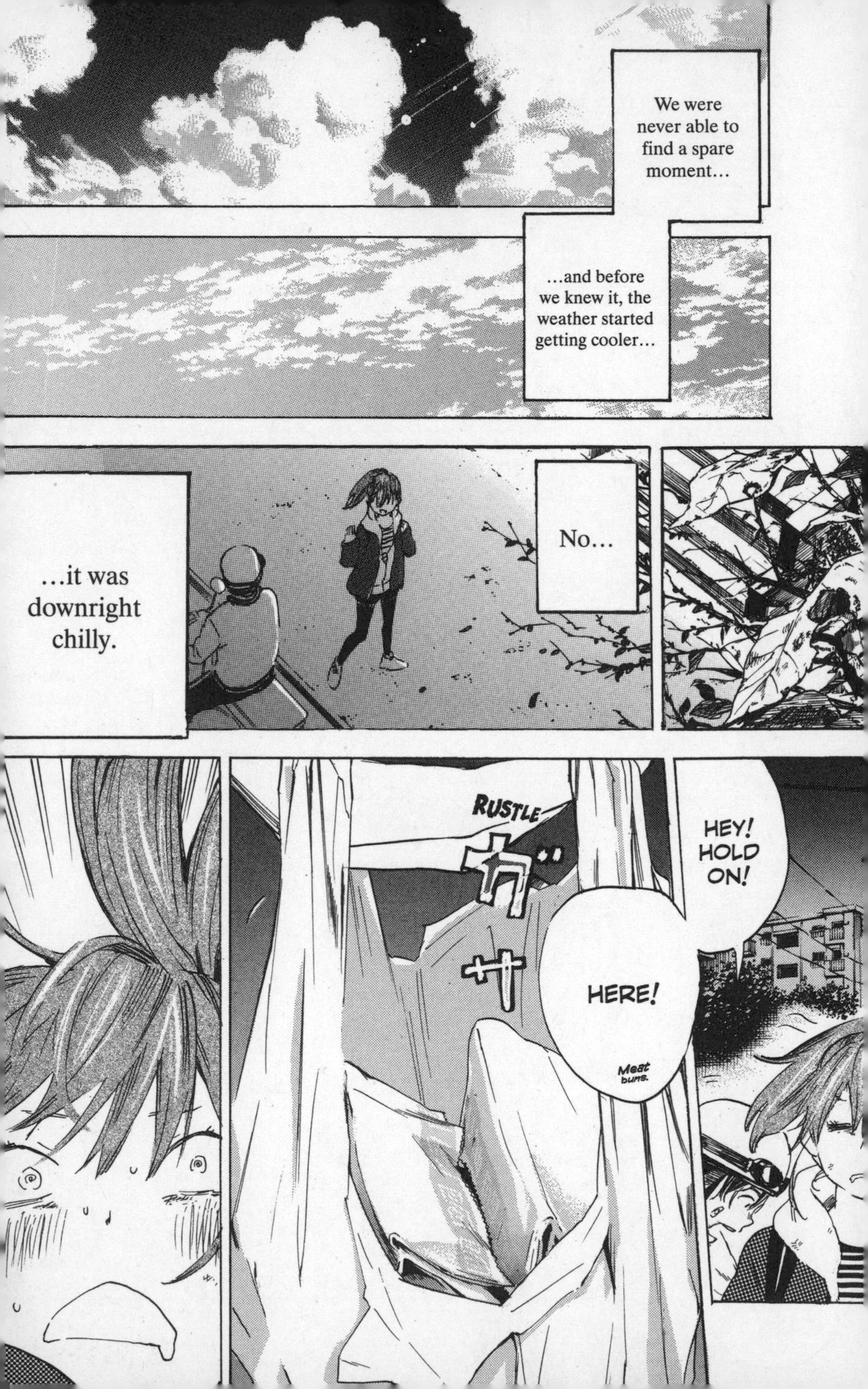
We were never able to find a spare moment…
…and before we knew it, the weather started getting cooler…
No…
…it was downright chilly.
HEY! HOLD ON!
HERE!
Meat buns.
RUSTLE
ガ
サ

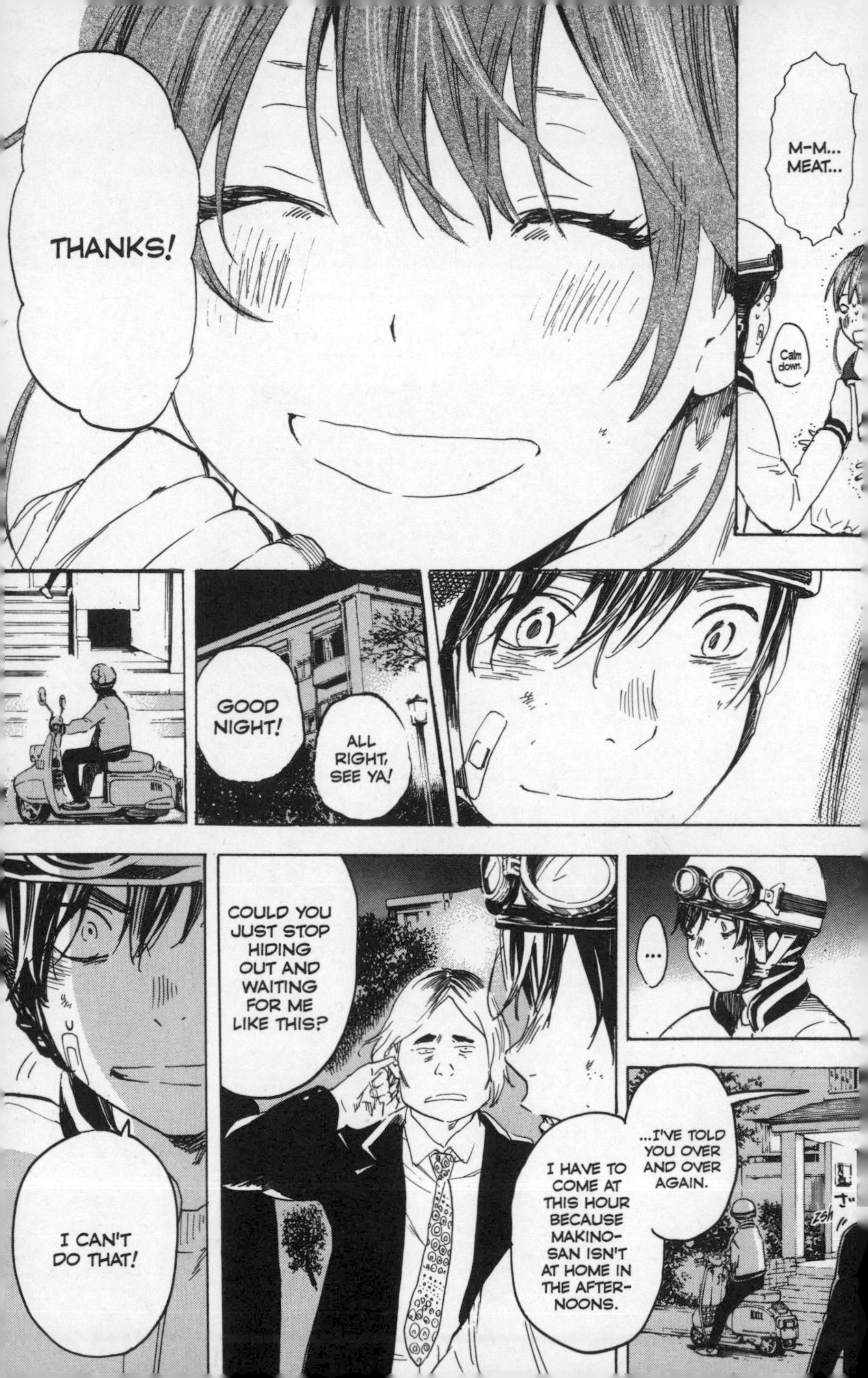
M-M... MEAT...
Calm down.
THANKS!
GOOD NIGHT!
ALL RIGHT, SEE YA!
...
...I'VE TOLD YOU OVER AND OVER AGAIN.
I HAVE TO COME AT THIS HOUR BECAUSE MAKINO-SAN ISN'T AT HOME IN THE AFTER-NOONS.
ZSH
COULD YOU JUST STOP HIDING OUT AND WAITING FOR ME LIKE THIS?
I CAN'T DO THAT!

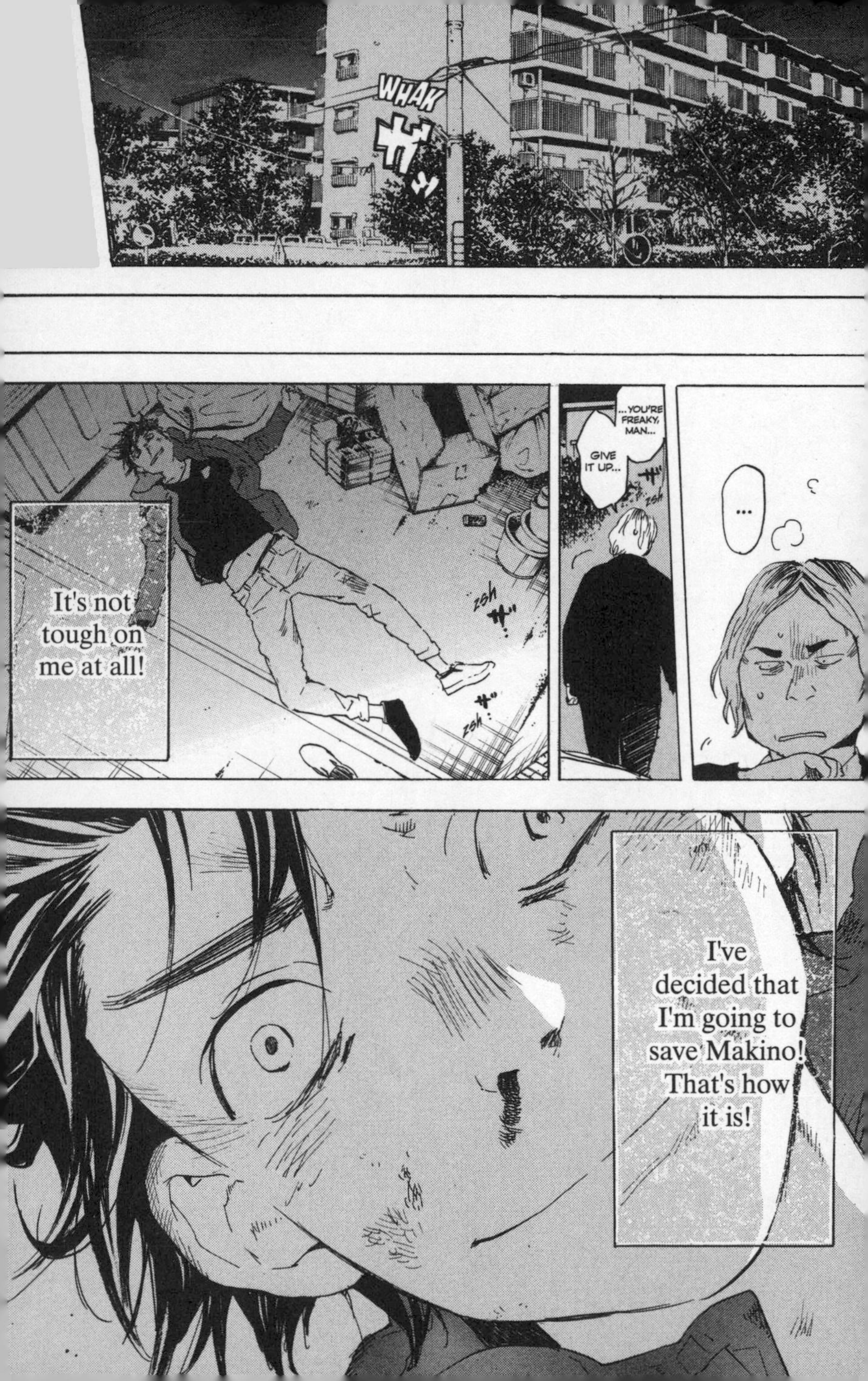
WHAK
...
...YOU'RE FREAKY, MAN...
GIVE IT UP...
zsh
zsh
zsh
It's not tough on me at all!
I've decided that I'm going to save Makino! That's how it is!

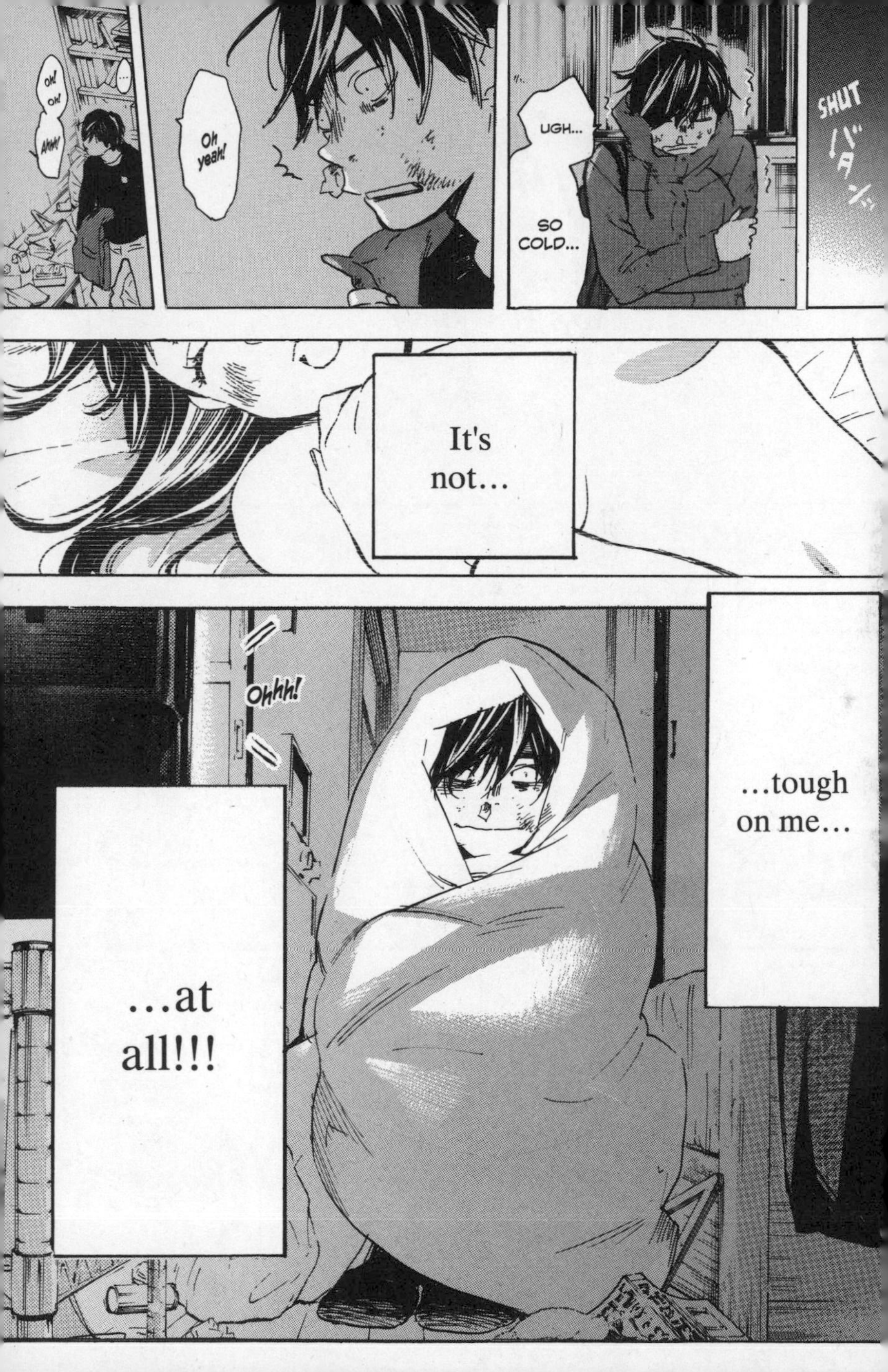
SHUT
UGH...
SO COLD...
Oh yeah!
...
Oh! Oh! Ahhh!
It's not…
…tough on me…
Ohhh!
…at all!!!

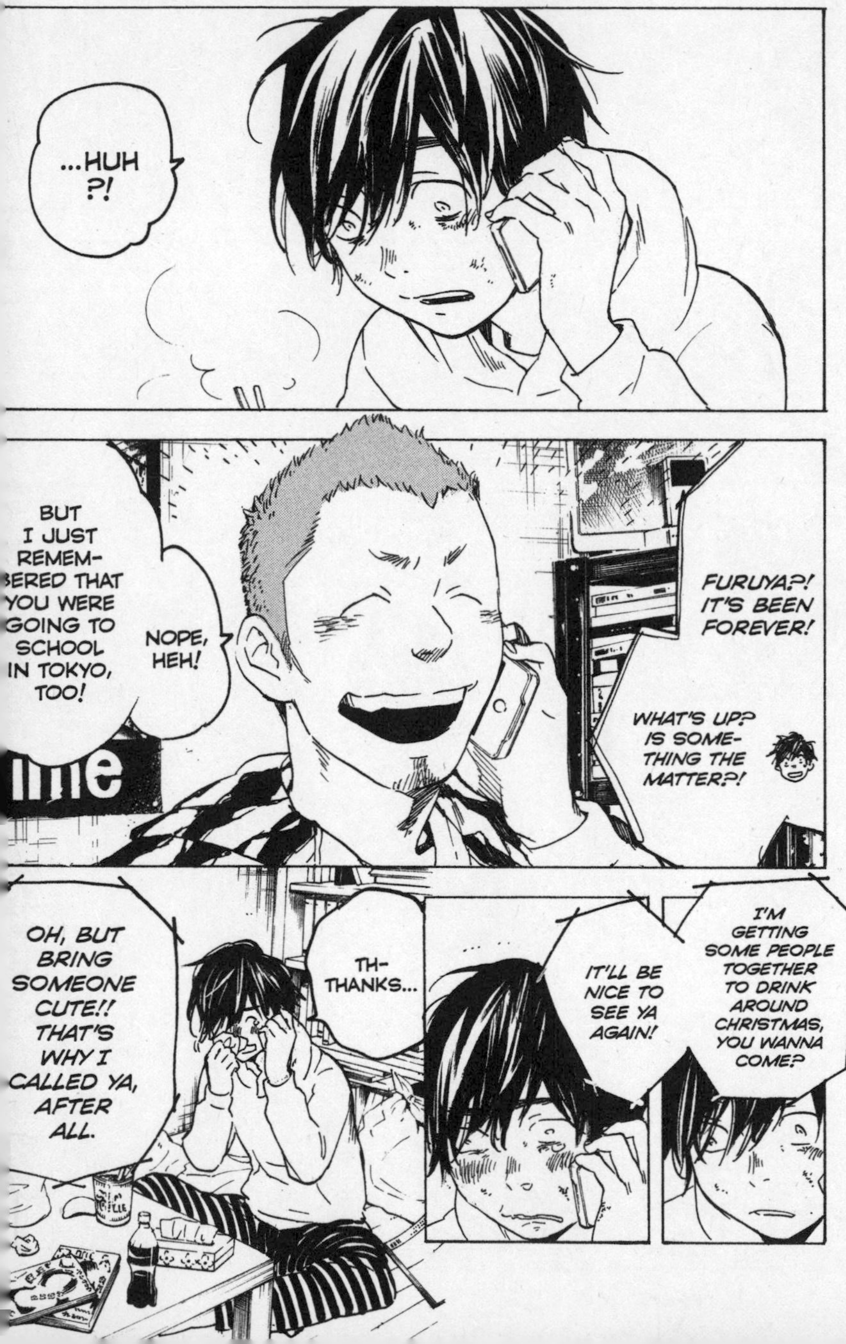
...HUH ?!
FURUYA?! IT'S BEEN FOREVER!
WHAT'S UP? IS SOMETHING THE MATTER?!
NOPE, HEH!
BUT I JUST REMEMBERED THAT YOU WERE GOING TO SCHOOL IN TOKYO, TOO!
I'M GETTING SOME PEOPLE TOGETHER TO DRINK AROUND CHRISTMAS, YOU WANNA COME?
IT'LL BE NICE TO SEE YA AGAIN!
...
TH-THANKS...
OH, BUT BRING SOMEONE CUTE!! THAT'S WHY I CALLED YA, AFTER ALL.

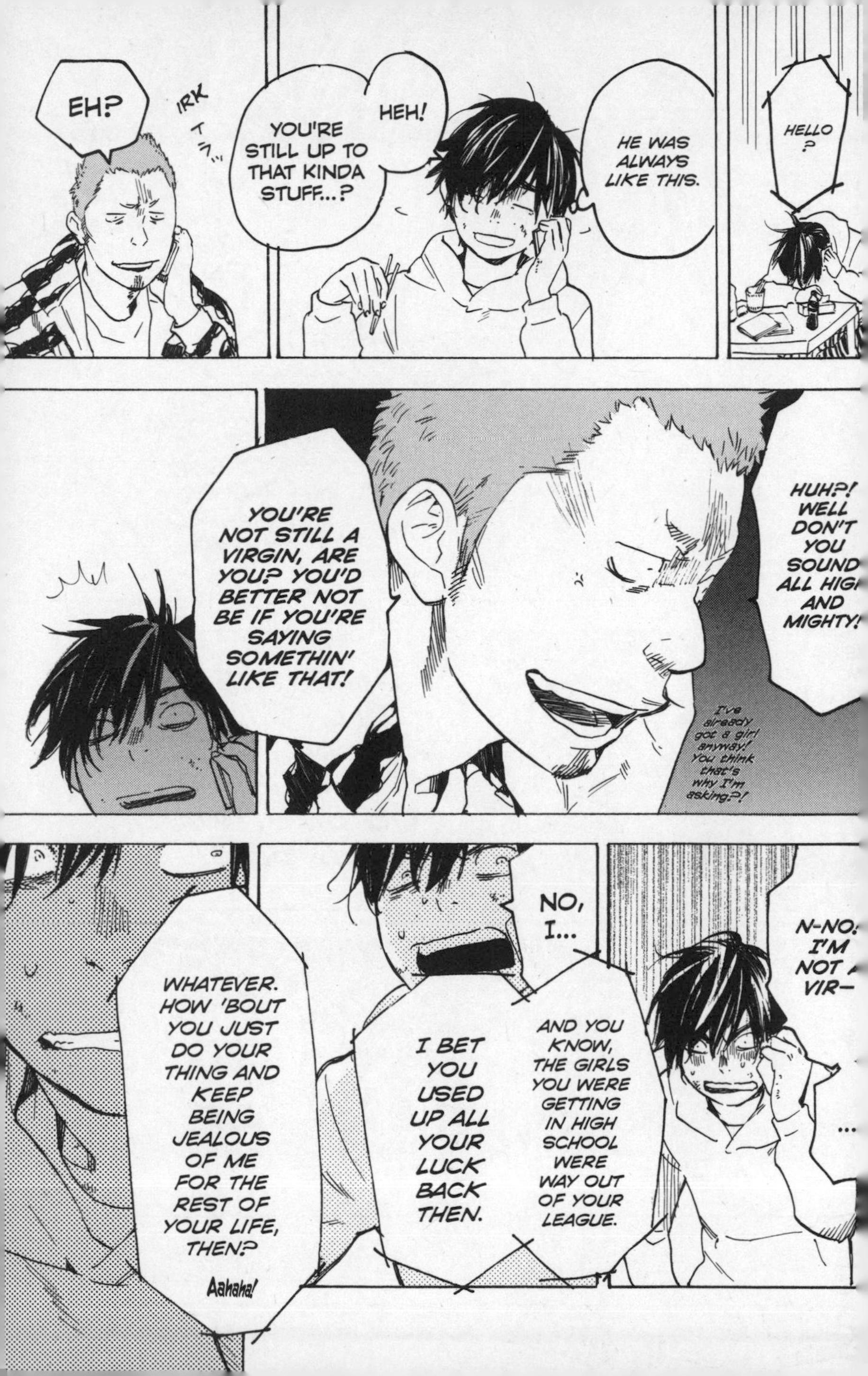
HELLO ?
HE WAS ALWAYS LIKE THIS.
HEH!
YOU'RE STILL UP TO THAT KINDA STUFF...?
IRK
EH?
HUH?! WELL DON'T YOU SOUND ALL HIG AND MIGHTY!
I've already got a girl anyway! You think that's why I'm asking?!
YOU'RE NOT STILL A VIRGIN, ARE YOU? YOU'D BETTER NOT BE IF YOU'RE SAYING SOMETHIN' LIKE THAT!
N-NO. I'M NOT VIR–
...
NO, I...
AND YOU KNOW, THE GIRLS YOU WERE GETTING IN HIGH SCHOOL WERE WAY OUT OF YOUR LEAGUE.
I BET YOU USED UP ALL YOUR LUCK BACK THEN.
WHATEVER. HOW 'BOUT YOU JUST DO YOUR THING AND KEEP BEING JEALOUS OF ME FOR THE REST OF YOUR LIFE, THEN?
Aahaha!

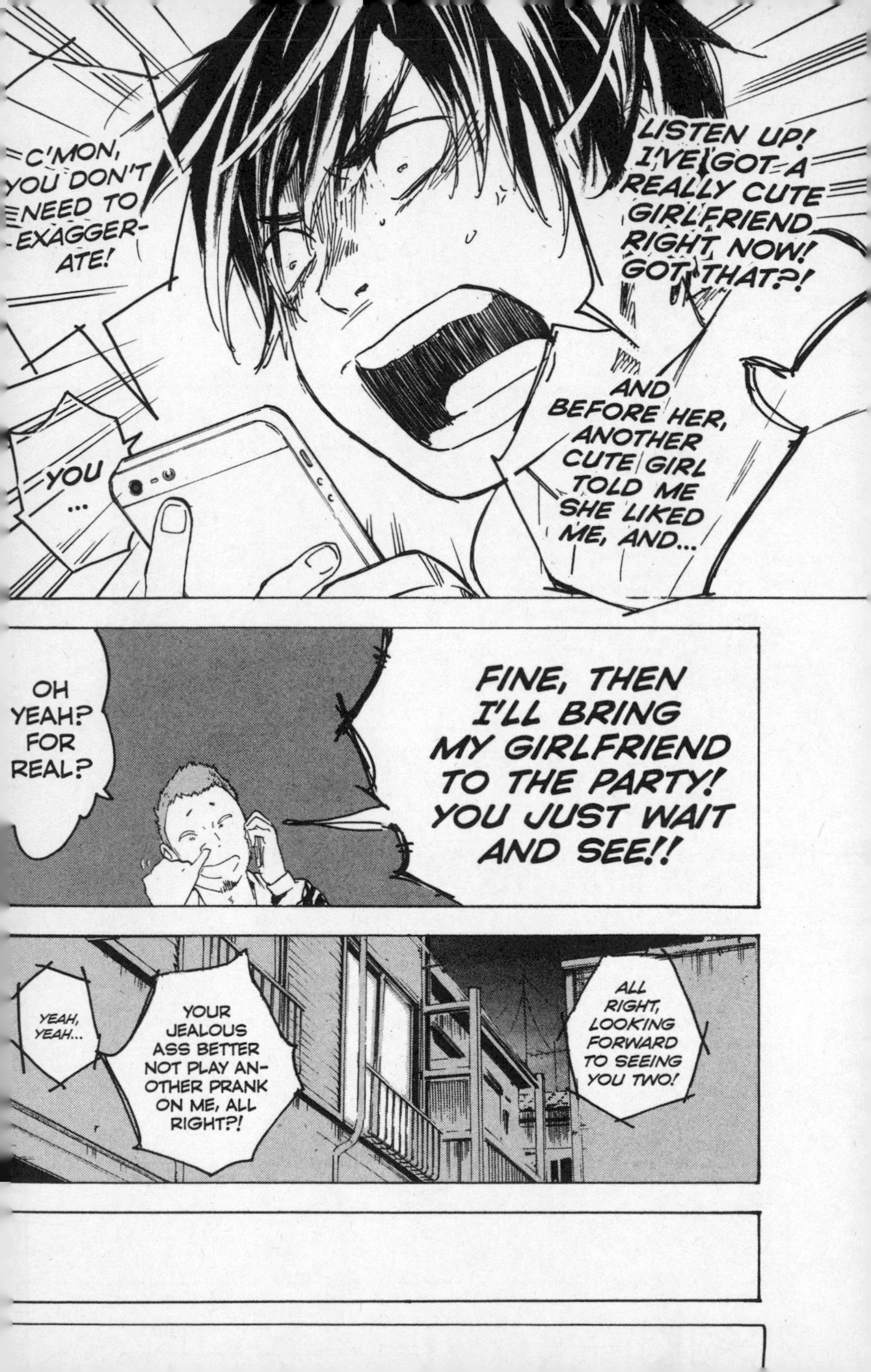
LISTEN UP! I'VE GOT A REALLY CUTE GIRLFRIEND RIGHT NOW! GOT THAT?!
C'MON, YOU DON'T NEED TO EXAGGER-ATE!
AND BEFORE HER, ANOTHER CUTE GIRL TOLD ME SHE LIKED ME, AND...
YOU ...
FINE, THEN I'LL BRING MY GIRLFRIEND TO THE PARTY! YOU JUST WAIT AND SEE!!
OH YEAH? FOR REAL?
ALL RIGHT, LOOKING FORWARD TO SEEING YOU TWO!
YOUR JEALOUS ASS BETTER NOT PLAY AN-OTHER PRANK ON ME, ALL RIGHT?!
YEAH, YEAH...

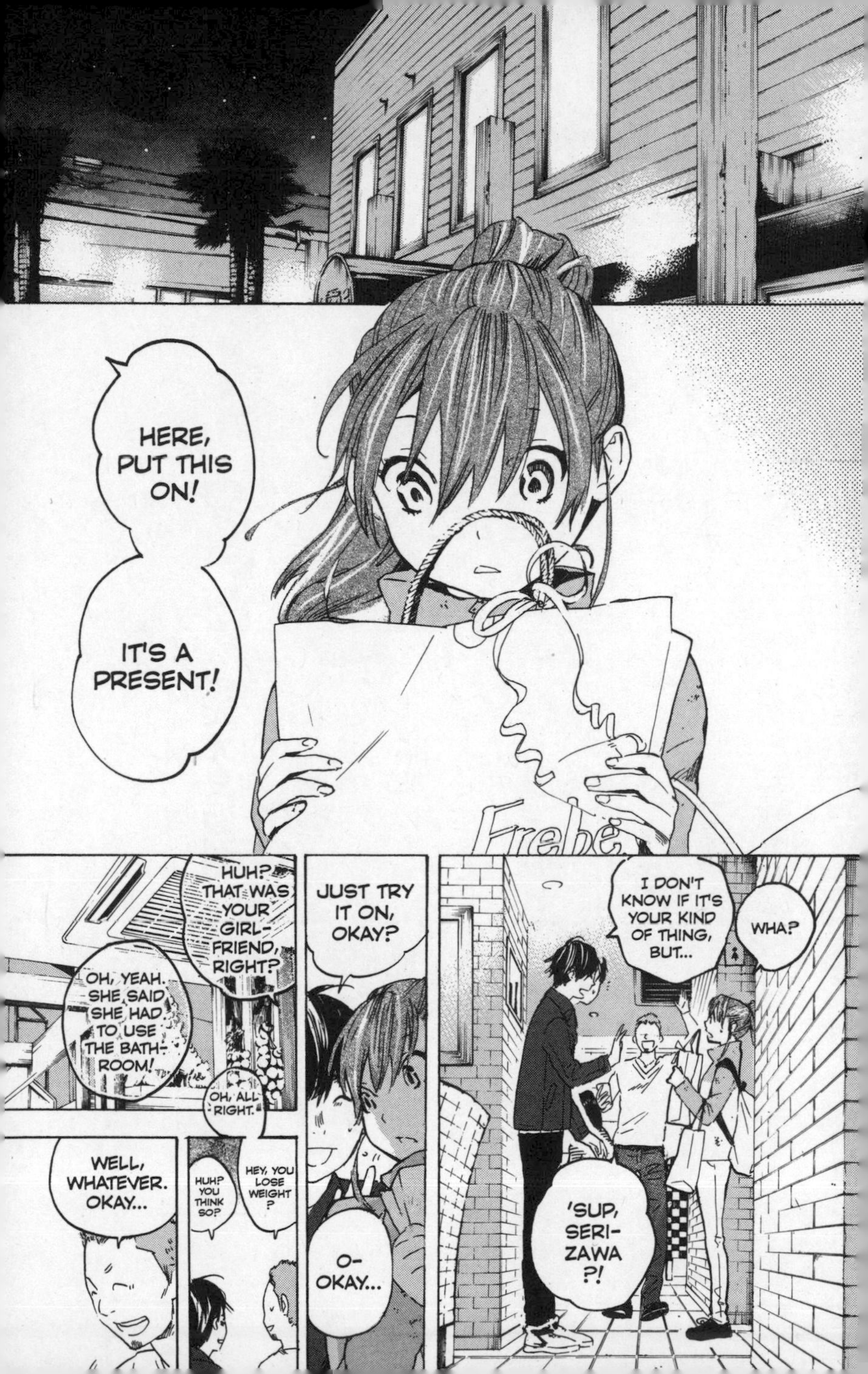
HERE, PUT THIS ON!
IT'S A PRESENT!
WHA?
I DON'T KNOW IF IT'S YOUR KIND OF THING, BUT...
'SUP, SERIZAWA?!
JUST TRY IT ON, OKAY?
O-OKAY...
HUH? THAT WAS YOUR GIRLFRIEND, RIGHT?
OH, YEAH. SHE SAID SHE HAD TO USE THE BATHROOM!
OH, ALL RIGHT.
HEY, YOU LOSE WEIGHT?
HUH? YOU THINK SO?
WELL, WHATEVER. OKAY...

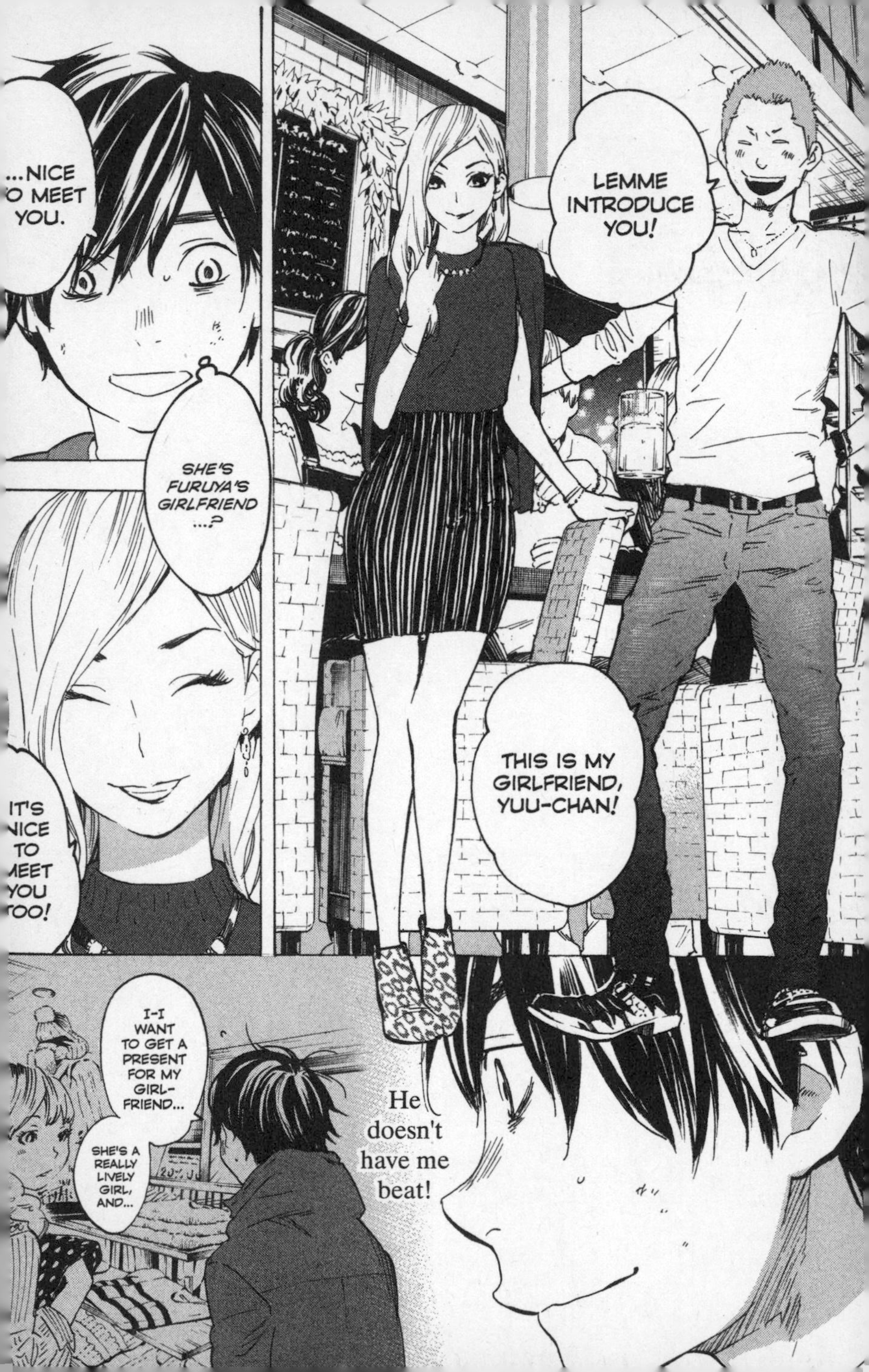
LEMME INTRODUCE YOU!
THIS IS MY GIRLFRIEND, YUU-CHAN!
...NICE O MEET YOU.
SHE'S FURUYA'S GIRLFRIEND ...?
IT'S NICE TO MEET YOU TOO!
He doesn't have me beat!
I-I WANT TO GET A PRESENT FOR MY GIRL-FRIEND...
SHE'S A REALLY LIVELY GIRL, AND...

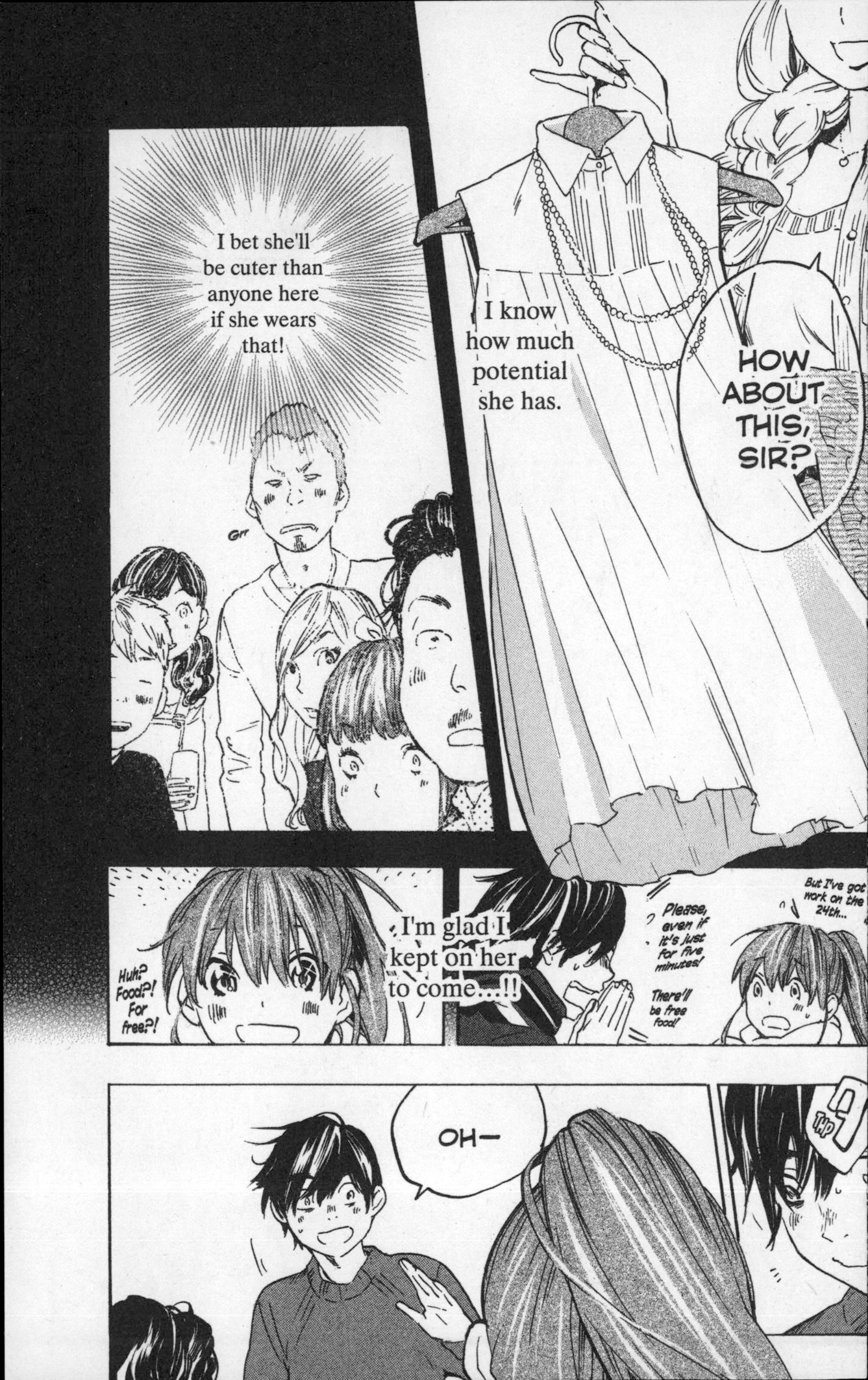
HOW ABOUT THIS, SIR?
I know how much potential she has.
I bet she'll be cuter than anyone here if she wears that!
Grr
But I've got work on the 24th...
Please, even if it's just for five minutes!
There'll be free food!
Huh? Food?! For free?!
I'm glad I kept on her to come...!!
THP
OH—

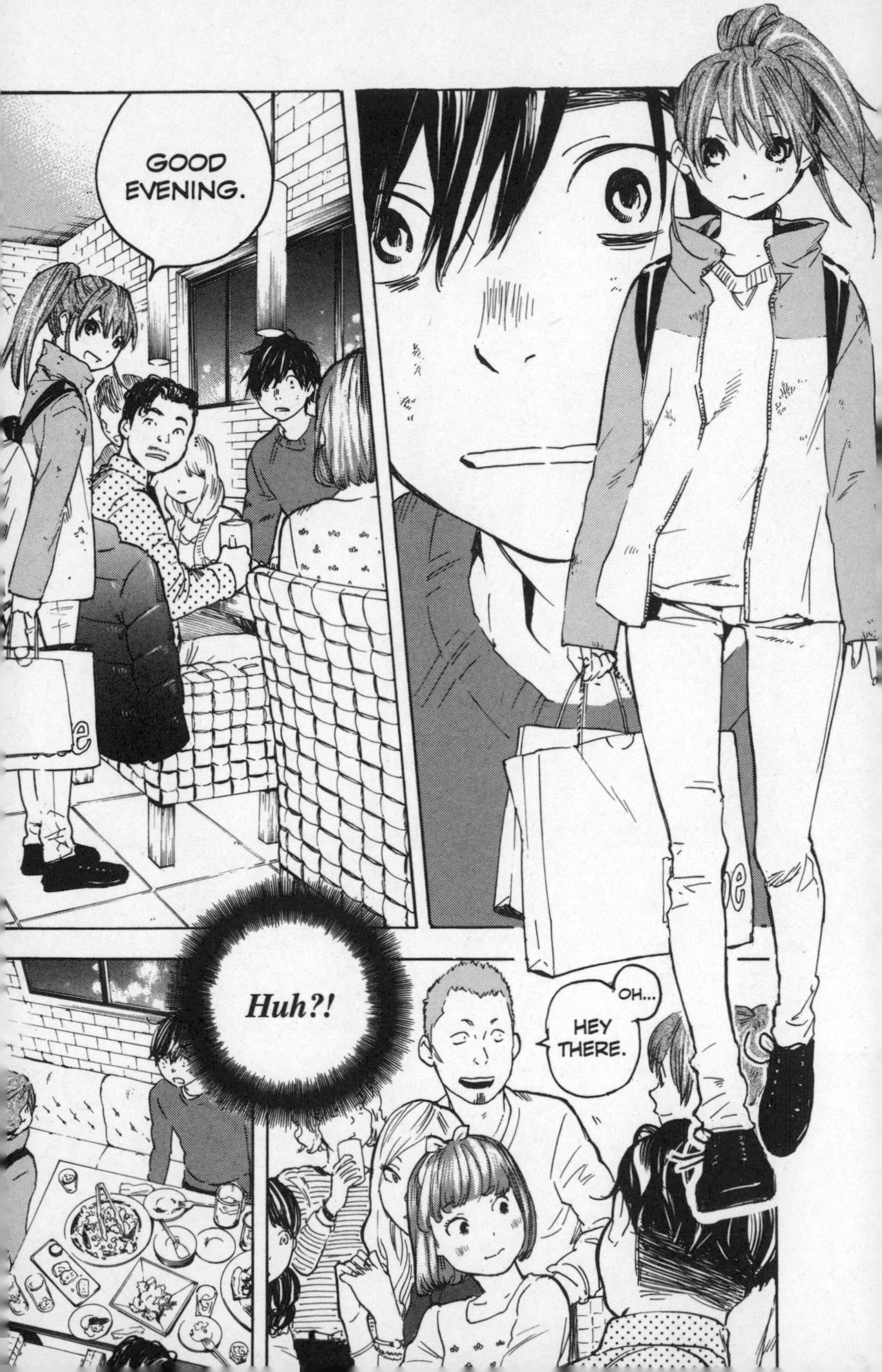
GOOD EVENING.
Huh?!
OH...
HEY THERE.

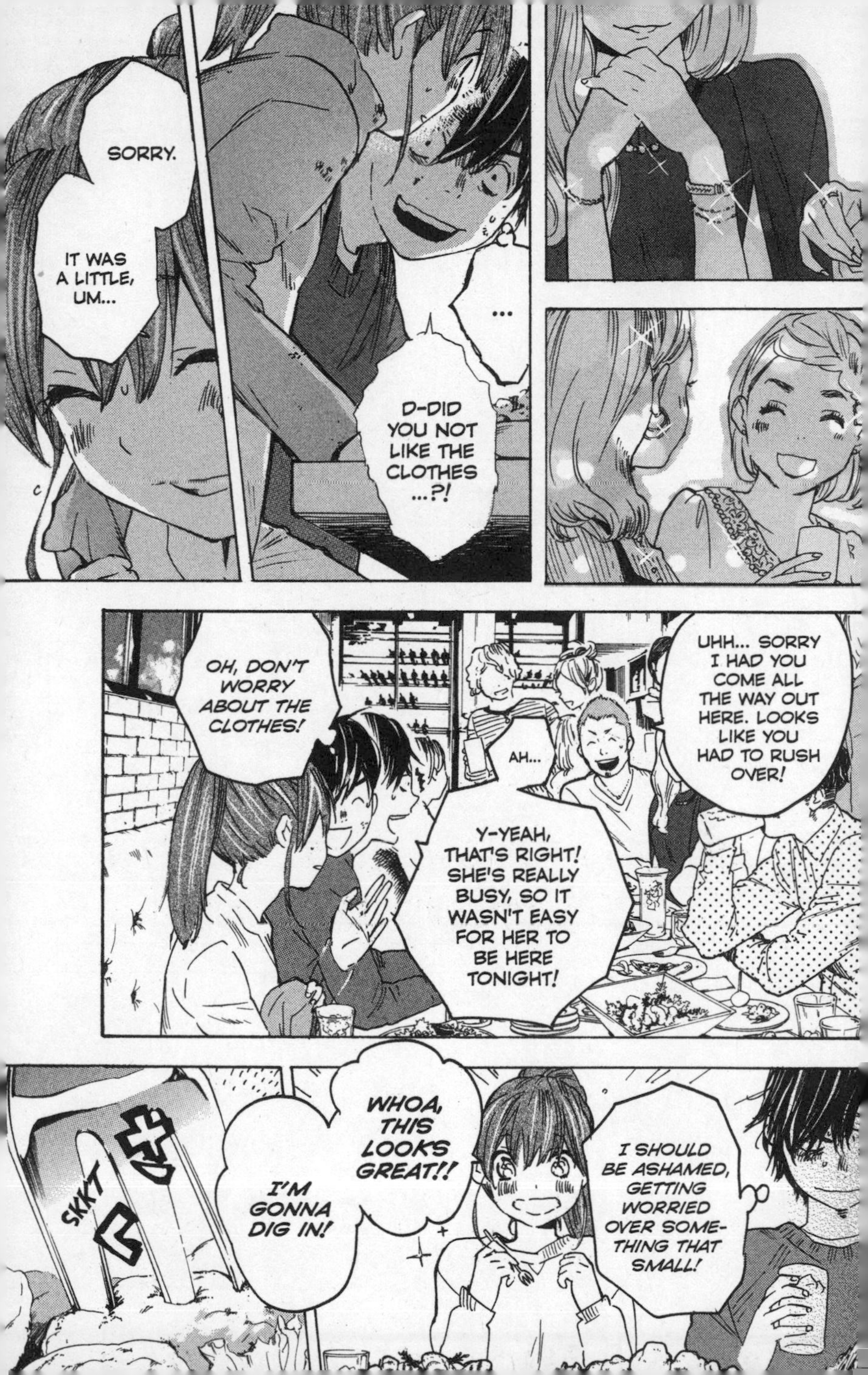
...
D-DID YOU NOT LIKE THE CLOTHES ...?!
SORRY.
IT WAS A LITTLE, UM...
UHH... SORRY I HAD YOU COME ALL THE WAY OUT HERE. LOOKS LIKE YOU HAD TO RUSH OVER!
AH...
OH, DON'T WORRY ABOUT THE CLOTHES!
Y-YEAH, THAT'S RIGHT! SHE'S REALLY BUSY, SO IT WASN'T EASY FOR HER TO BE HERE TONIGHT!
I SHOULD BE ASHAMED, GETTING WORRIED OVER SOME-THING THAT SMALL!
WHOA, THIS LOOKS GREAT!!
I'M GONNA DIG IN!
SKKT

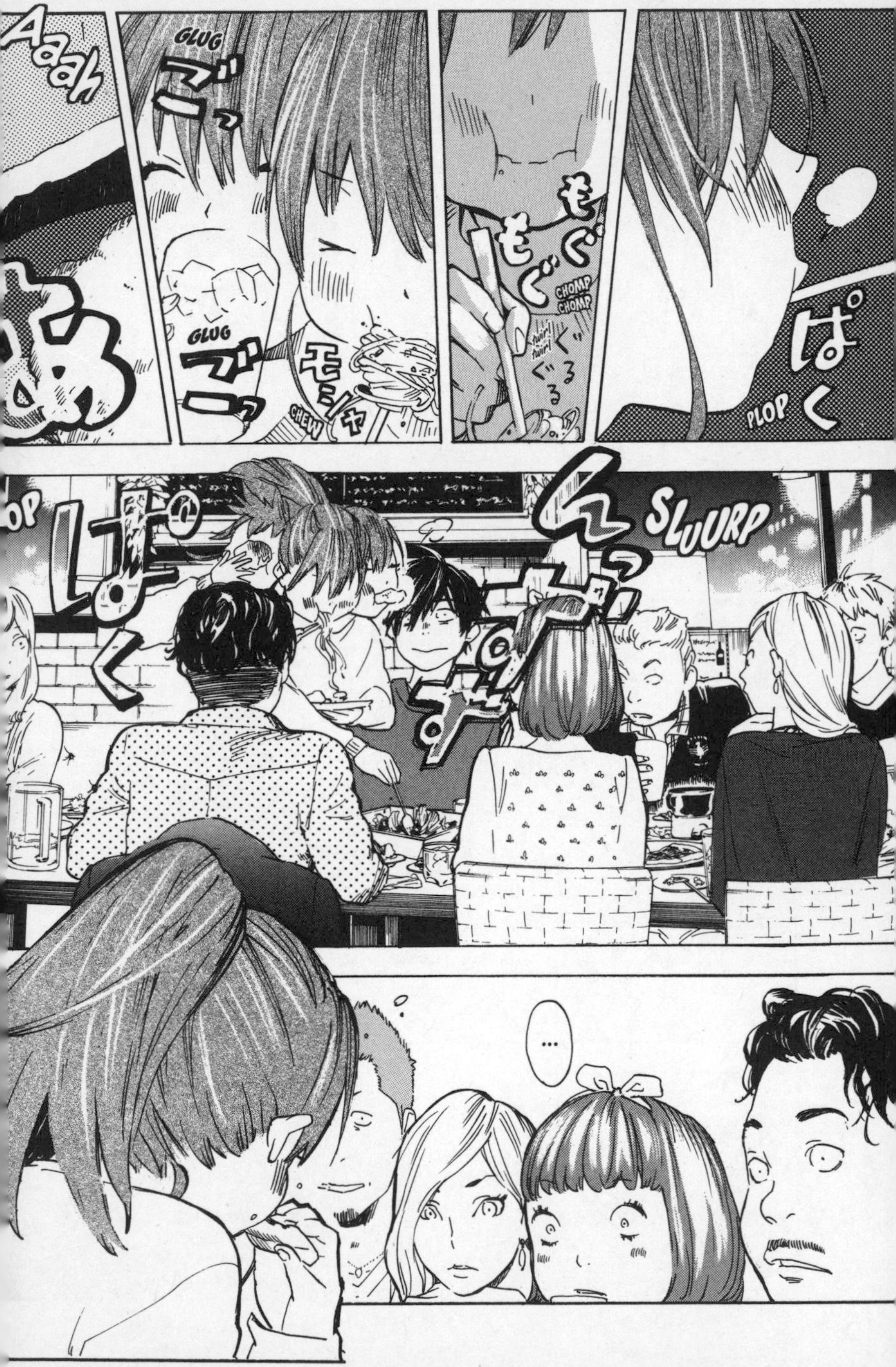
ぱく
PLOP
もぐもぐ
CHOMP CHOMP
ぐるぐる
twirl twirl
GLUG
GLUG
CHEW
Aaah
SLUURP
ぱく
POP
...

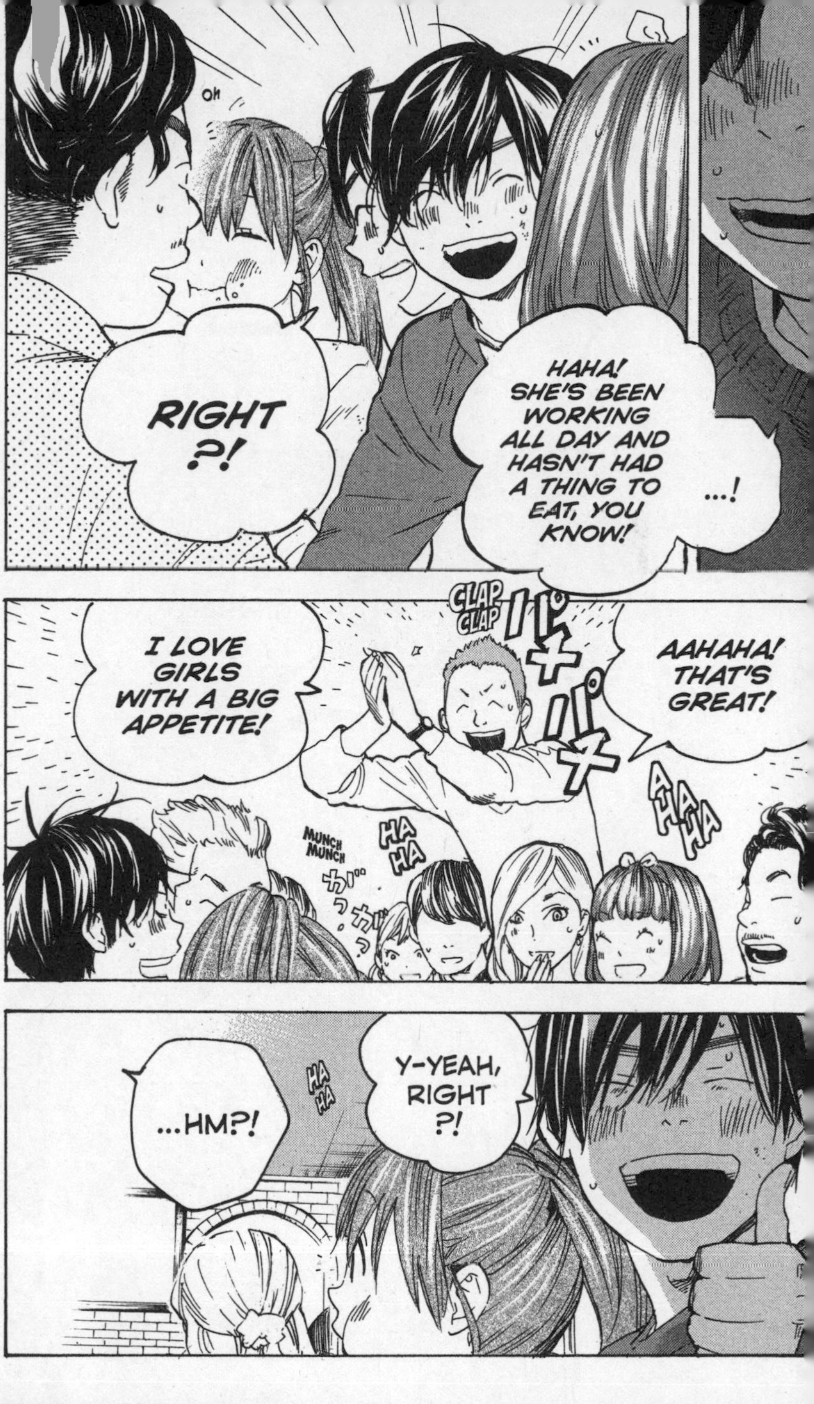
...!
HAHA! SHE'S BEEN WORKING ALL DAY AND HASN'T HAD A THING TO EAT, YOU KNOW!
RIGHT?!
Oh
AAHAHA! THAT'S GREAT!
AHAHA
CLAP CLAP
パチ パチ
I LOVE GIRLS WITH A BIG APPETITE!
HA HA
MUNCH MUNCH
ガッ ガッ
Y-YEAH, RIGHT?!
HA HA
...HM?!

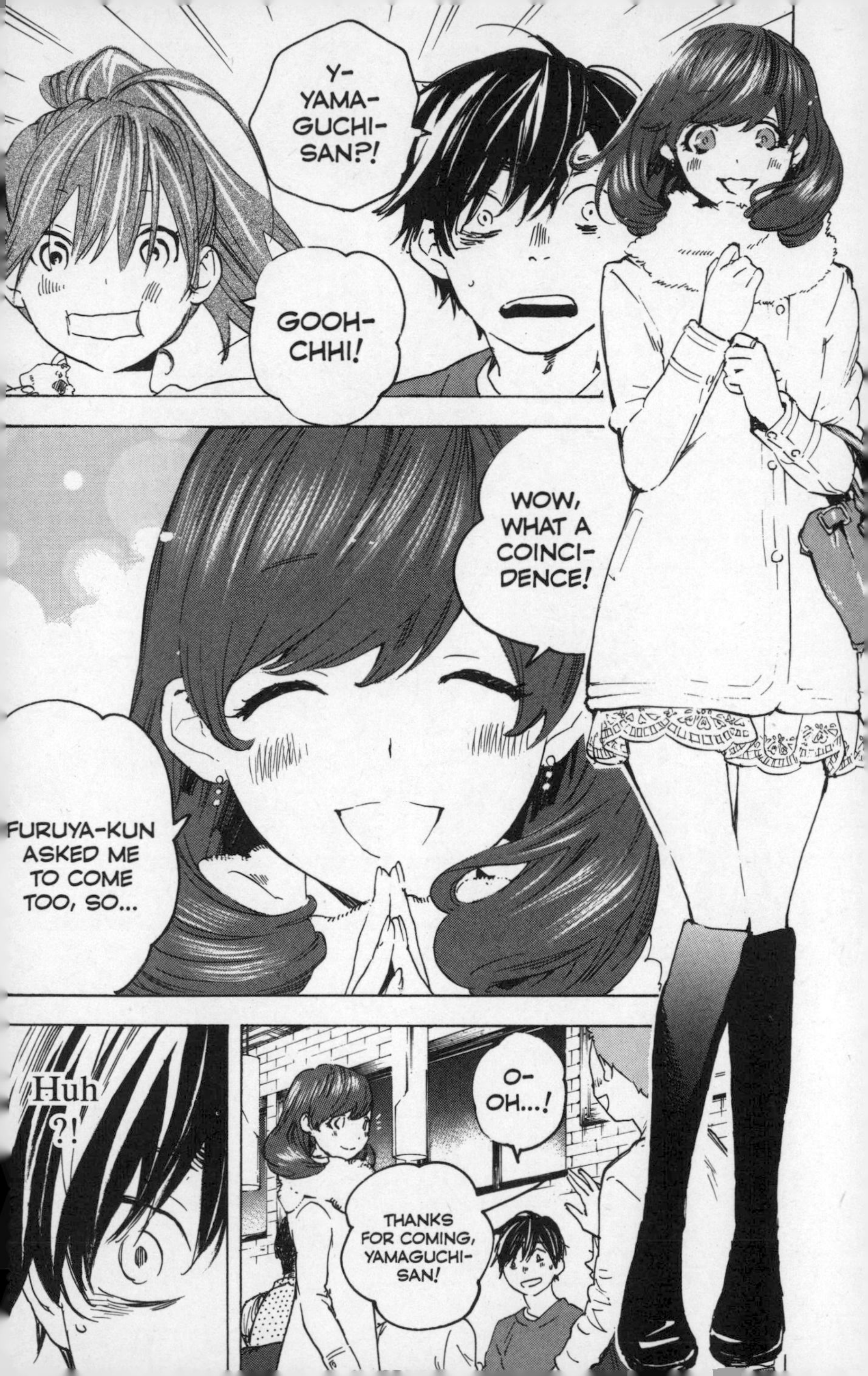
Y-YAMAGUCHI-SAN?!
GOOH-CHHI!
WOW, WHAT A COINCIDENCE!
FURUYA-KUN ASKED ME TO COME TOO, SO...
O-OH...!
THANKS FOR COMING, YAMAGUCHI-SAN!
Huh?!

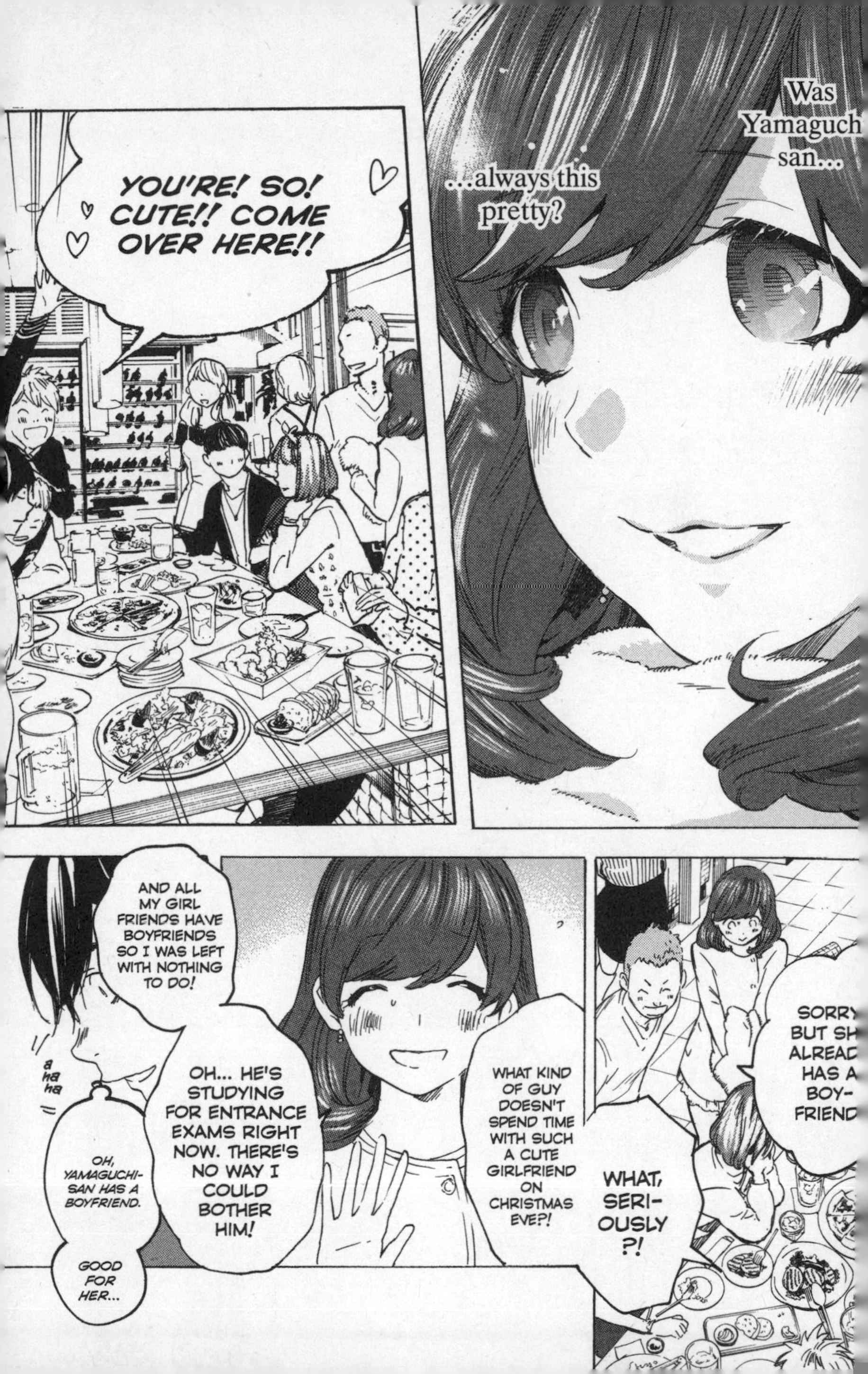
Was Yamaguch san...
...always this pretty?
YOU'RE! SO! CUTE!! COME OVER HERE!!
SORRY BUT SH ALREAD HAS A BOY-FRIEND
WHAT, SERI-OUSLY ?!
WHAT KIND OF GUY DOESN'T SPEND TIME WITH SUCH A CUTE GIRLFRIEND ON CHRISTMAS EVE?!
OH... HE'S STUDYING FOR ENTRANCE EXAMS RIGHT NOW. THERE'S NO WAY I COULD BOTHER HIM!
AND ALL MY GIRL FRIENDS HAVE BOYFRIENDS SO I WAS LEFT WITH NOTHING TO DO!
a ha ha
OH, YAMAGUCHI-SAN HAS A BOYFRIEND.
GOOD FOR HER...

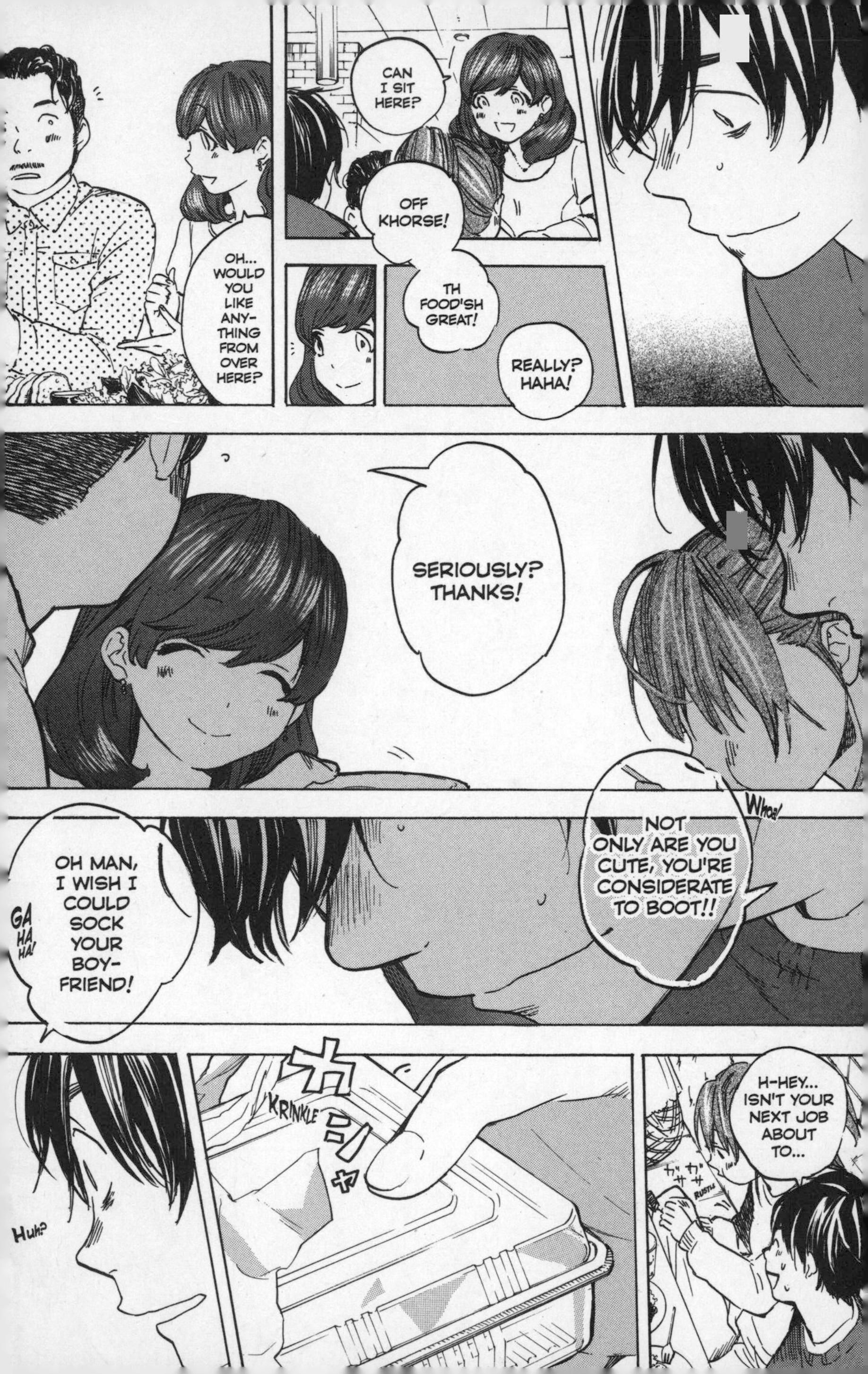
CAN I SIT HERE?
OFF KHORSE!
TH FOOD'SH GREAT!
REALLY? HAHA!
OH... WOULD YOU LIKE ANYTHING FROM OVER HERE?
SERIOUSLY? THANKS!
Whoa!
NOT ONLY ARE YOU CUTE, YOU'RE CONSIDERATE TO BOOT!!
OH MAN, I WISH I COULD SOCK YOUR BOY-FRIEND!
GA HA HA!
H-HEY... ISN'T YOUR NEXT JOB ABOUT TO...
RUSTLE
KRINKLE
Huh?

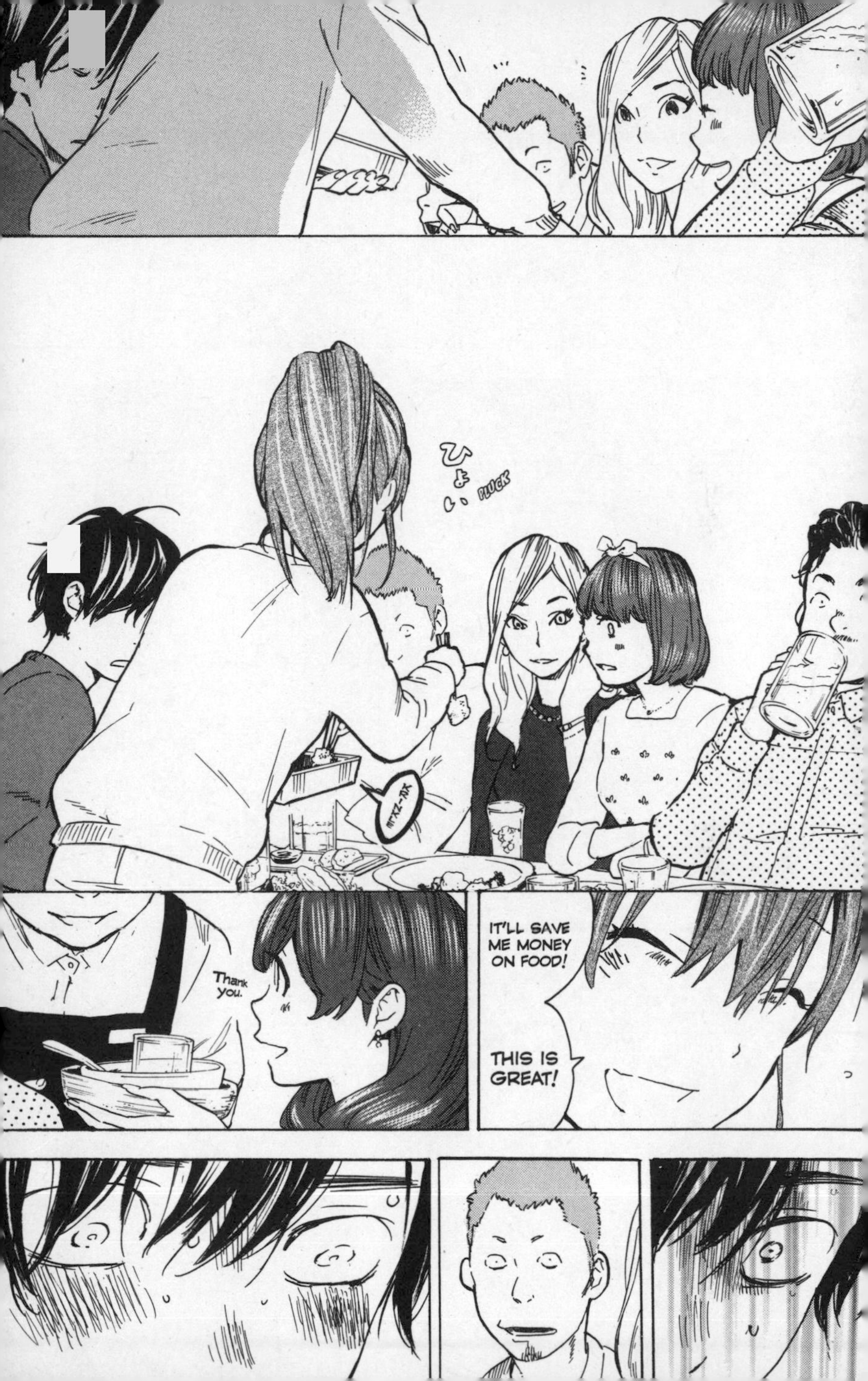
ひょい
PLUCK
IT'LL SAVE ME MONEY ON FOOD!
THIS IS GREAT!
Thank you.

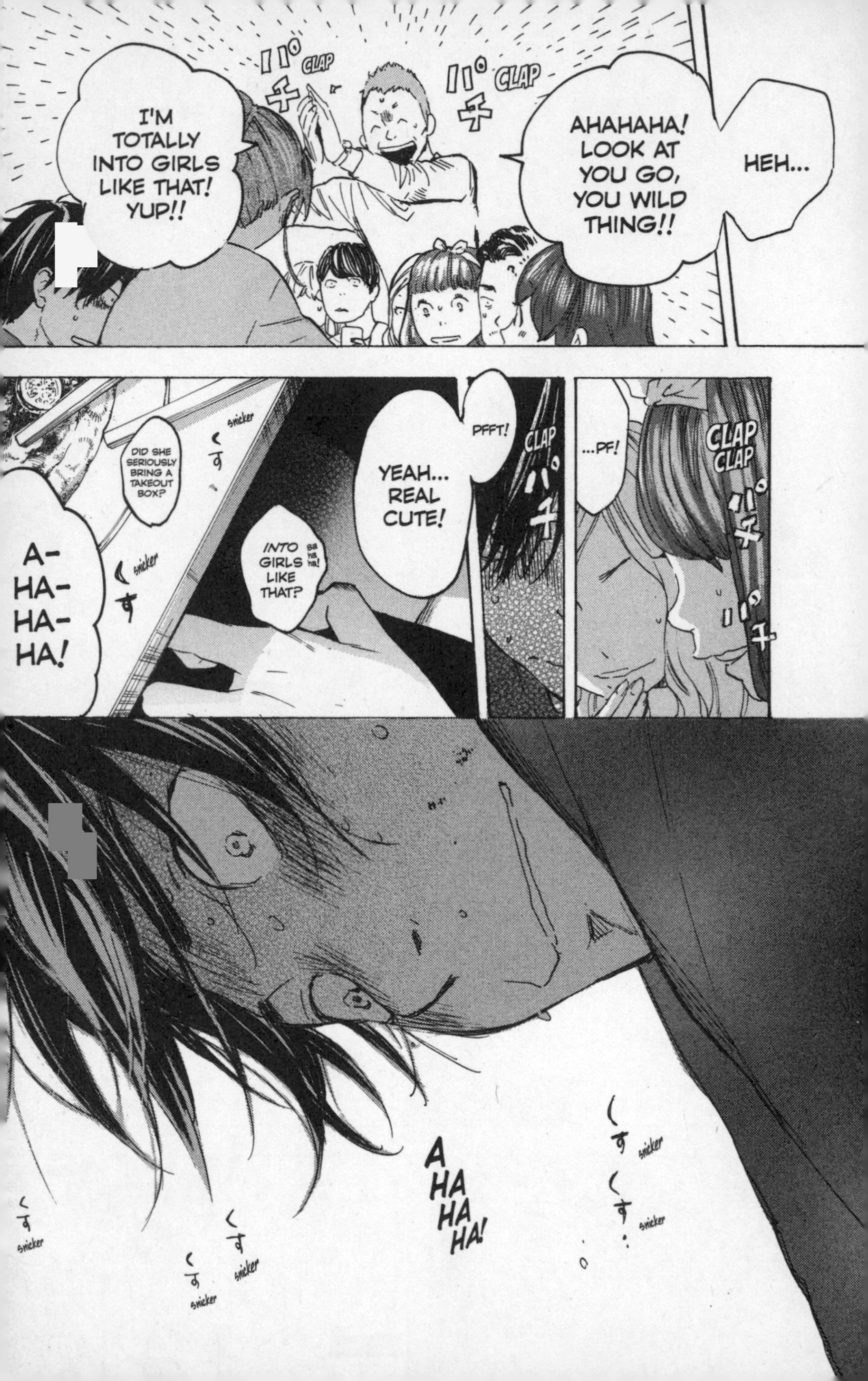
HEH...
AHAHAHA! LOOK AT YOU GO, YOU WILD THING!!
CLAP
CLAP
I'M TOTALLY INTO GIRLS LIKE THAT! YUP!!
CLAP CLAP
...PF!
CLAP
PFFT!
YEAH... REAL CUTE!
INTO GIRLS LIKE THAT?
ha ha ha!
snicker
DID SHE SERIOUSLY BRING A TAKEOUT BOX?
snicker
A-HA-HA-HA!
snicker
snicker
AHAHAHA!
snicker
snicker
snicker

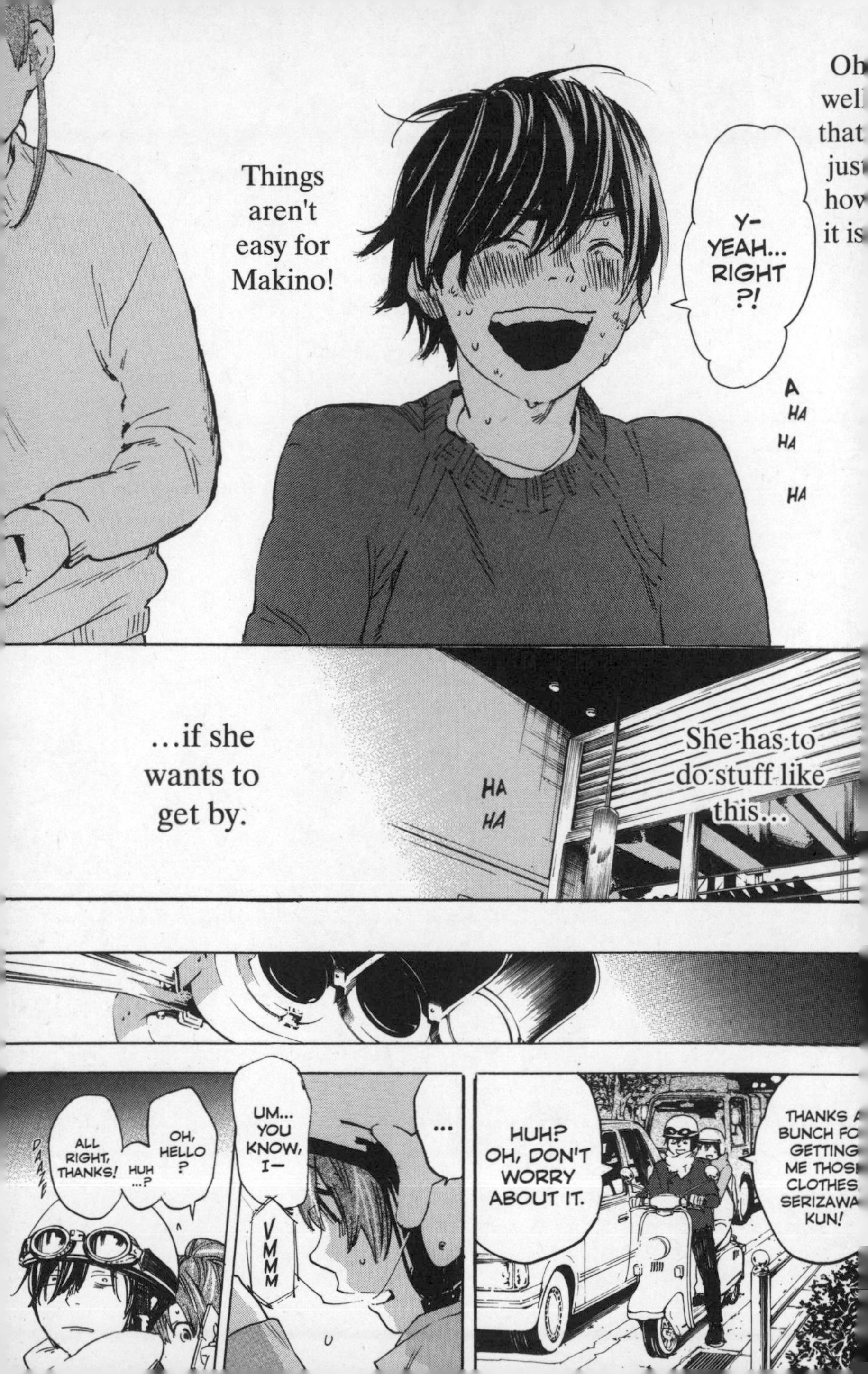
Oh wel that jus hov it is
Y-YEAH... RIGHT ?!
A HA HA HA
Things aren't easy for Makino!
She has to do stuff like this...
HA HA
...if she wants to get by.
THANKS A BUNCH FO GETTING ME THOS CLOTHES SERIZAWA KUN!
HUH? OH, DON'T WORRY ABOUT IT.
...
UM... YOU KNOW, I—
VMMM
OH, HELLO ?
HUH ...?
ALL RIGHT, THANKS!

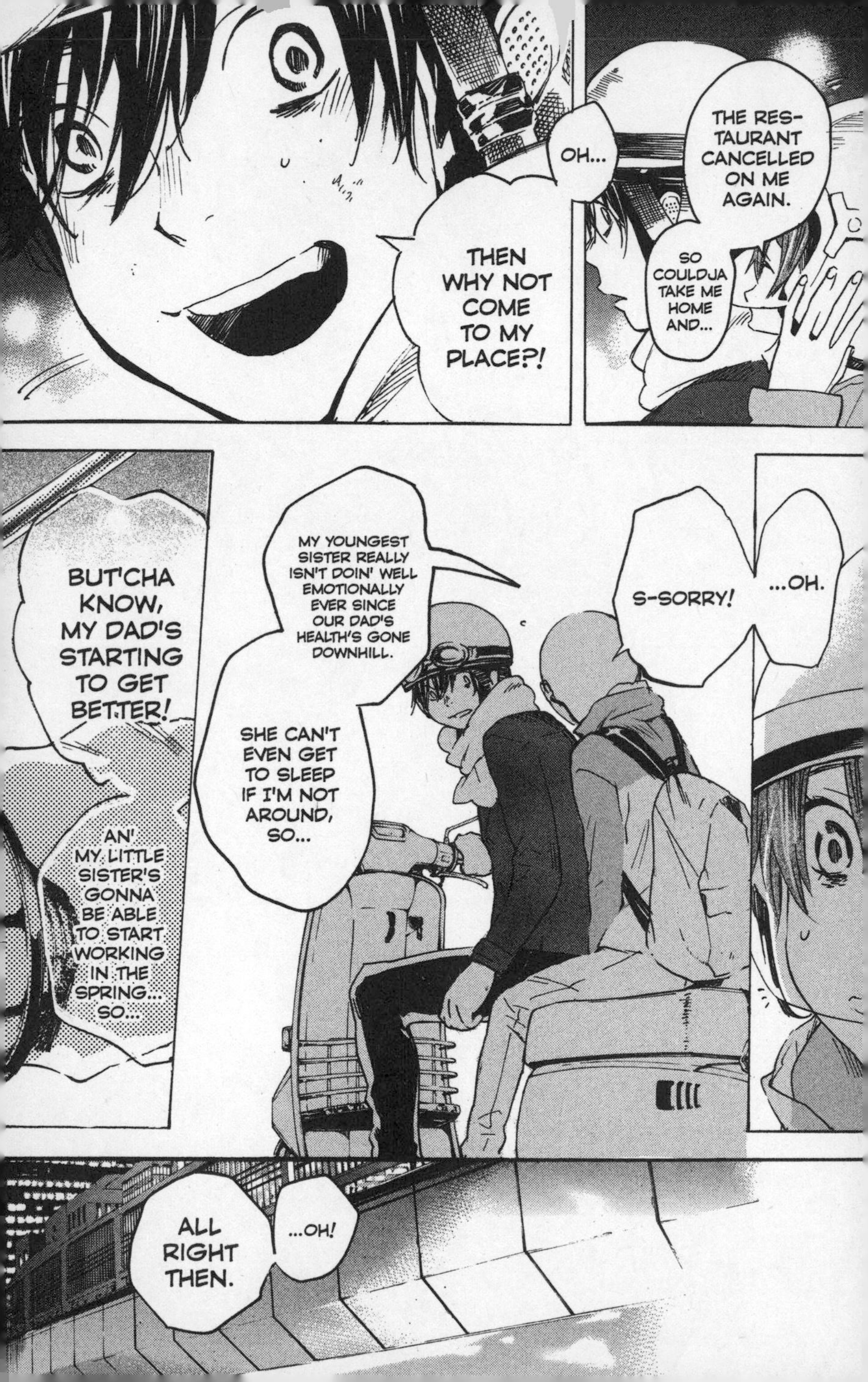
THE RES-TAURANT CANCELLED ON ME AGAIN.
SO COULDJA TAKE ME HOME AND...
OH...
THEN WHY NOT COME TO MY PLACE?!
...OH.
S-SORRY!
MY YOUNGEST SISTER REALLY ISN'T DOIN' WELL EMOTIONALLY EVER SINCE OUR DAD'S HEALTH'S GONE DOWNHILL.
SHE CAN'T EVEN GET TO SLEEP IF I'M NOT AROUND, SO...
BUT'CHA KNOW, MY DAD'S STARTING TO GET BETTER!
AN' MY LITTLE SISTER'S GONNA BE ABLE TO START WORKING IN THE SPRING... SO...
...OH!
ALL RIGHT THEN.

That's just how it is.

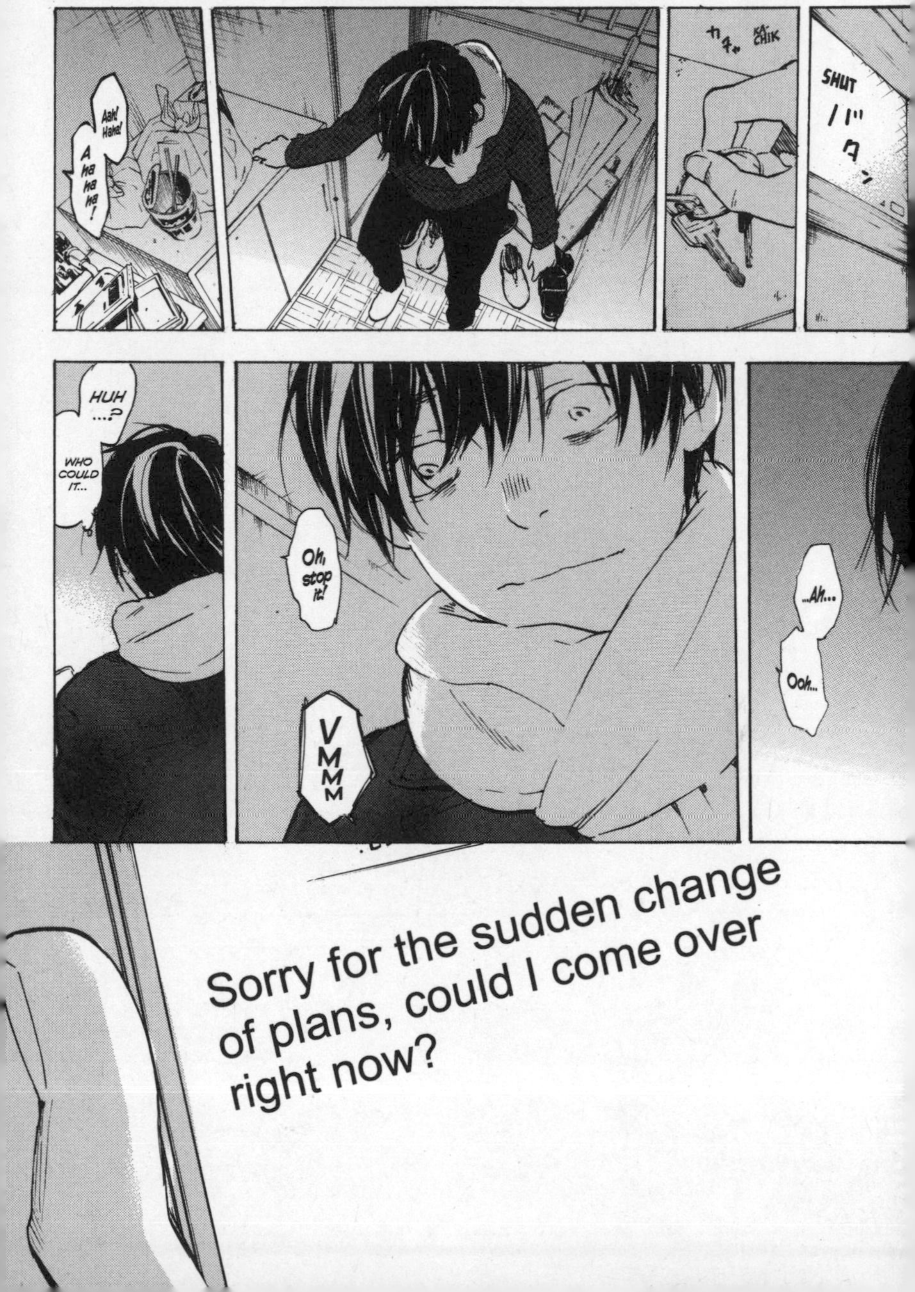

SHUT
バタン
カチャ
KA-CHIK
Aah! Haha!
A ha ha ha!
...Ah...
Ooh...
Oh, stop it!
VMMM
HUH ...?
WHO COULD IT...
Sorry for the sudden change of plans, could I come over right now?

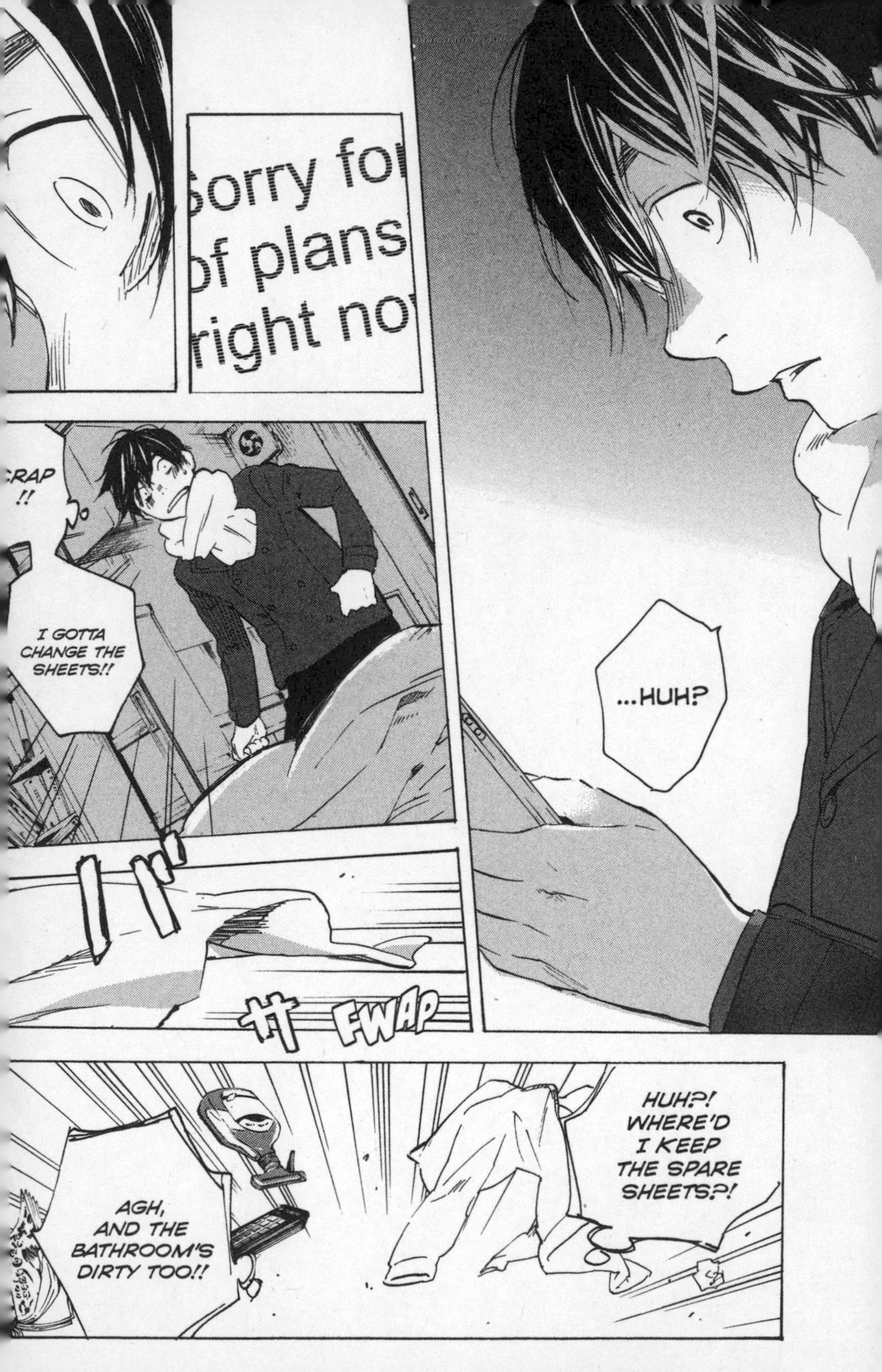
...HUH?
Sorry fo
of plans
right no
CRAP !!
I GOTTA CHANGE THE SHEETS!!
FWAP
HUH?! WHERE'D I KEEP THE SPARE SHEETS?!
AGH, AND THE BATHROOM'S DIRTY TOO!!

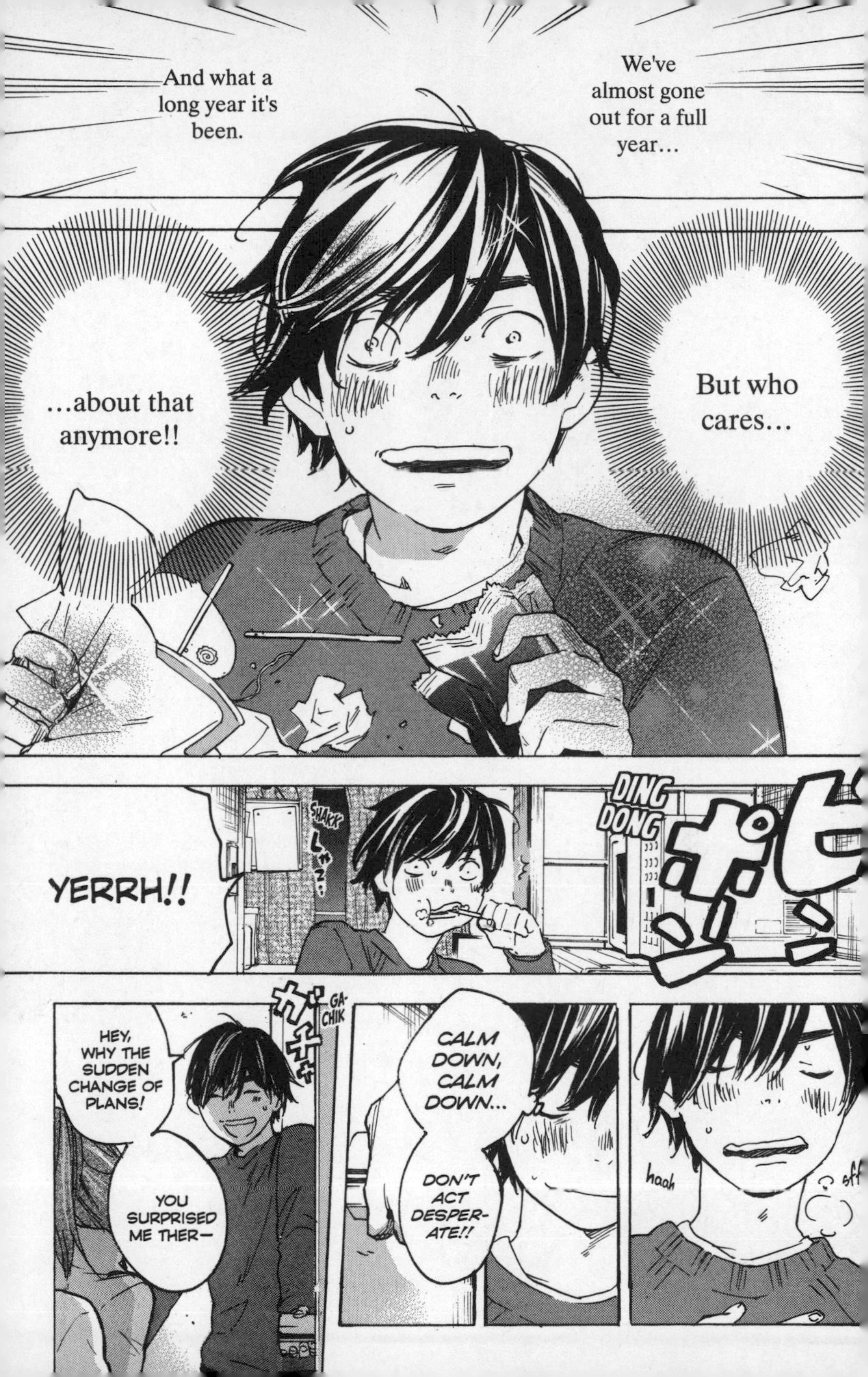
We've almost gone out for a full year…
And what a long year it's been.
But who cares…
…about that anymore!!
DING DONG
SHAKK
YERRH!!
haah
sff
CALM DOWN, CALM DOWN…
DON'T ACT DESPERATE!!
GA-CHIK
HEY, WHY THE SUDDEN CHANGE OF PLANS!
YOU SURPRISED ME THER—

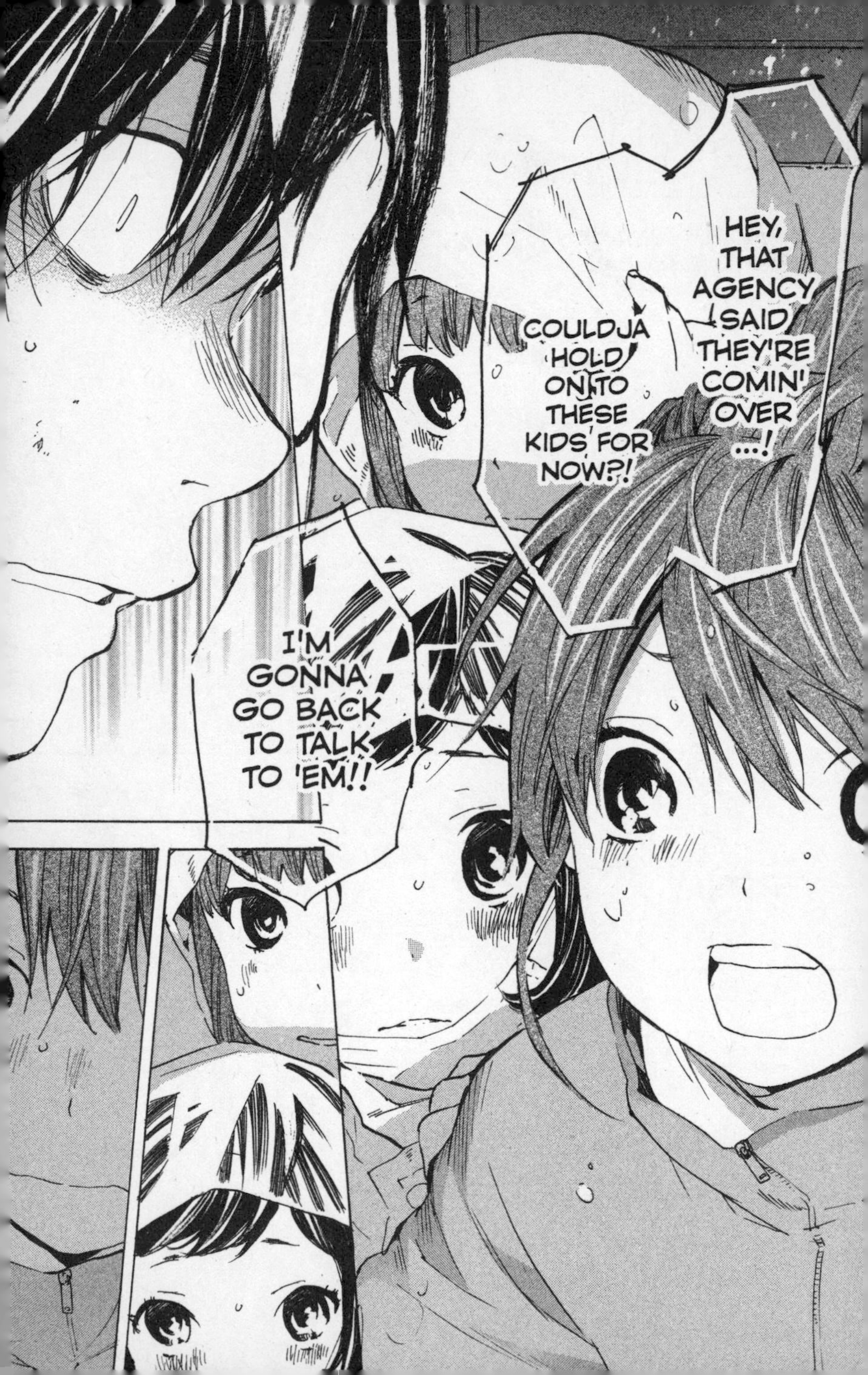
HEY, THAT AGENCY SAID THEY'RE COMIN' OVER ...!
COULDJA HOLD ON TO THESE KIDS FOR NOW?!
I'M GONNA GO BACK TO TALK TO 'EM!!

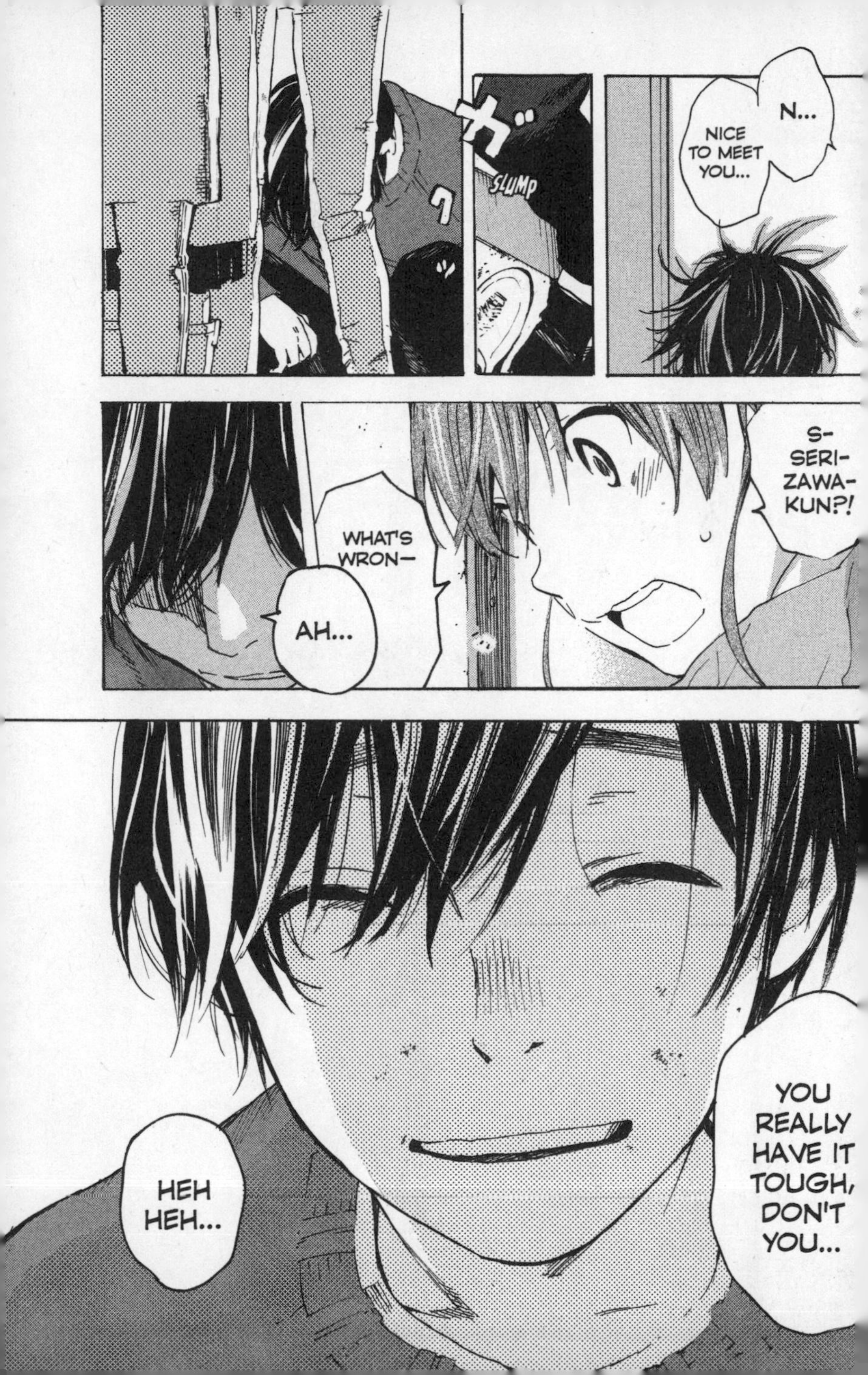
N...
NICE TO MEET YOU...
ガク
SLUMP
S-SERI-ZAWA-KUN?!
WHAT'S WRON—
AH...
YOU REALLY HAVE IT TOUGH, DON'T YOU...
HEH HEH...

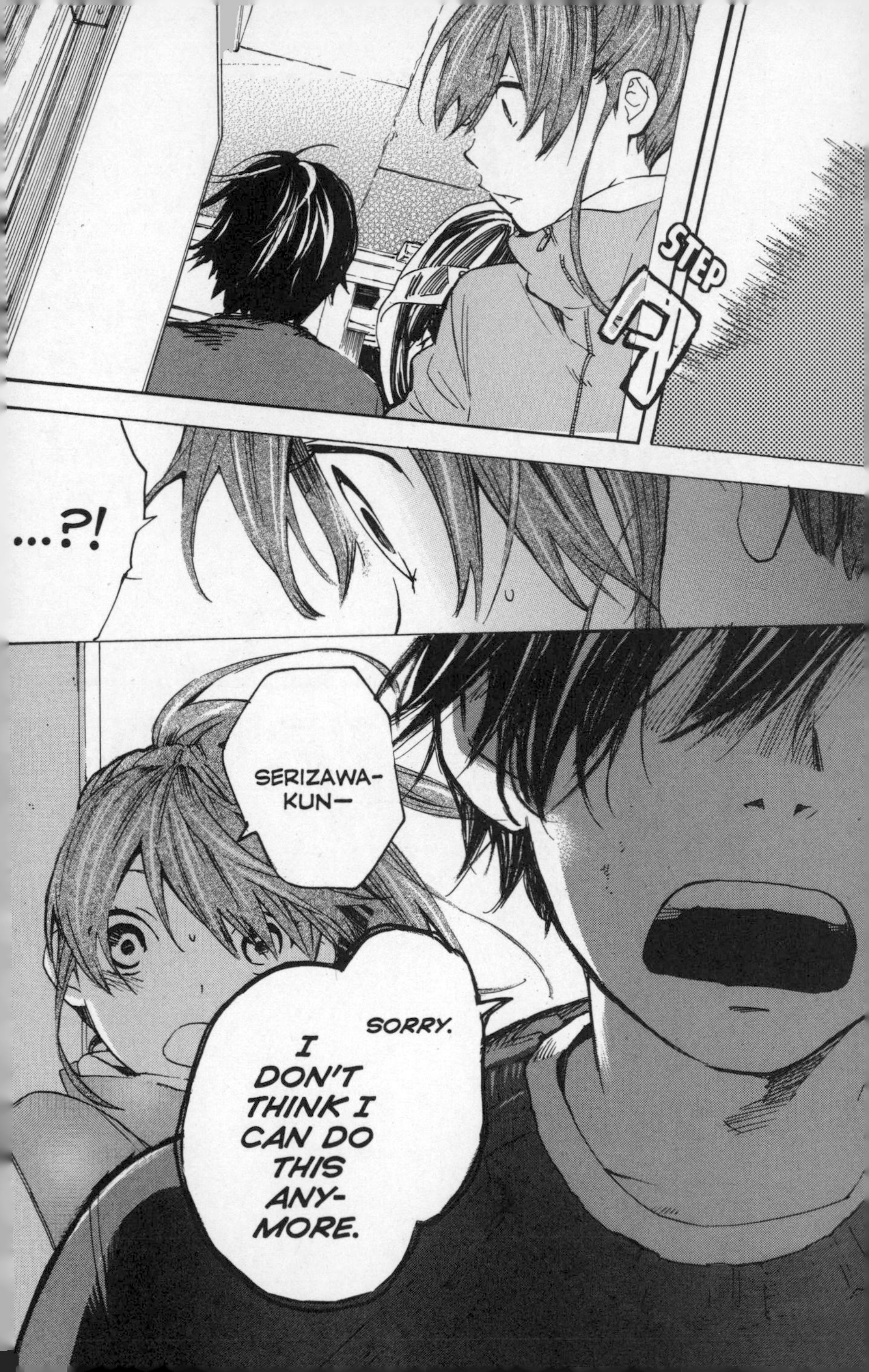
STEP
...?!
SERIZAWA-KUN—
SORRY.
I DON'T THINK I CAN DO THIS ANYMORE.

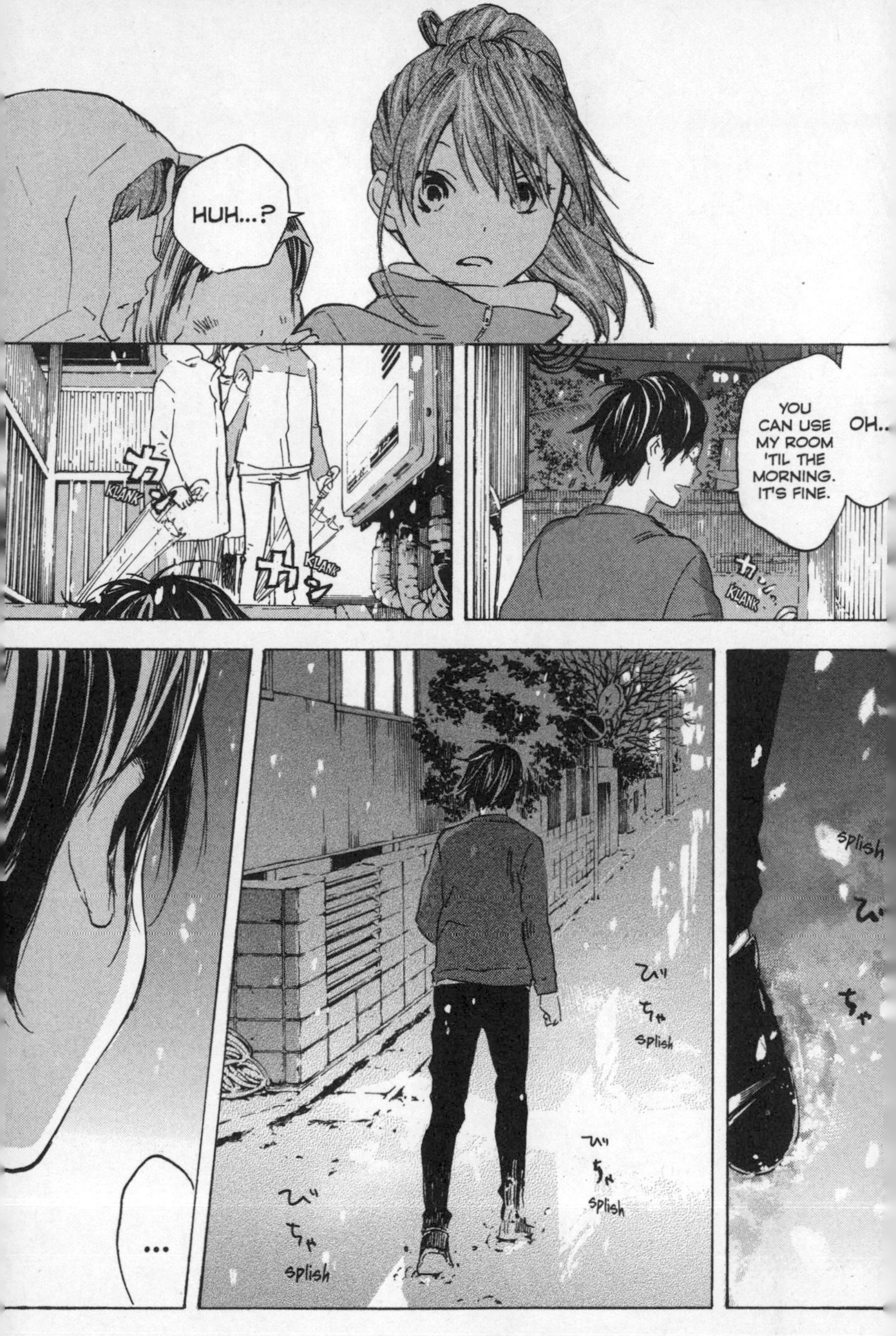
HUH...?
OH..
YOU CAN USE MY ROOM 'TIL THE MORNING. IT'S FINE.
KLANK
カ
KLANK
カ
KLANK
splish
びちゃ
splish
びちゃ
splish
びちゃ
splish
...

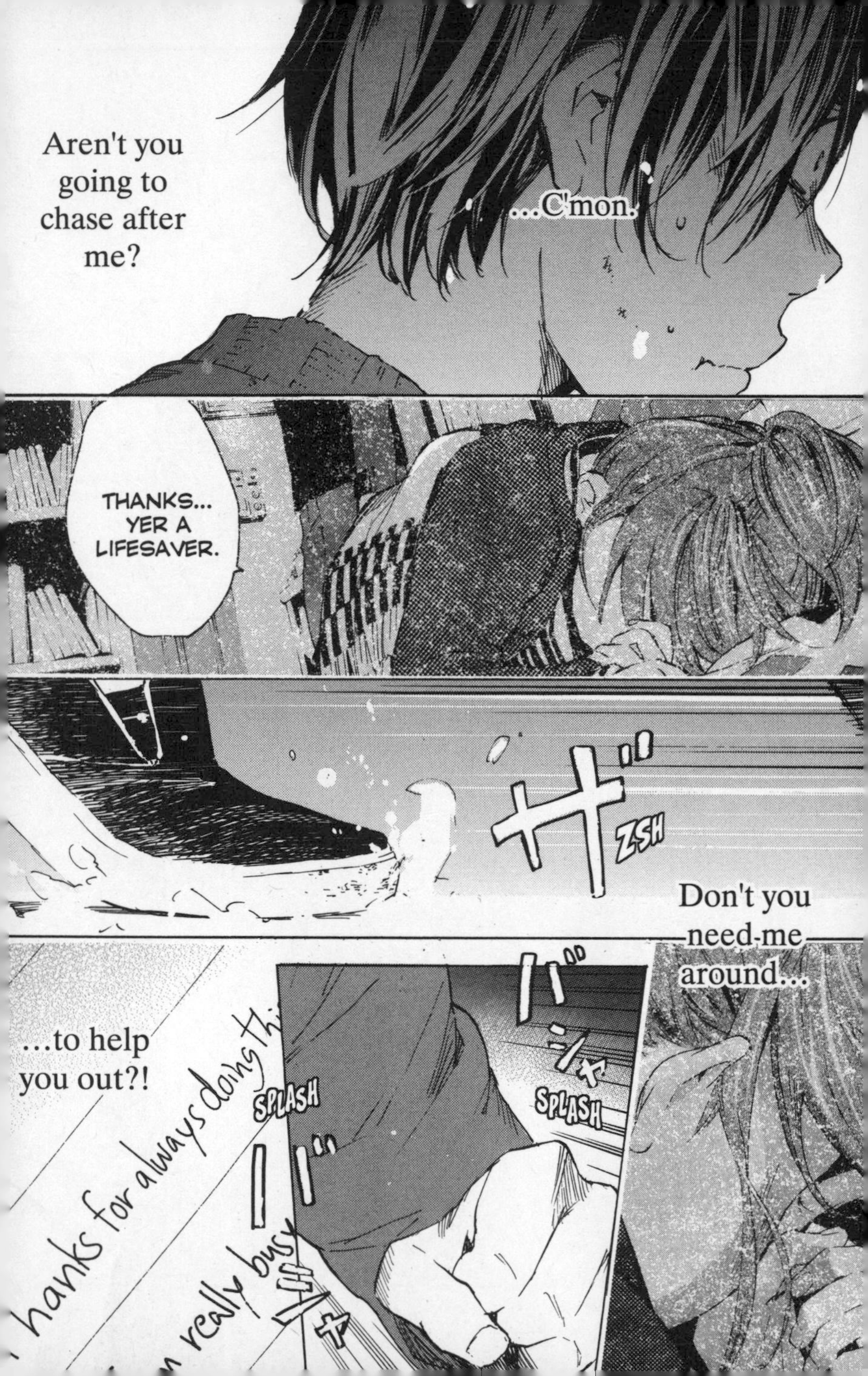
...C'mon.
Aren't you going to chase after me?
THANKS... YER A LIFESAVER.
ZSH
Don't you need me around...
SPLASH
SPLASH
...to help you out?!

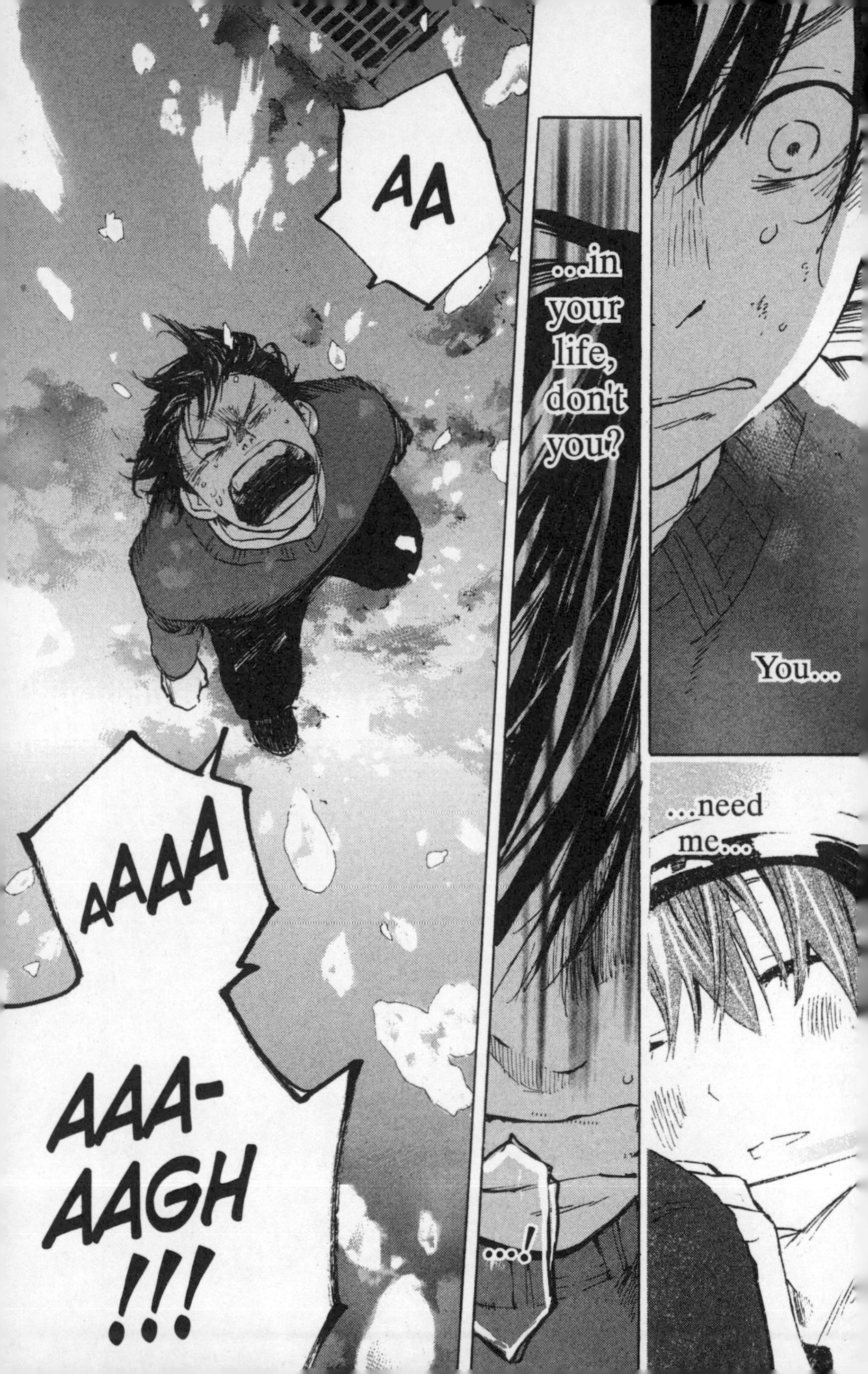
You...
...need me...
...in your life, don't you?
...!
AA
AAAA
AAA-AAGH!!!

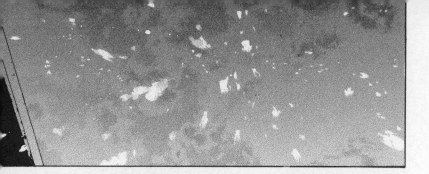

...

SIGH

Makino...

SPLASH

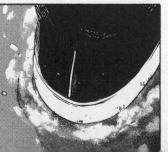

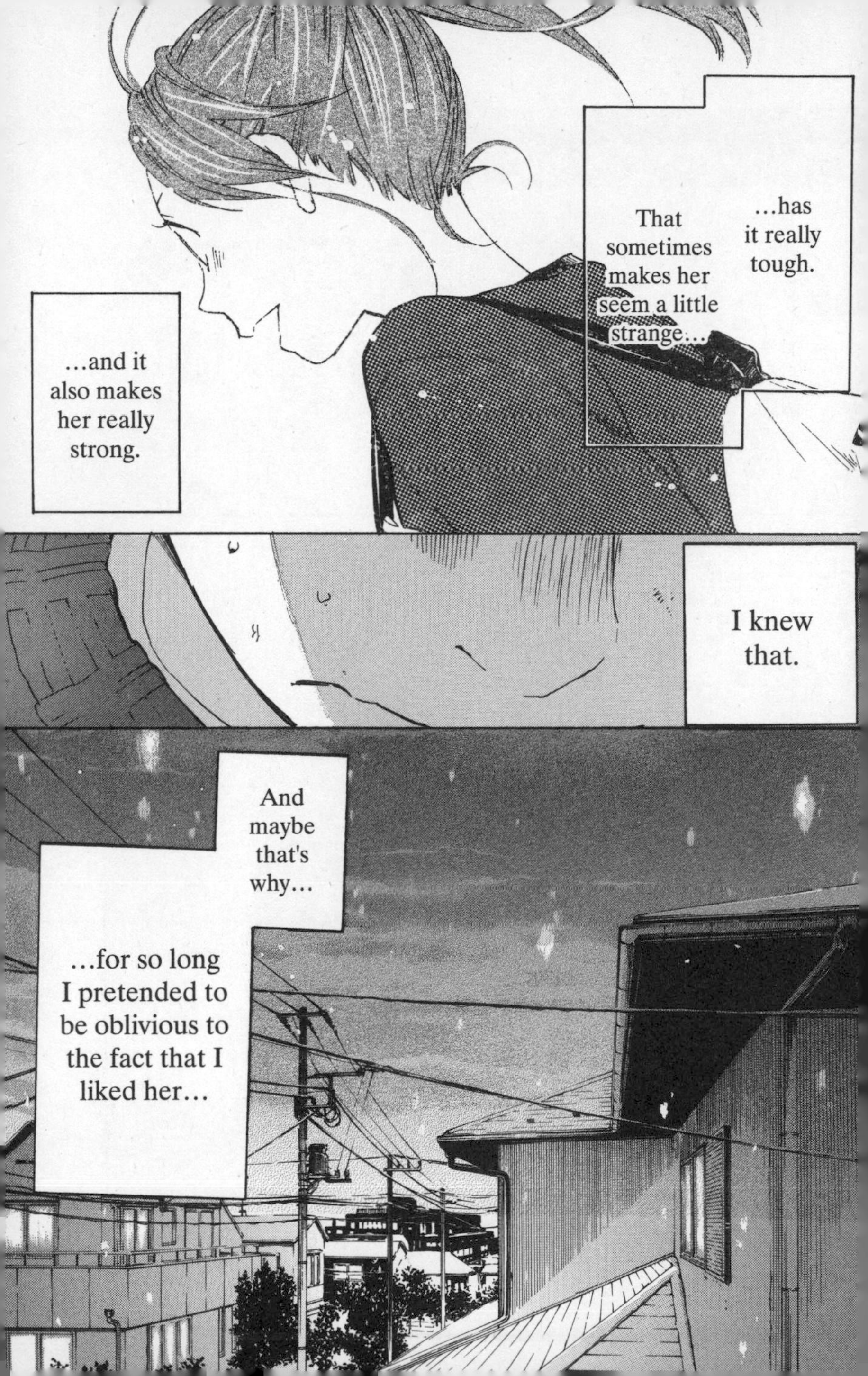
...has it really tough.
That sometimes makes her seem a little strange...
...and it also makes her really strong.
I knew that.
And maybe that's why...
...for so long I pretended to be oblivious to the fact that I liked her...

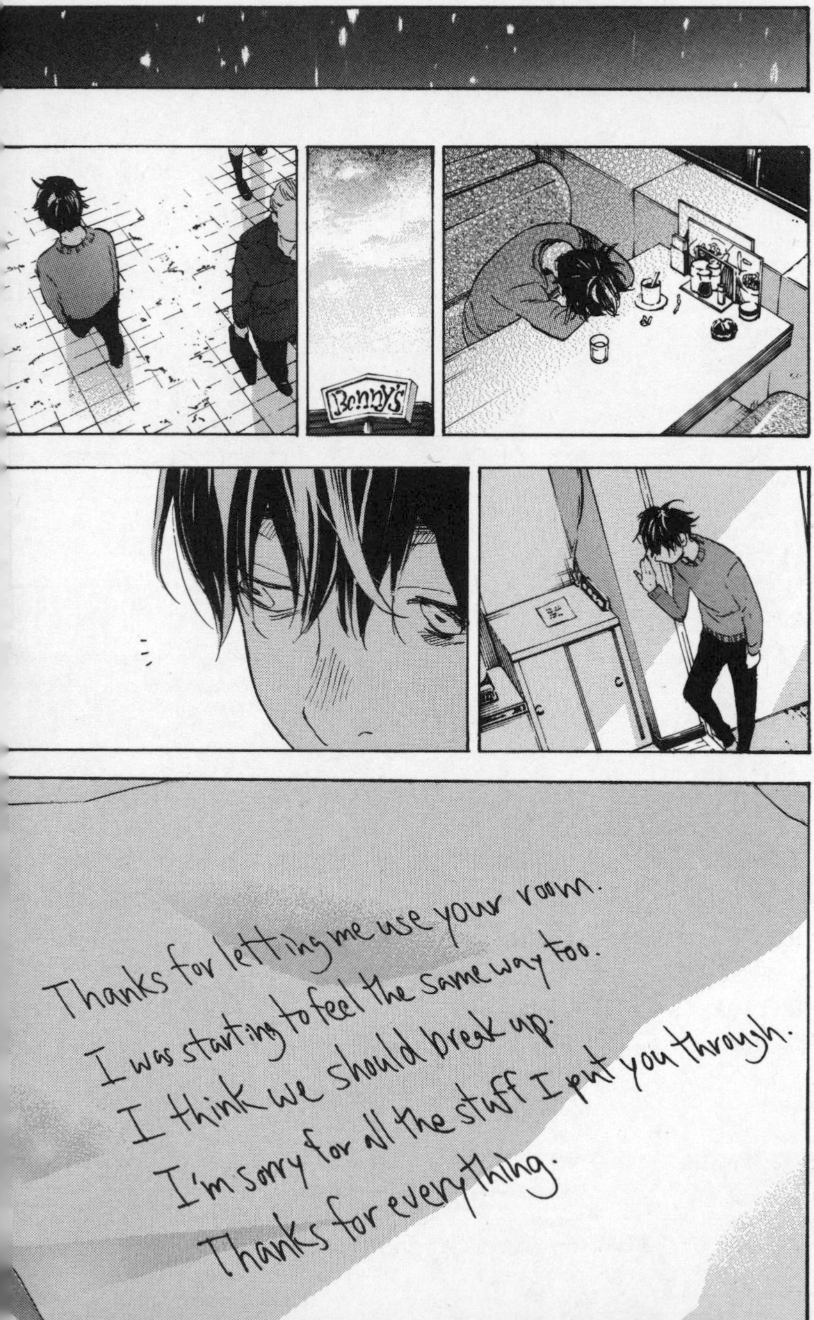
Benny's
Thanks for letting me use your room.
I was starting to feel the same way too.
I think we should break up.
I'm sorry for all the stuff I put you through.
Thanks for everything.

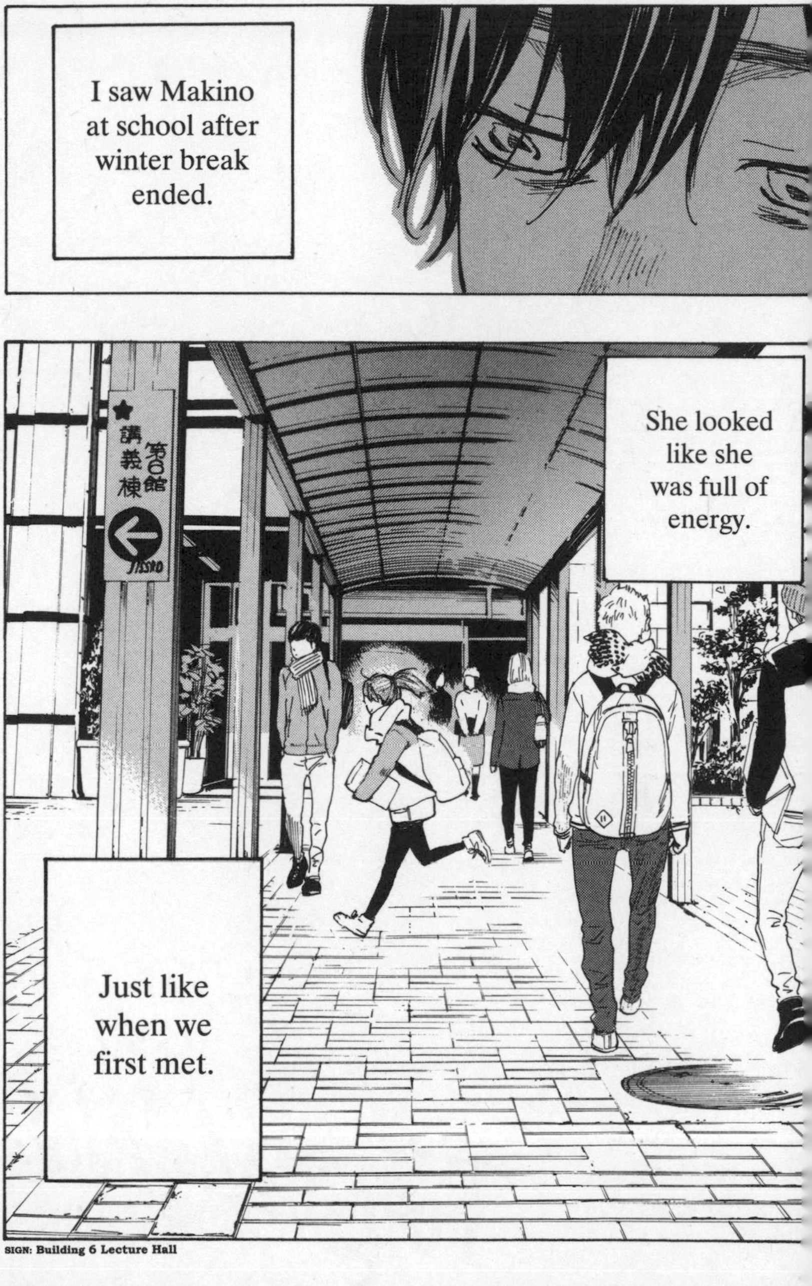
I saw Makino at school after winter break ended.
She looked like she was full of energy.
Just like when we first met.

SIGN: Building 6 Lecture Hall

Forget Me Not

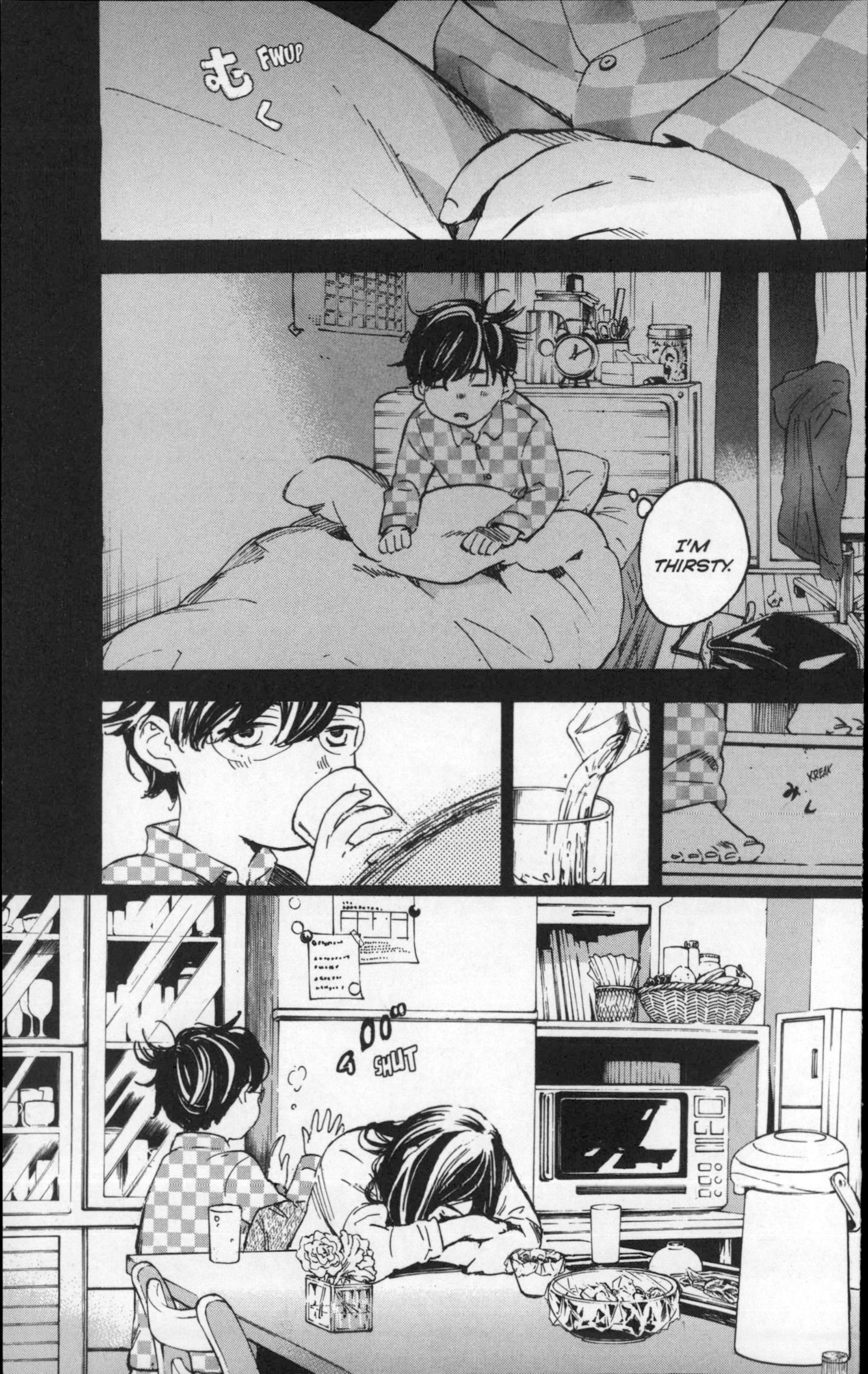
むく
FWUP
I'M THIRSTY.
みし
KREAK
SHUT

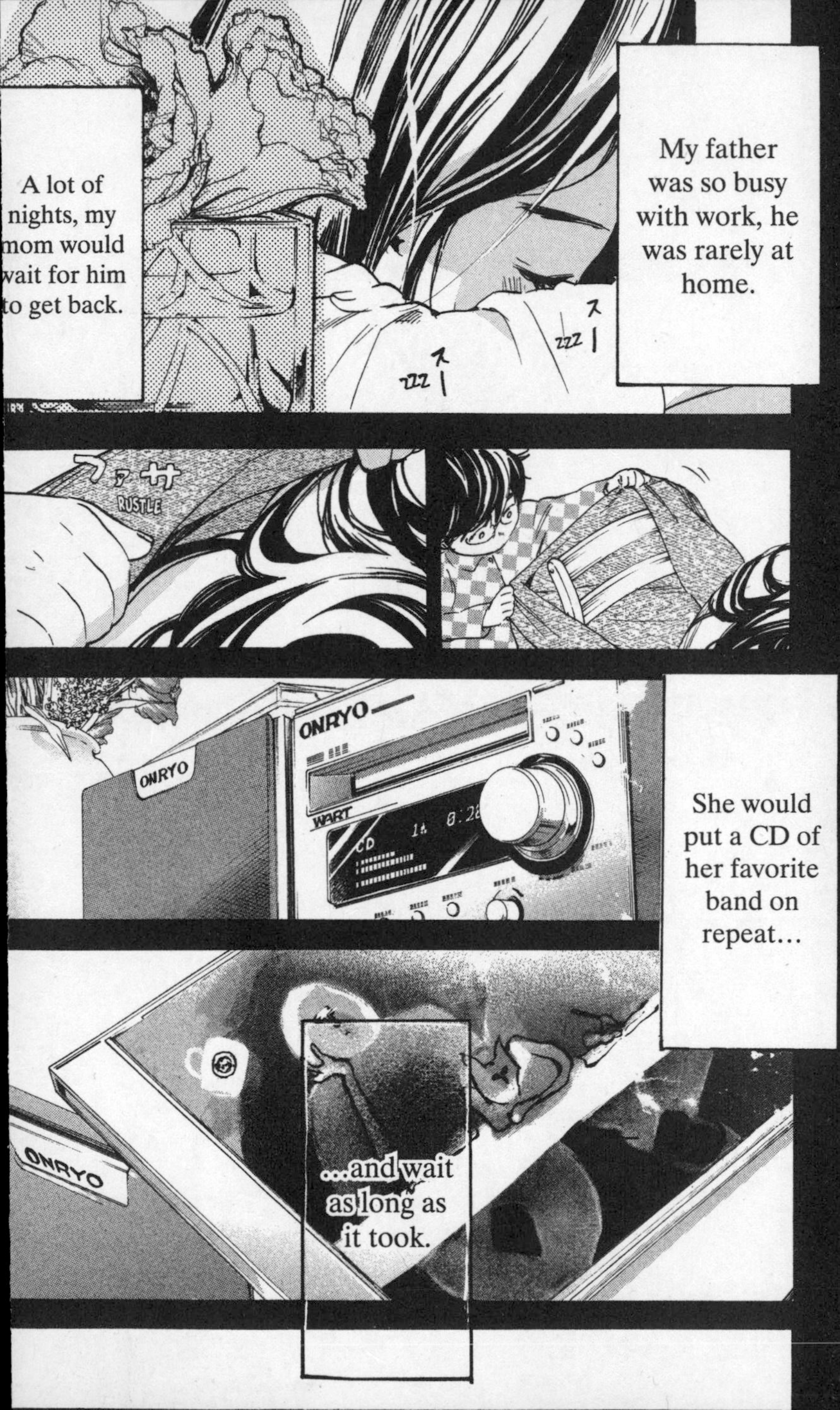
My father was so busy with work, he was rarely at home.
ZZZ
ZZZ
A lot of nights, my mom would wait for him to get back.
RUSTLE
ONRYO
ONRYO
She would put a CD of her favorite band on repeat...
ONRYO
...and wait as long as it took.

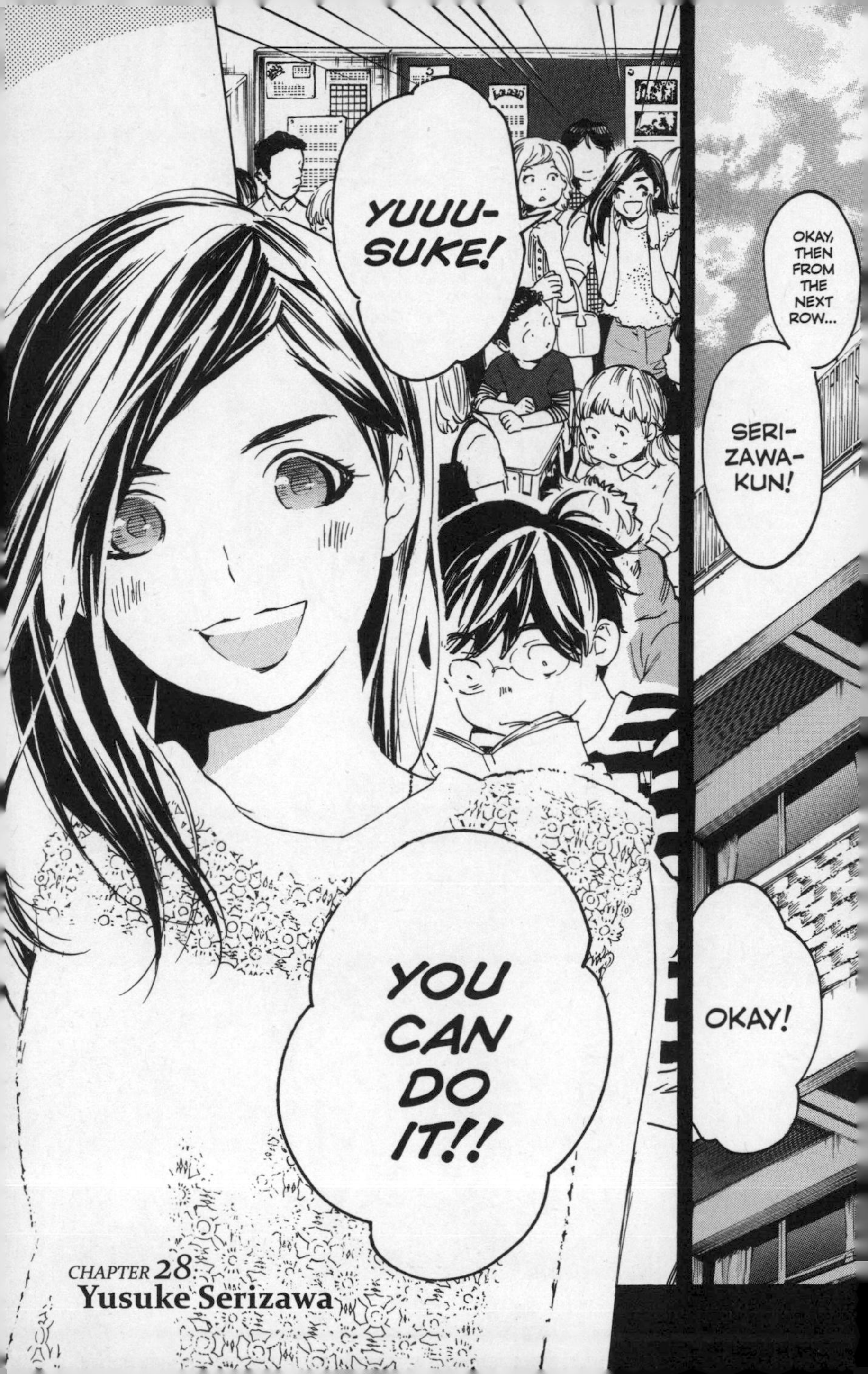
OKAY, THEN FROM THE NEXT ROW...
SERI-ZAWA-KUN!
OKAY!
YUUUU-SUKE!
YOU CAN DO IT!!

CHAPTER 28: Yusuke Serizawa

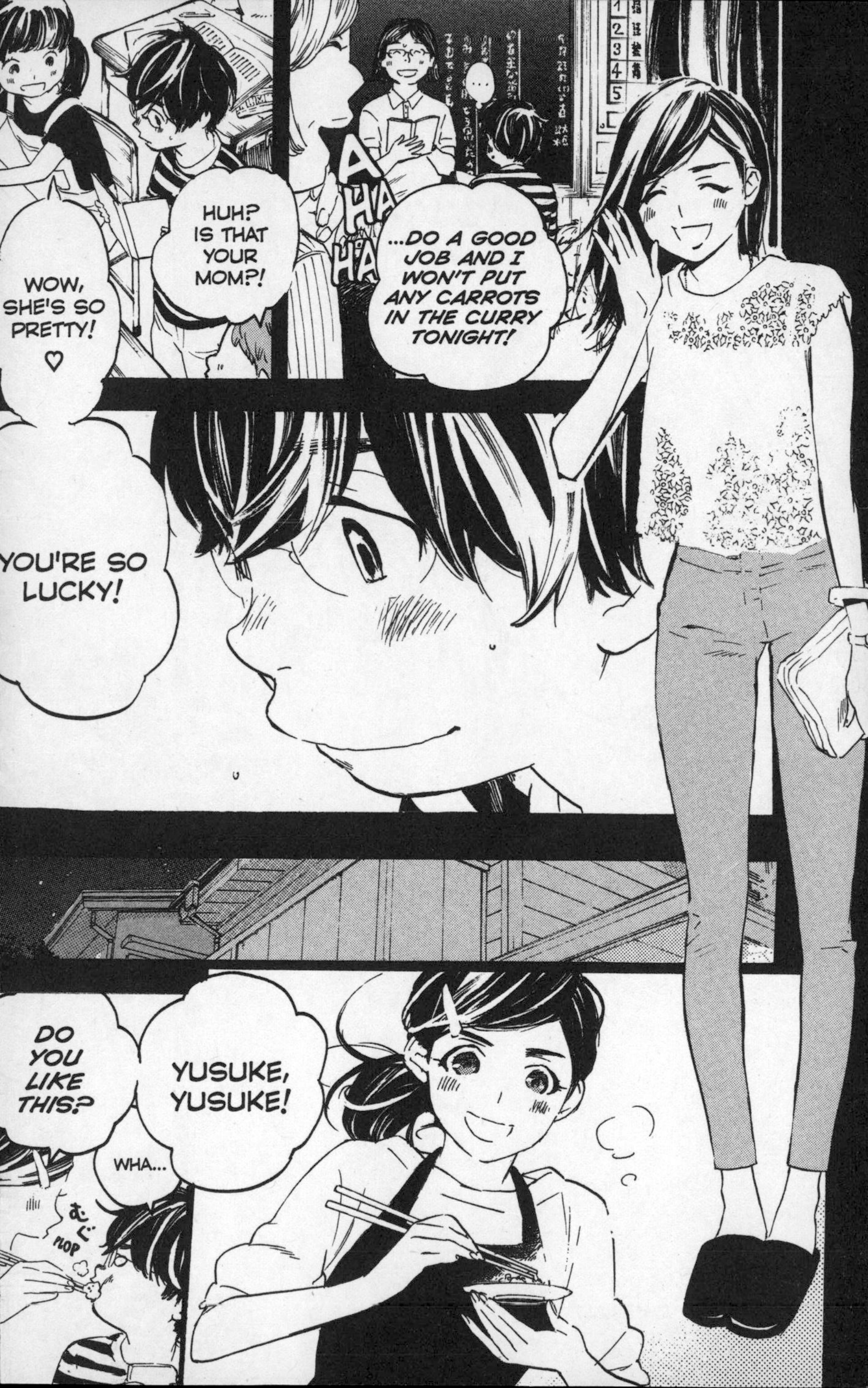
AHAHA
...DO A GOOD JOB AND I WON'T PUT ANY CARROTS IN THE CURRY TONIGHT!
HUH? IS THAT YOUR MOM?!
WOW, SHE'S SO PRETTY! ♡
YOU'RE SO LUCKY!
YUSUKE, YUSUKE!
DO YOU LIKE THIS?
WHA...
むぐ
PLOP

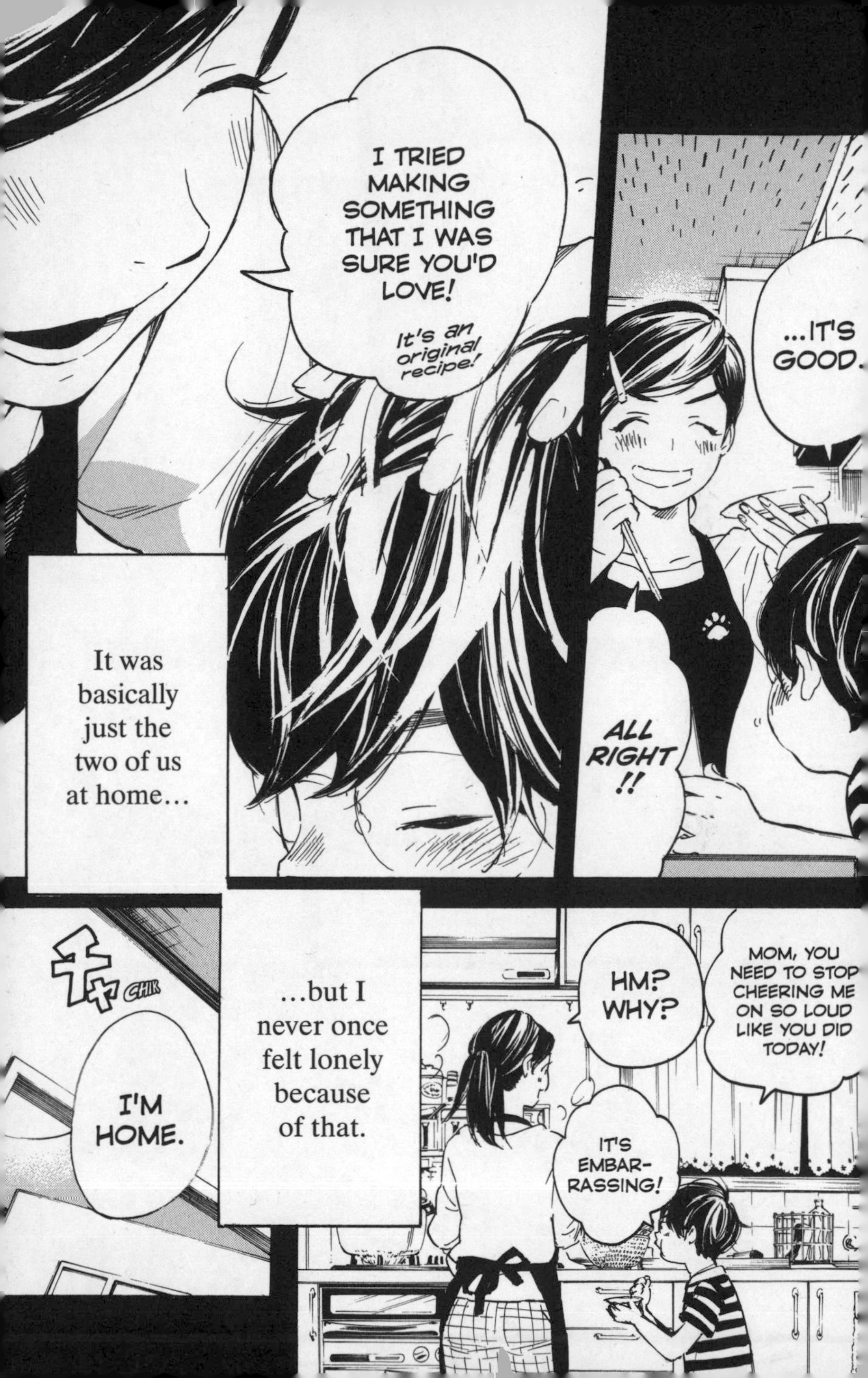
...IT'S GOOD.
ALL RIGHT!!
I TRIED MAKING SOMETHING THAT I WAS SURE YOU'D LOVE!
It's an original recipe!
It was basically just the two of us at home...
MOM, YOU NEED TO STOP CHEERING ME ON SO LOUD LIKE YOU DID TODAY!
HM? WHY?
IT'S EMBAR-RASSING!
...but I never once felt lonely because of that.
チャ CHIK
I'M HOME.

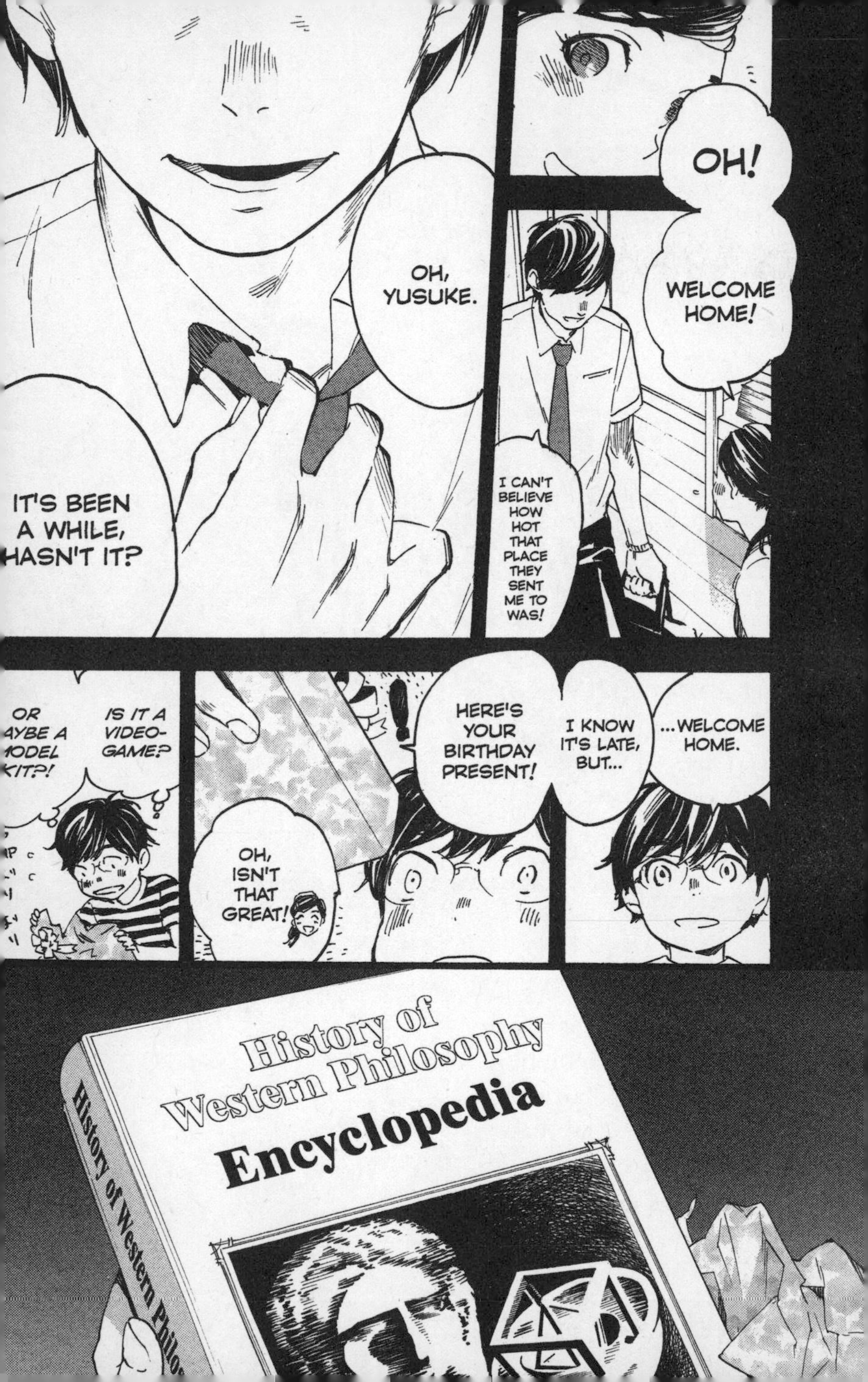
OH!
WELCOME HOME!
I CAN'T BELIEVE HOW HOT THAT PLACE THEY SENT ME TO WAS!
OH, YUSUKE.
IT'S BEEN A WHILE, HASN'T IT?
...WELCOME HOME.
I KNOW IT'S LATE, BUT...
HERE'S YOUR BIRTHDAY PRESENT!
OH, ISN'T THAT GREAT!
IS IT A VIDEO-GAME?
OR AYBE A ODEL KIT?!
History of Western Philosophy Encyclopedia
History of Western Philos

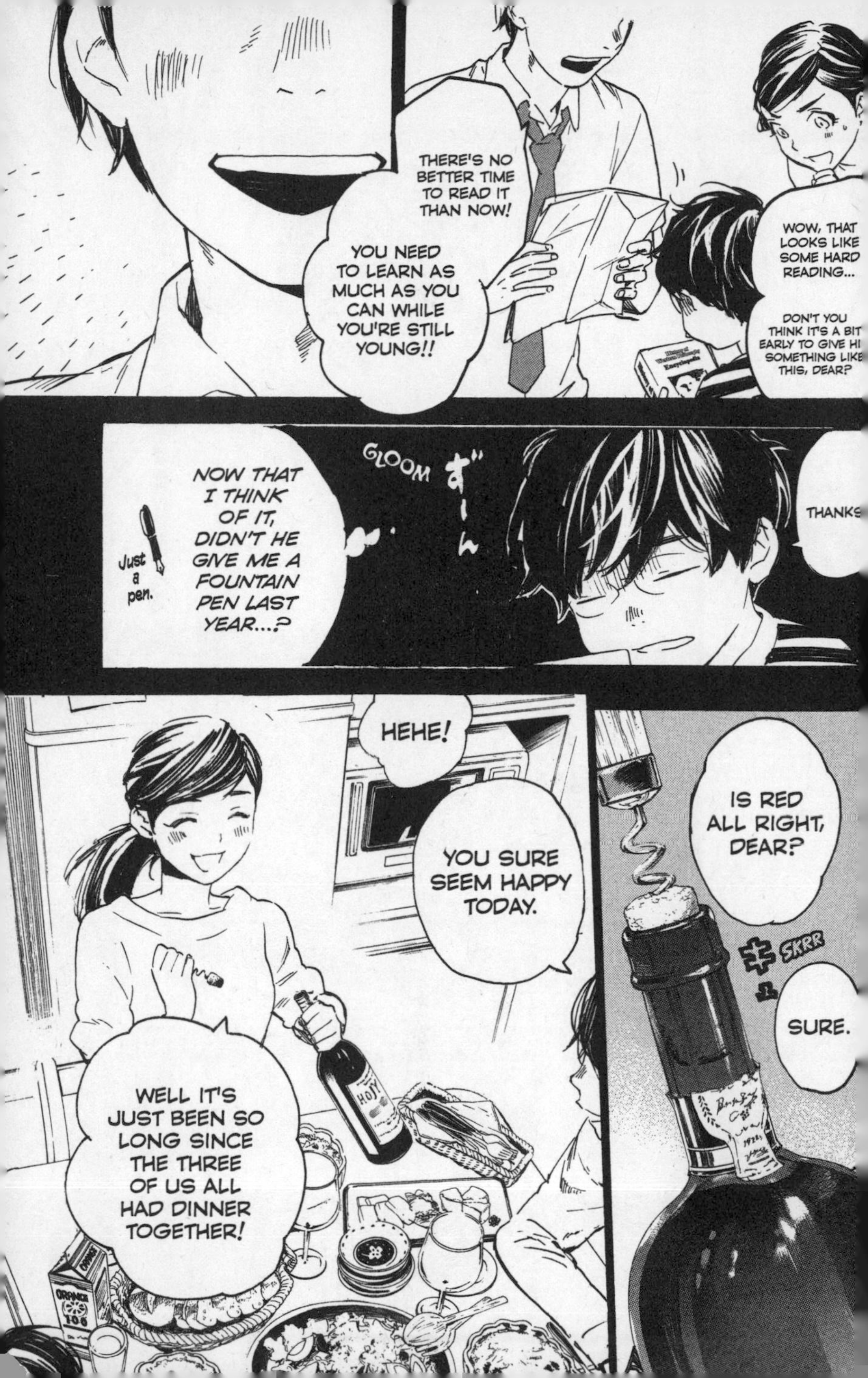
WOW, THAT LOOKS LIKE SOME HARD READING...
DON'T YOU THINK IT'S A BIT EARLY TO GIVE HI SOMETHING LIKE THIS, DEAR?
THERE'S NO BETTER TIME TO READ IT THAN NOW!
YOU NEED TO LEARN AS MUCH AS YOU CAN WHILE YOU'RE STILL YOUNG!!
THANKS
GLOOM ずーん
NOW THAT I THINK OF IT, DIDN'T HE GIVE ME A FOUNTAIN PEN LAST YEAR...?
Just a pen.
IS RED ALL RIGHT, DEAR?
キュ SKRR
SURE.
YOU SURE SEEM HAPPY TODAY.
HEHE!
WELL IT'S JUST BEEN SO LONG SINCE THE THREE OF US ALL HAD DINNER TOGETHER!

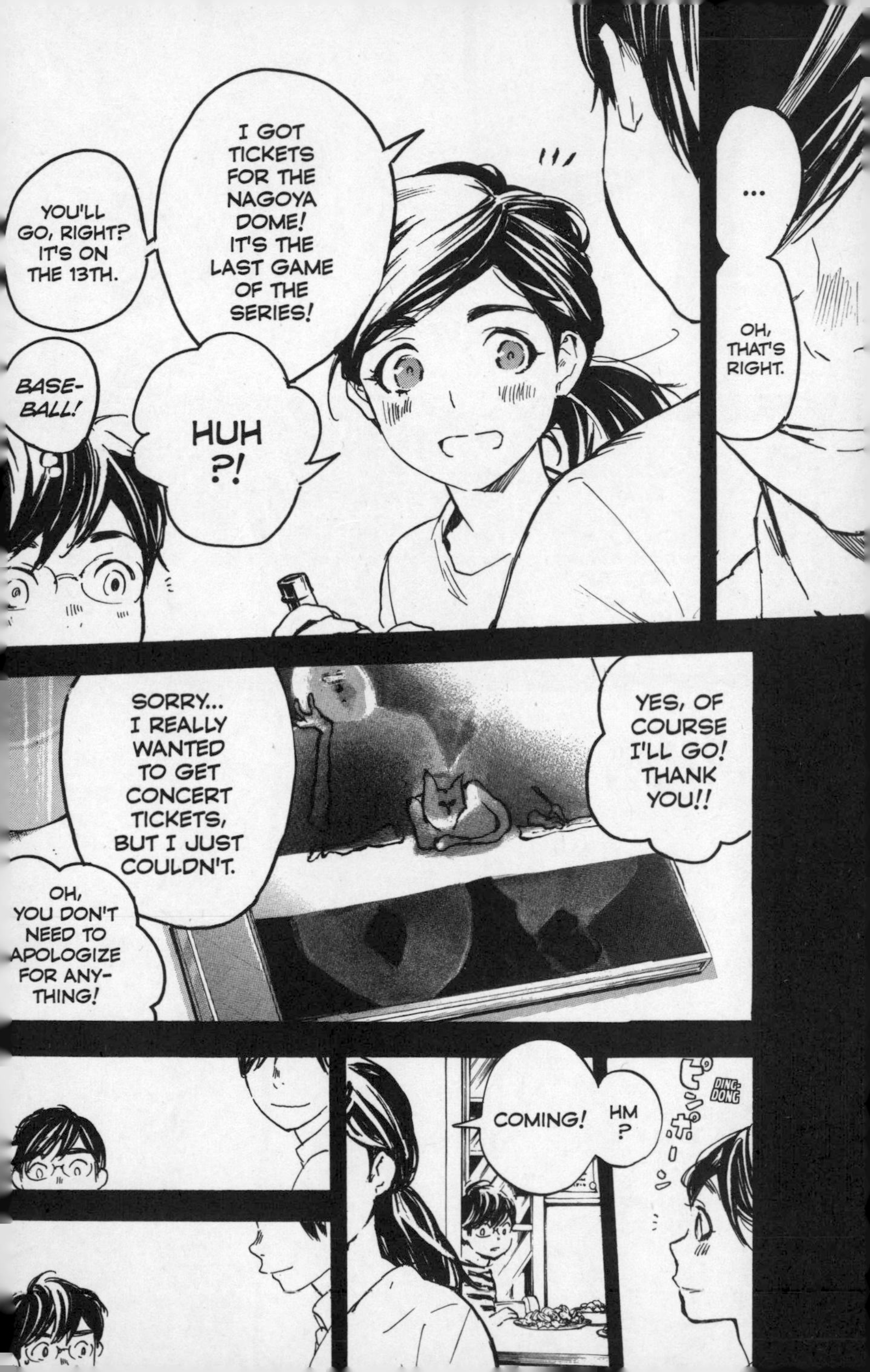
...
OH, THAT'S RIGHT.
I GOT TICKETS FOR THE NAGOYA DOME! IT'S THE LAST GAME OF THE SERIES!
YOU'LL GO, RIGHT? IT'S ON THE 13TH.
HUH ?!
BASE-BALL!
YES, OF COURSE I'LL GO! THANK YOU!!
SORRY... I REALLY WANTED TO GET CONCERT TICKETS, BUT I JUST COULDN'T.
OH, YOU DON'T NEED TO APOLOGIZE FOR ANY-THING!
DING-DONG
HM ?
COMING!

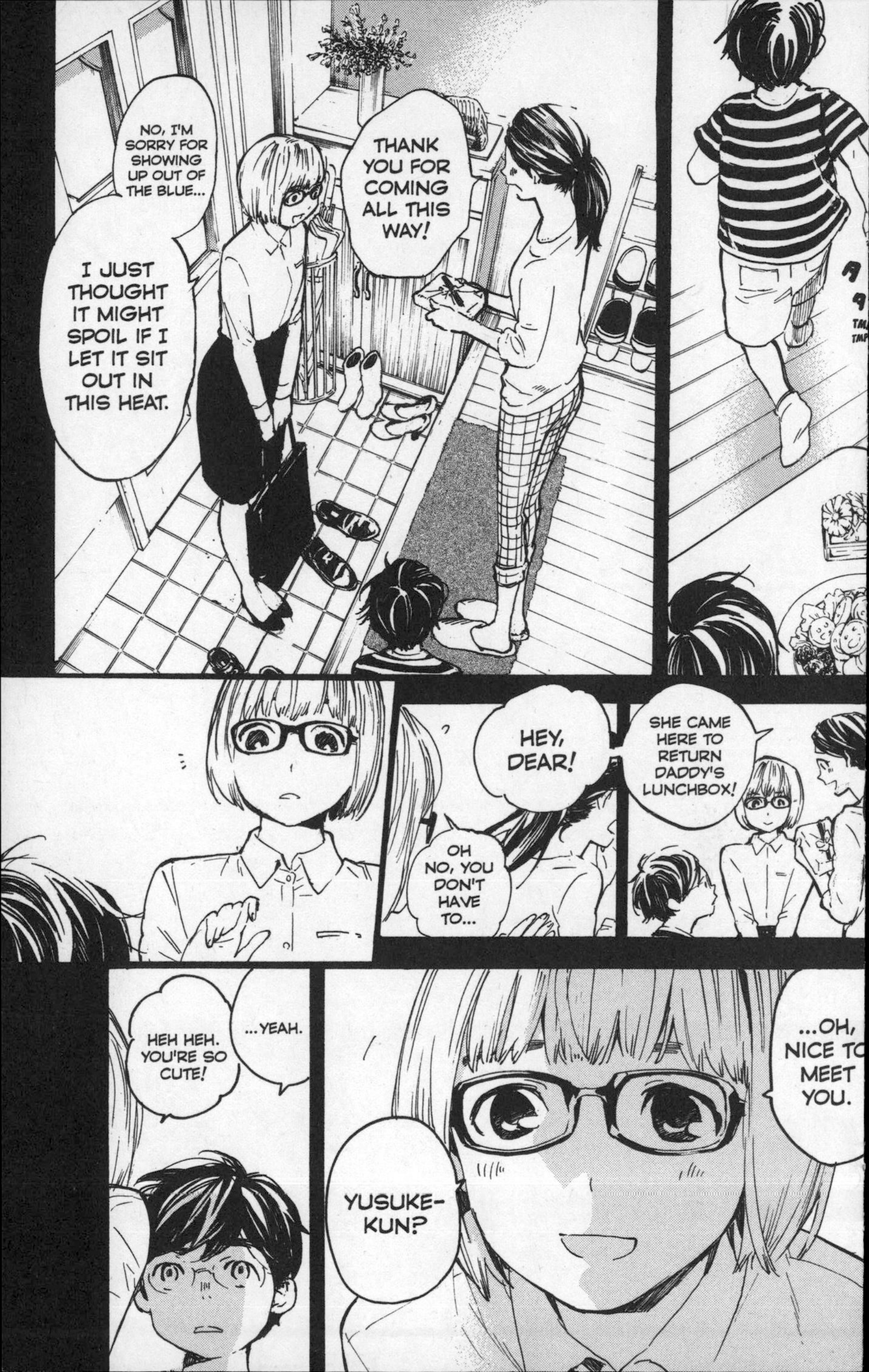
THANK YOU FOR COMING ALL THIS WAY!
NO, I'M SORRY FOR SHOWING UP OUT OF THE BLUE...
I JUST THOUGHT IT MIGHT SPOIL IF I LET IT SIT OUT IN THIS HEAT.
SHE CAME HERE TO RETURN DADDY'S LUNCHBOX!
HEY, DEAR!
OH NO, YOU DON'T HAVE TO...
...OH, NICE TO MEET YOU.
YUSUKE-KUN?
...YEAH.
HEH HEH. YOU'RE SO CUTE!

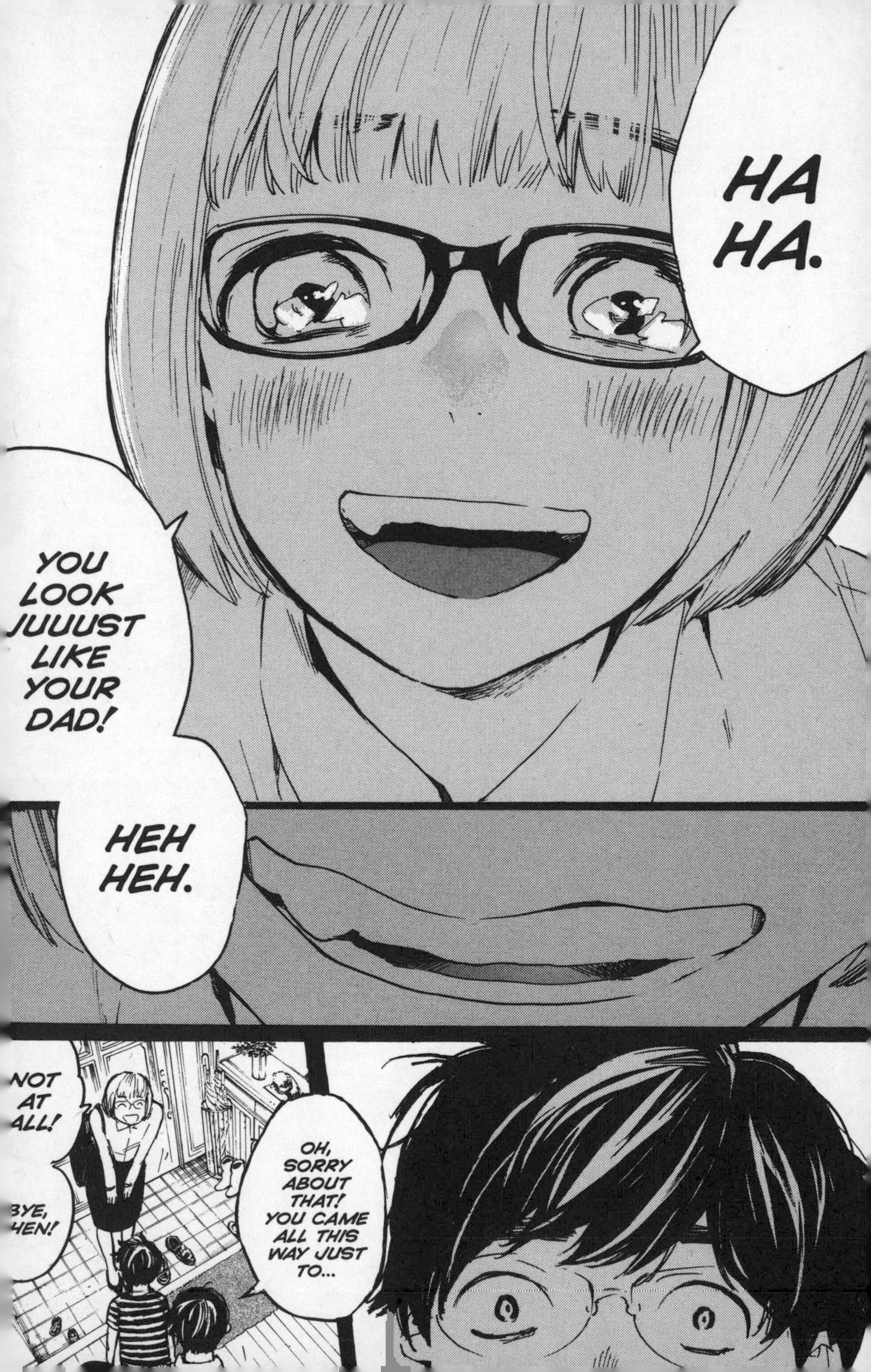
HA HA.
YOU LOOK JUUUST LIKE YOUR DAD!
HEH HEH.
OH, SORRY ABOUT THAT! YOU CAME ALL THIS WAY JUST TO...
NOT AT ALL!
BYE, HEN!

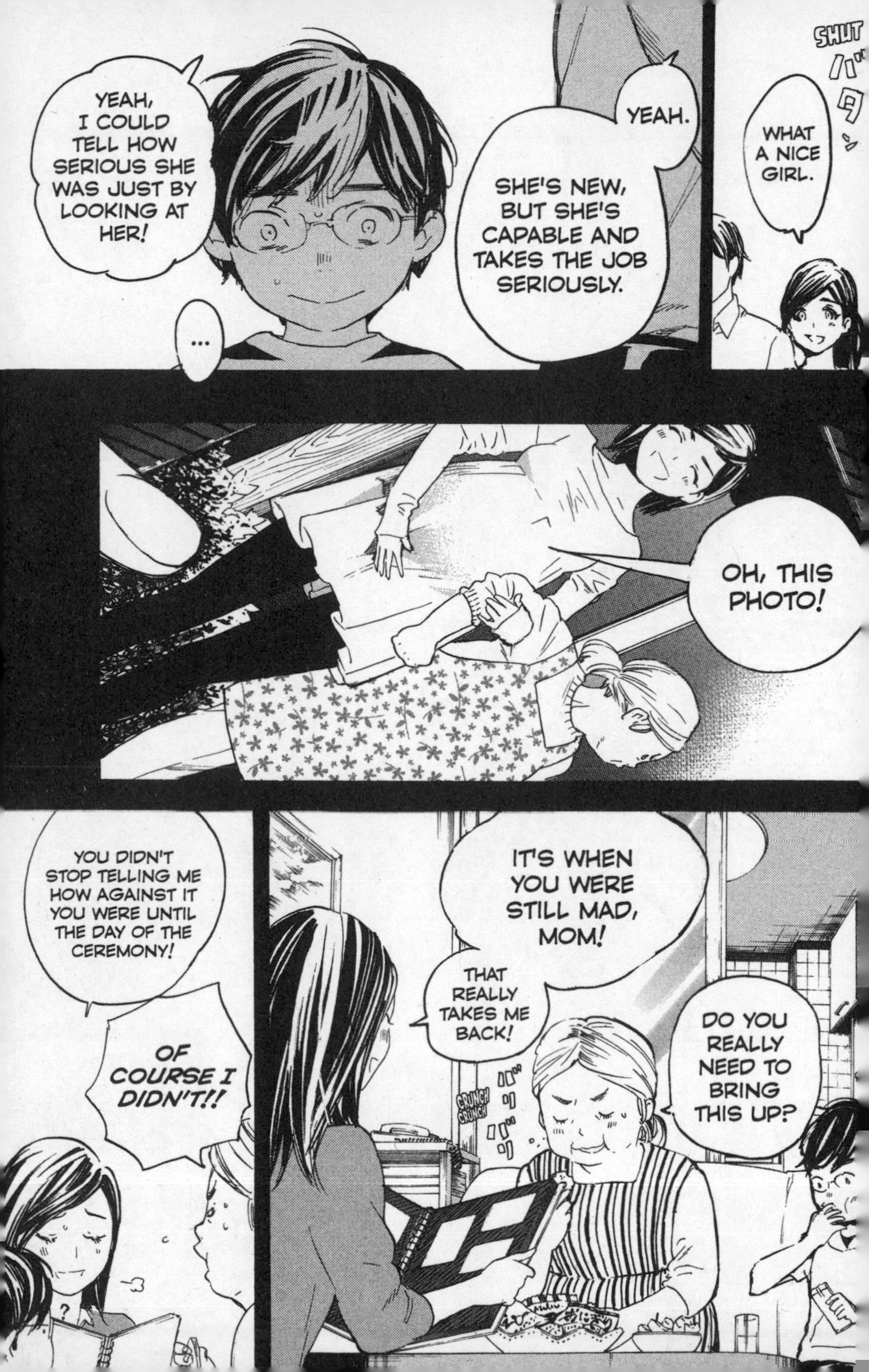
SHUT
WHAT A NICE GIRL.
YEAH.
SHE'S NEW, BUT SHE'S CAPABLE AND TAKES THE JOB SERIOUSLY.
YEAH, I COULD TELL HOW SERIOUS SHE WAS JUST BY LOOKING AT HER!
...
OH, THIS PHOTO!
IT'S WHEN YOU WERE STILL MAD, MOM!
THAT REALLY TAKES ME BACK!
DO YOU REALLY NEED TO BRING THIS UP?
CRUNCH CRUNCH
YOU DIDN'T STOP TELLING ME HOW AGAINST IT YOU WERE UNTIL THE DAY OF THE CEREMONY!
OF COURSE I DIDN'T!!
?

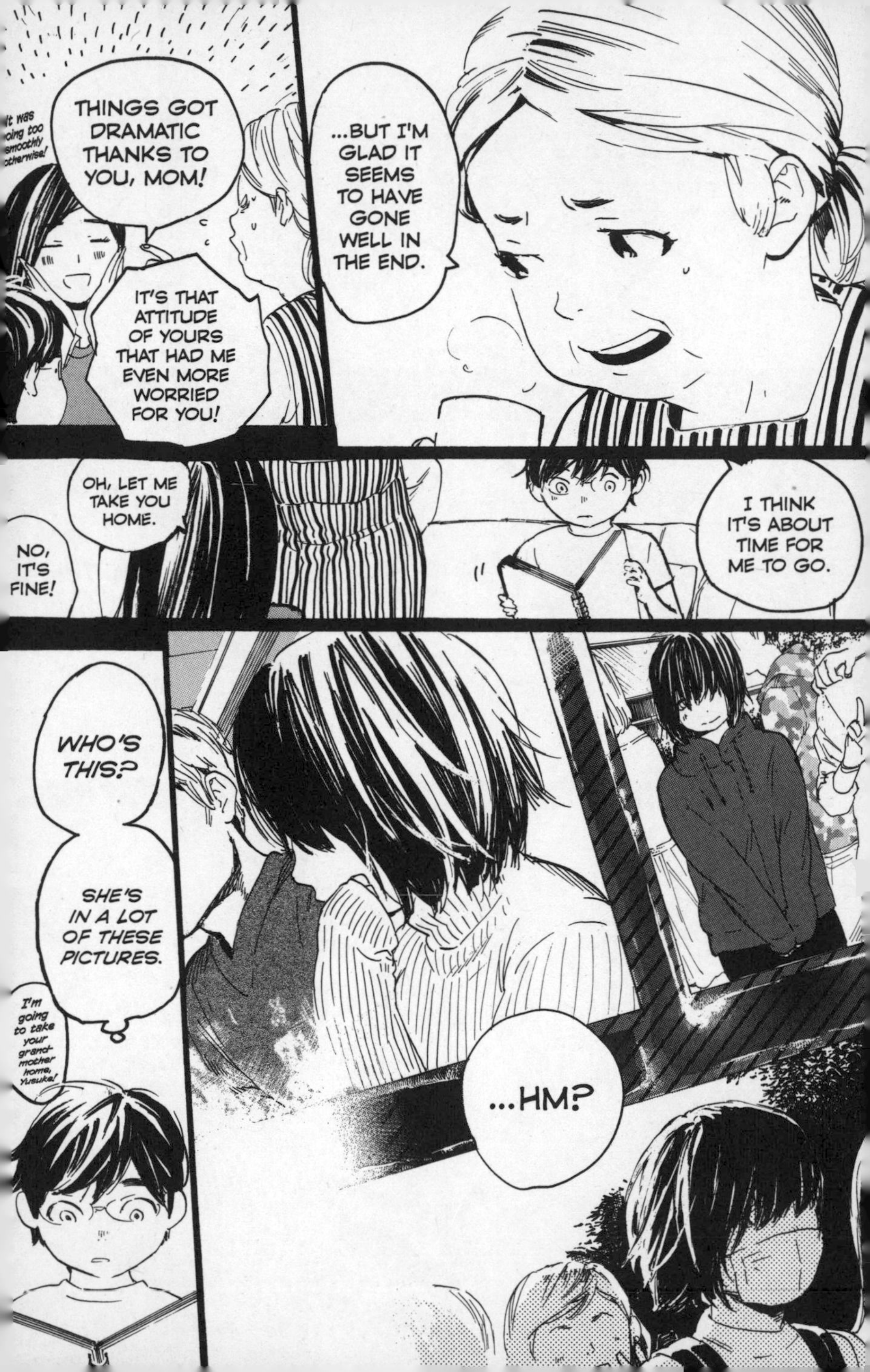
...BUT I'M GLAD IT SEEMS TO HAVE GONE WELL IN THE END.
THINGS GOT DRAMATIC THANKS TO YOU, MOM!
it was oing too smoothly otherwise!
IT'S THAT ATTITUDE OF YOURS THAT HAD ME EVEN MORE WORRIED FOR YOU!
I THINK IT'S ABOUT TIME FOR ME TO GO.
OH, LET ME TAKE YOU HOME.
NO, IT'S FINE!
...HM?
WHO'S THIS?
SHE'S IN A LOT OF THESE PICTURES.
I'm going to take your grand-mother home, Yusuke!

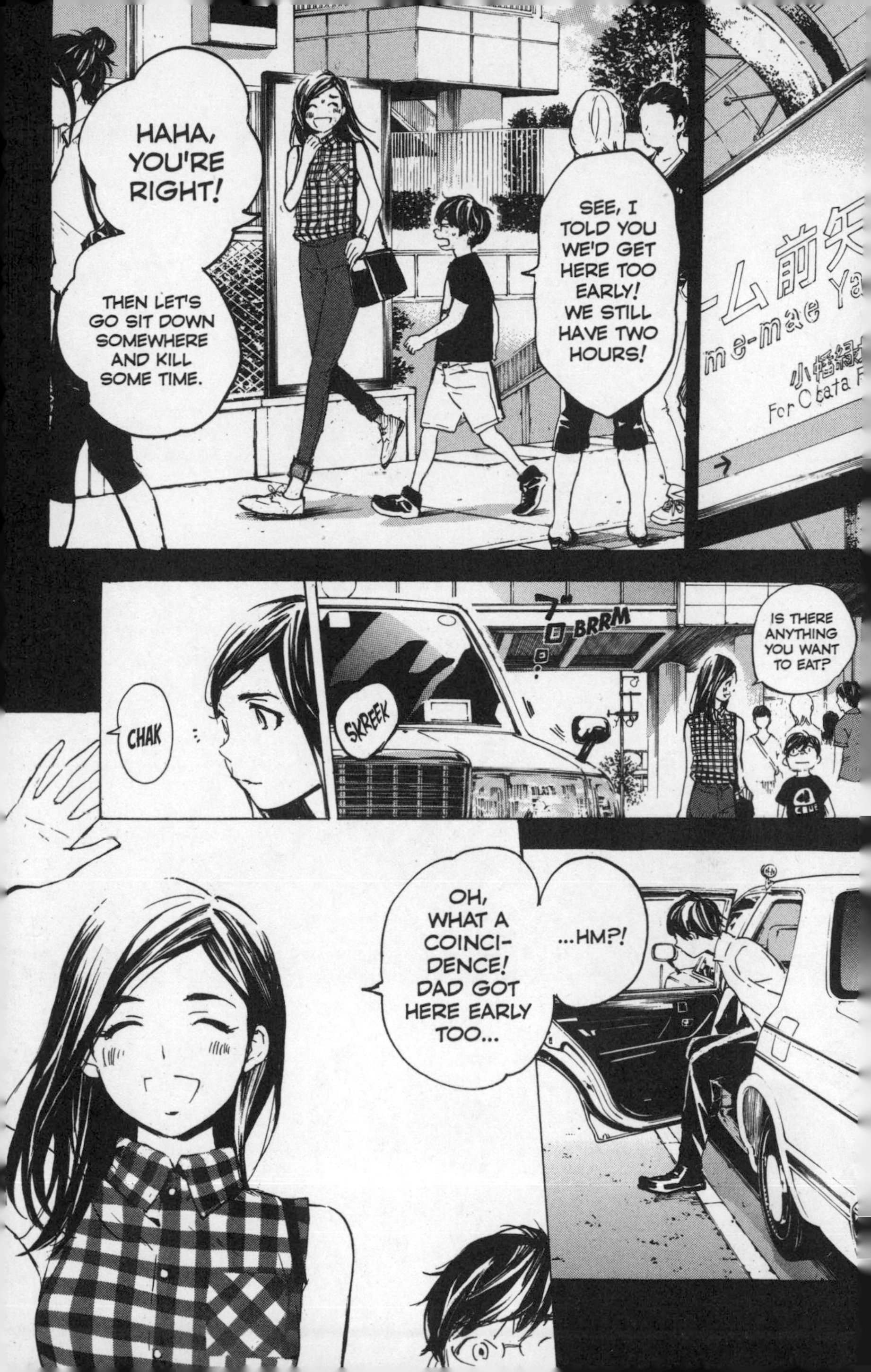
SEE, I TOLD YOU WE'D GET HERE TOO EARLY! WE STILL HAVE TWO HOURS!
HAHA, YOU'RE RIGHT!
THEN LET'S GO SIT DOWN SOMEWHERE AND KILL SOME TIME.
IS THERE ANYTHING YOU WANT TO EAT?
BRRM
SKREEK
CHAK
...HM?!
OH, WHAT A COINCIDENCE! DAD GOT HERE EARLY TOO...

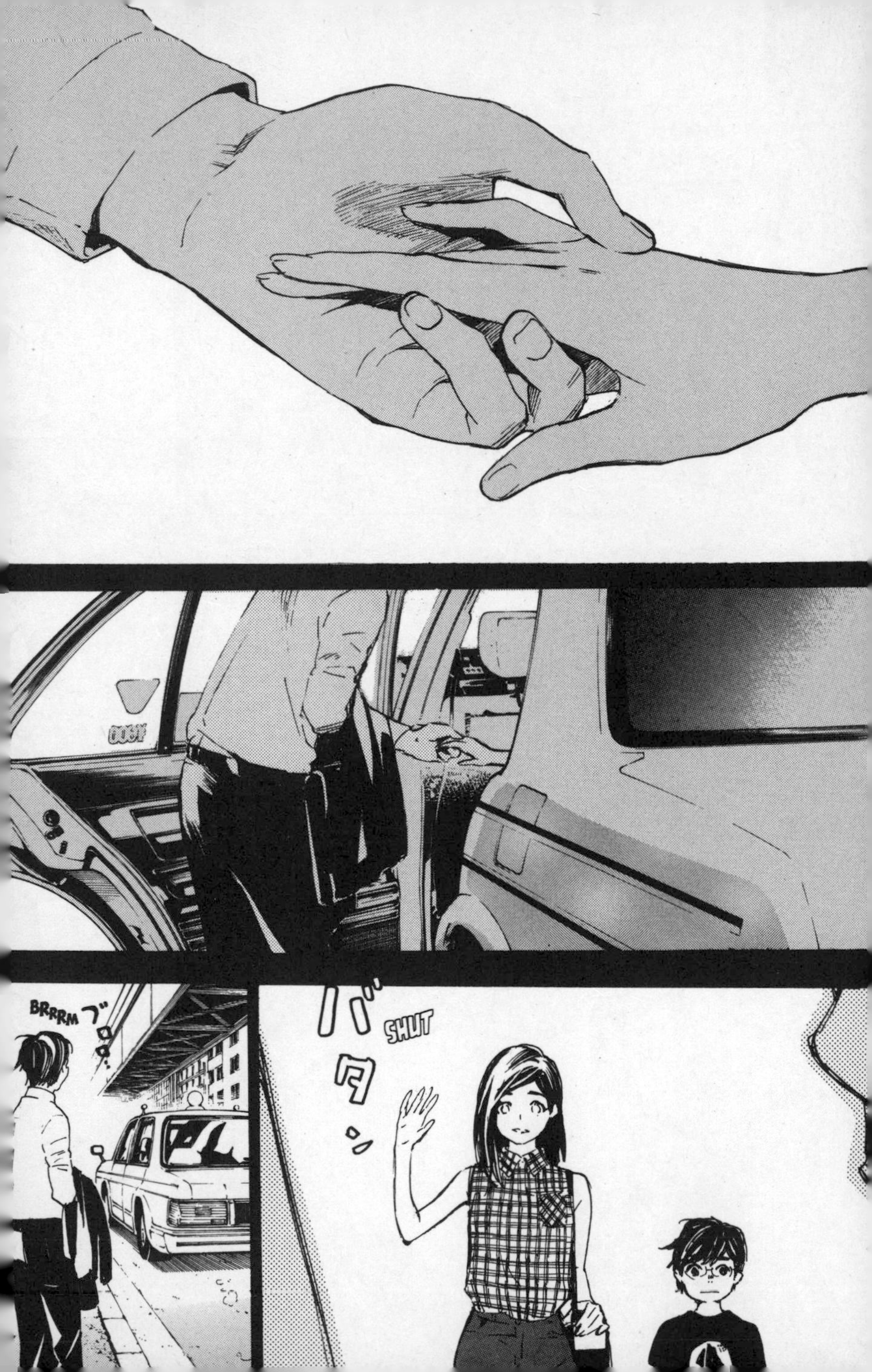
バタン
SHUT
BRRRM
ブロロ

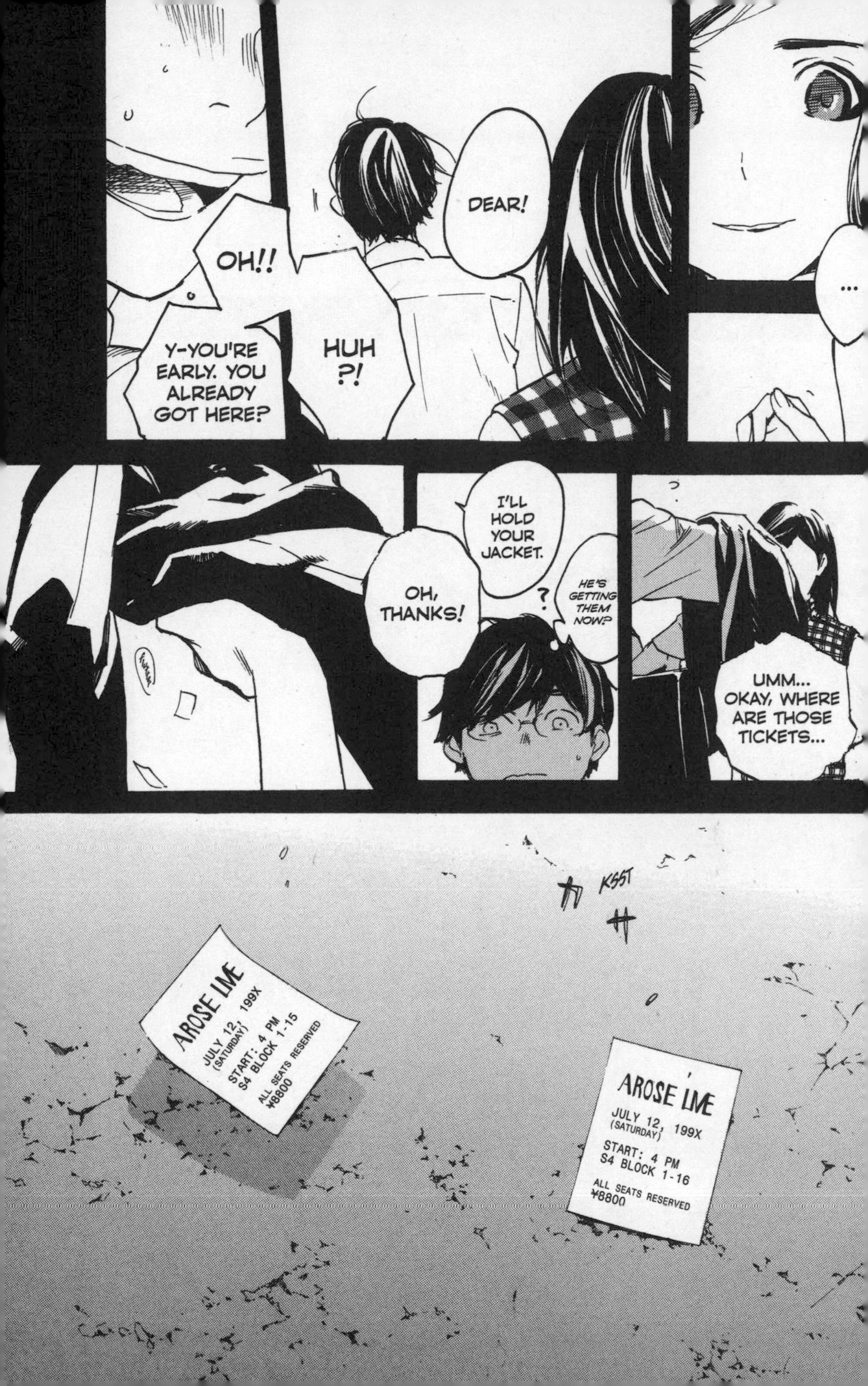
...
DEAR!
HUH ?!
OH!!
Y-YOU'RE EARLY. YOU ALREADY GOT HERE?
UMM... OKAY, WHERE ARE THOSE TICKETS...
I'LL HOLD YOUR JACKET.
HE'S GETTING THEM NOW?
?
OH, THANKS!
KSST
AROSE LIVE
JULY 12, 199X (SATURDAY)
START: 4 PM
S4 BLOCK 1-16
ALL SEATS RESERVED
¥8800
AROSE LIVE
JULY 12, 199X (SATURDAY)
START: 4 PM
S4 BLOCK 1-15
ALL SEATS RESERVED
¥8800

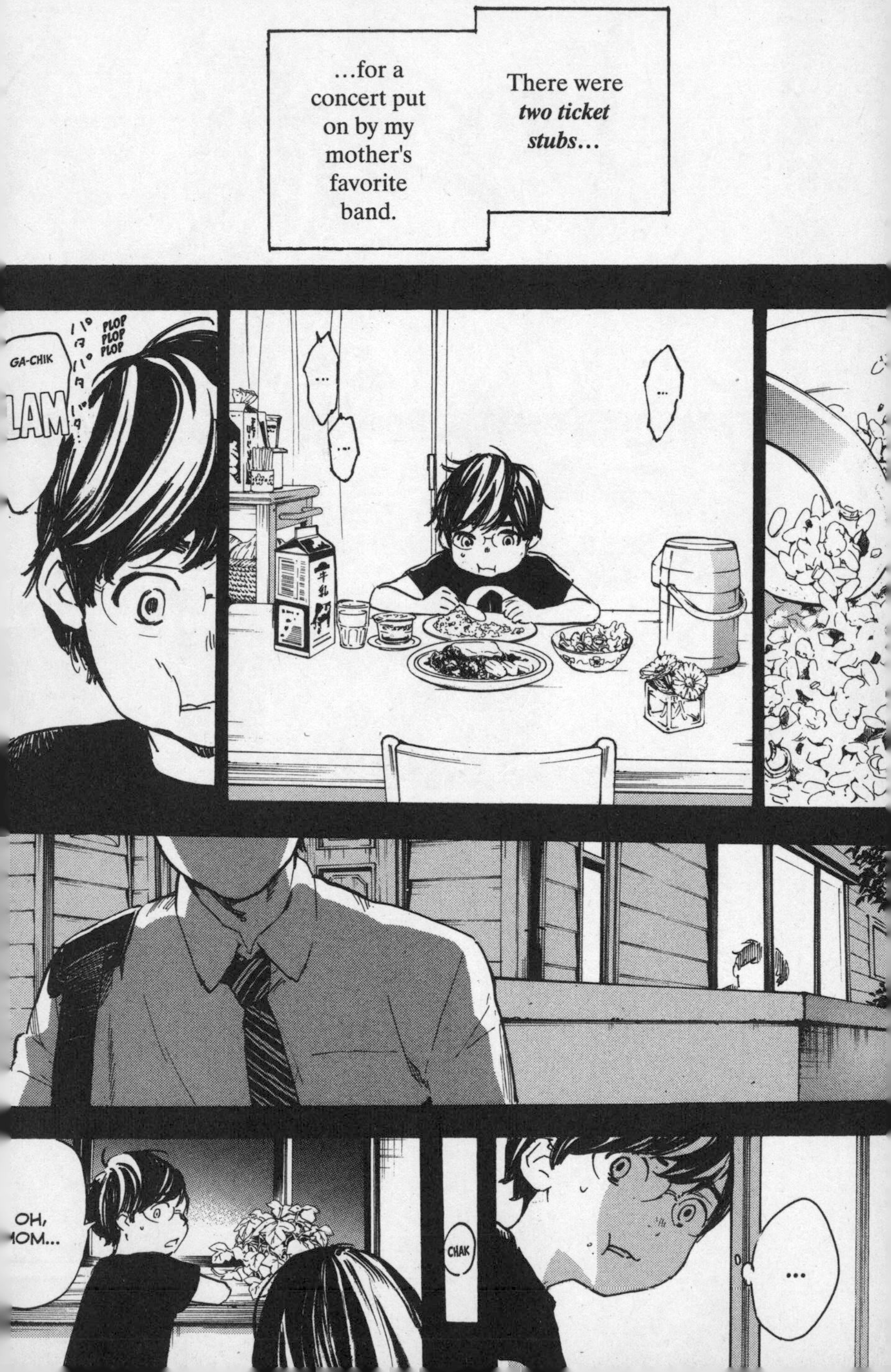
There were *two ticket stubs*...
...for a concert put on by my mother's favorite band.
...
...
...
PLOP PLOP PLOP
GA-CHIK
LAM
...
CHAK
OH, MOM...

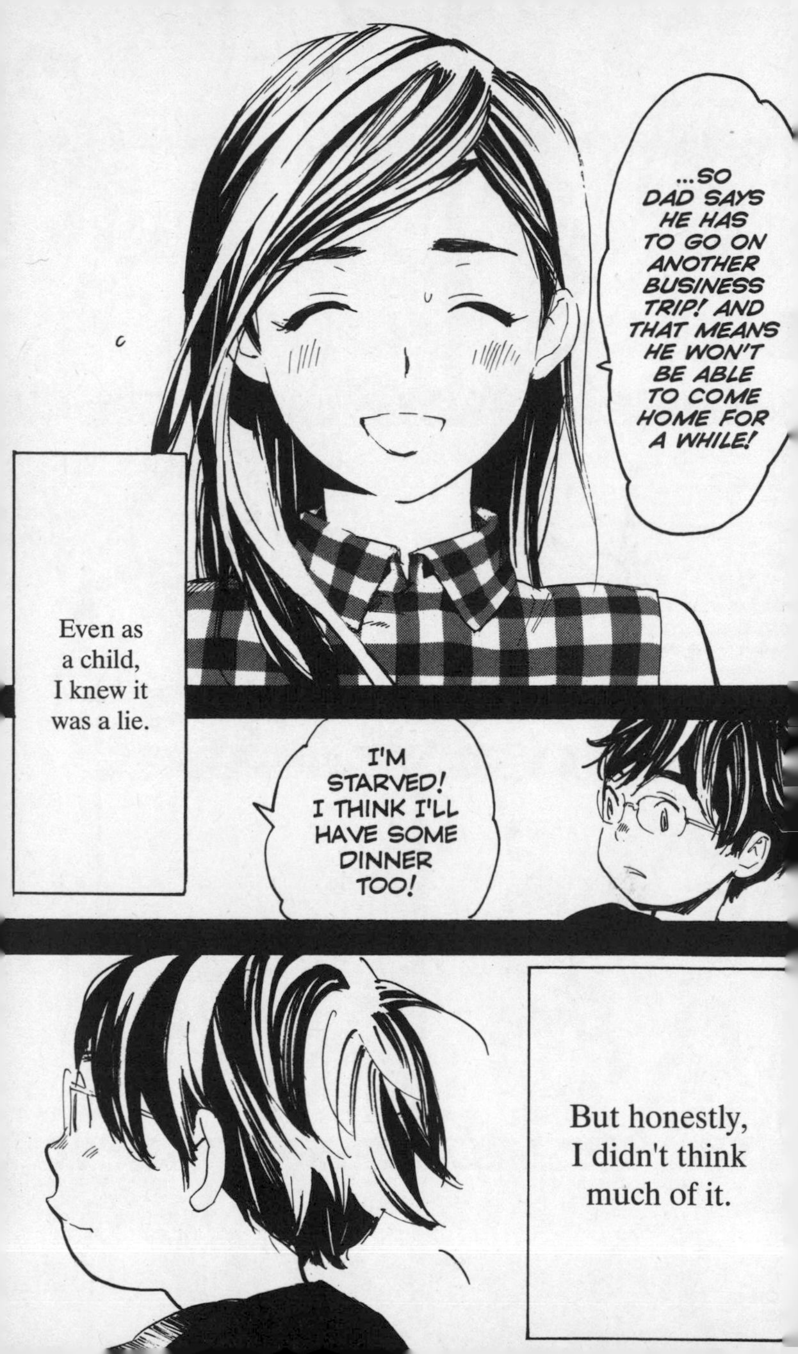
...SO DAD SAYS HE HAS TO GO ON ANOTHER BUSINESS TRIP! AND THAT MEANS HE WON'T BE ABLE TO COME HOME FOR A WHILE!
Even as a child, I knew it was a lie.
I'M STARVED! I THINK I'LL HAVE SOME DINNER TOO!
But honestly, I didn't think much of it.

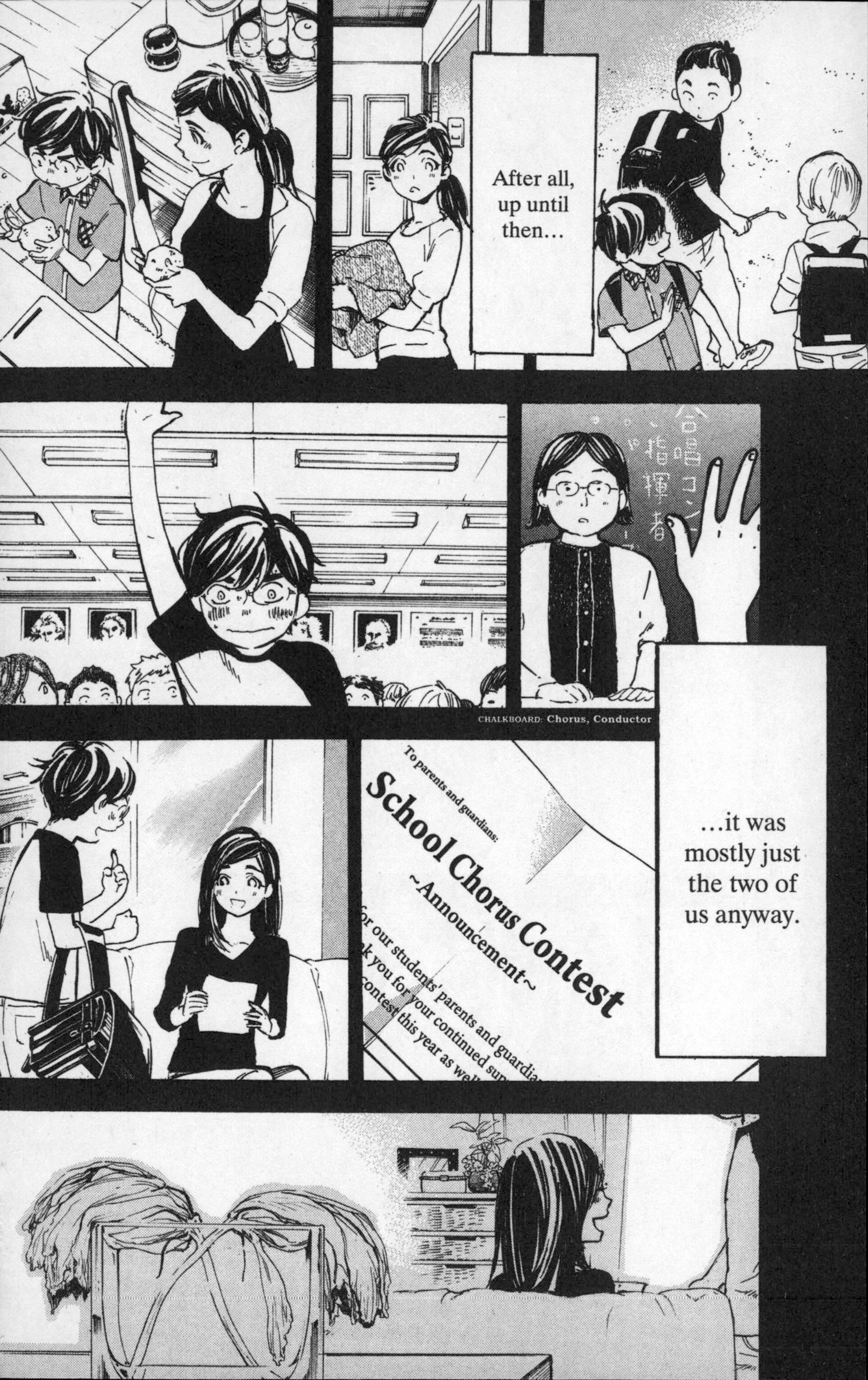
After all, up until then…
合唱コン
指揮者
CHALKBOARD: Chorus, Conductor
…it was mostly just the two of us anyway.
To parents and guardians:
School Chorus Contest
~Announcement~
for our students' parents and guardia
k you for your continued su
contest this year as wel

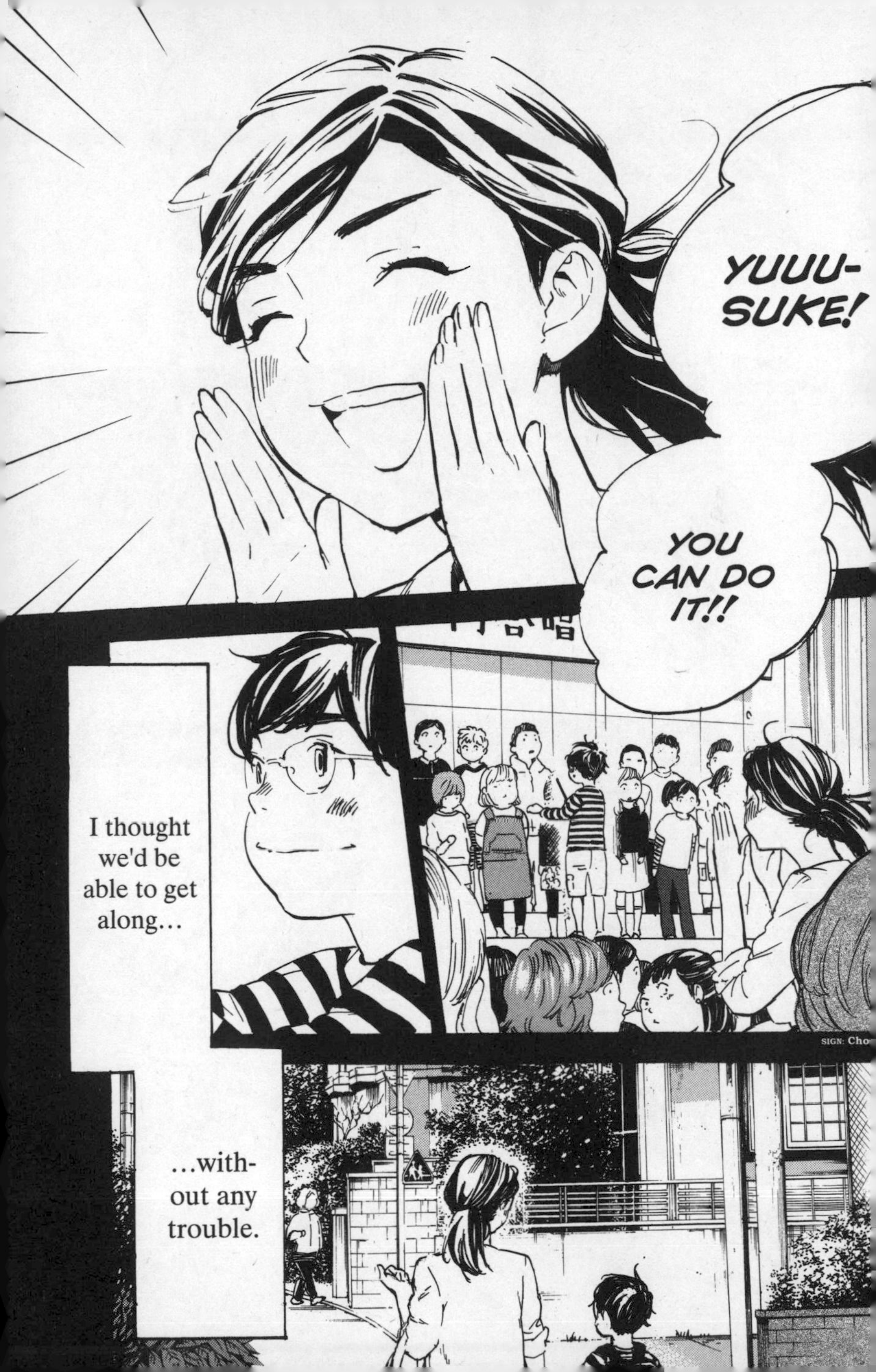
YUUUU-SUKE!
YOU CAN DO IT!!
SIGN: Cho
I thought we'd be able to get along…
…with-out any trouble.

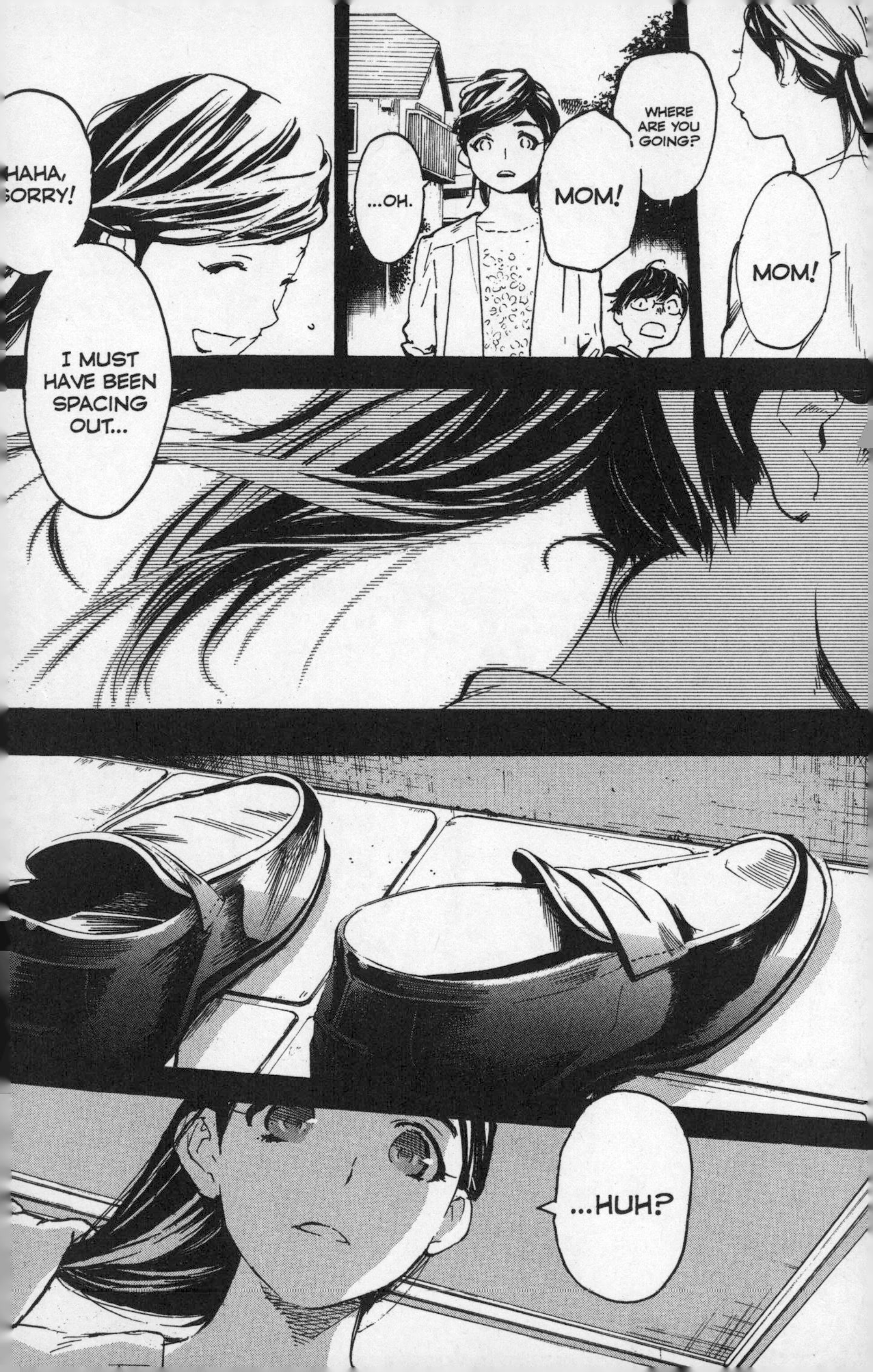
MOM!
WHERE ARE YOU GOING?
MOM!
...OH.
HAHA, SORRY!
I MUST HAVE BEEN SPACING OUT...
...HUH?

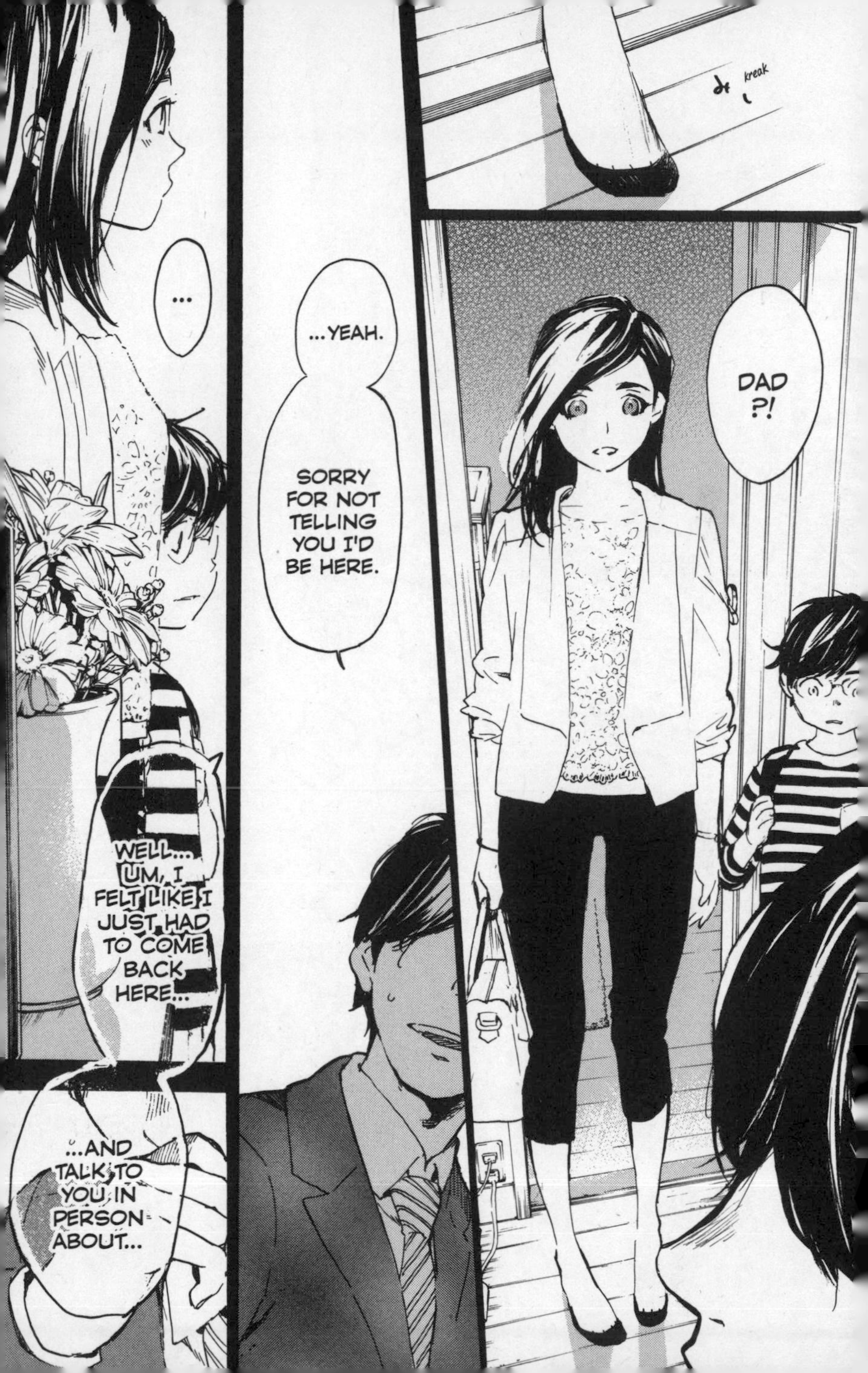
kreak
DAD ?!
...YEAH.
SORRY FOR NOT TELLING YOU I'D BE HERE.
...
WELL... UM, I FELT LIKE I JUST HAD TO COME BACK HERE...
...AND TALK TO YOU IN PERSON ABOUT...

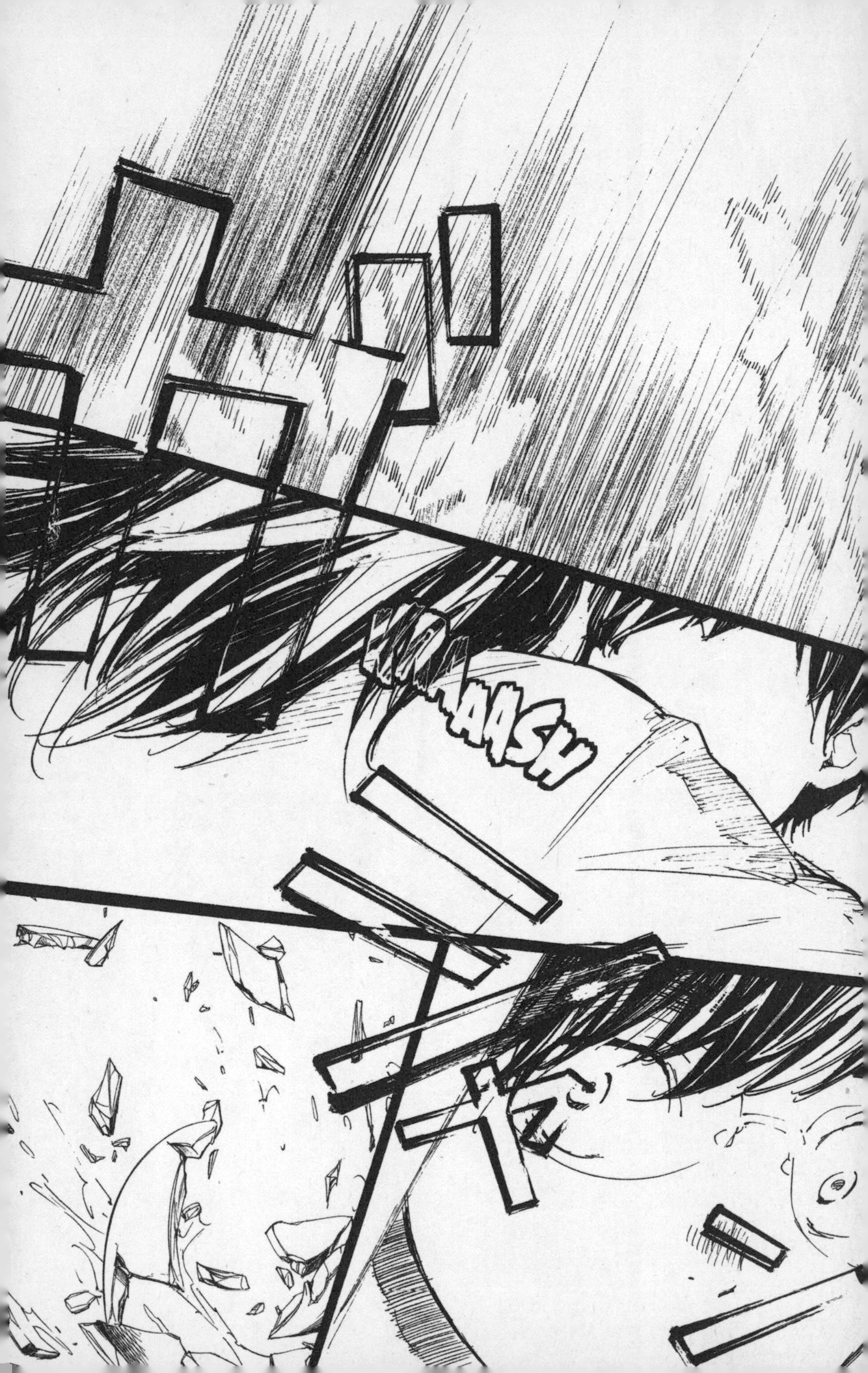
AASH

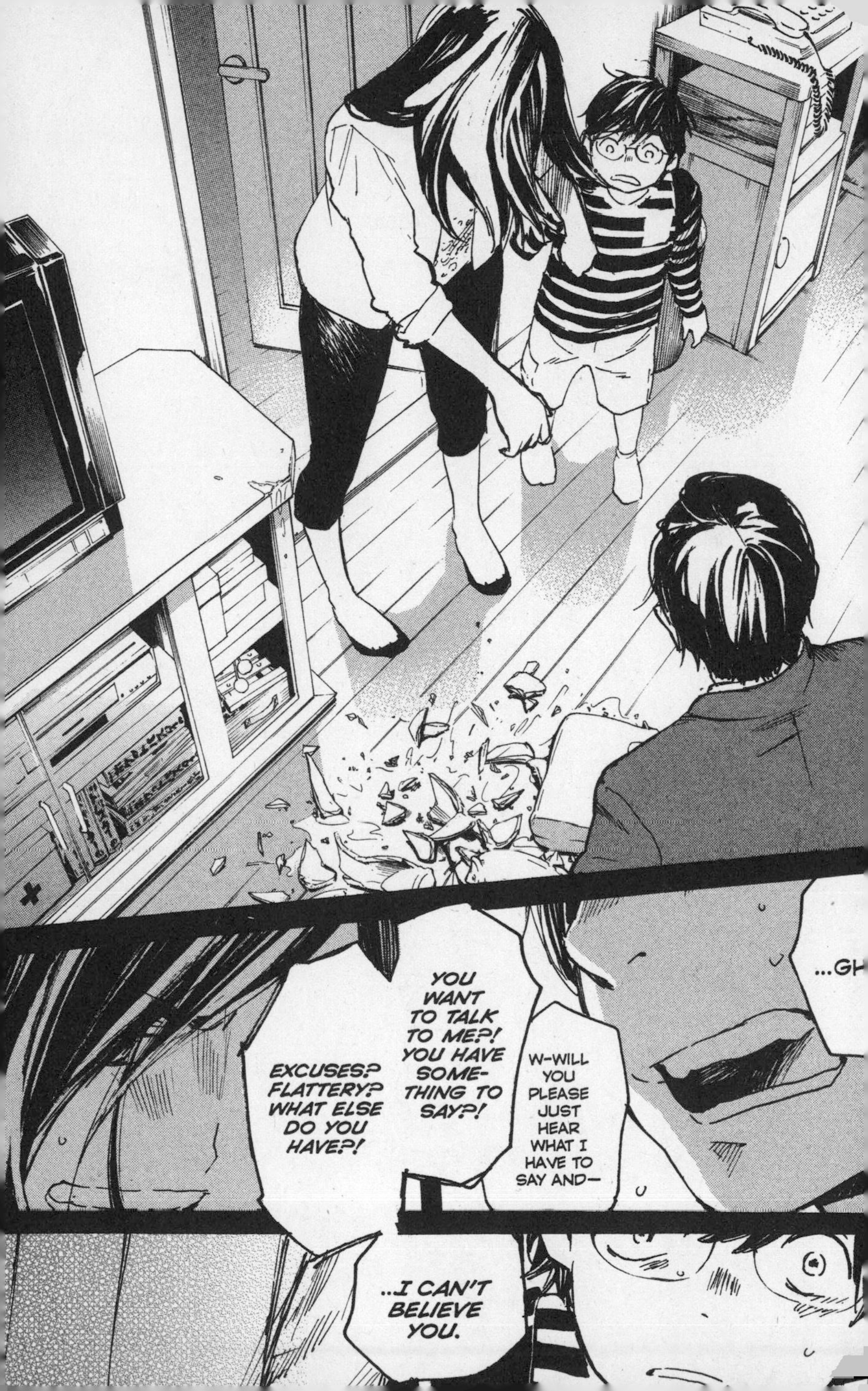
...GH
W-WILL YOU PLEASE JUST HEAR WHAT I HAVE TO SAY AND—
YOU WANT TO TALK TO ME?! YOU HAVE SOME-THING TO SAY?!
EXCUSES? FLATTERY? WHAT ELSE DO YOU HAVE?!
...I CAN'T BELIEVE YOU.

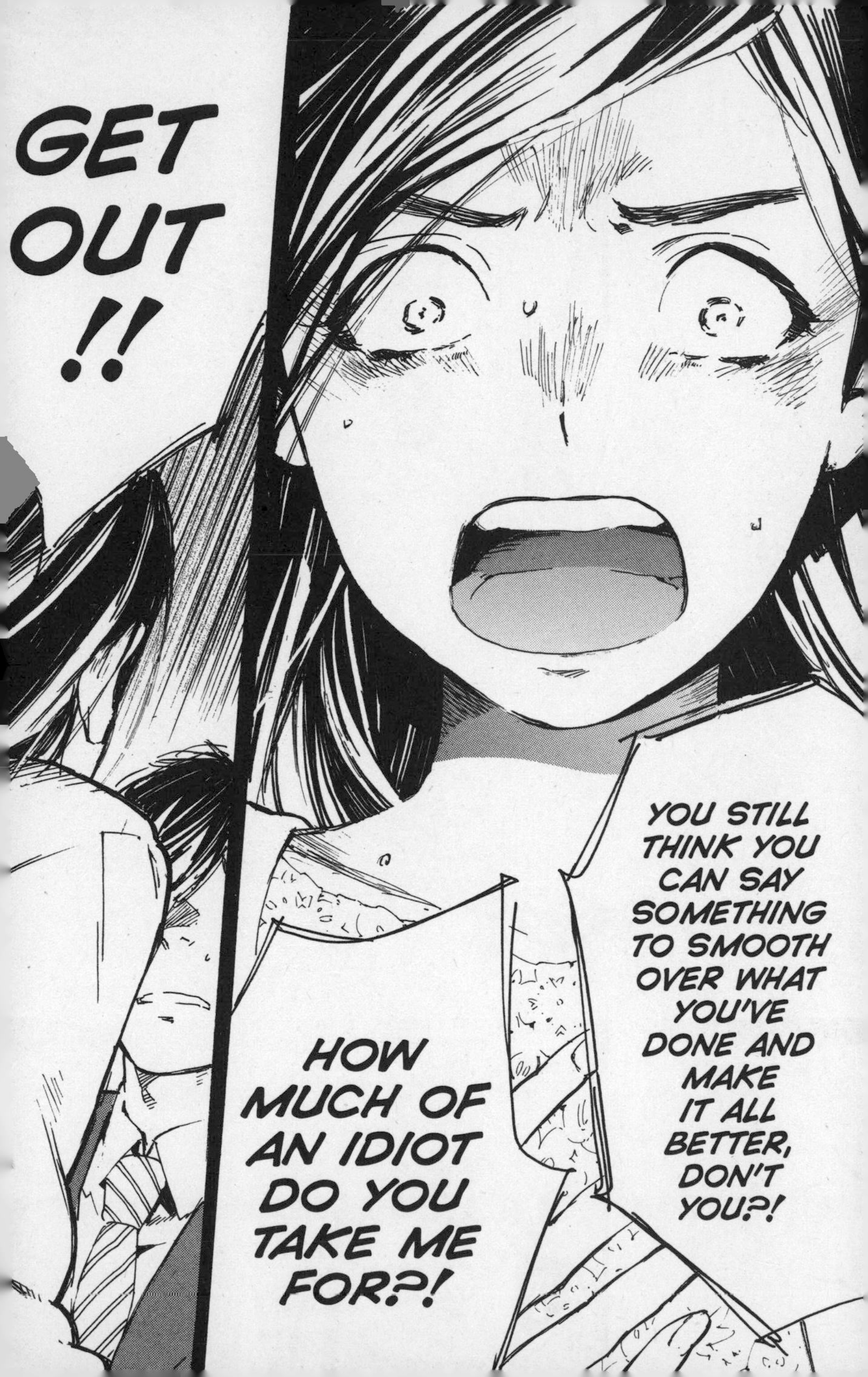
YOU STILL THINK YOU CAN SAY SOMETHING TO SMOOTH OVER WHAT YOU'VE DONE AND MAKE IT ALL BETTER, DON'T YOU?!
HOW MUCH OF AN IDIOT DO YOU TAKE ME FOR?!
GET OUT!!

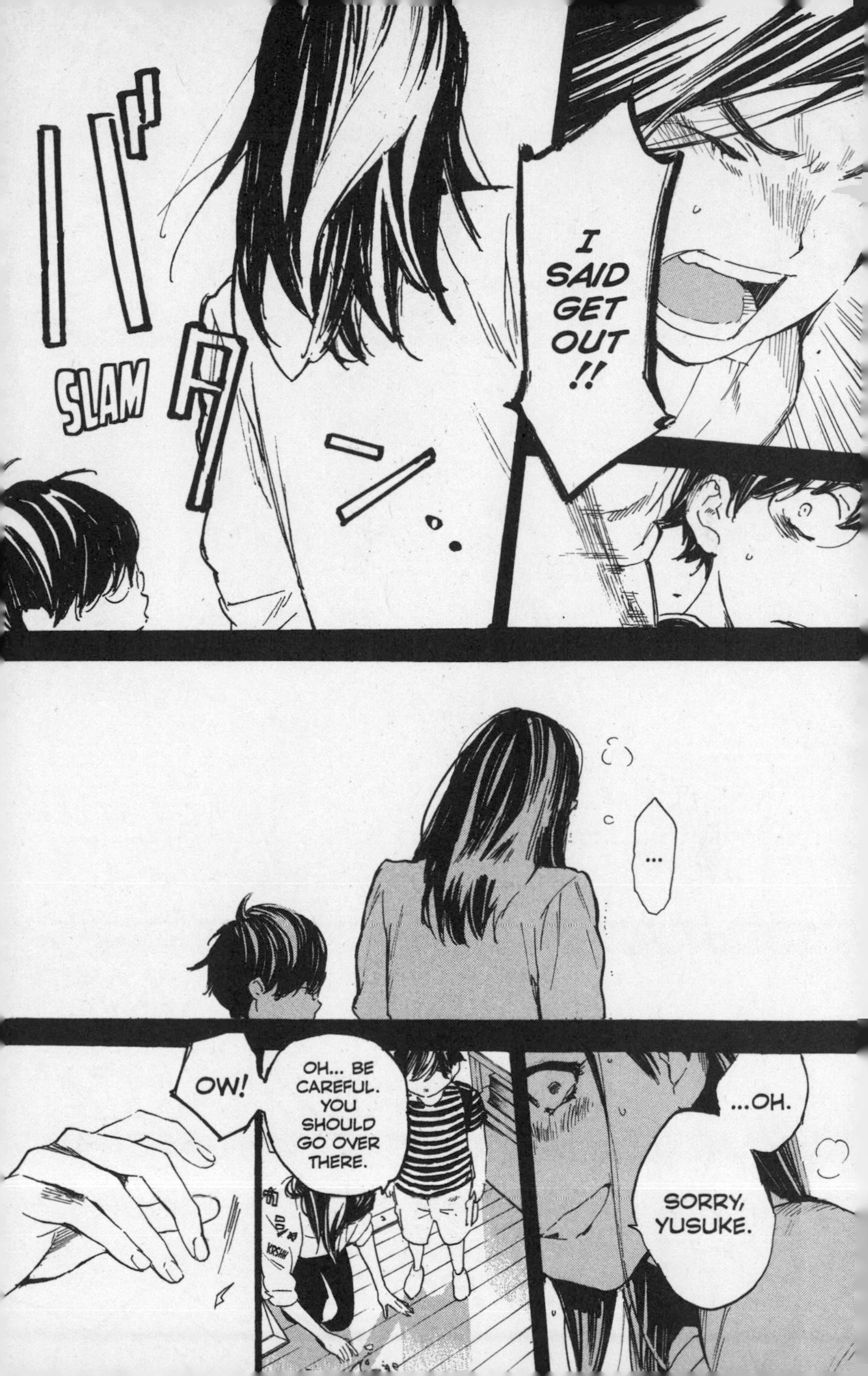
I SAID GET OUT!!
SLAM
...
...OH.
SORRY, YUSUKE.
OH... BE CAREFUL. YOU SHOULD GO OVER THERE.
KRSH
OW!

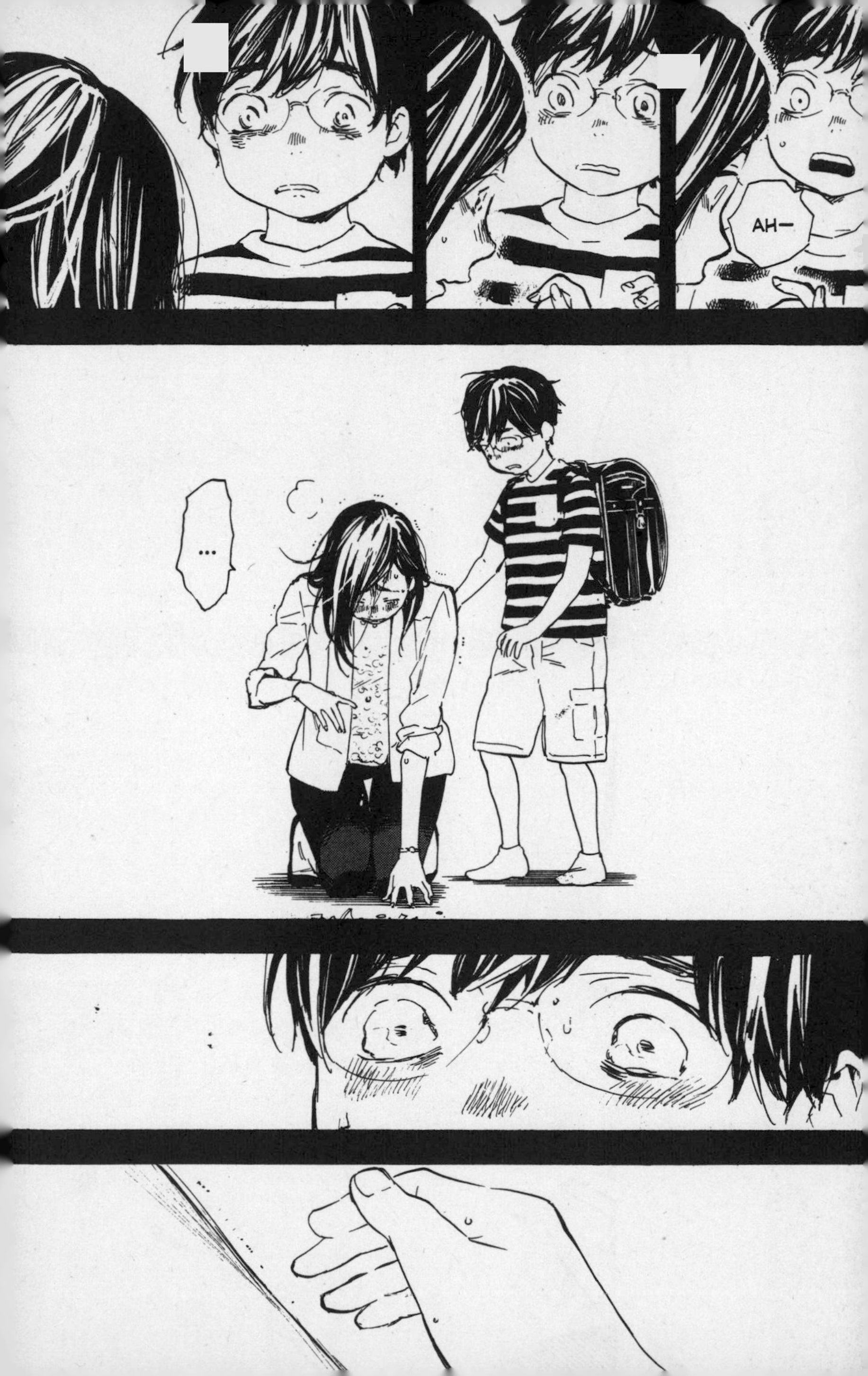
AH—
...

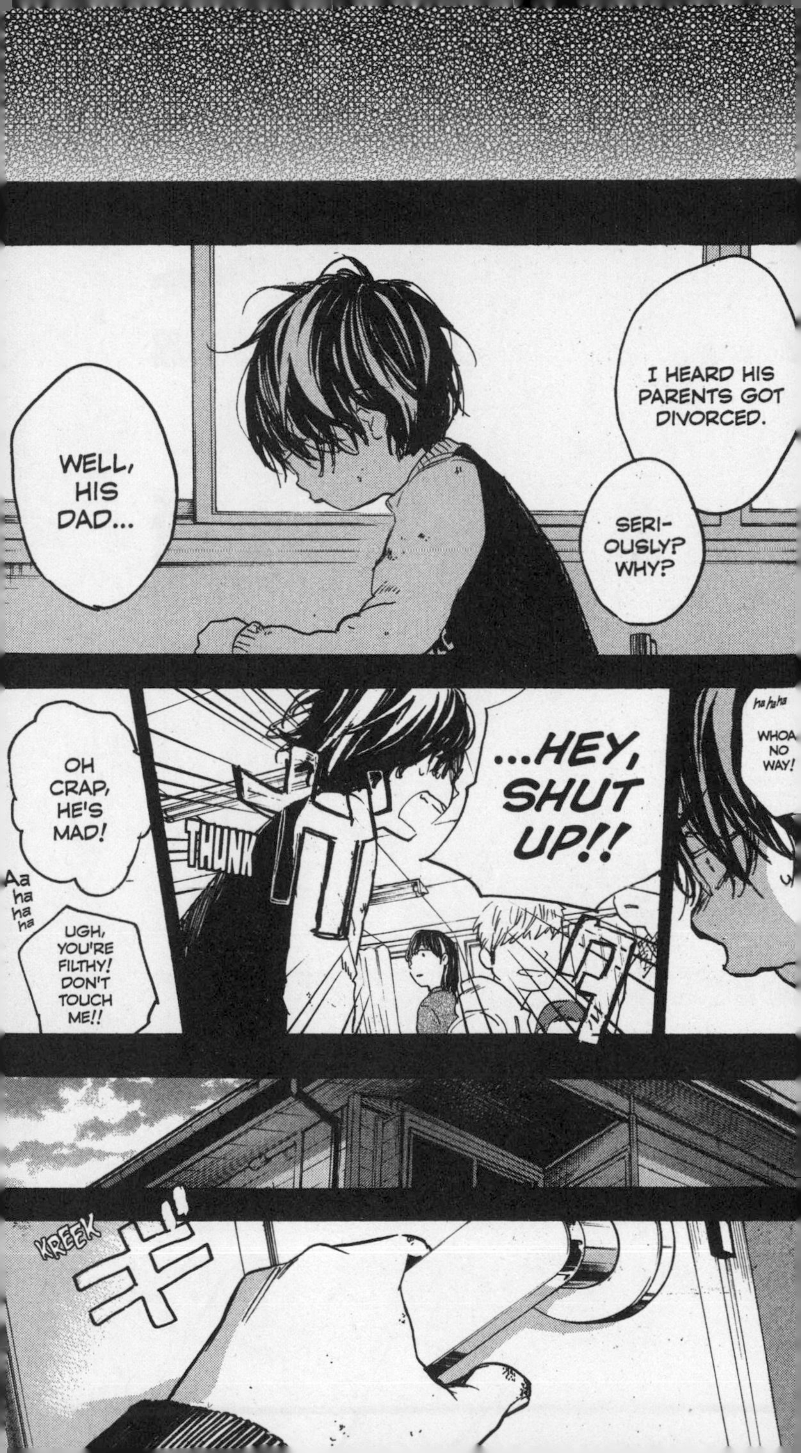
I HEARD HIS PARENTS GOT DIVORCED.
SERI-OUSLY? WHY?
WELL, HIS DAD...
ha ha ha
WHOA NO WAY!
...HEY, SHUT UP!!
THUNK
OH CRAP, HE'S MAD!
Aa ha ha ha
UGH, YOU'RE FILTHY! DON'T TOUCH ME!!
KREEK
ギ

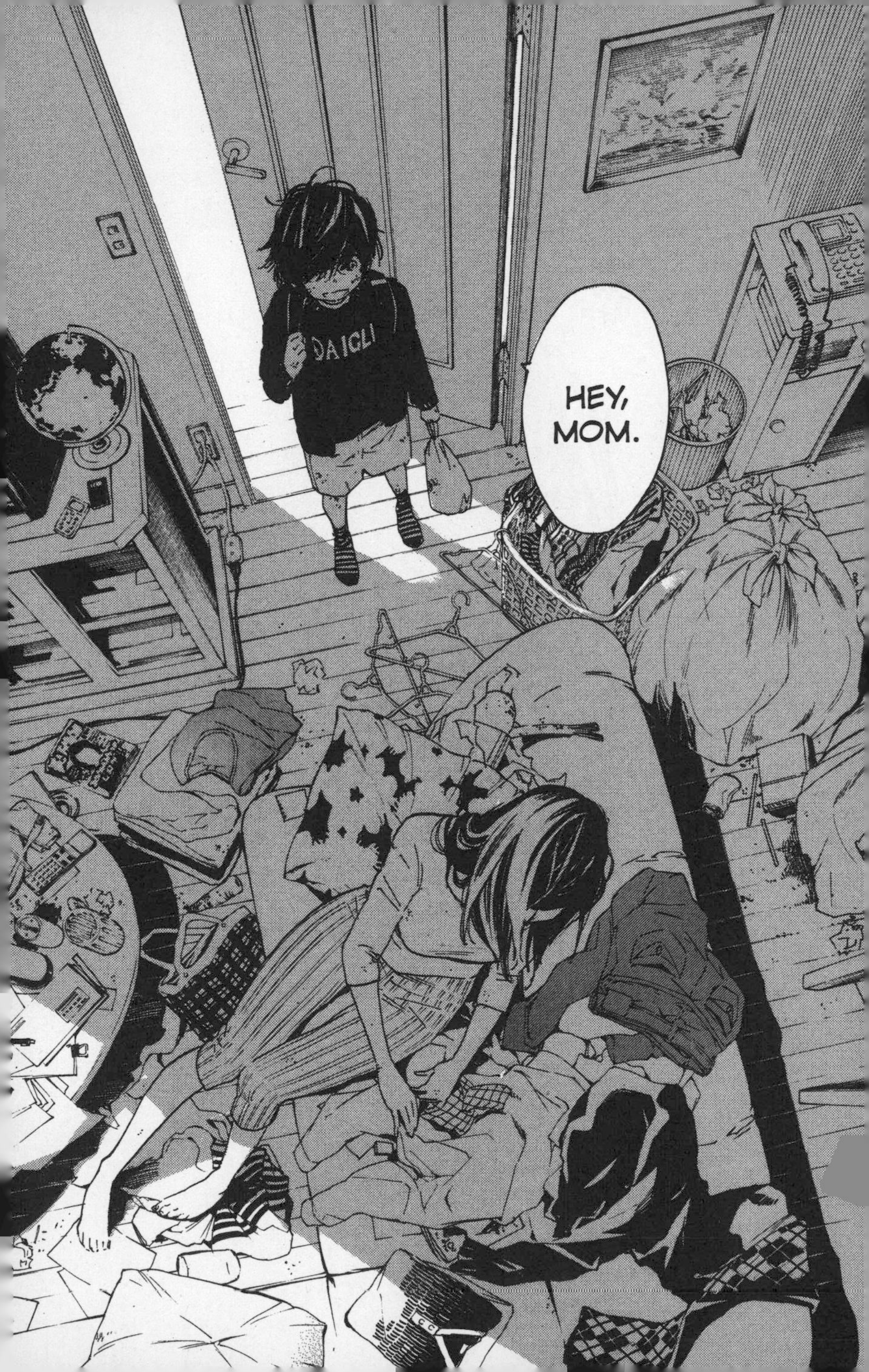
HEY, MOM.

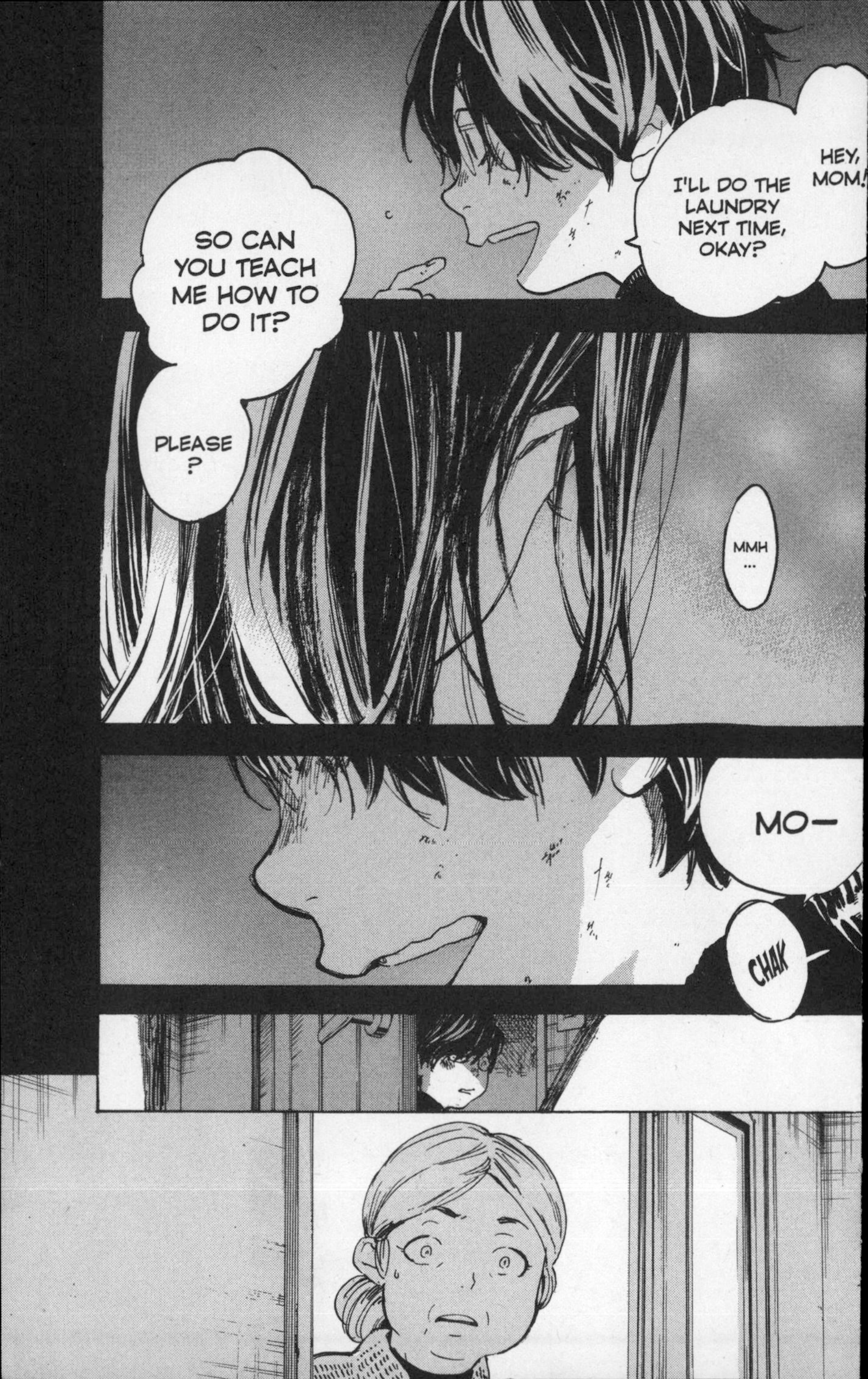
HEY, MOM!
I'LL DO THE LAUNDRY NEXT TIME, OKAY?
SO CAN YOU TEACH ME HOW TO DO IT?
PLEASE?
MMH ...
MO—
CHAK

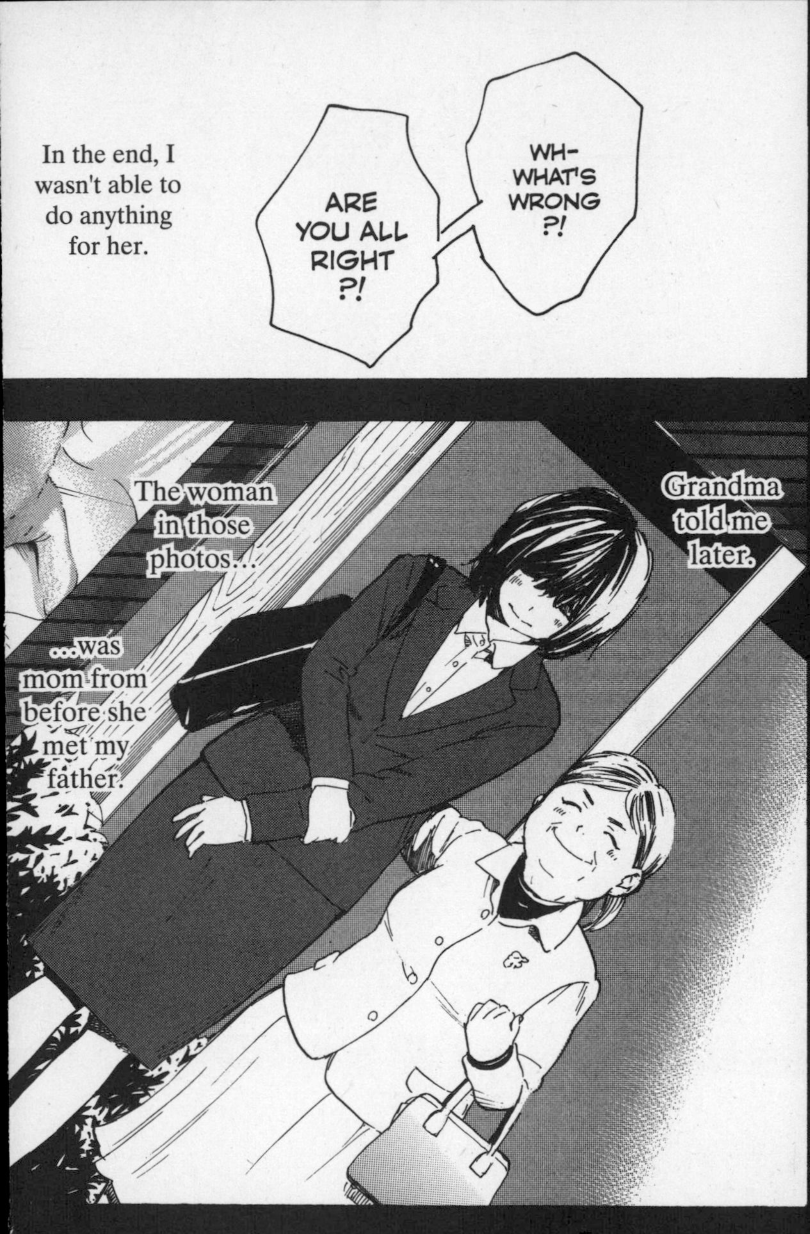
WH- WHAT'S WRONG ?!
ARE YOU ALL RIGHT ?!
In the end, I wasn't able to do anything for her.
Grandma told me later.
The woman in those photos...
...was mom from before she met my father.

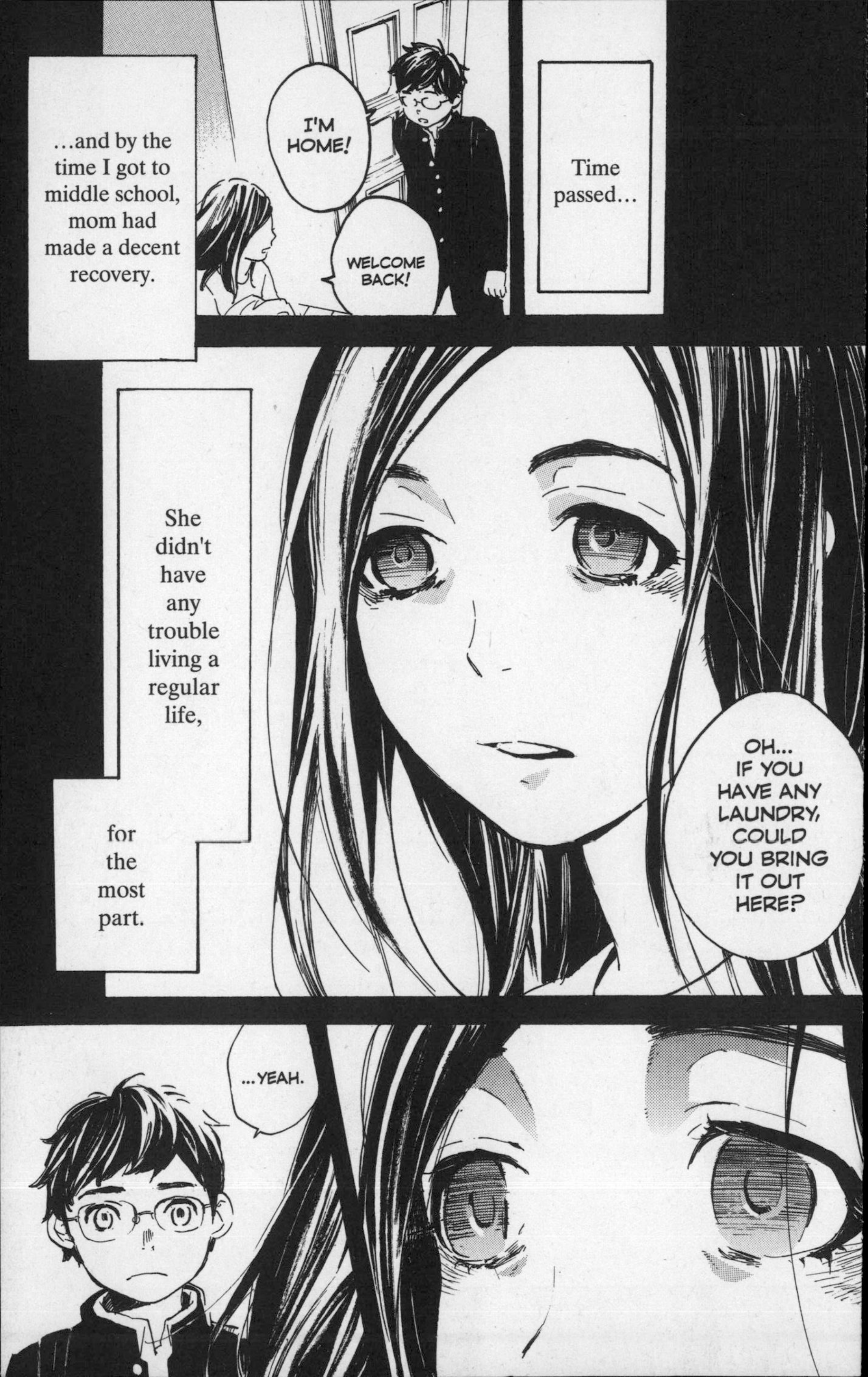
Time passed…
…and by the time I got to middle school, mom had made a decent recovery.
I'M HOME!
WELCOME BACK!
OH... IF YOU HAVE ANY LAUNDRY, COULD YOU BRING IT OUT HERE?
She didn't have any trouble living a regular life,
for the most part.
...YEAH.

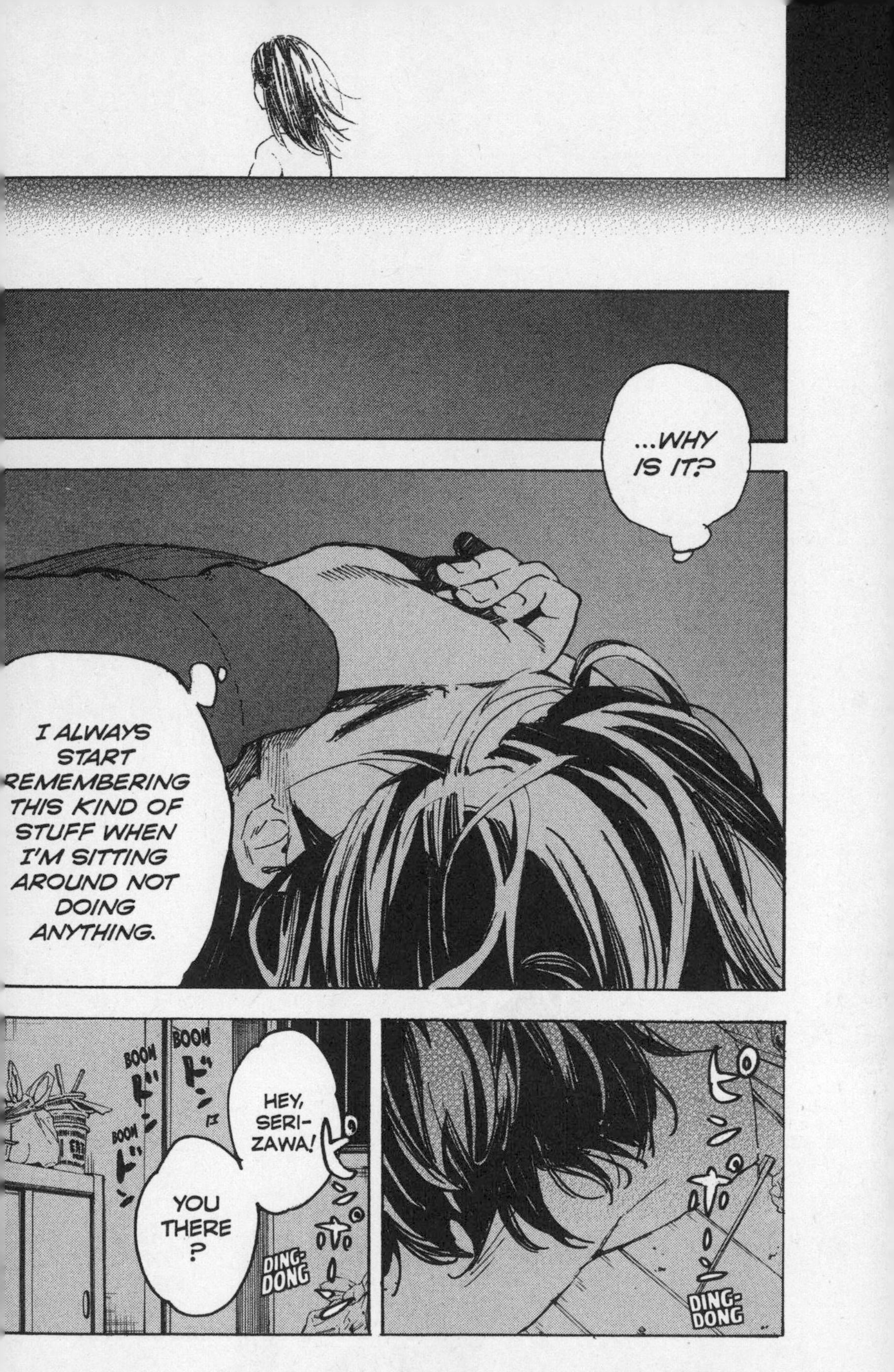
...WHY IS IT?
I ALWAYS START REMEMBERING THIS KIND OF STUFF WHEN I'M SITTING AROUND NOT DOING ANYTHING.
DING-DONG
HEY, SERI-ZAWA!
YOU THERE?
DING-DONG
BOOM
BOOM
BOOM

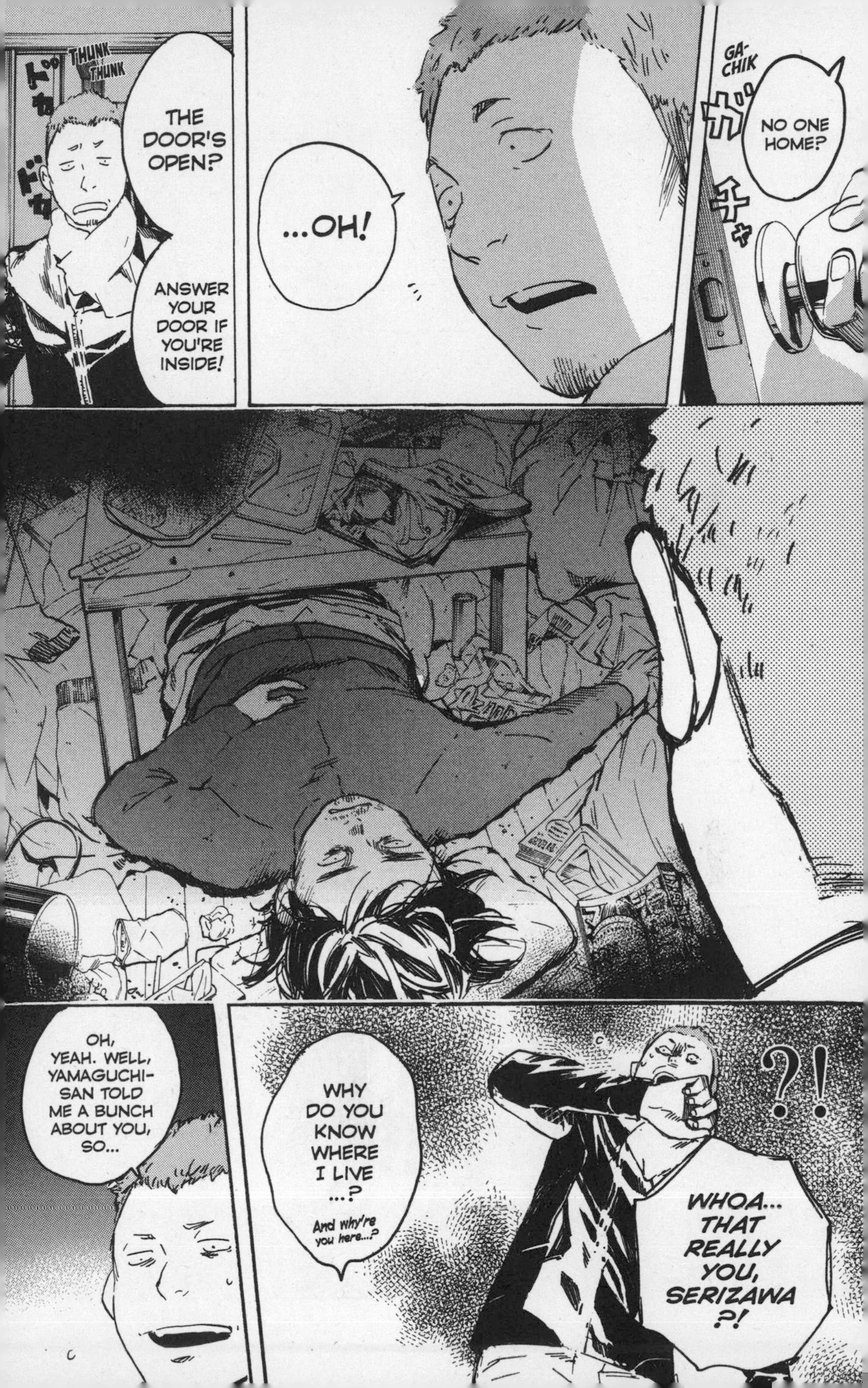
GA-CHIK
NO ONE HOME?
...OH!
THUNK THUNK
THE DOOR'S OPEN?
ANSWER YOUR DOOR IF YOU'RE INSIDE!
?!
WHOA... THAT REALLY YOU, SERIZAWA?!
WHY DO YOU KNOW WHERE I LIVE ...?
And why're you here...?
OH, YEAH. WELL, YAMAGUCHI-SAN TOLD ME A BUNCH ABOUT YOU, SO...

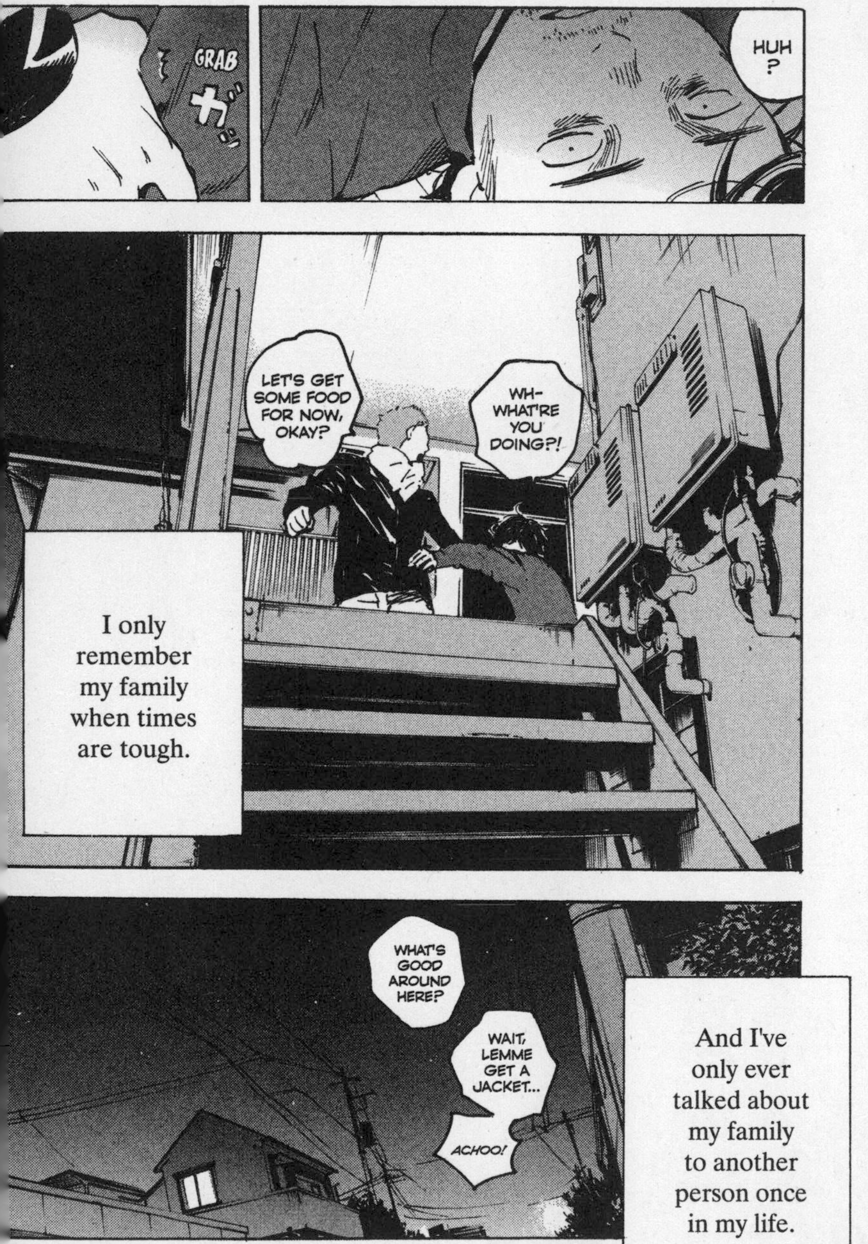
HUH?
GRAB
ガッ
WH- WHAT'RE YOU DOING?!
LET'S GET SOME FOOD FOR NOW, OKAY?
I only remember my family when times are tough.
And I've only ever talked about my family to another person once in my life.
WHAT'S GOOD AROUND HERE?
WAIT, LEMME GET A JACKET...
ACHOO!

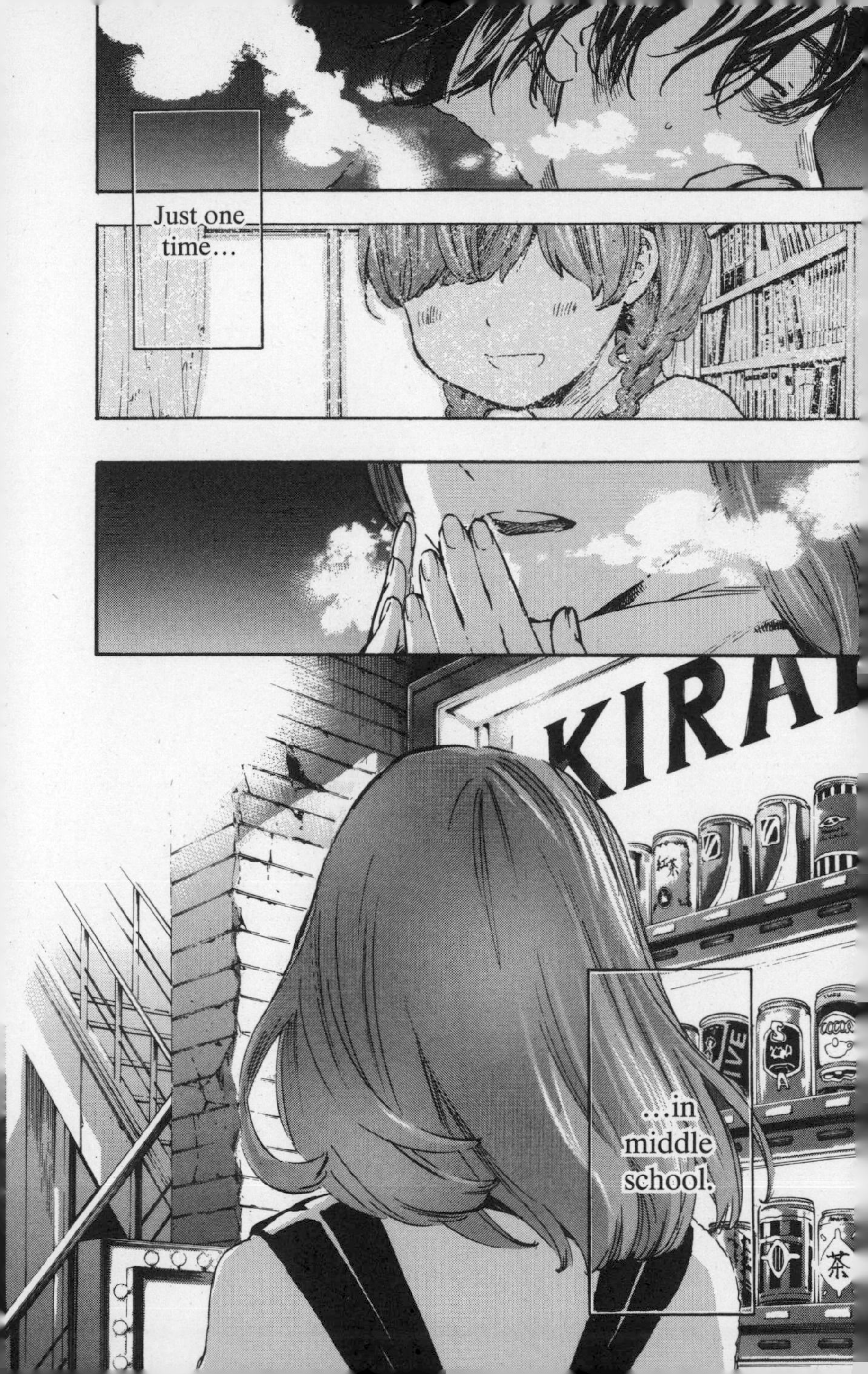
Just one time…
KIRA
…in middle school.

Forget Me Not

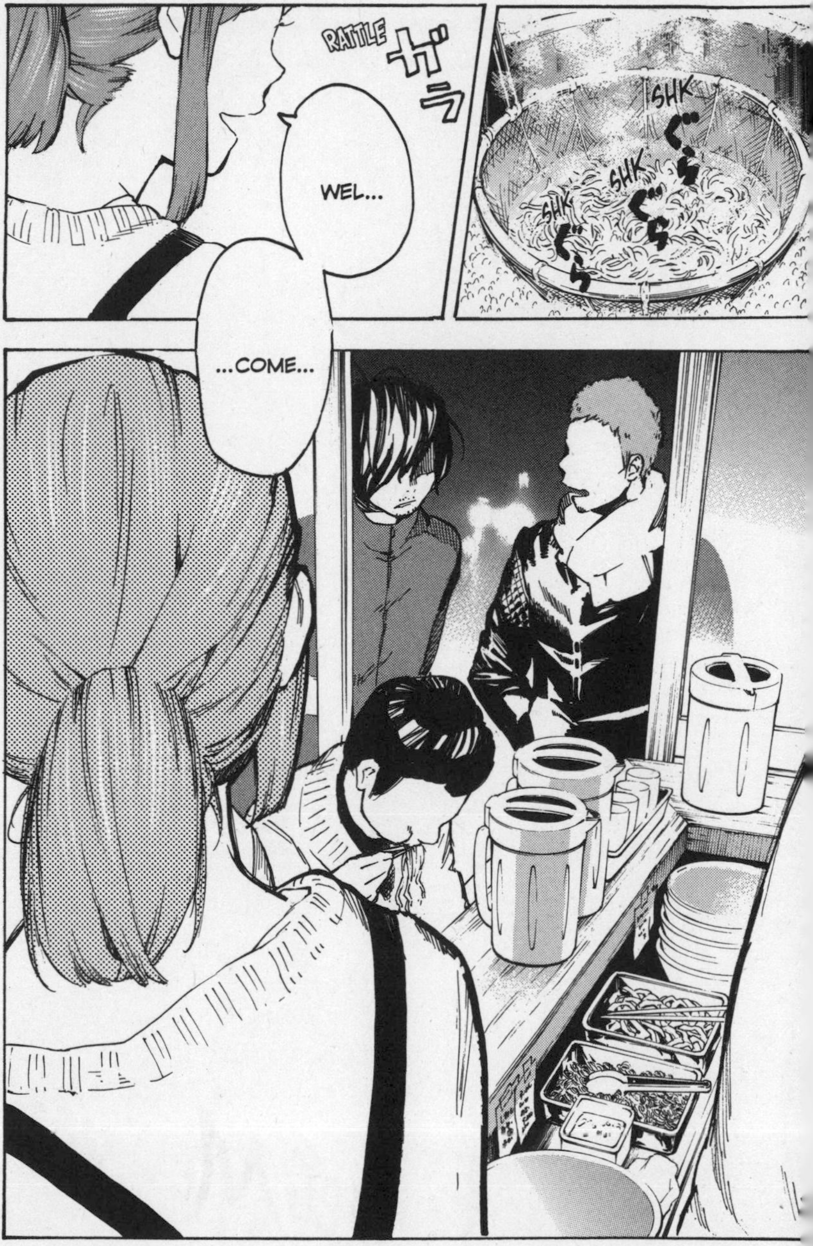
SHK
ぐ
SHK
ぐ
SHK
ぐ
RATTLE
ガラ
WEL...
...COME...

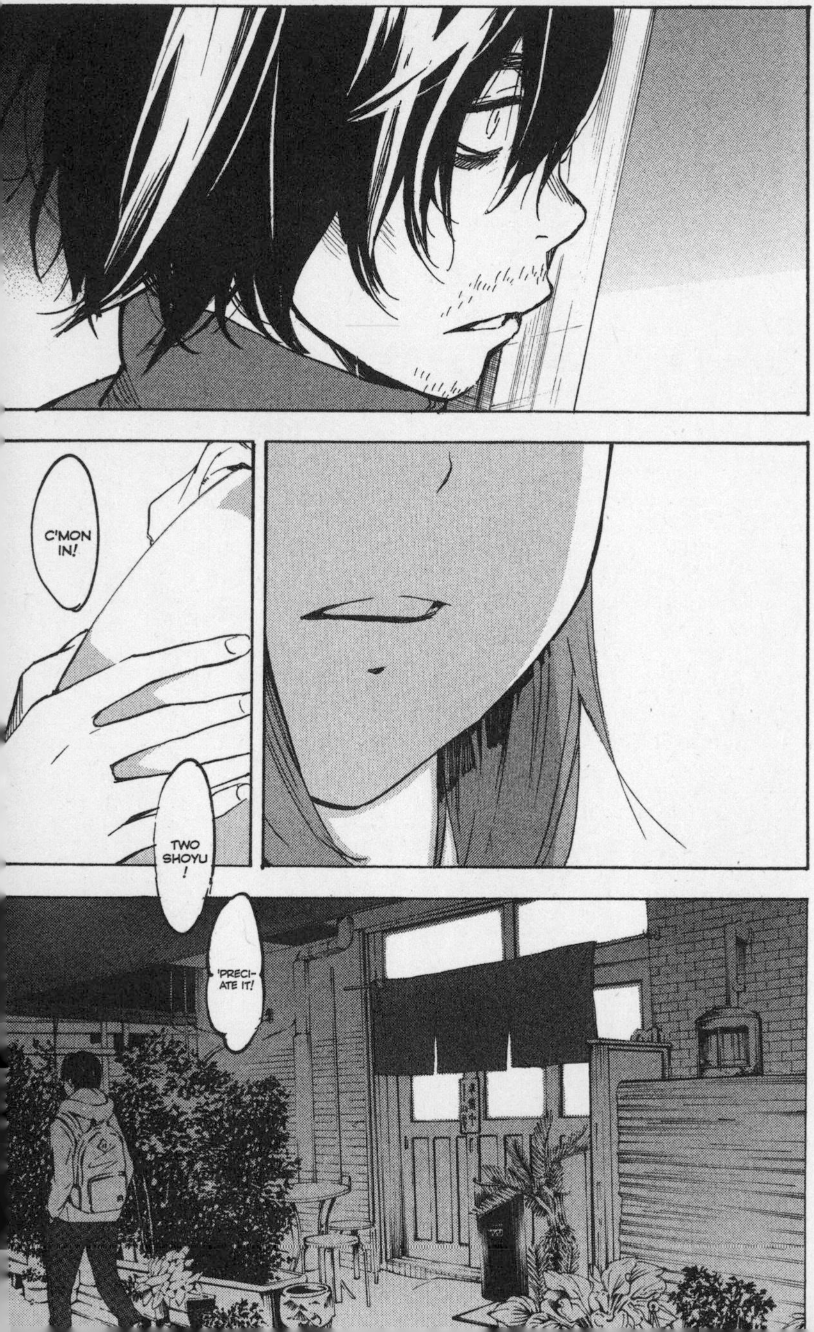
C'MON IN!
TWO SHOYU!
'PRECI-ATE IT!

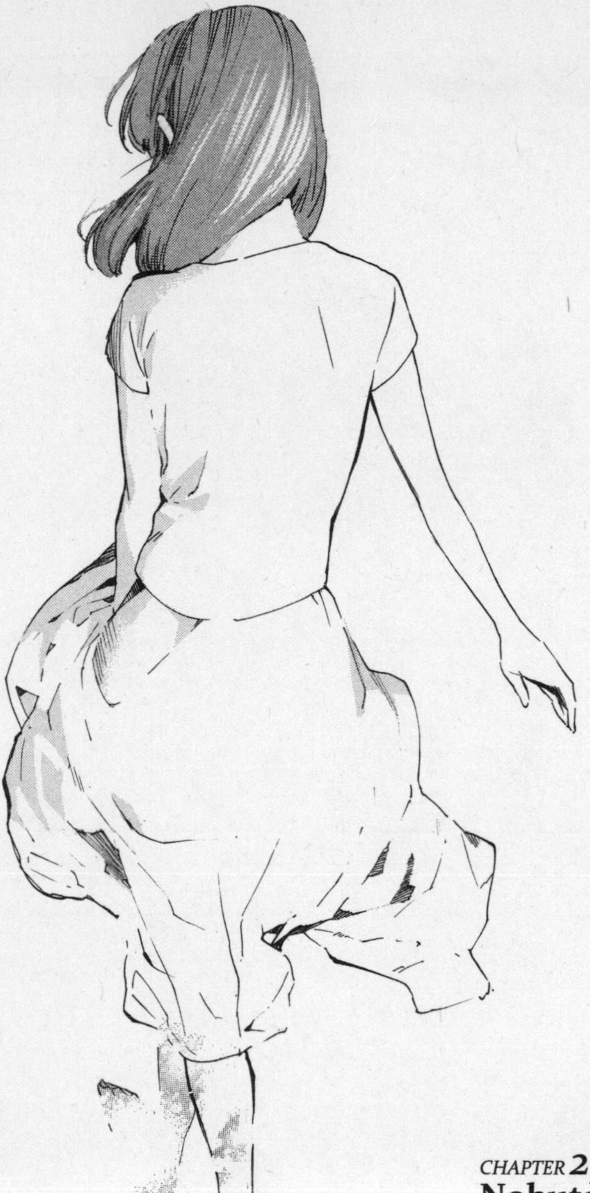

CHAPTER 29:
Nobuta 2

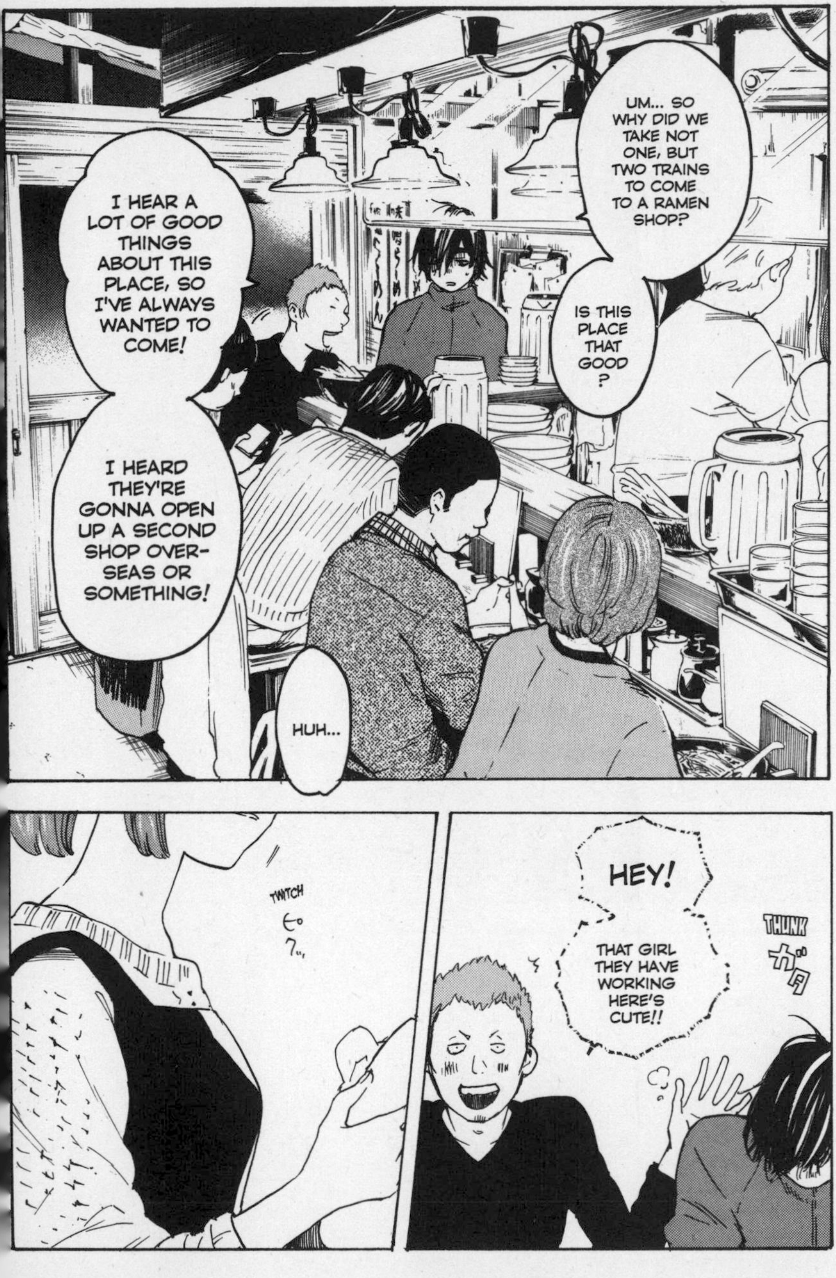

UM... SO WHY DID WE TAKE NOT ONE, BUT TWO TRAINS TO COME TO A RAMEN SHOP?
IS THIS PLACE THAT GOOD?
I HEAR A LOT OF GOOD THINGS ABOUT THIS PLACE, SO I'VE ALWAYS WANTED TO COME!
I HEARD THEY'RE GONNA OPEN UP A SECOND SHOP OVER-SEAS OR SOMETHING!
HUH...
HEY!
THAT GIRL THEY HAVE WORKING HERE'S CUTE!!
THUNK
ガタ
TWITCH

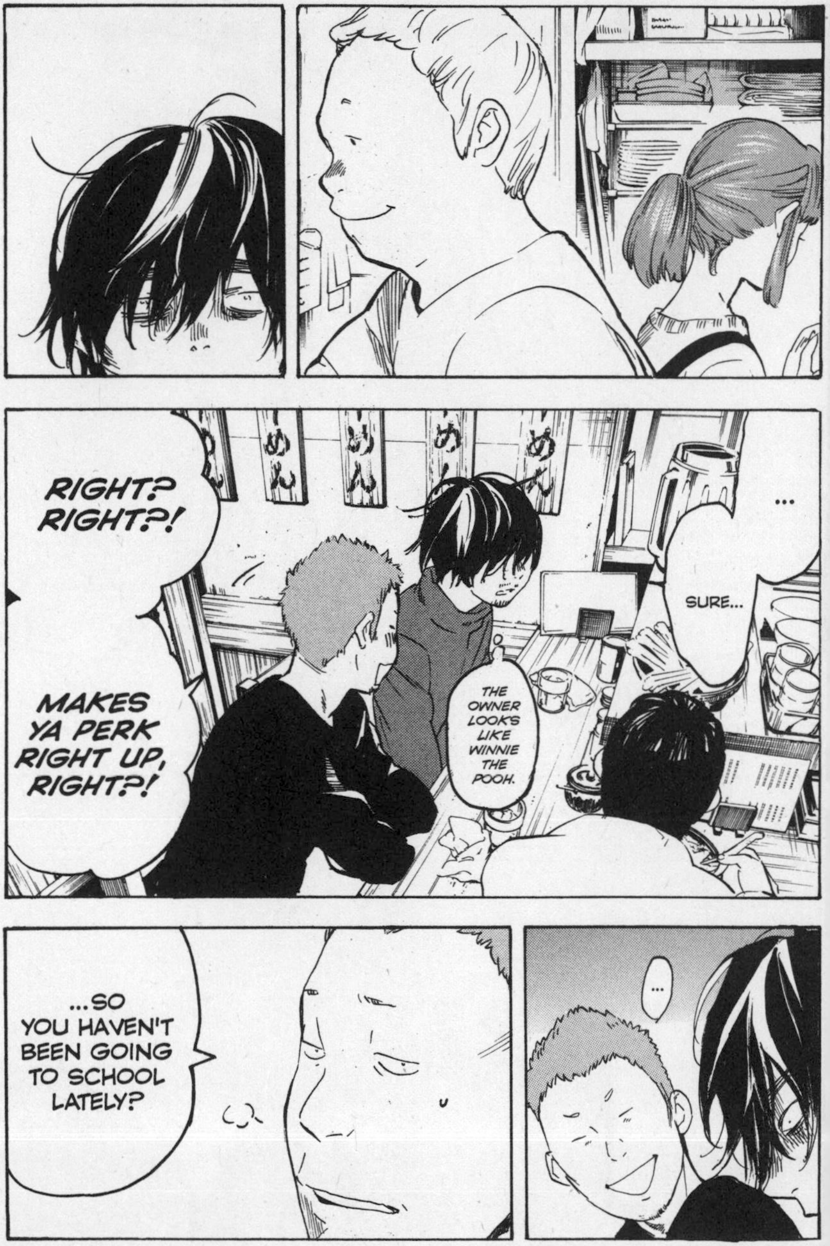
... SURE...
RIGHT? RIGHT?! MAKES YA PERK RIGHT UP, RIGHT?!
THE OWNER LOOKS LIKE WINNIE THE POOH.
...
...SO YOU HAVEN'T BEEN GOING TO SCHOOL LATELY?

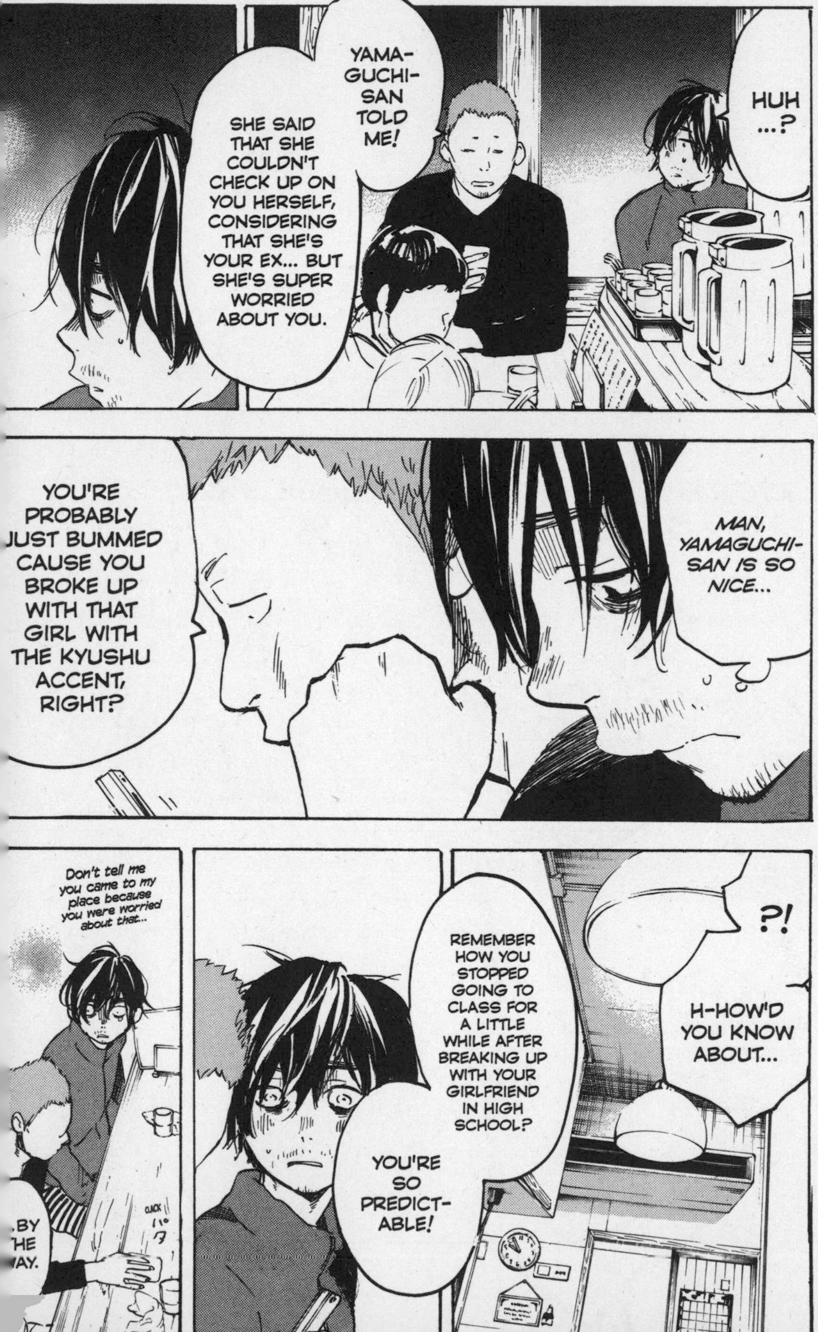

HUH ...?
YAMA-GUCHI-SAN TOLD ME!
SHE SAID THAT SHE COULDN'T CHECK UP ON YOU HERSELF, CONSIDERING THAT SHE'S YOUR EX... BUT SHE'S SUPER WORRIED ABOUT YOU.
MAN, YAMAGUCHI-SAN IS SO NICE...
YOU'RE PROBABLY JUST BUMMED CAUSE YOU BROKE UP WITH THAT GIRL WITH THE KYUSHU ACCENT, RIGHT?
?!
H-HOW'D YOU KNOW ABOUT...
REMEMBER HOW YOU STOPPED GOING TO CLASS FOR A LITTLE WHILE AFTER BREAKING UP WITH YOUR GIRLFRIEND IN HIGH SCHOOL?
YOU'RE SO PREDICT-ABLE!
Don't tell me you came to my place because you were worried about that...
CLACK
.BY THE WAY.

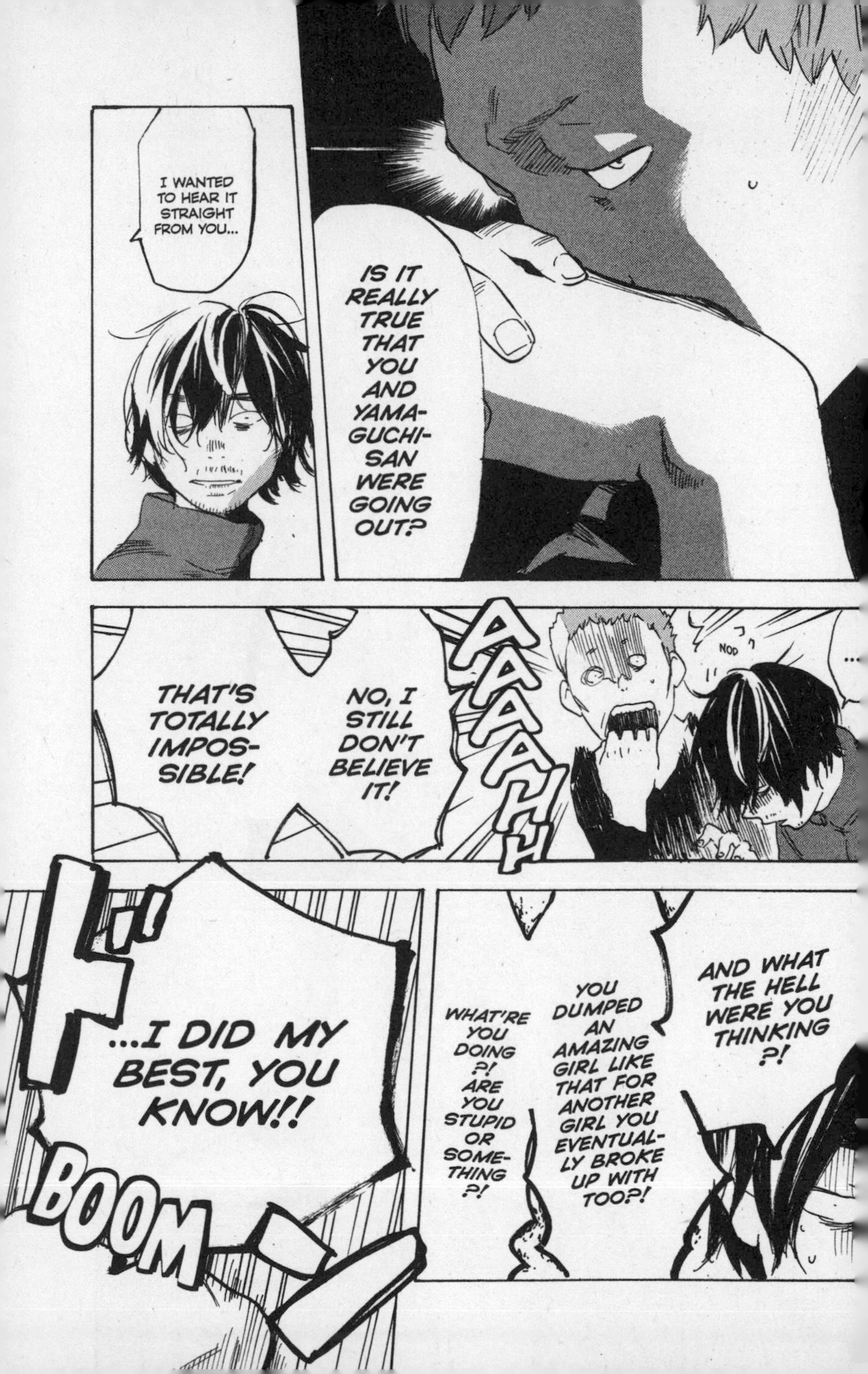
IS IT REALLY TRUE THAT YOU AND YAMAGUCHI-SAN WERE GOING OUT?
I WANTED TO HEAR IT STRAIGHT FROM YOU...
...
NOD
AAAAAHH
NO, I STILL DON'T BELIEVE IT!
THAT'S TOTALLY IMPOSSIBLE!
AND WHAT THE HELL WERE YOU THINKING?!
YOU DUMPED AN AMAZING GIRL LIKE THAT FOR ANOTHER GIRL YOU EVENTUALLY BROKE UP WITH TOO?!
WHAT'RE YOU DOING?! ARE YOU STUPID OR SOMETHING?!
...I DID MY BEST, YOU KNOW!!
BOOM

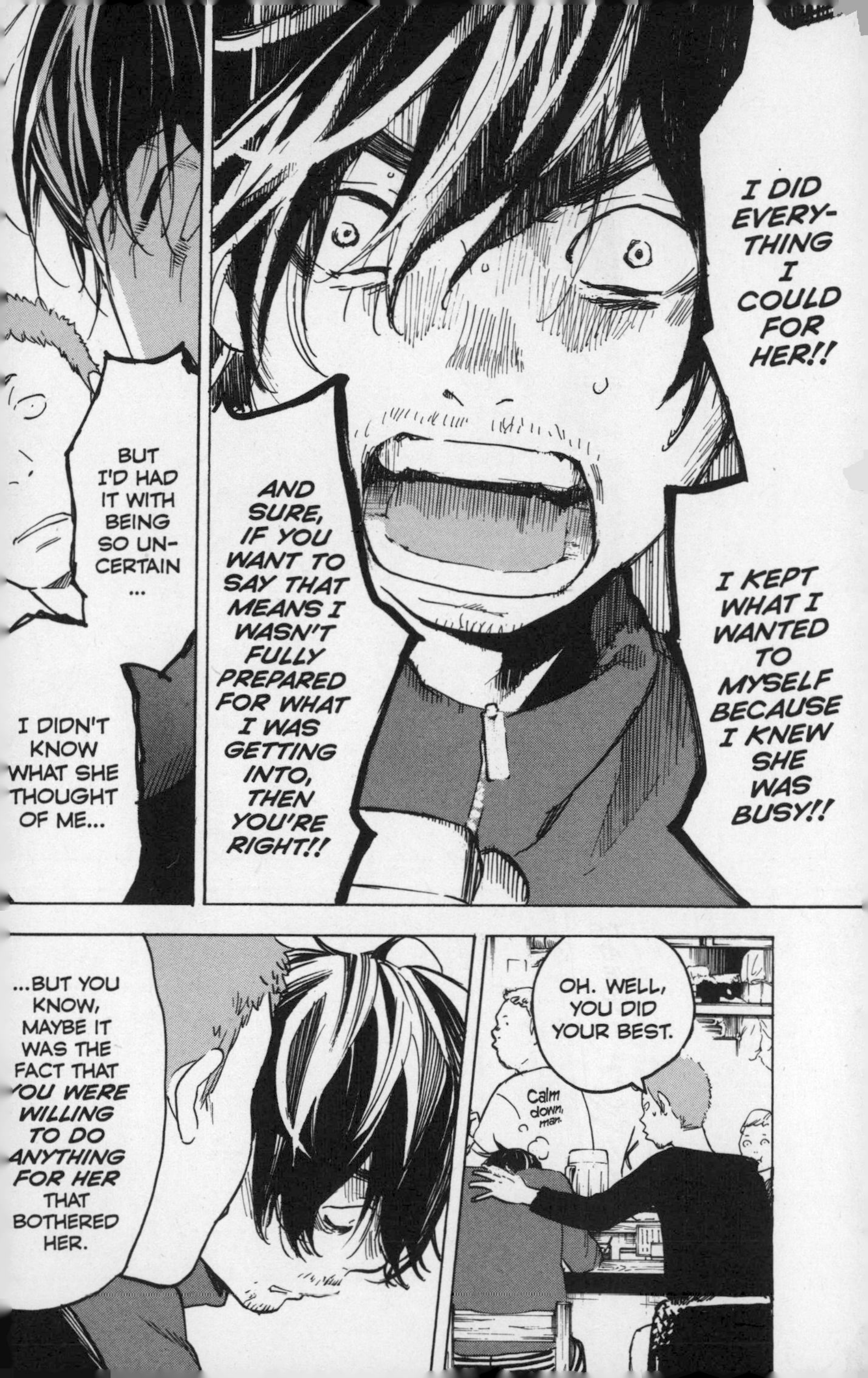
I DID EVERY-THING I COULD FOR HER!!
I KEPT WHAT I WANTED TO MYSELF BECAUSE I KNEW SHE WAS BUSY!!
AND SURE, IF YOU WANT TO SAY THAT MEANS I WASN'T FULLY PREPARED FOR WHAT I WAS GETTING INTO, THEN YOU'RE RIGHT!!
BUT I'D HAD IT WITH BEING SO UN-CERTAIN ...
I DIDN'T KNOW WHAT SHE THOUGHT OF ME...
OH. WELL, YOU DID YOUR BEST.
Calm down, man.
...BUT YOU KNOW, MAYBE IT WAS THE FACT THAT YOU WERE WILLING TO DO ANYTHING FOR HER THAT BOTHERED HER.

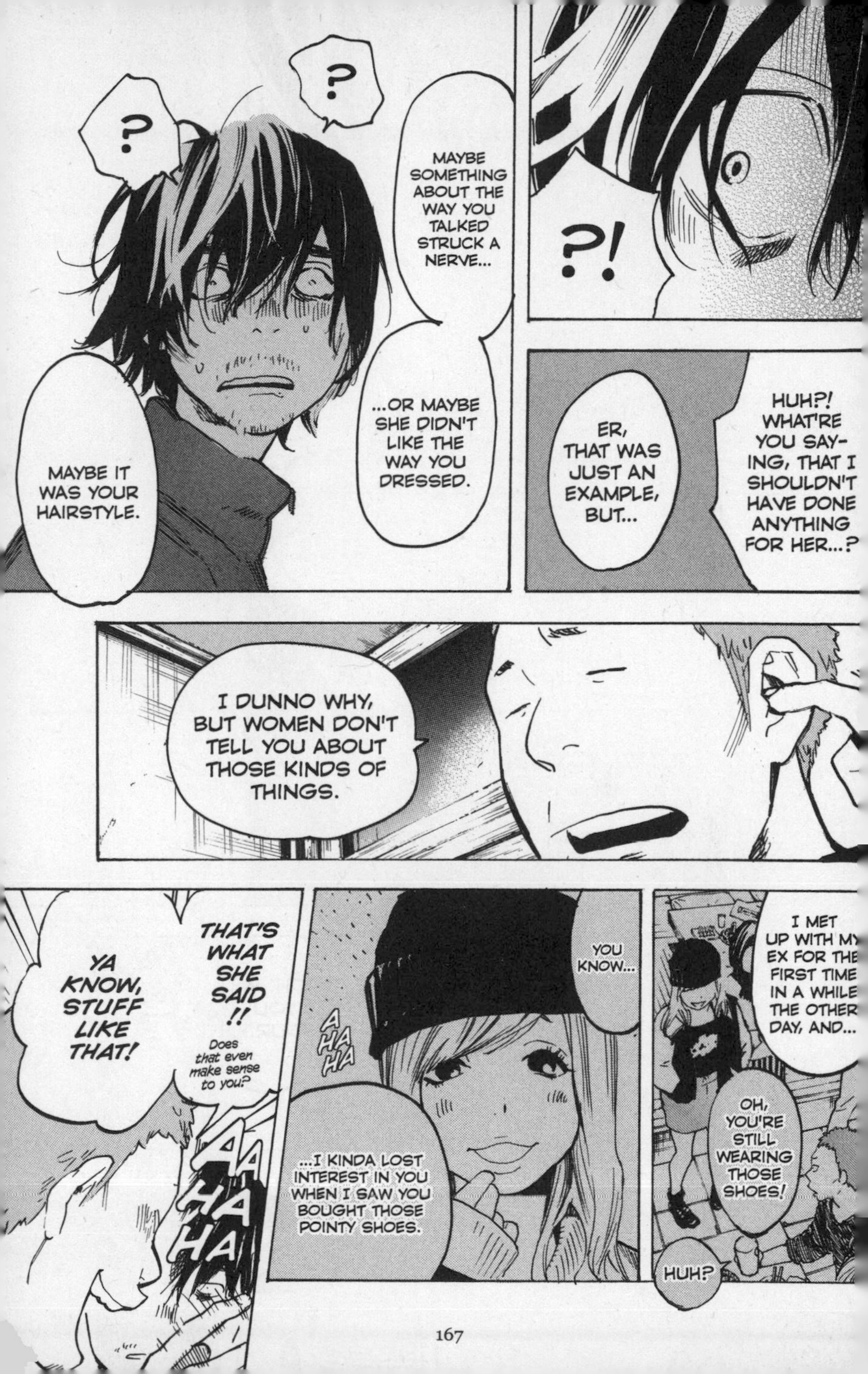
?!
HUH?! WHAT'RE YOU SAY-ING, THAT I SHOULDN'T HAVE DONE ANYTHING FOR HER...?
ER, THAT WAS JUST AN EXAMPLE, BUT...
?
?
MAYBE SOMETHING ABOUT THE WAY YOU TALKED STRUCK A NERVE...
...OR MAYBE SHE DIDN'T LIKE THE WAY YOU DRESSED.
MAYBE IT WAS YOUR HAIRSTYLE.
I DUNNO WHY, BUT WOMEN DON'T TELL YOU ABOUT THOSE KINDS OF THINGS.
I MET UP WITH MY EX FOR THE FIRST TIME IN A WHILE THE OTHER DAY, AND...
OH, YOU'RE STILL WEARING THOSE SHOES!
HUH?
YOU KNOW...
AHAHA
...I KINDA LOST INTEREST IN YOU WHEN I SAW YOU BOUGHT THOSE POINTY SHOES.
THAT'S WHAT SHE SAID!!
Does that even make sense to you?
YA KNOW, STUFF LIKE THAT!
AAHAHA

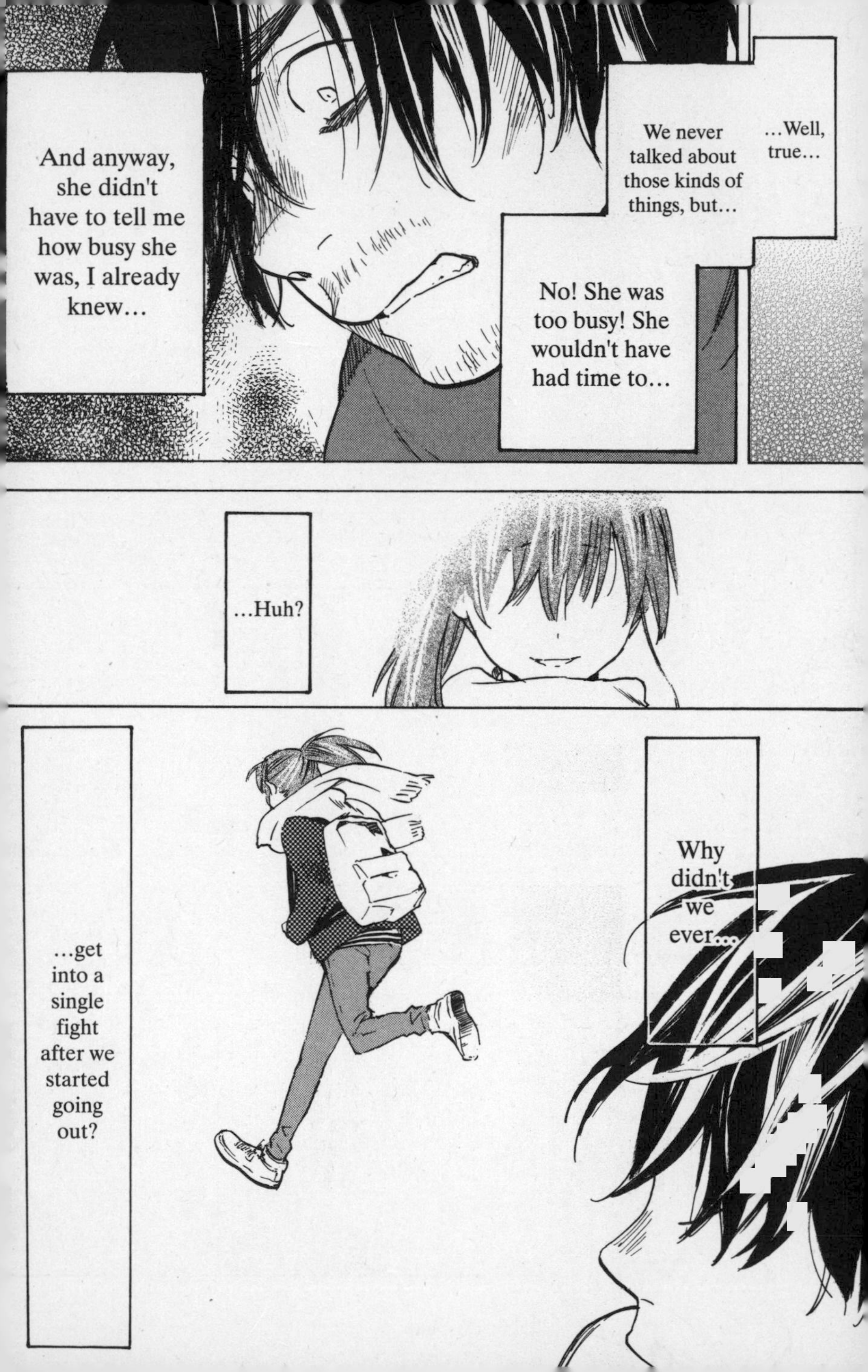
...Well, true...
We never talked about those kinds of things, but...
No! She was too busy! She wouldn't have had time to...
And anyway, she didn't have to tell me how busy she was, I already knew...
...Huh?
Why didn't we ever...
...get into a single fight after we started going out?

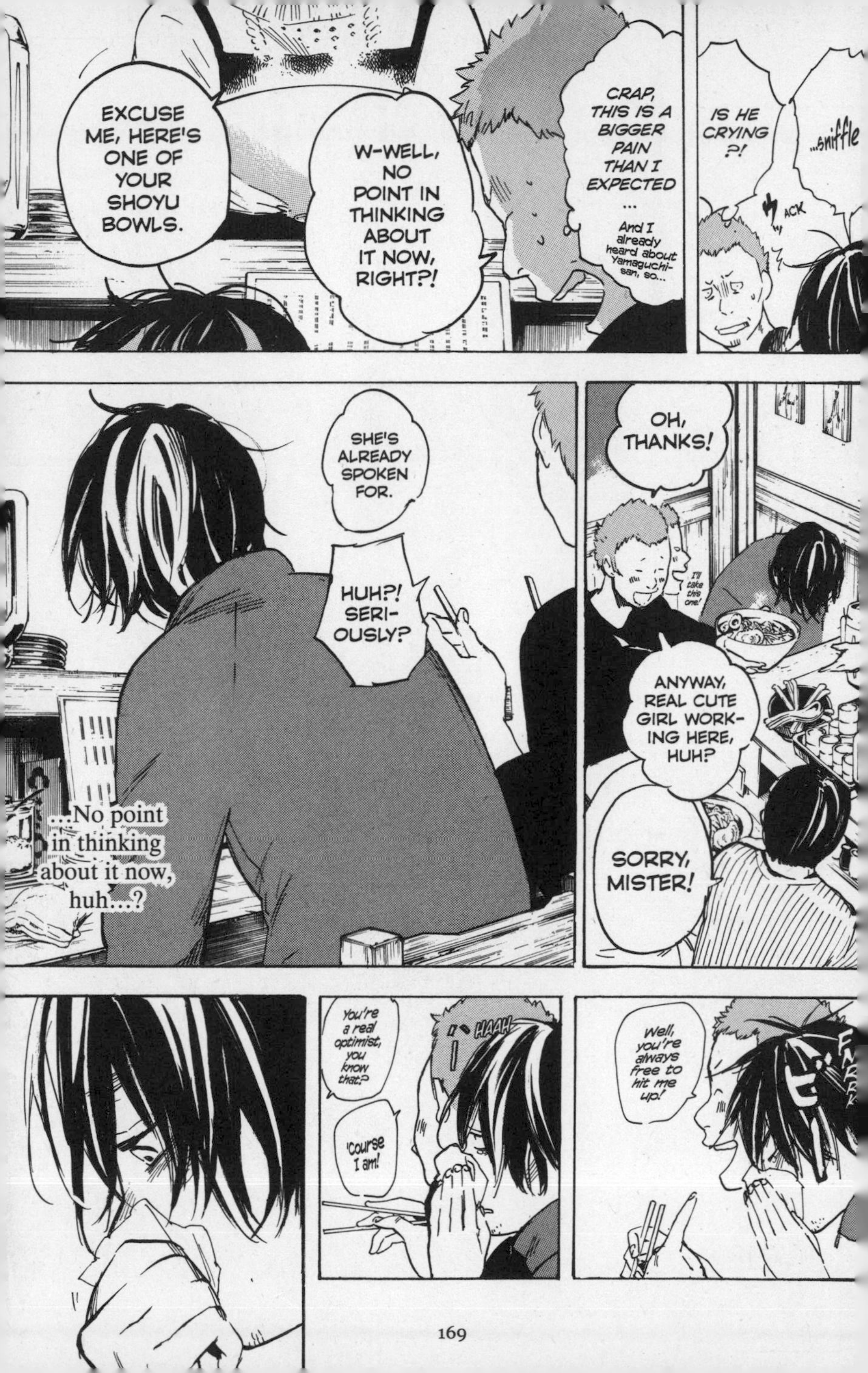
IS HE CRYING ?!
...sniffle
ACK
CRAP, THIS IS A BIGGER PAIN THAN I EXPECTED ...
And I already heard about Yamaguchi-san, so...
W-WELL, NO POINT IN THINKING ABOUT IT NOW, RIGHT?!
EXCUSE ME, HERE'S ONE OF YOUR SHOYU BOWLS.
OH, THANKS!
I'll take this one!
ANYWAY, REAL CUTE GIRL WORK-ING HERE, HUH?
SORRY, MISTER!
SHE'S ALREADY SPOKEN FOR.
HUH?! SERI-OUSLY?
...No point in thinking about it now, huh...?
Well, you're always free to hit me up!
FNRRK
HAAH
You're a real optimist, you know that?
'Course I am!

HEY, COULD YOU TAKE THIS FIRST?

OKAY!

N—

No way.
No way.

She looks exactly like...

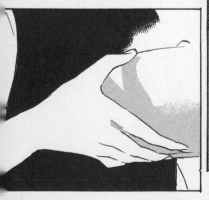

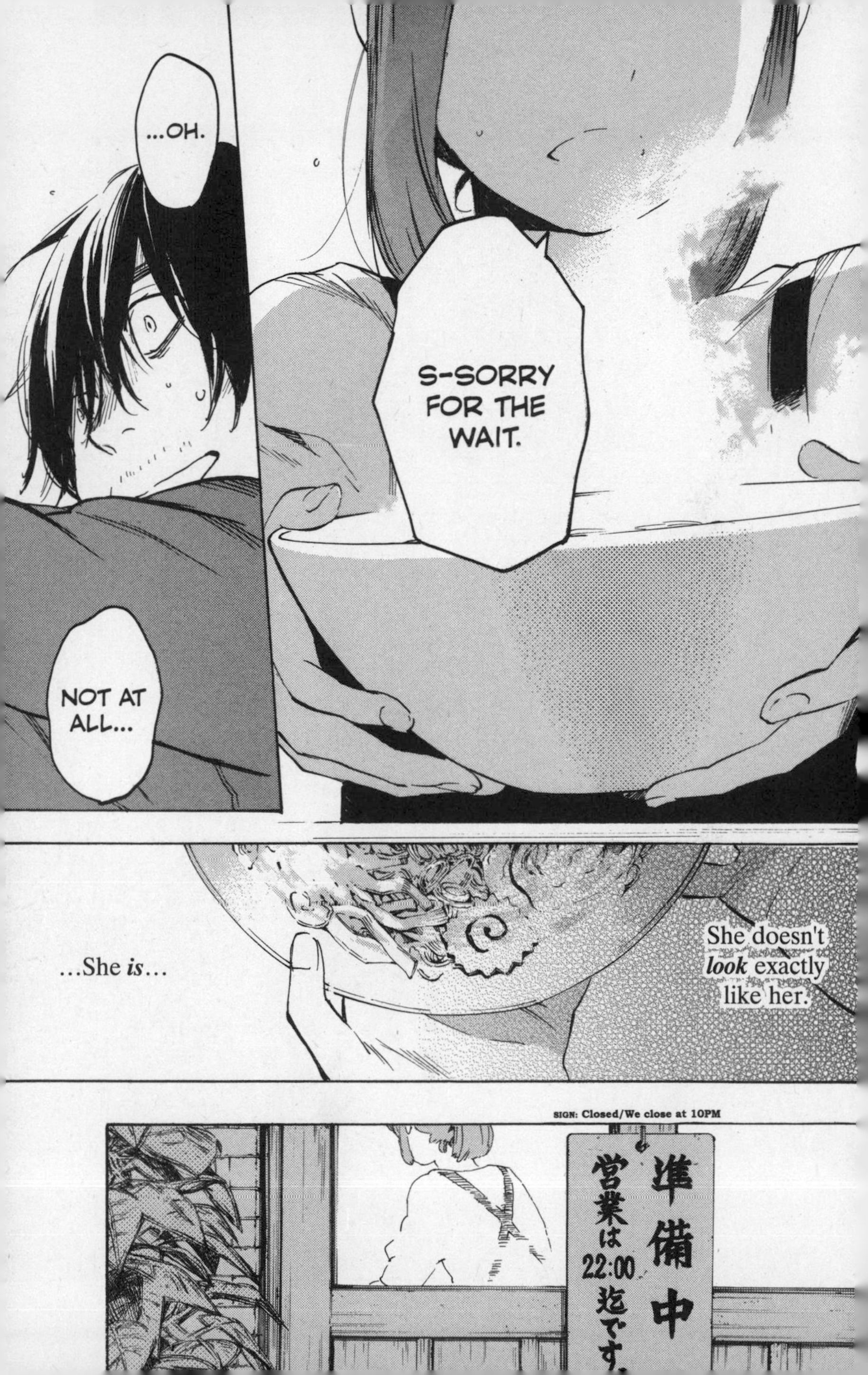
S-SORRY FOR THE WAIT.
...OH.
NOT AT ALL...
She doesn't *look* exactly like her.
...She *is*...
SIGN: Closed/We close at 10PM
準備中
営業は22:00迄です。

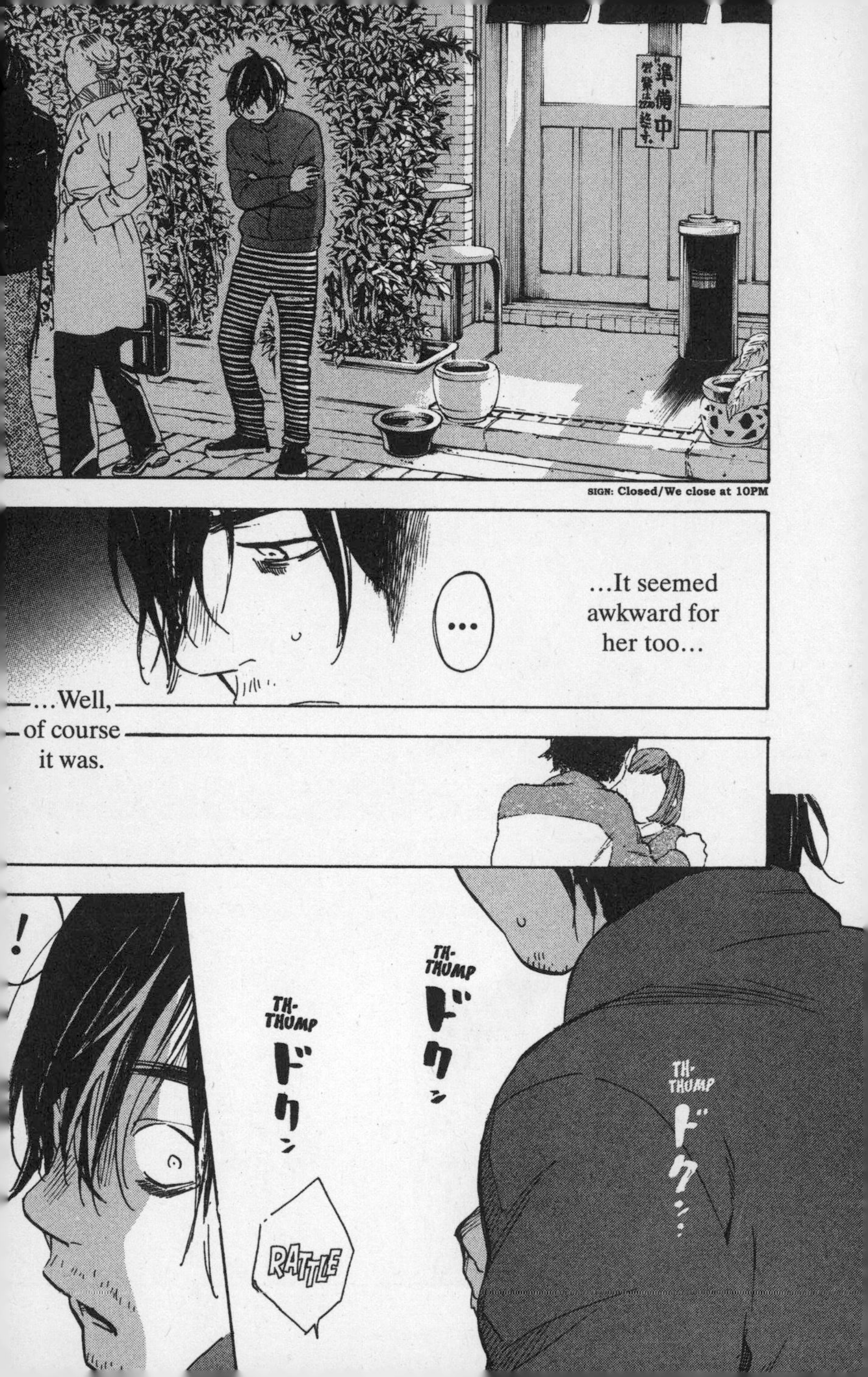
準備中
営業は22:00迄です。
SIGN: Closed/We close at 10PM
...It seemed awkward for her too...
...
...Well, of course it was.
TH-THUMP
ドクン
TH-THUMP
ドクン
TH-THUMP
ドクン
!
RATTLE

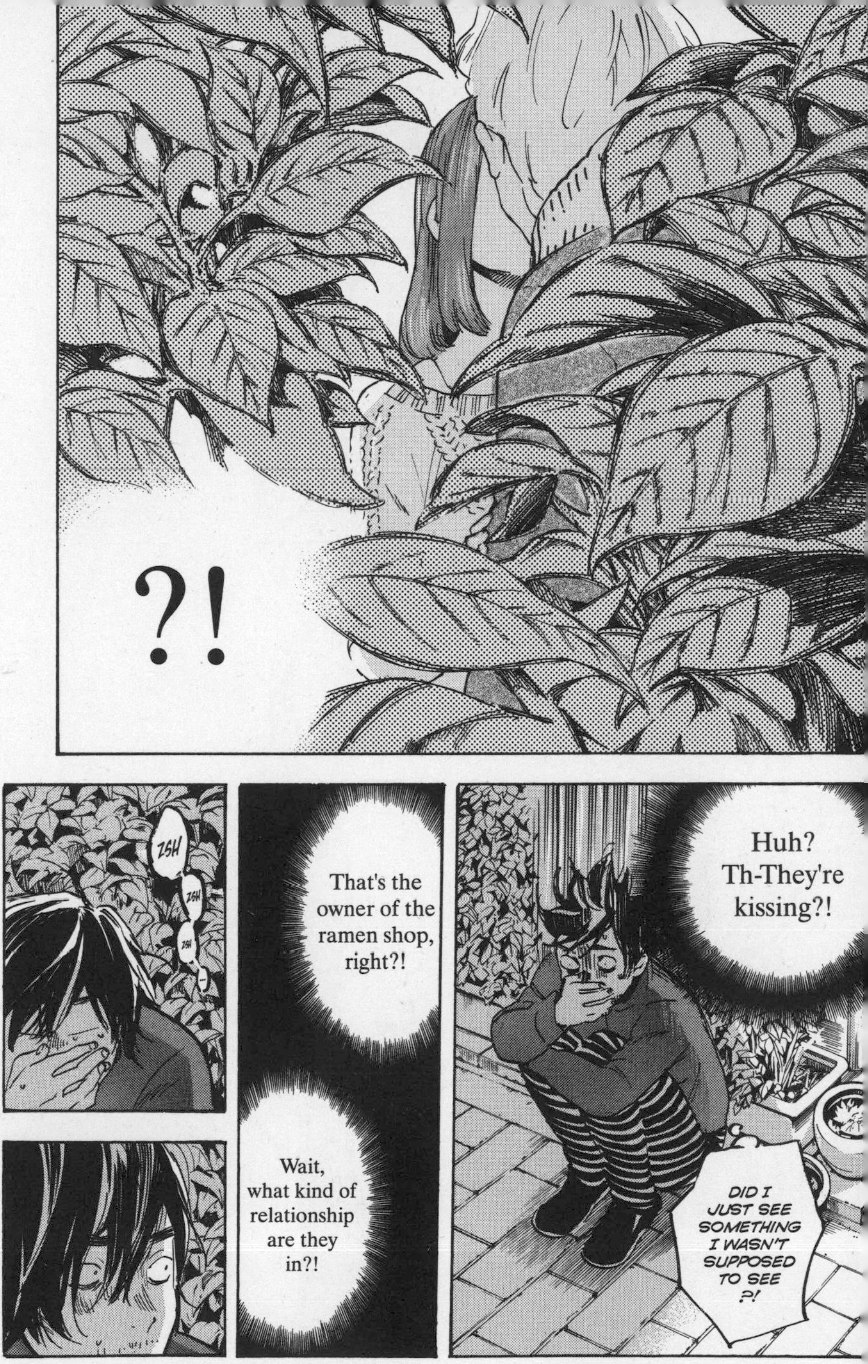
?!
Huh? Th-They're kissing?!
DID I JUST SEE SOMETHING I WASN'T SUPPOSED TO SEE?!
That's the owner of the ramen shop, right?!
Wait, what kind of relationship are they in?!
ZSH
ZSH
ZSH

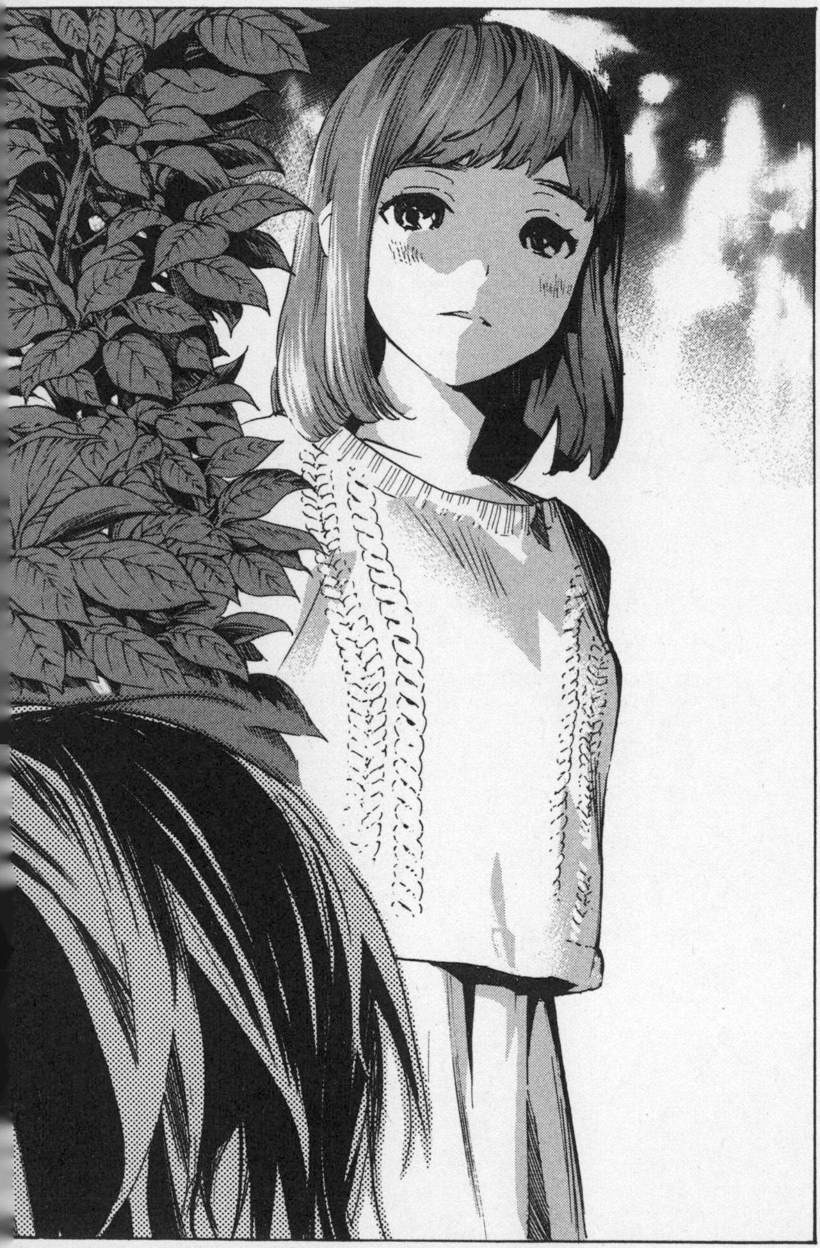

TO BE CONTINUED IN VOLUME 5.

Forget Me Not

── TRANSLATION NOTES ──

COLLECTING ON DEBTS AFTER 9 page 57

Like in the United States, debt collectors can sometimes go to extreme lengths to collect money from debtors, so various laws have been set up to protect consumers. In Japan, under Article 21 of the Money Lending Business Act, it is illegal for collectors to intimidate debtors. Included in the guidelines for not intimidating debtors is a section that states a debt collector cannot contact or personally engage that debtor at inappropriate times, which have been determined to be between the hours of 9 pm and 8 am. Incidentally, this is the same in the United States under the Fair Debt Collection Practices Act (FDCPA).

CHIIIIRUP page 86

These are the sounds of cicadas chirping, which is often indicative of summer in Japan.

A Kodansha Comics Trade Paperback Original.

Forget Me Not volume 4 copyright © 2015 Mag Hsu & Nao Emoto
Original title "My Girls!: dedicated to those of you whom I love and hurt"
published in Taiwan 2011 by TITAN Publishing Co., Ltd.
English translation copyright © 2016 Mag Hsu & Nao Emoto

Published in the United States by Kodansha Comics,
an imprint of Kodansha USA Publishing, LLC, New York.

Publication rights for this English edition arranged through Kodansha Ltd.,
Tokyo.

First published in Japan in 2015 by Kodansha Ltd., Tokyo, as *Sore Demo
Boku Wa Kimi Ga Suki* volume 4.

ISBN 978-1-63236-314-5

Printed in the United States of America.

www.kodanshacomics.com

9 8 7 6 5 4 3 2 1

Translation: Ko Ransom
Lettering: Evan Hayden
Editing: Ajani Oloye
Kodansha Comics edition cover design: Phil Balsman